MUSEUM OF ANTHROPOLOGY, THE UNIVERSITY OF MICHIGAN

TECHNICAL REPORTS

Number 11

RESEARCH REPORTS IN ARCHAEOLOGY

Contribution 6

PREHISTORIC SOCIAL, POLITICAL, AND ECONOMIC DEVELOPMENT IN THE AREA OF THE TEHUACAN VALLEY

SOME RESULTS OF THE PALO BLANCO PROJECT

Edited by

Robert D. Drennan

With Contributions by

John R. Alden
Elsa M. Redmond
Judith E. Smith
and
Charles S. Spencer

Spanish Text Translated by
Verónica Kennedy

ANN ARBOR
1979

© 1979 Regents of The University of Michigan
The Museum of Anthropology
All rights reserved

Printed in the
United States of America

ISBN 0-932206-82-4

TABLE OF CONTENTS

LIST OF FIGURES. iv
LIST OF TABLES vi
1. INTRODUCTION
        by Robert D. Drennan 1
   INTRODUCCION 8

2. IRRIGATION, ADMINISTRATION, AND SOCIETY IN FORMATIVE TEHUACAN
        by Charles S. Spencer 13
   IRRIGACION, ADMINISTRACION, Y SOCIEDAD EN EL FORMATIVO DE
        TEHUACAN, SUMARIO 76
   APPENDIX TO CHAPTER 2 81

3. A TERMINAL FORMATIVE CERAMIC WORKSHOP IN THE TEHUACAN VALLEY
        by Elsa M. Redmond 111
   UN TALLER DE CERAMICA DEL FORMATIVO TERMINAL EN EL VALLE DE
        TEHUACAN, SUMARIO 126

4. SYSTEMATIC SURFACE SURVEY AT QUACHILCO (Ts218)
        by John R. Alden 129
   RECONOCIMIENTO DE SUPERFICIE SISTEMATICO EN QUACHILCO, SUMARIO . . 155
   APPENDIX TO CHAPTER 4 159

5. EXCAVATIONS AT CUAYUCATEPEC (Ts281): A PRELIMINARY REPORT
        by Robert D. Drennan 169
   EXCAVACIONES EN CUAYUCATEPEC (Ts281): INFORME PRELIMINAR,
        SUMARIO 196

6. FORMATIVE AND CLASSIC DEVELOPMENTS IN THE CUICATLAN CAÑADA: A
        PRELIMINARY REPORT
        by Charles S. Spencer and Elsa M. Redmond 201
   DESARROLLO FORMATIVO Y CLASICO EN LA CAÑADA DE CUICATLAN:
        INFORME PRELIMINAR, SUMARIO 213

7. CARBONIZED BOTANICAL REMAINS FROM QUACHILCO, CUAYUCATEPEC,
        AND LA COYOTERA: A PRELIMINARY REPORT
        by Judith E. Smith 217
   RESTOS BOTANICOS CARBONIZADOS PROVENIENTES DE QUACHILCO,
        CUAYUCATEPEC, Y LA COYOTERA: INFORME PRELIMINAR, SUMARIO . 247

REFERENCES CITED 251

LIST OF FIGURES

1.1	Ceramic chronology for the Tehuacán Valley.	2
1.2	Map of the Tehuacán Valley showing archeological sites mentioned in the text and the Lencho Diego survey area.	4-5
2.1	Plan of the Purrón Dam complex.	20
2.2	Elevation and cross section views of the Purrón Dam	21
2.3	Early Santa María settlement in the Arroyo Lencho Diego	23
2.4	Site map of Ts449	25
2.5	Middle Santa María settlement in the Arroyo Lencho Diego.	29
2.6	Site map of Ts452	31
2.7	Site map of Ts450 and Ts67	32
2.8	Late Santa María settlement in the Arroyo Lencho Diego.	34
2.9	Site map of Ts131	35
2.10	Site map of Ts451	37
2.11	Early Palo Blanco settlement in the Arroyo Lencho Diego	39
2.12	Site map of Ts73.	40-41
2.13	Site map of Ts79a	43
2.14	Site map of Ts79b	44
2.15	Site map of Ts79c	46
2.16	Histogram of mound heights at Ts73/79	51
2.17	Proposed administrative hierarchy at Ts73/79.	52
2.18	Estimated population and predicted carrying capacity for 950 years of development in the Arroyo Lencho Diego	64
3.1	Plans of ceramic workshop features.	112
3.2	Lumps of fired clay	114
3.3	Angular fracture patterns on misfired jar rims and bowl rims	116
3.4	Spalled surfaces.	116
3.5	Mineral inclusions.	117
3.6	Bubbled surface and porous surfaces	118
3.7	Porous core and pocketed cores.	118
3.8	Deformed sherds	119
3.9	Sherd with a hard-burned loam cover	120
4.1	Contour map of the central area of Quachilco, showing the locations of the surface collection squares	131
4.2	A typical lot card, showing the data collected in the field during the surface survey	132
4.3	The procedure followed in recording data from the surface collections	133
4.4	Sherd counts and weights for the north-south transect samples	134
4.5	Sherd counts and weights for the east-west transect samples	134
4.6	Approximate boundaries of the site and its core area as defined by the transect samples.	136
4.7	Sherd density across the Late Santa María/Early Palo Blanco occupation at Quachilco.	140

LIST OF FIGURES

4.8	Sherd density across the Late Palo Blanco occupation at Quachilco.	141
4.9	Sherd density across the Venta Salada occupation at Quachilco	142
4.10	Histograms of diagnostic sherd count in each collection square.	143
4.11	Histogram of weights of fist-sized or larger stones from the collection squares	145
4.12	Scatter plot of rim sherd counts and weights.	146
4.13	Scatter plot of obsidian counts and weights	149
5.1	View of Cuayucatepec from southeast	172
5.2	Map of Cuayucatepec	174
5.3	View to the west across Sector I to the Valle de Cinco Señores	176
5.4	Plan and section of Area A excavations.	177
5.5	Plan and section of Area B excavations.	178-179
5.6	Plan and section of Area F excavations.	181
5.7	Plan and section of Area E excavations.	183
5.8	Plan and section of Area H excavations.	184
5.9	Plan and section of Area G excavations.	186-187
5.10	Plan and section of Area C excavations.	191
5.11	Plan and section of Area D excavations.	192
6.1	Location of the Cuicatlán Cañada between Tehuacán and Oaxaca.	202
6.2	Map of the Cuicatlán Cañada	203
6.3	Correspondence of ceramic phases in the Valley of Oaxaca, the Cuicatlán Cañada, and the Tehuacán Valley	206
6.4	Aerial photograph of the excavated Perdido phase residential compound at La Coyotera	209
7.1	Partial chile pepper seed from Quachilco.	221
7.2	Avocado seeds from Quachilco.	222
7.3	Black zapote seeds from Quachilco	224
7.4	Beans from Cuayucatepec	231
7.5	Coyol palm endocarps from Lomas phase midden at La Coyotera	239
7.6	Ciruela from Lomas phase midden at La Coyotera.	242
7.7	Seed fragments of unidentified fruit from Lomas phase midden at La Coyotera	244

LIST OF TABLES

2.1	Site sizes and population estimates for The Arroyo Lencho Diego.	26
2.2	Artifact distributions at Ts449 (Early Santa María Phase)	27
2.3	Artifact distributions for Middle and Late Santa María sites).	30
2.4	Distribution of mounded residences and obsidian blades at Ts452.	33
2.5	Distribution of obsidian in Late Santa María sites.	38
2.6	Residential areas of Ts73/79 (Early Palo Blanco Phase).	42
2.7	Artifact distributions at Ts73/79 (Early Palo Blanco Phase).	47
2.8	Manpower requirements of dam construction	57
2.9	Available manpower and manpower stress index.	58
2.10	Manpower stress and administrative complexity	59
2.11	Social differentiation and number of households dependent upon irrigation system.	61
2.12	Maize productivity.	66
2.13	Carrying capacity estimates	66
2.14	Reconstructed diets of occupants of Purrón Cave	67
2.15	Regional population estimates for the Tehuacán Valley	69
3.1	Fire-cracked rock at Ts73	113
3.2	Density of sherds in ceramic workshop	115
3.3	Distribution of firing accidents among vessel forms	121
3.4	Relation between firing accidents and surface colors.	121
3.5	Proportions of misfired bowls and jars in ceramic workshop collection squares	124
4.1	Definitions of ceramic type groups used in this report.	137
4.2	Frequencies of type groups from excavation units.	138
4.3	Population estimates for the three occupations at Quachilco	144
4.4	Mean proportions of three well-dated ceramic categories in surface strata and t-Test comparisons of strata.	147
7.1	_Persea americana_ seed measurements.	223
7.2	Tentative varieties of _Phaseolus_ at Cuayucatepec.	232

1. INTRODUCTION

by Robert D. Drennan

During the past four years the Palo Blanco Project has conducted fieldwork in and around the Tehuacán Valley with the objective of contributing to a better understanding of the processes of social, political, and economic development by which complex societies emerge. To this end we have focussed on the Late and Terminal Formative and Early Classic periods. In terms of the ceramic chronology established by MacNeish, Peterson, and Flannery (1970), these include the Late Santa María and the Early and Late Palo Blanco phases (Fig. 1.1). Before this time the Tehuacán Valley was the scene of a series of relatively autonomous, egalitarian farming villages. At the beginning of the period we study, a primitive "central place" was founded and became the geographical focus of a society which included a number of villages subsidiary to the central place. During the Early Palo Blanco phase this pattern crystalized and spread throughout the Tehuacán Valley, with the result that some half-dozen polities, each focussed on a central place of moderate size, divided the valley among themselves. No one of these polities seems ever to have dominated the entire valley, although competition among them and consequent waxing and waning of various centers are apparent.

It is this process of sociopolitical change we seek to understand in terms of the region in which it developed and in terms of its relationship to the sociopolitical developments apparent in the nearby and contemporaneous but much more spectacular centers of Teotihuacán and Monte Albán. Our preliminary reconstruction of the sociopolitical development in the Tehuacán Valley is described in greater detail in Drennan (1978:1-7) as are the issues involved in coming to an understanding of it.

The several chapters in this volume are reports on various portions of the studies we have carried out during a number of field seasons. These reports vary considerably in nature. Some are final reports of discrete segments of our work, while others are preliminary reports on more recent seasons. At this writing, then, we stand in the middle of the project. Some parts of the project have been completed, and the results are presented here. Fieldwork for other parts of the project has been completed but analysis of data has only begun; these parts are described in preliminary form, as has been done previously (Drennan, ed., 1977 and Drennan 1978), so that their immediate results may be made available as soon as possible. And still more fieldwork is planned for several parts of the project.

The chapters are arranged roughly in chronological order, according to the archeological phases with which they deal. First, because it reaches farthest back in time, comes a final report by Charles Spencer on surface survey conducted during 1976 in the area of the Arroyo Lencho Diego at the downstream end of the Tehuacán Valley (Fig. 1.2). The arroyo is spanned by the impressive irrigation structure called the Purrón Dam. This dam was studied by Woodbury and Neely (1972:82-99), and habitation sites in the adjacent region were further described by MacNeish et al. (1972:393-428). Spencer conducted more intensive surface survey, including detailed mapping and controlled surface collection, at these habitation sites. His study spans the entire period during which the dam was in use, from the Early Santa María phase through the Early Palo Blanco phase (Fig. 1.1). As such it shows in microcosm the sociopolitical development outlined above in general terms for the Tehuacán Valley as a whole. Small, apparently egalitarian villages of the Early Santa María phase gave way to more complex social forms, culminating during the Early Palo Blanco phase in a hilltop "town" (central place for one of the half-dozen polities which existed in the valley at this time) before the dam ceased to function and the immediate area was abandoned. Because of the evidence available from the dam, a unique data set for its time period in Mesoamerica, Spencer is able to study in unprecedented detail the relationship between this sociopolitical development and the development of the system of irrigated agriculture which sustained it. He can thus offer some unusually well-documented

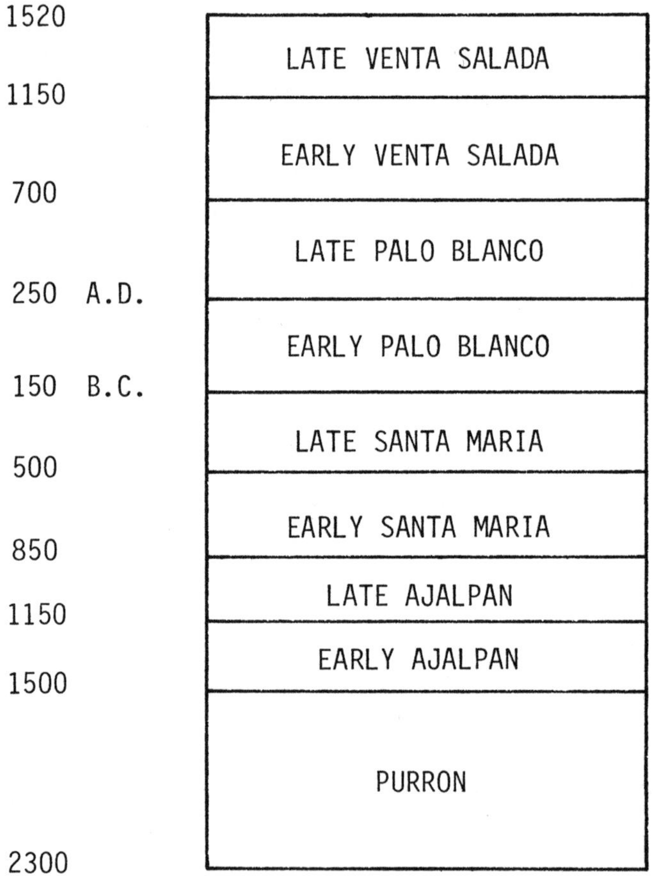

Date	Phase
1520	LATE VENTA SALADA
1150	EARLY VENTA SALADA
700	LATE PALO BLANCO
250 A.D.	EARLY PALO BLANCO
150 B.C.	LATE SANTA MARIA
500	EARLY SANTA MARIA
850	LATE AJALPAN
1150	EARLY AJALPAN
1500	PURRON
2300	

Fig. 1.1. Ceramic chronology for the Tehuacán Valley.

1. INTRODUCTION

conclusions concerning this much-discussed relationship.

Chapter 3 relates to Chapter 2, since it is a detailed study of the evidence for ceramic production at the Early Palo Blanco hilltop town in the Arroyo Lencho Diego survey area. The contribution of this study by Elsa Redmond is twofold. First, it provides fundamental information concerning the organization of production in this area during the Early Palo Blanco phase. Such information contributes materially to Spencer's study in Chapter 2 and to our understanding of sociopolitical development in the Tehuacán Valley in general. Second, it outlines the kind of evidence for ceramic production available for this period in Mesoamerica. Despite the heavy reliance of archeologists on the study of ceramics and the number of implicit assumptions we make concerning the organization of production of ceramics, actual archeological evidence bearing upon this organization is extremely scarce for Mesoamerica. Mesoamericanists have not been unaware of the problems created by this scarcity of evidence, as the attention to ethnographic studies of pottery manufacture shows. But concrete archeological data on pottery manufacture have been difficult to locate. An occasional feature from a later time period has been interpreted as a ceramic kiln (see, for example, Winter and Payne 1976), but the direct artifactual evidence of pottery manufacture has received almost no attention. As Redmond shows, Mesoamericanists need not nurse a concealed envy of colleagues who work in regions such as the Near East where "kiln wasters" are well known, although we may have to hide some embarrassment at our failure up to now to make more of evidence that is, under some circumstances at least, available in Mesoamerica.

Chapter 4 is out of place chronologically in that it deals with an earlier phase than the most recent developments discussed in Chapters 2 and 3. John Alden presents a final report on systematic surface survey conducted in 1975 at Quachilco, the Late Santa María phase site representing the earliest "town" in the Tehuacán Valley (see above). It is located in the center of a broad level expanse of alluvial farmland in the central section of the valley (site 218 in Fig. 1.2). Here are found the earliest indications of the more centralized kind of sociopolitical organization which characterized the Classic period. On the one hand, Alden's survey served as a guide for the 1977 excavations at Quachilco (Drennan 1978), suggesting notions about the organization of the site to be pursued by collecting data through excavation. On the other hand, the data from the surface collections complement the excavation data by providing a view of the site more extensive and complete than one attained through limited excavation at a large site, although subject to all the problems inherent in dealing with material not in primary context.

Beginning in Chapter 5 we turn to preliminary reports with a description of 1978 excavations at Cuayucatepec (site 281 in Fig. 1.2). Founded during the Early Palo Blanco phase and occupied into the Late Palo Blanco phase, Cuayucatepec represents the period during which the pattern of "town" organization was replicated throughout the Tehuacán Valley. Cuayucatepec was a second generation central place, one of the half-dozen which, like the hilltop town in the Lencho Diego survey area, succeeded Quachilco. The excavations here were explicitly intended to

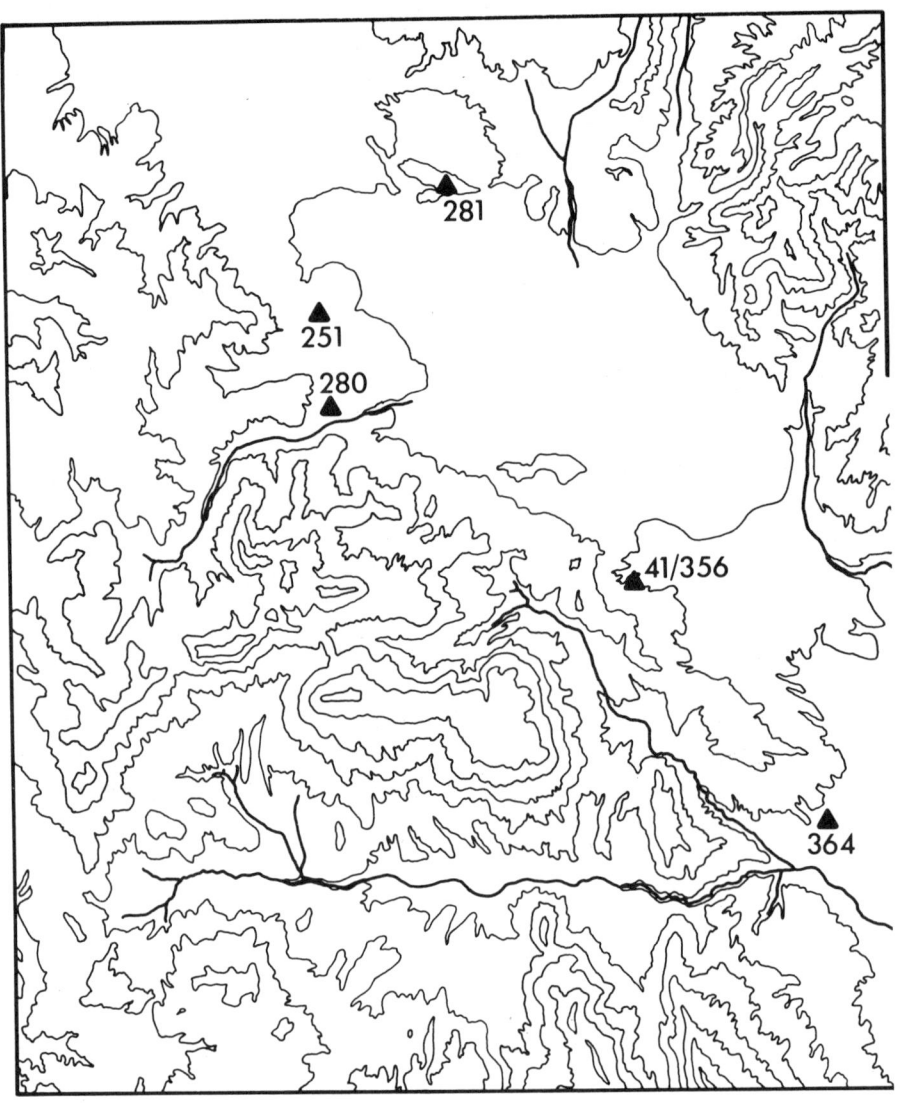

Fig. 1.2. Map of the Tehuacán Valley showing archeological sites mentioned in the text and the Lencho Diego survey area. Quachilco is site 218; Cuayucatepec is site 281. The Cañada (Fig. 6.2) lies to the south of this map.

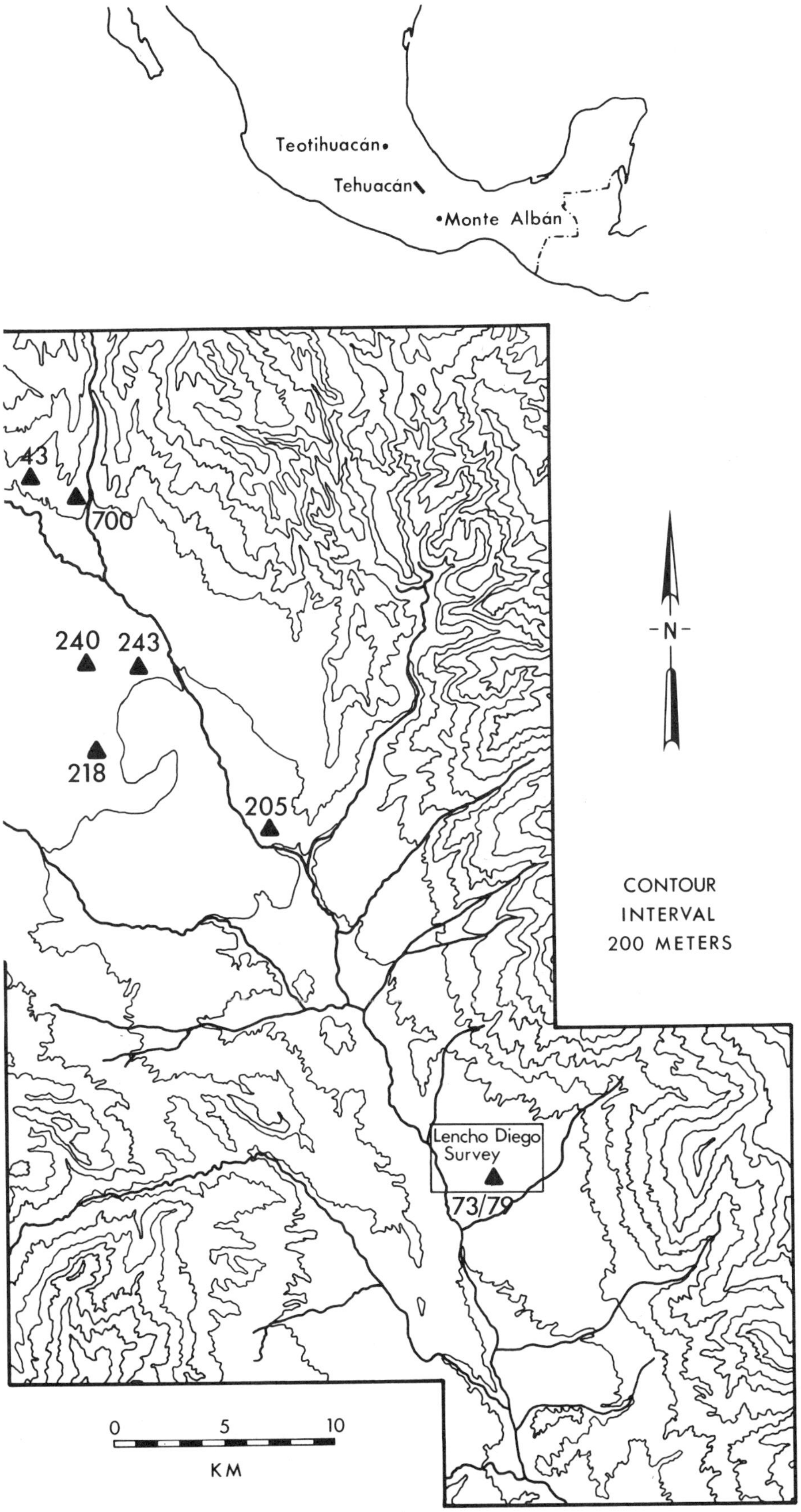
Teotihuacán
Tehuacán
Monte Albán
43
700
240
243
218
205
Lencho Diego Survey
73/79
N
CONTOUR INTERVAL 200 METERS
0 5 10
KM

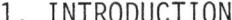

extend into the next period the view of Tehuacán Valley society provided by the excavations at Quachilco. Cuayucatepec, both more nucleated and more populous than Quachilco, suggests in its hilltop location and walled central sector a less than peaceful period. Although contemporaneous with major powers centered at Monte Albán, Teotihuacán, and perhaps Cholula, its ceramics show no strong stylistic similarities to theirs.

In another preliminary report in Chapter 6, Spencer and Redmond describe a program of surface survey and excavation in the Cuicatlán Cañada, a low-lying region just to the south of the map in Fig. 1.2. Although the Cañada is outside the Tehuacán Valley proper, Spencer's and Redmond's work there falls squarely within the interests of the Palo Blanco Project since it deals most directly with one of the important factors in the Classic period sociopolitical development of the region—its relations with the more complex societies of neighboring regions. The surface survey in the Cañada, directed by Redmond during 1977, recorded sites of all periods, although the principal focus, like that of all the work described in this volume, was on the Late and Terminal Formative and Classic periods. Spencer directed excavations during 1977 and 1978 at the site of La Coyotera, a center of the Late and Terminal Formative. The preliminary interpretations Spencer and Redmond present concern the political domination of the Cañada by Monte Albán. The survey documents the extent of such domination—it seems to have included the Cañada but not the Tehuacán Valley. Both survey and excavation trace some of the social, political, and economic effects of this domination on the Cañada by comparing the periods before, during, and after its existence. It is thus possible to deal with the impact of Monte Albán on the Cañada, to contrast the Cañada with the Tehuacán Valley where this kind of domination by outside powers seems not to have occurred, and to gain insight into the nature of the political unit centered at Monte Albán itself.

Finally, in Chapter 7, Judith Smith gives a preliminary account of the botanical remains encountered in all the excavations thus far conducted by the Palo Blanco Project. Because they come from open sites which were, from the Formative onward, the principal human occupations in the Tehuacán Valley, these remains provide an important complement to those recovered by MacNeish's Tehuacán Archaeological-Botanical Project. Although preservation of organic material in the open sites does not compare with that in the dry caves excavated by MacNeish et al. (1972), substantial quantities of carbonized botanical remains have been recovered from these open sites through flotation. The view of subsistence from these sites is crucial to a complete understanding of the systems which supplied Tehuacán's earliest complex societies with their food, because Tehuacán's inhabitants spent almost all of their time after the beginning of the Formative period in these villages and towns, making only short-term, special-purpose camps in the caves which have hitherto provided the only subsistence data for the valley. Smith points out some interesting parallels and differences between the patterns of plant use at the three main excavated sites of the Palo Blanco Project, and notes some of the directions her continuing analysis is taking to elucidate the reasons for these parallels and differences.

We all wish to stress that Chapters 5, 6, and 7 are preliminary re-

1. INTRODUCTION

ports. Considerable further analysis remains to be done for these portions of the project—analysis which may lead us to alter some of our preliminary interpretations.

All site numbers used in this report correspond to those assigned by MacNeish et al. (1972:341-495). We have not, however, attempted to maintain the distinction between surface sites (designated by the prefix "Ts") and "ruins" (designated by the prefix "Tr"). In general, we have given the prefix "Ts" to all sites not in caves. The prefix makes no difference in the identification of sites in any event, since numbers have been assigned to sites by order of discovery, regardless of prefix. That is, Ts218 and Tr218 are in no case different sites.

The work of the Palo Blanco Project from 1975 through 1978, a part of which is described in this volume, has been made possible through the kindness, cooperation, and generosity of a number of institutions and individuals. The project began with funding from the Robert S. Peabody Foundation for Archaeology whose director, Dr. Richard S. MacNeish, has also been most generous with the data collected by his earlier Tehuacán Archaeological-Botanical Project. The continuation of the Palo Blanco Project has been under the auspices of the University of Michigan Museum of Anthropology, and its work has been supported by the National Science Foundation under Grant No. BNS76-82651. Any opinions, findings, and conlusions expressed in this publication are, of course, those of the authors and do not necessarily reflect the views of the National Science Foundation.

Drs. Richard I. Ford and Robert E. Whallon, Jr., of the University of Michigan Museum of Anthropology, have greatly facilitated the work of the project and the publication of its results. Thanks are also due to Drs. James B. Richardson, III, and James M. Adovasio of the University of Pittsburgh Department of Anthropology for the use which the project has made of the equipment, facilities, and services of that institution. Permission for the fieldwork in Mexico has been granted by the Instituto Nacional de Antropología e Historia. The Project has benefited greatly from the cooperation, assistance, and advice of many individuals from that institution, including Dr. Ignacio Bernal, Prof. Manuel Esparza, Arqga. Diana López, Prof. José L. Lorenzo, Arqgo. Eduardo Matos M., Arqgo. Daniel Molina, Lic. Ariel Valencia R., and Dr. Marcus C. Winter.

All parts of the Palo Blanco Project owe a debt to these individuals and institutions for the very existence of the project and the logistical base from which we all have worked. Other persons, institutions, and funding sources have been involved in various parts of the project as well, not the least of whom are the people who have actively participated in the fieldwork in addition to the authors of the chapters of this volume. Funding sources and individuals particularly involved in one part or other of the project, in addition to those already mentioned, receive acknowledgement in the chapters which follow.

1. INTRODUCCION

por Robert D. Drennan

Durante los últimos cuatro años el Proyecto Palo Blanco ha conducido trabajos de campo en el Valle de Tehuacán con el objetivo de contribuir a un mejor entendimiento del proceso por medio del cual se desarrollan sociedades complejas. Hacia este fin nuestros estudios se han enfocado tanto en el Formativo Tardío y Terminal así como también en el Clásico Temprano. Con referencia a la cronología cerámica establecida por MacNeish, Peterson, y Flannery (1970) este período es el de las fases Santa María Tardía y Palo Blanco Temprana y Tardía (Fig. 1.1). Antes de este tiempo el Valle de Tehuacán estaba poblado por una serie de aldeas agrícolas que eran relativamente autónomas y egalitarias. Al comienzo del período que estudiamos, un "lugar central" primitivo fue fundado, y se convirtió en el centro geográfico de una sociedad que incluía un número de aldeas subordinadas. Durante la fase Palo Blanco Temprana este patrón de asentamiento se cristalizó y se extendió por todo el Valle de Tehuacán, con el resultado que una media docena de entidades políticas, cada una enfocada en un lugar central de tamaño moderado, se dividieron el valle entre ellas. Aparentemente ninguna de estas entidades políticas dominó todo el valle en este período, aunque competencia entre ellas y consecuentemente el incremento o disminución del poder de una u otra, es aparente.

Este proceso de cambio socio-político es el que tratamos de entender con relación a la región en el cual fue desarrollado, así como también en término de su relación con los desarrollos socio-políticos aparentes en los sitios cercanos y contemporáneos, pero mucho más espectaculares, de Teotihuacán y Monte Albán. Nuestra reconstrucción preliminar de los desarrollos socio-políticos en el Valle de Tehuacán está descripta en mucho más detalle en Drennan (1978:1-7), así como también los problemas en llegar a un entendimiento de estos procesos.

Los varios capítulos en este volumen son informes sobre varias partes de los estudios que hemos llevado a cabo durante varias temporadas de trabajo de campo. Estos informes varían considerablemente. Algunos son informes finales de partes de nuestro trabajo, mientras que otros son informes preliminares sobre trabajos más recientes. Estamos pues en el punto medio de nuestro trabajo, algunas partes del proyecto han sido completadas y los resultados son presentados aquí, mientras que para otras partes del proyecto aunque el trabajo de campo está terminado, el análisis de los datos aún está en su fase inicial. Estas últimas partes están descriptas solamente en una manera preliminar, tal como se ha hecho en el pasado (Drennan, ed., 1977 y Drennan 1978), para que sus resultados inmediatos estén al alcance de todos lo más pronto posible. Se debe agregar que para algunas partes del proyecto se tiene planeado aún más trabajo de campo.

Los capítulos se han organizado aproximadamente en orden cronológico,

1. INTRODUCTION

según las fases arqueológicas con que tratan. Primeramente, porque pertenece a la época más temprana, se encuentra el informe final por Charles Spencer sobre el reconocimiento de superficie efectuado en el Arroyo Lencho Diego, en el área río abajo del Valle de Tehuacán (Fig. 1.2). El arroyo está cortado por la magnífica estructura de irrigación conocida como la presa Purrón. Esta presa fue estudiada por Woodbury y Neely (1972:82-99), y los sitios de habitación en su vecindad descriptos por MacNeish et al. (1972:393-428). Spencer condujo un reconocimiento de superficie más intenso, haciendo mapas detallados y colección de superficie controlada en estos sitios de habitación. Su estudio cubre todo el período en que la presa fue usada, desde la fase Santa María Temprana hasta, e incluyendo la fase Palo Blanco Temprana (Fig. 1.1). Su estudio muestra en microcosmo los desarrollos socio-políticos descriptos en términos generales para el Valle de Tehuacán. Las pequeñas, aparentemente egalitarias, aldeas de la fase Santa María Temprana dan paso a una organización social más compleja que culmina durante la fase Palo Blanco Temprana en un "centro" situado en la cima de una colina (este es un lugar central para una de las entidades políticas que existían en el valle en este período) antes que la presa dejara de funcionar y el área inmediata fuera abandonada. Por medio de la evidencia disponible en la presa, un grupo singular de datos para este período en Mesoamérica, Spencer ha podido estudiar en gran detalle la relación entre el desarrollo socio-político y el desarrolla de la agricultura irrigada que lo mantuvo. El puede, entonces, llegar a unas conclusiones muy bien documentadas en lo que concierne a esta muy discutida relación.

El Capítulo 3 está relacionado al Capítulo 2, ya que es un estudio detallado de la producción de cerámica en el centro situado en la cima de la colina en el área del Arroyo Lencho Diego. La contribución de este estudio por Elsa Redmond es de doble importancia. Primero, nos da información fundamental en lo que concierne a la organización de la producción en esta área durante la fase Palo Blanco Temprana. Esta información contribuye materialmente al estudio de Spencer en el Capítulo 2, así como a nuestro entendimiento del desarrollo socio-político en el Valle de Tehuacán en general. En segundo lugar, nos delinea el tipo de evidencia para la producción de cerámica que se encuentra disponible para este período en Mesoamérica. A pesar del fuerte énfasis que los arqueólogos ponen sobre los estudios de cerámica, y el número de suposiciones implícitas que hacemos en lo que concierne a la organización de la producción de cerámica, evidencia arqueológica relacionada con esta organización es muy escasa en Mesoamérica. Mesoamericanistas no han estado concientes de los problemas creados por esta escacez de evidencia, tal como la atención a estudios etnográficos de la producción de cerámica nos enseña. Pero hay que añadir que evidencia arqueológica sobre la producción de cerámica ha sido difícil de localizar. Ocasionalmente un elemento arqueológico de períodos más tardíos ha sido identificado como un horno de cerámica (véase, por ejemplo, Winter y Payne 1976), pero evidencia directa sobre la producción de cerámica ha recibido muy poca atención. Como Redmond nos enseña, Mesoamericanistas no tienen porqué tener envidia de colegas que trabajan en regiones tales como el Medio Oriente, donde evidencia para la producción de cerámica es bien conocida, aunque tal vez tengamos que estar un poco avergonzados por nuestra inabilidad de tomar ventaja, hasta ahora, de la evidencia disponible bajo algunas circunstancias en Mesoamérica.

El Capítulo 4 no está exactamente en orden cronológico ya que trata con una fase más temprana que los hechos más recientes descriptos en los Capítulos 2 y 3. John Alden presenta un reporte final sobre el reconocimiento de superficie que tomó lugar en Quachilco en 1975 y que trata con la fase Santa María Tardía y representa la primera "ciudad" en el Valle de Tehuacán (ver arriba). Quachilco está localizado en medio de una gran área de tierra aluvial agrícola en la región central del valle (sitio 218 en Fig. 1.2). Aquí se encontraron los indicios más tempranos del tipo de organización socio-política que caracterizó el período Clásico. El reconocimiento hecho por Alden sirvió como una guía a las excavaciones efectuadas en Quachilco en 1977 (Drennan 1978), sugiriendo nociones sobre la organización del sitio que necesitaban ser investigadas por medio de excavaciones. Además los datos de la colección de superficie complementan los datos de la excavación, proporcionándonos una vista del sitio más extensa y completa que la proporcionada por excavaciones limitadas en un sitio de grandes proporciones, aunque siempre limitada por los problemas inherentes en el tratamiento de materiales fuera de su contexto principal.

Comenzando con el Capítulo 5 tratamos con reportes preliminares. Primeramente tenemos una descripción de las excavaciones en el sitio de Cuayucatepec durante 1978 (sitio 281 en Fig. 1.2). Fundada durante la fase Palo Blanco Temprana y ocupada hasta la fase Palo Blanco Tardía, Cuayucatepec representa el período durante el cual la organización de "centros" fue replicada en todo el Valle de Tehuacán. Cuayucatepec fue un lugar central de la segunda generación, una entre la media docena que, como la ciudad situada en la cima de la colina en la región de Lencho Diego, sucedió a Quachilco. Las excavaciones en Cuayucatepec tuvieron la intención explícita de extender al período siguiente las ideas sobre la sociedad del Valle de Tehuacán que nos proporcionaron las excavaciones en Quachilco. Cuayucatepec, un sitio más nucleado y con una población más grande que Quachilco, nos sugiere, con su localidad en la cima y su sector central amurallado, un período menos pacífico que los anteriores. Aunque este sitio es contemporáneo con los poderes mayores centrados en Monte Albán, Teotihuacán, y tal vez Cholula, sus cerámicas no tienen similitudes estilísticas fuertes con las de ellos.

En otro informe preliminar en el Capítulo 6, Spencer y Redmond describen un programa de reconocimiento de superficie y excavación en la Cañada de Cuicatlán, una región bajía, justamente al sur del mapa en la Fig. 1.2. Aunque la Cañada está afuera del propio Valle de Tehuacán, el trabajo de Spencer y Redmond coincide con los intereses del Proyecto Palo Blanco, ya que trata directamente con uno de los factores importantes en el desarrollo socio-político de la región durante el período Clásico: su relación con las sociedades más complejas de las regiones cercanas. El reconocimiento de superficie en la Cañada bajo la direccion de Redmond llevado a cabo durante 1977, tomó nota de sitios de todos los períodos, aunque el enfoque principal, como el de todos los trabajos descriptos en este volumen, fue sobre los períodos Formative Tardío y Terminal, así como también el Clásico. Spencer dirigió excavaciones durante 1977 y 1978 en el sitio de la Coyotera, un centro de los períodos Formativo Tardío y Terminal. Las

1. INTRODUCTION

interpretaciones preliminares que Spencer y Redmond presentan conciernen la dominación política de la Cañada por Monte Albán. El reconocimiento de superficie documenta la extención de esta dominación, la cual parece haber incluído la Cañada, pero no el Valle de Tehuacán. Tanto el reconocimiento como las excavaciones trazan algunos de los efectos sociales, políticos, y económicos de esta dominación en la Canñada por medio de comparaciones de los períodos antes, durante, y después de su existencia. De esta manera es posible lidear con el impacto de Monte Albán sobre la Cañada, contrastar la Cañada con el Valle de Tehuacán donde este dominio por poderes extranjeros parece no haber sucedido, y lograr un discernimiento sobre la naturaleza del poder centrado en el propio Monte Albán.

Finalmente en el Capítulo 7, Judith Smith da un informe preliminar sobre los restos botánicos encontrados en todas las excavaciones conducidas hasta ahora por el Proyecto Palo Blanco. Dado el caso que estos restos provienen de sitios abiertos, los cuales, comenzando en el Formativo, son los sitios principales de ocupación humana en el Valle de Tehuacán, estos restos proporcionan un complemento importante a esos recogidos por MacNeish en el Proyecto Arqueológico-Botánico de Tehuacán, a pesar de que la preservación de materiales orgánicos en sitios abiertos no se compare con la de las cuevas secas excavadas por MacNeish (1972). A pesar de la diferencia en preservación, cantidades de material orgánico carbonizado se ha recuperado por medio de flotación. El tener una idea completa de la subsistencia de estos sitios abiertos es importante para un entendimiento completo de los sistemas que proveían las sociedades complejas más tempranas en Tehuacán, porque fue en estas aldeas y centros que los habitantes de Tehuacán pasaron casi todo su tiempo después del comienzo del período Formativo. Estos habitantes solamente acampaban por cortos períodos, y por razones específicas, en las cuevas que hasta ahora han sido las únicas fuentes de información sobre la subsistencia del valle. Smith nos presenta con paralelos y diferencias interesantes entre los patrones de uso de vegetales en los tres sitios principales excavados por el Proyecto Palo Blanco, y nota algunas de las direcciones que lleva su análisis para esclarecer estos paralelos y diferencias.

Todos nosotros deseamos enfatizar que los capítulos 5, 6, y 7 son informes preliminares. Todavía nos falta una considerable parte del análisis para completar estas partes del proyecto, el cual nos puede llevar a cambiar algunas de nuestras interpretaciones preliminares.

Todos los números de sitios usados en este informe corresponden a los asignados por MacNeish et al. (1972:341-495). No hemos, sin embargo, mantenido la distinción entre sitios de superficie (designados por el prefijo "Ts") y ruinas (designadas por el prefijo "Tr"). En general hemos dado el prefijo "Ts" a todos los sitios que no se encuentran en cuevas. En todo caso el prefijo no hace ninguna diferencia en la identificación de sitios, ya que números han sido asignados a sitios en el orden de su descubrimiento sin tener en cuenta el prefijo. Es decir Ts218 y Tr218 no son, en ningún caso, sitios diferentes.

El trabajo del Proyecto Palo Blanco desde 1975 hasta, e incluyendo 1978, parte del cual está descripta en este volumen, ha sido posible por medio de la generosidad, cooperación y gentileza de un número de individuos e instituciones. El proyecto comenzó con fondos del Robert S. Peabody Foundation for Archaeology, cuyo director, Dr. Richard S. MacNeish, nos ha demostrado gran generosidad con los datos coleccionados por su Proyecto Arqueológico-Botánico de Tehuacán. La continuación del Proyecto Palo Blanco ha sido bajo los auspicios del University of Michigan Museum of Anthropology con financiamiento del National Science Foundation bajo Grant No. BNS76-82651. El proyecto y la publicación de los resultados han sido facilitados por los Drs. Richard I. Ford y Robert E. Whallon del University of Michigan Museum of Anthropology. También se le deben gracias a los Drs. James B. Richardson, III, y James M. Adovasio del Departamento de Antropología de la University of Pittsburgh, por su generosidad con equipo, facilidades, y servicios de esa institución. El permiso para el trabajo de campo en México fue dado por el Instituto Nacional de Antropología e Historia. El proyecto se ha beneficiado mucho por la cooperación, asistencia y consejos de muchos individuos en esa institución, entre los que se encuentran el Dr. Ignacio Bernal, Prof. Manuel Esparza, Arqga. Diana López, Prof. José L. Lorenzo, Arqgo. Eduardo Matos M., Arqgo. Daniel Molina, Lic. Ariel Valencia R., y el Dr. Marcus C. Winter.

El Proyecto Palo Blanco tiene una gran deuda con todos estos individuos e instituciones, para la existencia misma del proyecto, y para la base logística de la cual trabajamos. Otras personas, instituciones, y fuentes de financiamiento han sido partes del proyecto en sus varias fases, sin dejar de notar las personas que han participado en los trabajos de campo, además de las que han contribuído capítulos a este volumen. Fuentes de financiamiento e individuos que han contribuído a una u otra parte del proyecto, además de los ya mencionados, serán agradecidos en los varios capítulos que siguen.

2. IRRIGATION, ADMINISTRATION, AND SOCIETY IN FORMATIVE TEHUACAN

by Charles S. Spencer

This chapter deals with a large prehistoric irrigation system and the sociopolitical organization of the people who used it. The setting is the Arroyo Lencho Diego, a major tributary barranca in the southeastern part of the Tehuacán Valley. Here members of R.S. MacNeish's Tehuacán Archaeological-Botanical Project discovered an impressive water-control feature, the Purrón Dam, as well as a number of archeological sites. Woodbury and Neely (1972) studied the dam itself in 1964 and found that it had been constructed in four stages, beginning with a small structure built around 700 B.C. The last stage brought the dam to truly monumental proportions: some 400 m long, 20 m high, and 100 m thick at the base. The capacity of the reservoir associated with this last stage is estimated at 2,640,000 m^3. The dam functioned until ca. A.D. 250, when both it and the surrounding area were abandoned. The dam was used, maintained, and enlarged during the Middle and Late Formative period when sociopolitical organization throughout Mesoamerica was rapidly becoming more complex. The Purrón Dam and Arroyo Lencho Diego consequently have a key role to play in the long-standing anthropological debate over the importance of large-scale irrigation works in cultural evolution.

During the summer of 1976, the author conducted an archeological survey in the Arroyo Lencho Diego as part of the University of Michigan's Palo Blanco Project. This work was aimed at defining the nature and extent of human settlement in the arroyo for the periods when the dam was in use. In this chapter, an attempt will be made to relate changes in the scale of the irrigation system, determined by variation in dam size and reservoir capacity over time, to concurrent developments in social, political, and economic organization, determined by an analysis of the associated settlement patterns. A set of four hypotheses dealing with large-scale irrigation systems and the organization of the people who use them will be tested with these data.

Theoretical Background and Presentation of Hypotheses

The idea that irrigation and politics are functionally related is not new. As Karl Wittfogel himself has pointed out (Wittfogel 1972:62), Karl Marx was perhaps the first social theorist to consider the political

---

I would like to thank the following people for reading and making useful comments on this chapter: Robert Drennan, Kent Flannery, Richard Ford, Joyce Marcus, Jeffrey Parsons, Elsa Redmond, and Henry Wright. While these people have contributed much to the clarity of this presentation, only I am responsible for its shortcomings.

implications of large-scale waterworks. Nevertheless, it was Wittfogel who coined the term "hydraulic society" and presented the concept as a developed formulation (1938; 1957).

A central theme in this formulation is that water has certain unique properties as a flowing resource which demand cooperative labor from the people who use it in constructing and maintaining dams, canals, and other water-control features. This need for cooperation encourages in turn the development of an administrative bureaucracy to direct and monitor the cooperative endeavors. Wittfogel also explicated the relationship of water-control institutions to other aspects of culture such as property laws, class structure, and religion. He specified how the effects of large-scale water control might vary with the scale of the irrigation system and under different environmental conditions. The development of the centralized control characteristic of hydraulic society would, he felt, be most likely to occur in situations where aridity necessitated irrigation for all agricultural activity, and where the scale of the irrigation system was quite large.

There is possibly no social-scientific concept that has excited more controversy and certainly none that has sent more archeologists to the field than the hydraulic theory. A polarization of opinion has resulted, with some archeologists adamantly supporting the Wittfogelian position and others just as adamantly opposing it. One of the more vigorous opponents of the classic hydraulic formulation has been Robert Adams (1966). He argued that small-scale irrigation preceded the state in Mesopotamia by many centuries, and truly large-scale irrigation systems were not built until long after early state developments. Adams highlighted a different aspect of irrigation: its ability to increase greatly the potential yields of the productive base. This characteristic, he felt, stimulated social stratification by increasing the amount of absolute surplus that could be manipulated by an emergent elite bent on increasing its power and prestige. (See also Friedman 1974:463 for a similar position.)

The Wittfogelian formulation has also been criticized from an ethnographic perspective. Studies by Millon, Hall, and Díaz (1962), Millon (1962), and Leach (1959 and 1961) considered the wide variety of social and political forms associated with irrigation agriculture in the ethnographic present, and Millon (1962:56) concluded that "there is no clear relationship between degree of centralization of authority and the size of the irrigation system and the number of persons it supports." But in spite of these objections it was still an undeniable fact that many early civilizations were economically based on irrigation agriculture. Furthermore, the irrigation cooperatives studies by these authors were often imbedded in a larger political system, the modern nation-state, and thus did not strictly refute the hydraulic theory as it pertained to early state formation. (See Sanders and Price 1968:182.)

In Mesoamerica, the anthropological investigation of irrigation agriculture has a fairly lengthy history. Pedro Armillas (1949 and 1951), Angel Palerm (1955 and Palerm and Wolf 1957), and Eric Wolf (1959) proposed the existence of a significant relationship between irrigation agriculture and the emergence of precolumbian civilization. In a conference organized by Julian Steward (Steward, ed., 1955), Palerm pointed to the present-day correlation in Mexico between population density and degree of agricultural intensity. Although no evidence had been found for Formative or Classic irrigation works, he surmised that an intensive mode of production like irrigation agriculture must have been the economic base of Classic Mesoamerican civilization in the highlands. "It seems rather obvious that rainfall agriculture, never extensive in Mesoamerica, could not accumulate an adequate and consistent surplus to maintain the urban centers" (Palerm 1955:31).

This "must have been" argument failed to convince many archeologists, particularly in the absence of substantive data on early irrigation systems. But in the 1960's several excavations finally produced evidence for irrigation works in the Formative period (Brunet 1967, Neely 1967, Flannery et al. 1967, Orlandini 1967, and Woodbury and Neely 1972). These discoveries brought the hydraulic theory onto center stage and several prominent theorists sought to work it into complex explanatory models of culture change. One of these, William Sanders, argued that hydraulic agriculture along with "economic symbiosis" was a major selective agent in the genesis of early Mesoamerican civilization (Sanders 1968 and 1972). Sanders and Price (1968:181) asserted that "over a long period of time the practice of irrigation presents certain problems and stimuli, and that there is a strong selective force analogous to biological natural selection in favor of centralized control." In addition to the problem of cooperative construction and maintenance of waterworks, Sanders stressed the potential for conflict over water allocation between upstream and downstream irrigators as a condition that might select for more centralized control. (See also Lees 1973.)

Why a human group would decide to intensify agricultural production in the first place is also a subject of debate. Sanders and Price (1968) felt that the major factor prompting such a decision was population pressure, coming about when the size of the human population approached the carrying capacity of the subsistence procurement regime as defined in terms of environmental variables and technological factors. One adaptive response to such population pressure would be a decision to intensify agricultural production through irrigation. Problems contingent on such a decision (organizing mass labor, allocating water and irrigable land, etc.) would select for more centralized control. Millon (1973 and 1976) has been a vigorous opponent of this approach. He felt that Mesoamerican civilization could not be understood by considering merely demographic and techno-economic variables. Political and ideological factors, he insisted, must be incorporated into any comprehensive explanation of the rise of Mesoamerican civilization.

A real difficulty confronting theorists of all persuasions, however, has been a lack of pertinent archeological data to which the various versions of the hydraulic theory could be applied. As Sanders and Price (1968:180) admitted, "the major problem has been archaeological, that of establishing the antiquity of irrigation and of hydraulic society and of evaluating their roles in the genesis and growth of Mesoamerican society as a whole." In spite of years of research on the topic, we have made very little progress toward a true understanding of irrigation's role in the development of complex society in Mesoamerica, and Wittfogel's theory remains essentially untested.

Recently, Hunt and Hunt (1976) have presented a critique and programmatic statement dealing with current work on irrigation and society. They pointed out that Wittfogel's formulation is basically concerned with historical development, and a proper test of his theory ought to be carried out in a diachronic frame of reference. Nearly all current studies and so-called "tests" of the hydraulic theory have been synchronic comparisons of contemporary systems (cf. Kappel 1974). Furthermore, Wittfogel consistently maintained that his theory applied to hydraulic societies in arid environments, and many anthropologists have ignored this. The Hunts also stressed that a concept central to the hydraulic theory is change in the scale of the irrigation system.

> Another variable is 'scale' which may be taken to mean the scale of the physical works associated with water control, the population served, the acreage irrigated, the length of canals, and so on. Measurement of these in avilable studies is generally no better than an intuitive ordinal scale. (Hunt and Hunt 1976:390)

A proper test of the hydraulic theory, said the Hunts, demands long-term diachronic data on changes in the scale of an irrigation system combined with information on concurrent variability in human demography, economics, and sociopolitical organization. "Until such data are generally available, a test of Wittfogel's hypothesis from anthropological field studies is out of the question" (Hunt and Hunt 1976:390).

The Hunts' message has special significance for archeologists interested in the sociopolitical implications of early canal irrigation in Mesoamerica. Although a number of prehistoric water-control features have been located and chronologically placed (cf. Fowler 1969 and Neely 1967), there are at this writing no archeological data available on diachronic variability in the scale of an early Mesoamerican irrigation system coupled with data on concurrent variability in, for example, settlement patterns which might provide information about social and political organization. This lack of pertinent data has hindered all attempts by archeologists to understand the role of irrigation in the evolution of sociopolitical complexity in highland Mesoamerica.

The discovery in the 1960's that the Purrón Dam was built in four stages over a 950-year period was an important development in Mesoamerican irrigation studies. Furthermore, an analysis of silt deposits behind the dam provided farily accurate volume estimates for the reservoirs associated with the various construction phases. Here finally was a way to measure long-term diachronic variability in the scale of an early Mesoamerican irrigation system. What remained to be collected was information on concurrent variability in the associated patterns of settlement. The Arroyo Lencho Diego Survey conducted by the author in the summer of 1976 was explicitly designed to compile the kinds of information necessary for a test of the hydraulic theory.

2. IRRIGATION, ADMINISTRATION, AND SOCIETY

The present study monitors several aspects of the Arroyo Lencho Diego irrigation community for the 950 years of its growth and development. For each of the four ceramic phases that together span this period, an attempt will be made to define and, where appropriate, to quantify the following variables:

1. <u>The physical size of the Purrón Dam and reservoir</u>. This is taken from Woodbury and Neely (1972).

2. <u>The size and distribution of human population</u>. Population size estimates are based on the number of house mounds and house foundations on the site maps. These same maps are used to assess the distribution of population in the arroyo.

3. <u>The nature and degree of social differentiation</u>. The controlled surface collections are used to make quantitative comparisons among households and groups of households on the basis of associated artifact distributions. Modes of household construction also provide insight into the nature of social differentiation in the arroyo.

4. <u>The degree of economic specialization</u>. This is approached primarily by examining the distributions of waste materials from certain craft activities, though other lines of evidence are also used.

5. <u>The degree of differential participation in ritual activities</u>. A "contextual analysis" (Flannery 1976a) of ritual paraphernalia is carried out to discover whether certain rituals were performed more often by some members of arroyo society than by others.

6. <u>The degree of complexity in administrative structure</u>. This is approached by an examination of the use of public space for each phase, since the quantity, morphology, and distribution of public architecture on a site reflect the nature of that community's administrative structure (Flannery and Marcus 1976). In this analysis we employ the concept of administration in its general sense, that is, as the decision-making apparatus of a cultural system (Flannery 1972, Wright 1977, and Johnson 1978). In Mesoamerica, as elsewhere, decision making was comprised of both religious and secular mechanisms and sanctions. This distinction, however, does not greatly concern us here, as we deal with public architecture in the arroyo more in terms of its administrative function than its ideological matrix. Following Johnson (1978), we assess the complexity of administration according to the degree of vertical and horizontal specialization in the organization of decision making. Vertical specialization refers to the number of formalized, hierarchically arranged orders of decision making, that is, the number of formalized levels of decision making above the level of the primary producers in society. Horizontal specialization, on the other hand, refers to the number of formalized decision-making units in a given level of administration.

The Arroyo Lencho Diego as described above is used in a diachronic frame of reference to evaluate the following set of four hypotheses distilled from the continuing debate over the hydraulic theory.

Hypothesis 1. There is a positive covariant relationship between the physical size and complexity of an irrigation system and the degree of administrative complexity in the society that uses it. The development of complex administration is primarily a response to the problems of organizing mass labor for the construction and maintenance of the irrigation facilities. (This is a major element in the Wittfogelian formulation.) Administrative complexity should increase when these organizational problems are most acute, when, for example, there is an imbalance between the manpower requirements of the task at hand and the size of the available work force.

Hypothesis 2. In a system where irrigation is necessary for agricultural production and there is but one water source, the opportunity exists for an emergent elite to gain control over the distribution of water and use this power in an entrepreneurial fashion to regulate the surplus production of the rest of the population (Adams 1966 and Friedman 1974:463). As more and more households are incorporated into such an irrigation system, the amount of absolute surplus that the elite can mobilize for its own aggrandizement will correspondingly increase. We would consequently expect a positive covariant relationship between the number of primary production units (that is, households) incorporated into the irrigation system and the degree to which society is characterized by differential access to power and desired resources.

Hypothesis 3. In situations where two or more communities are using the same water source for irrigation, there is the potential for conflict between upstream and downstream users over water rights. This sort of conflict is a major selective agent in the development of administrative complexity and centralized authority (Sanders and Price 1968 and Lees 1973). We would expect the addition of a downstream community to be followed rather quickly by increased administrative complexity in the system as a whole.

Hypothesis 4. The final hypothesis is based on the assumption that people will intensify production only if they are forced to by population pressure (Boserup 1965 and Sanders and Price 1968). Consequently, we would expect to find that every decision to expand the irrigation system was prompted by a stressful relationship between the productive potential of the existing mode of production and the nutritional requirements of the population.

The Arroyo Lencho Diego: Environment and Previous Work

The Arroyo Lencho Diego is located in the southeastern part of the Tehuacán Valley (see Fig. 1.2). According to MacNeish et al. (1972:67), it owes its name to one Lencho Diego, a local bandit who used a cave in the arroyo as his hideout. The arroyo begins in the southern slopes of the Cerro Chichiltepec, flowing southwest and then west through a hilly piedmont area composed of alternating cretaceous beds of sandstone and limestone interspersed with gypsum. For the last 1.5 km of its flow, the arroyo crosses the flat alluvial terraces of the Río Salado. There are

2. IRRIGATION, ADMINISTRATION, AND SOCIETY

about 425 ha of prime alluvium in the vicinity of the arroyo, between the two places where the piedmont intrudes nearly to the banks of the river. (See, for example, Fig. 2.3.)

The arroyo is in one of the warmest parts of the Tehuacán Valley. The mean annual temperature is about 25° C, and it ranges from 4° C in the wintertime to 45° C in the summer. This is also one of the drier parts of the valley. Rainfall averages between 400 and 500 mm per year but is extremely variable. When figures on evapo-transpiration are taken into consideration, a farmer near San Rafael can count on an 80% probability of useful rainfall between only 132 and 168 mm per annum (Byers 1967:54). This is far below the amounts needed for successful rainfall farming (cf. Kirkby 1973), and all agricultural production in the arroyo today is completely dependent upon irrigation.

The natural vegetation of the arroyo is not particularly dense. But mala mujer, prickly pear cactus, organ cactus, and maguey are fairly abundant, and there are moderate amounts of mesquite and acacia. The fauna of the region (evidently much reduced in numbers since prehistoric times) includes white-tailed deer, lynx, striped and spotted skunk, cottontail, kangaroo rat, gray fox, and various mice and lizards.

Although the agricultural potential of the area today is totally dependent upon irrigation, there is no useful, permanent, running water here. The Río Salado, which does flow most of the year, is true to its name by this point in the Tehuacán Valley: it is so salty that the farmers from San Rafael today do not use its water for irrigation. Instead, they rely upon run-off that courses through the tributary barrancas during the rainy season (from June to September). This water is not salty like that of the Salado, but harnessing it presents a significant problem. Today the people who farm the alluvium near San Rafael get their irrigation water by canal from a large barranca that enters the Valley near Coxcatlán, about 12 km to the north.

If the fertile alluvium of the Salado is irrigated with fresh water from the tributary barrancas, agriculture here can be quite productive. At present, the alluvium near San Rafael is entirely given over to cash cropping, and great quantities of sugar cane are produced. During the 1976 field season, however, we located two older men who remembered when some maize had been grown on the alluvium. One was a former ejido official who lived in San Rafael; the other was the present ejido sub-commissioner in Tilapa (the ejido headquarters for the area). Both men independently recalled that two crops of maize per year had been grown with irrigation on the alluvium near San Rafael. Each crop, they said, had averaged about 800 kg of shelled maize per ha.

While farmers now consider only the alluvium worth the effort of cultivation, the the ancient past some limited planting probably occurred in the tributary barrancas during the wet season. Plant remains from Purrón Cave (MacNeish et al. 1972:67-127) suggest that such seasonal cultivation had been practiced since at least 2,000 B.C., though it is unlikely that the yields from this cultivation would have been large or predictable enough to support a sedentary village. In fact, we shall see that the first sedentary settlement in the arroyo is associated with the first evidence for irrigation agriculture.

Perhaps the best known excavation in the arroyo is that conducted at Purrón Cave or Tc272. (See Fig. 2.3 for location.) MacNeish and his associates worked here in 1962 and 1963 and uncovered 31 occupations dating from 6,000 B.C. to A.D. 500. MacNeish estimated that the cave could have housed, on a seasonal basis, around four to five nuclear families. The great quantities of plant and animal remains found in Purrón Cave yielded information on season of occupation and subsistence activities (MacNeish et al. 1972:67-127).

Just a few hundred meters downstream from Purrón Cave is the Purrón Dam, an extremely large complex of water-control features (Fig. 2.1). Although parts of it had been discovered in 1961, not until 1962 was the complex recognized for what it truly was: a huge dam and associated reservoir. During 1964, a study of the dam complex was carried out by Richard Woodbury and James Neely (1972:82-99).

As Woodbury and Neely pointed out, the exact location chosen for the construction was ideal from an engineering viewpoint. The main structure

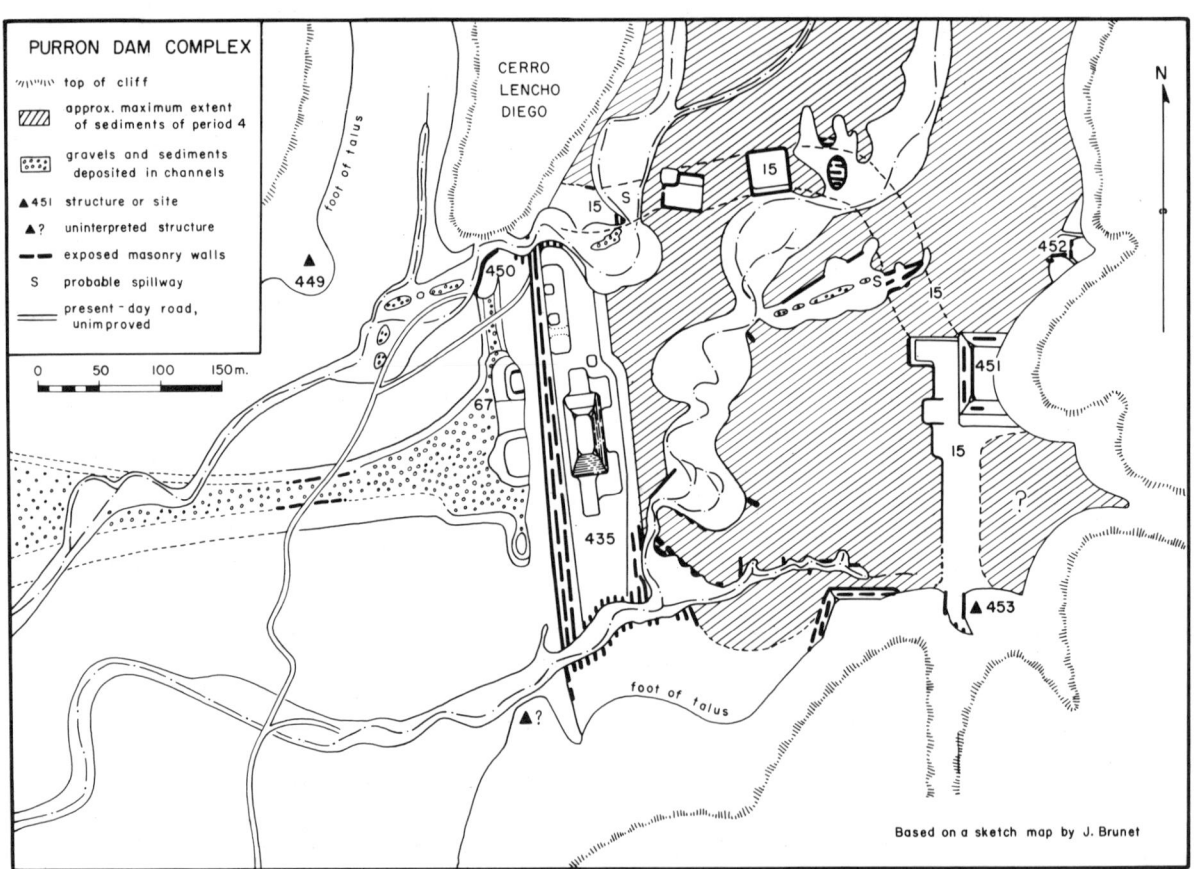

Fig. 2.1. Plan of the Purrón Dam complex. (From Woodbury and Neely 1972: Fig. 9.)

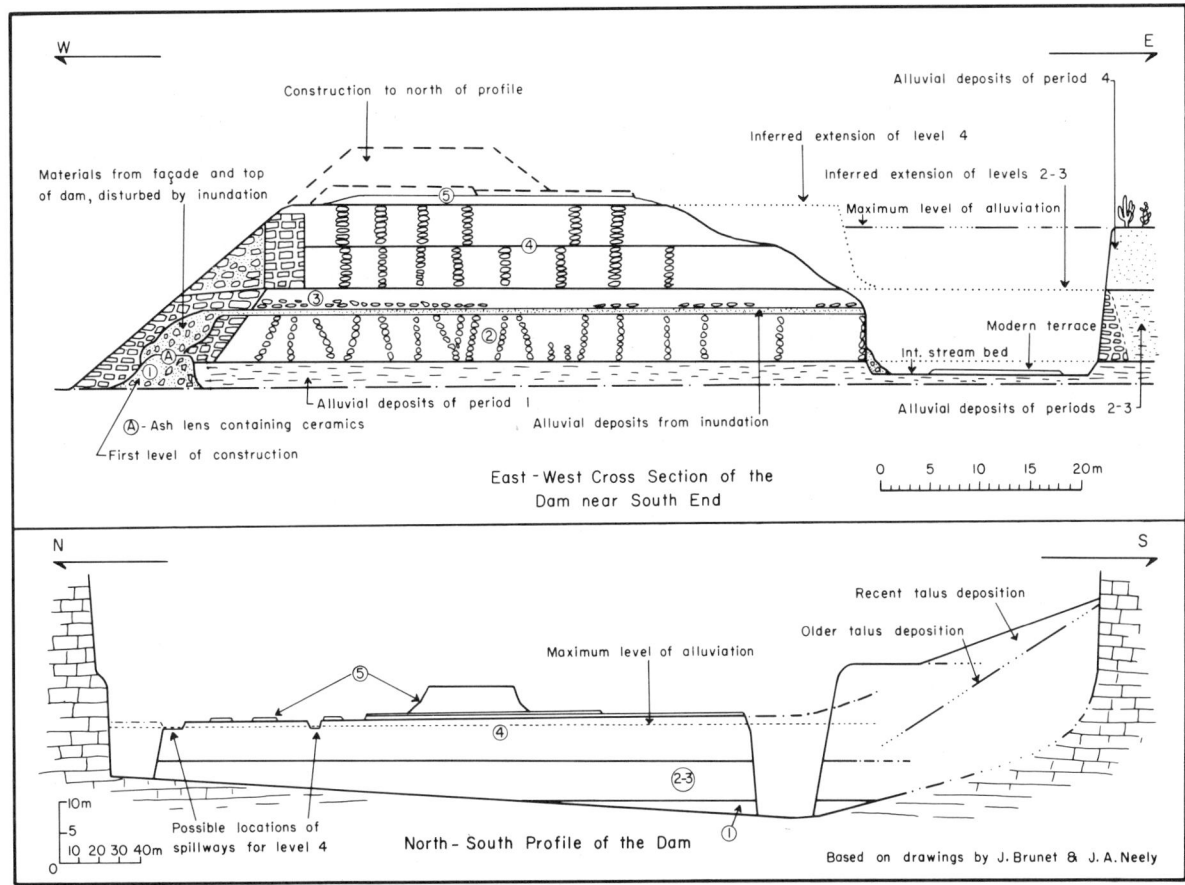

Fig. 2.2. Elevation and cross section views of the Purrón Dam. (From Woodbury and Neely 1972:Fig. 8.)

is strategically situated at a narrow point in the canyon. Here the arroyo constricts to less than half its previous width between two sheer cliffs 40 to 50 m high. By placing the dam at precisely this point, the builders got a sizeable collection basin through a minimum of construction effort.

In the years since the abandonment of the dam, run-off has cut two channels through the structure, one at each of the two places where the dam joins the canyon walls. The cut at the south end has provided the better cross section of the dam, and it was by studying this profile that Woodbury and Neely were able to determine that the dam had been built in four stages (Fig. 2.2). A fifth level consisting of some large mounded structures was added much later, during the Postclassic, long after the dam had ceased to function. Woodbury and Neely also made estimates of the amount of fill involved in each construction stage of the dam and of the capacity of the reservoir associated with each level. The estimates of capacity were based on a study of silt deposition behind the dam conducted by geologist Jean Brunet.

The 1976 Lencho Diego Survey

As of 1976, the archeology of the arroyo remained as described above. The dam had been dealt with extensively; Purrón and Abejas caves had been thoroughly excavated. In addition, a number of other sites in the vicinity had been located; but aside from rough chronological placement, very little had been done with these sites.

As part of the University of Michigan's Palo Blanco Project, we conducted a settlement pattern survey of those sites in the Arroyo Lencho Diego that had been occupied when the dam was functioning. We pursued a program of intensive mapping and controlled surface collecting (see Redman and Watson 1970) and surveyed a total of eight sites with occupations ranging over the four ceramic phases in question. We discovered that the arroyo was admirably suited to surface survey. It was possible to locate and map virtually all house mounds and other architectural features. This means that our population estimates (based on house mound counts) have a high degree of reliability. It also means that our surface collections in most cases can be directly associated with adjacent or nearby architectural units, allowing comparison of such units on the basis of their associated artifacts. Although it would have been desirable to map each site completely before selecting architectural units for collection by some random sampling procedure, limitations of time and personnel required us to map and collect in concert as we moved across a site. In selecting locations for collection, we followed two basic guidelines: we tried to place collection squares where the context was not ambiguous, and we tried to ensure more or less even coverage of each site. We were greatly aided by having copies of Frederick Peterson's and James Neely's original field notes concerning these sites. Although their survey was not designed to be as intensive as ours, they did locate all the sites in question, and their notes included rather precise instructions for reaching each site as well as some general information on settlement layout and chronology.

The sections which follow are organized according to the four ceramic phases during which the Purrón Dam was constructed and used. This chronology is that established by MacNeish, Peterson, and Flannery (1970) and illustrated in Fig. 1.1, except that it has been possible in the Lencho Diego material to divide the Santa María phase into three parts (Early, Middle, and Late) instead of the two used in the older chronology. As elsewhere in this report, the numbers of all sites not in caves are given with the prefix "Ts," although MacNeish et al. (1972:341-495) used the prefix "Tr" for some of them. But if the numbers match, the same site is meant, regardless of the prefix.

Early Santa María Phase (850-650 B.C.)

The first sedentary occupation in the Arroyo Lencho Diego was established at Ts449 during the Early Santa María phase. This is coeval with the first construction stage of the Purrón Dam (Fig. 2.3). Before this the arroyo had been visited on a seasonal basis by people who evidently lived

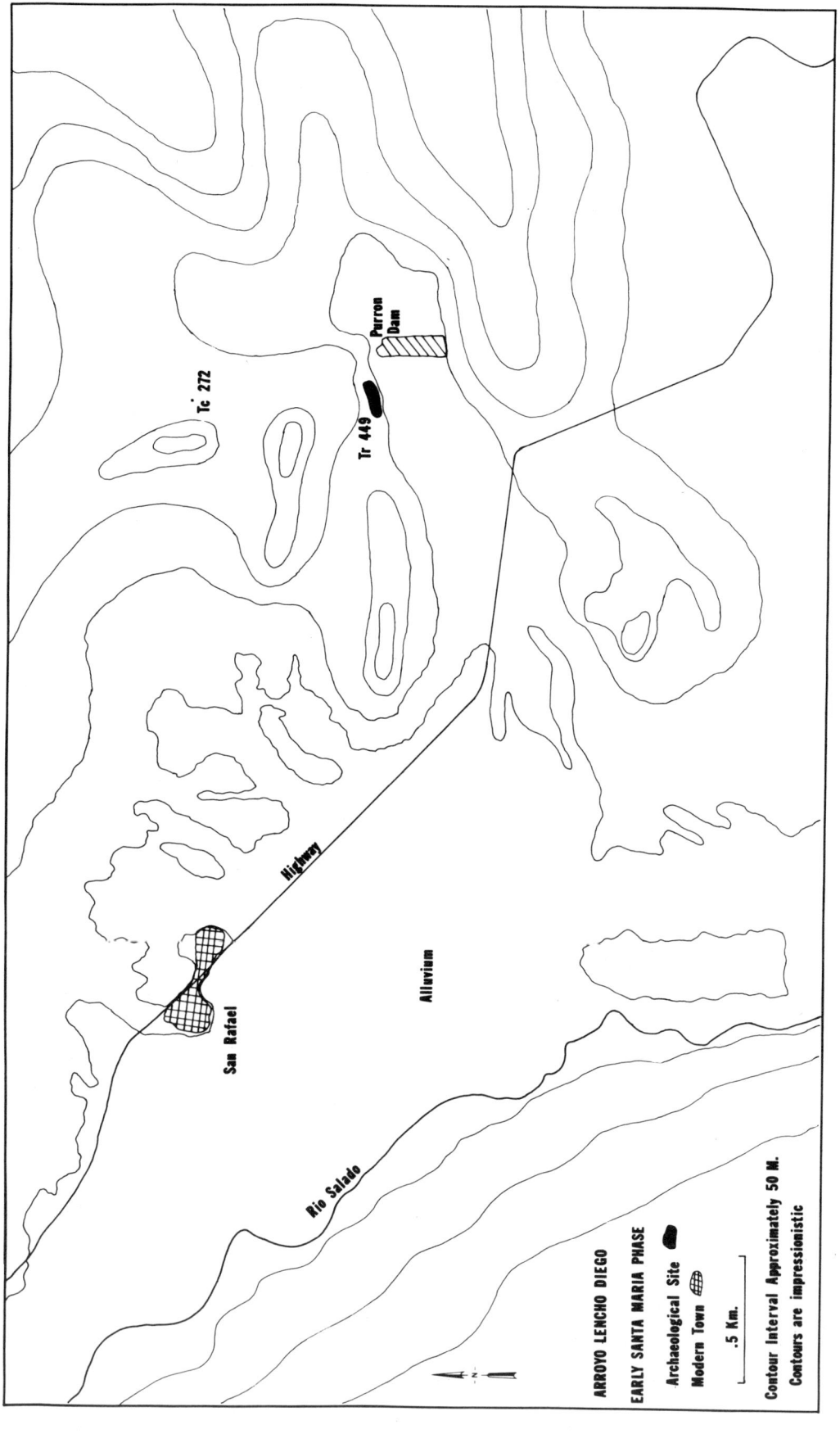

Fig. 2.3. Early Santa María settlement in the Arroyo Lencho Diego.

elsewhere for much of the year. Subsistence remains from Purrón Cave (Tc272) (MacNeish et al. 1972:73-97) suggest that they had engaged in some deer hunting, rabbit trapping, and collecting of various wild plants like agave and prickly pear cactus. This pattern of resource procurement is evident in the arroyo as far back as 6,000 B.C. Beginning around 2,000 B.C., however, the cultivation of maize became increasingly prominent. Limited planting probably occurred during the wet season in some of the moister nooks of the arroyo.

Then, sometime between 750 B.C. and 600 B.C., a small dam was built across part of the arroyo. This was Level 1 of the Purrón Dam (Fig. 2.2). Level 1 was dome-shaped in cross section. The structure was about 6 m wide, 2.8 m high, and 175 m long. Its 2,940 m^3 of fill were primarily composed of earth and fine gravels lying over a foundation of medium-sized river pebbles. The dam extended about halfway across the 400 m wide canyon. The lower elevation of the south side of the canyon resulted in a fair-sized collecting basin. Woodbury and Neely (1972:82-99) estimated the associated reservoir at about 140 m by 170 m, with a capacity of 37,000 m^3.

A map of Ts449 is presented in Fig. 2.4. Two houses with stone foundations were located on a large residential terrace. Scattered about these two houses were seven to ten additional residential terraces, each probably containing only one structure. On these other terraces we found domestic debris but no stone foundations. The total number of households at Ts449 was probably between nine and twelve. Allowing five persons per household would put 45 to 60 persons in about 1 ha of settlement, with an average population density of 52.5 persons per ha (Table 2.1).

Three intensive surface collections were made during the 1976 season at Ts449. Because of low sherd densities, we expanded our usual 5 by 5 m collection squares to a 25 by 25 m size. Fig. 2.4 shows the locations of the three collection squares. One collection is associated with the two structures having stone foundations. The other two collections were made on the residential terraces that lacked stone foundations. Table 2.2 presents some of the recovered data. One immediate point of interest in these data is that obsidian is not evenly distributed across the site. The collection associated with the masonry structures has a much higher ratio of obsidian fragments to chert and quartzite fragments than the two collections associated with residences lacking stone foundations (Table 2.2).

We suggest that the differential distribution of obsidian is related to status differences between the occupants of the structures with the stone foundations and those of the residential terraces without them. Obsidian was a resource highly prized and widely traded in ancient Mesoamerica. (See Pires-Ferreira 1975.) The sources closest to the Arroyo Lencho Diego are the Guadelupe Victoria source, 125 km away, and the Pico de Orizaba source, 100 km away. Both sources are well beyond the borders of the Tehuacán Valley. On the other hand, the chert and quartzite which make up the rest of the chipped stone assemblage are available in considerable abundance in the immediate vicinity of the Arroyo Lencho Diego. Differential access to a scarce resource like obsidian, therefore, can be construed as evidence for status differentiation within society. A further line of

2. IRRIGATION, ADMINISTRATION, AND SOCIETY

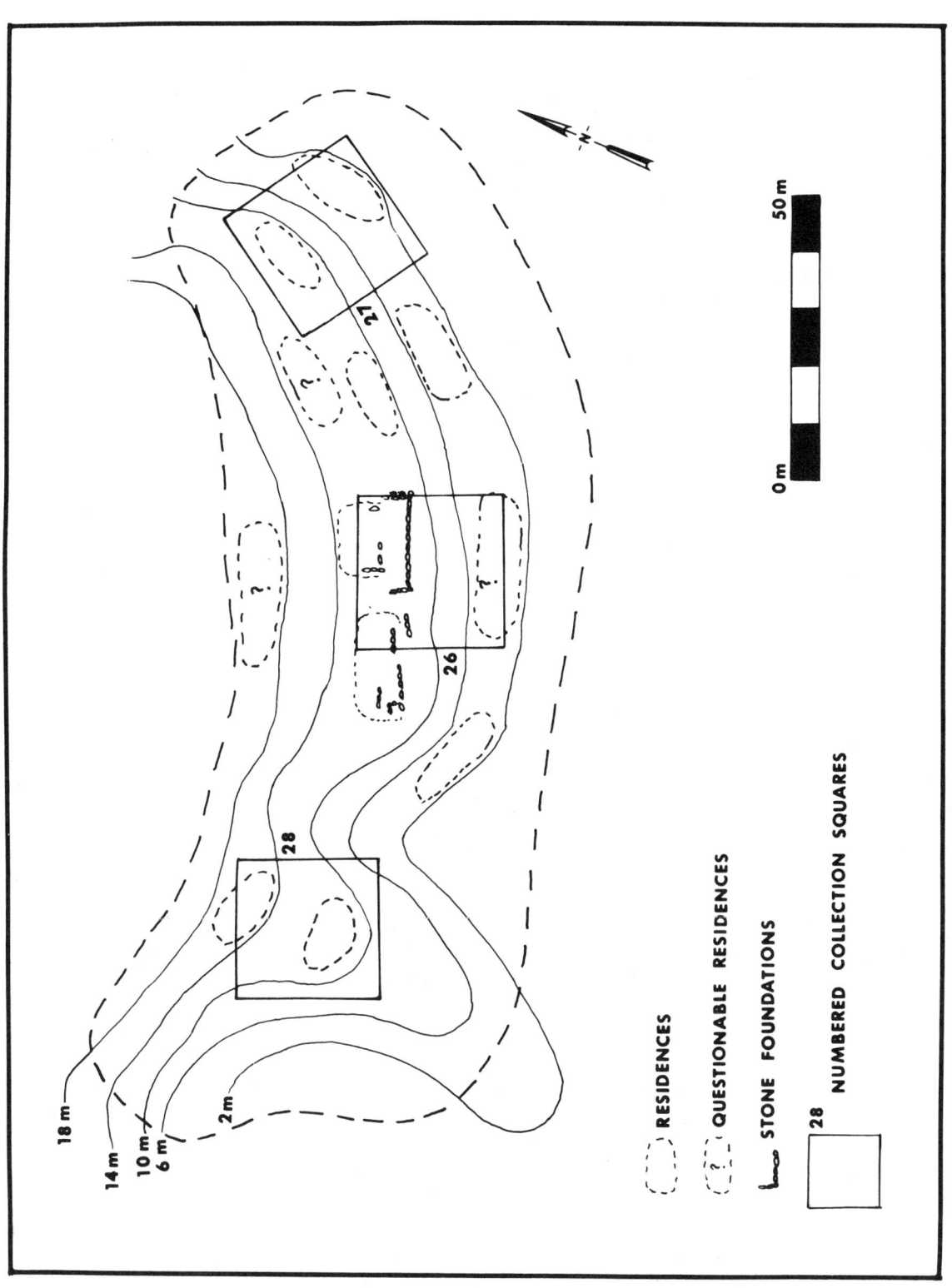

Fig. 2.4. Site map of Ts449.

TABLE 2.1
SITE SIZES AND POPULATION ESTIMATES FOR THE ARROYO LENCHO DIEGO

Site and Phase*		Occupied Area (ha)	Number of houses	Est. population at 5 persons/house	Mean pop. density (persons/ha)
Ts449	ESM	1.0	9-12	45-60	52.5
Ts67	MSM/LSM	2.2	25-27	125-135	59.1
Ts450	MSM/LSM	0.1	0	0	0.0
Ts452	MSM/LSM	0.4	5-7	25-35	75.0
Ts451	LSM	0.2	1	5	25.0
Ts131	LSM	5.1	65-70	325-350	66.2
Ts73	EPB	7.6	130-138	650-690	88.2
Ts79a	EPB	2.0	25-30	110-125	58.8
Ts79b	EPB	2.7	10-20?	50-100	27.8
Ts79c	EPB	1.8	30-(50?)	150-250	111.0
All ESM sites		1.0	9-12	45-60	52.5
All MSM sites		2.7	30-34	150-170	59.3
All LSM sites		8.0	96-105	480-525	62.8
All EPB sites		14.1	195-238	975-1190	76.8

* Phase abbreviations: ESM = Early Santa María; MSM = Middle Santa María; LSM = Late Santa María; EPB = Early Palo Blanco.

evidence is the ratio of bowl sherds to jar sherds. Drennan (1976a:77) has argued that this ratio may also be sensitive to status differences in society. The reasoning behind this is that although a given number of jars per household is probably required for normal domestic activities, it is likely that wealthier households had relatively more serving vessels. The distribution of bowls at Ts449 parallels that of obsidian: a higher proportion of bowls was found in the collection square associated with the stone foundations than in the collections associated with the residential terraces lacking stone foundations (Table 2.2). These several lines of evidence together suggest a definite status differential between the occupants of the two structures with stone foundations, who seem to have been of relatively higher status, and the occupants of the seven to ten residential terraces lacking stone foundations, who appear to have been of relatively lower status.

There are no structures on Ts449 that could be termed public buildings; domestic debris such as grinding stone fragments occurs throughout the site (Table 2.2). There is likewise no evidence for economic specialization at the site. There is, however, some evidence for differen-

2. IRRIGATION, ADMINISTRATION, and SOCIETY

TABLE 2.2
ARTIFACT DISTRIBUTIONS AT Ts449 (EARLY SANTA MARIA PHASE)

Artifact category or ratio	Square 26	Square 27	Square 28
Obsidian/other chipped stone	3.22	1.36	0.47
Obsidian blades/all chipped stone	0.29	0.12	0.05
Quartz fragments	1	4	4
Chert fragments	8	7	11
Obsidian fragments	29	15	7
Obsidian blade fragments	11	3	1
Bowl rims/jar rims	9.4	2.67	0.57
Ground stone fragments	2	3	1
Figurine fragments	1	0	0
Incense burner fragments	1	0	0

tial participation in ritual. The only figurine and the only incense burner fragments recovered from the surface of the site come from the collection suqare associated with the stone foundations. Further support comes from the distribution of obsidian blades on the site. It is quite likely that obsidian blades have important ritual significance in ancient Mesoamerica. Flannery (1976a:341), citing Nuttall (1904), suggested that they were used in self-sacrificial blood-letting. Furthermore, at the time of the conquest such self-sacrifice was more frequently practiced by the upper classes. "The higher the social position of the individual and the more he consequently knew of ritualistic observance, the more arduously he performed the fasts, penances, and tortures imposed by the religion" (Vaillant 1941:206). Thus the degree to which obsidian blades are differentially distributed across a site can be an indication of the degree to which participation in certain rituals was restricted to a segment of the total population. At Ts449 in the collection associated with the stone foundations, obsidian blades accounted for more of the chipped stone than in the two collections associated with the residential terraces lacking stone foundations (Table 2.2). This is consistent with the figurine and incense burner evidence and suggests some degree of differential participation in certain ritual activities at Ts449.

The absence, then, of any public architecture at Ts449 suggests that this Early Santa María community had no <u>formalized</u> administrative structure, be it religious or secular in nature. On the other hand, we do have evidence for a definite though small degree of social differentiation at the site expressed in terms of differential access to certain prized resources. It further appears that this social differentiation was somehow codified or mapped into the religious system of Ts449's inhabitants, because the same people who had greater access to prized resources were also the more active participants in various ritual activities. As we shall see, this pattern of differential participation in ritual according to social status continues all through the developmental sequence in the arroyo.

Middle Santa María Phase (650-450 B.C.)

Around 600 B.C., a decision was made to enlarge the Purrón Dam. Both Level 2 and Ts15 were built at this time (Figs. 2.1 and 2.2). The main dam was extended across the entire arroyo, bringing the structure to a length of 400 m, a width of 100 m, and a total height of 7.5 to 8 m. The fill of this second level totals about 123,000 m^3. Like the first level, the mass is composed of sandy earth, fine gravels, and small rock fragnebts. Beginning with this second level, however, the fill is compacted between retaining walls forming cubicle-like compartments within the dam. These walls are usually made from dry-laid river cobbles. Finally, in places a finished facade was created by placing slabs of locally available sedementary rock (limestone, sandstone, and gypsum) into clay mortar. The size of the reservoir associated with this dam is estimated at 500 by 400 m in area and 1,430,000 m^3 in volume, a thirty-fold increase in capacity over the previous phase (Woodbury and Neely 1972:82-99).

Just upstream from the main structure is Ts15 (Fig. 2.1), another water control feature built at about the same time as Level 2. A well-preserved spillway was found at the point where Ts15 joins the west side of the arroyo. Ts15 was about 330 m long by 30 m wide and 3 to 5 m high, with a total fill estimated at about 40,000 m^3. This feature was constructed in the same manner as Level 2. Woodbury and Neely (1972:96) felt that the function of Ts15 was not easily explained. Although it seemed to have impounded water at some time, its use as a dam had not been of long duration. They suggested that it had served either as a cofferdam or some sort of religious structure. We will return later to the problem of Ts15's function.

For the Middle Santa María phase, we have three occupation sites in the arroyo (in addition to Purrón Cave (Tc272) which continued to be used mainly as a hunting and gathering camp). These sites are Ts67, Ts450, and Ts452 (Fig. 2.5). The total area of settlement is about 2.7 ha, and the number of households is estimated to be between 30 and 34, about a 200% increase over the previous phase. At five persons per house, this would be a total Middle Santa María population of 150 to 170 persons. The average estimated density is 59.3 persons per ha of occupation (Table 2.1).

We made maps and surface collections at all three sites but encountered a serious problem with the surviving sherd coverage. These sites, which are located very close to the dam itself, had evidently been intensively collected by MacNeish and his associates. The remaining sherds, although adequate for dating the occupations, do not really constitute a sizeable enough sample for systematic comparisons between collections on the basis of vessel form, like those conducted with the Ts449 samples. Nevertheless, the sites can be compared in terms of architectural complexity and chipped stone artifact distributions.

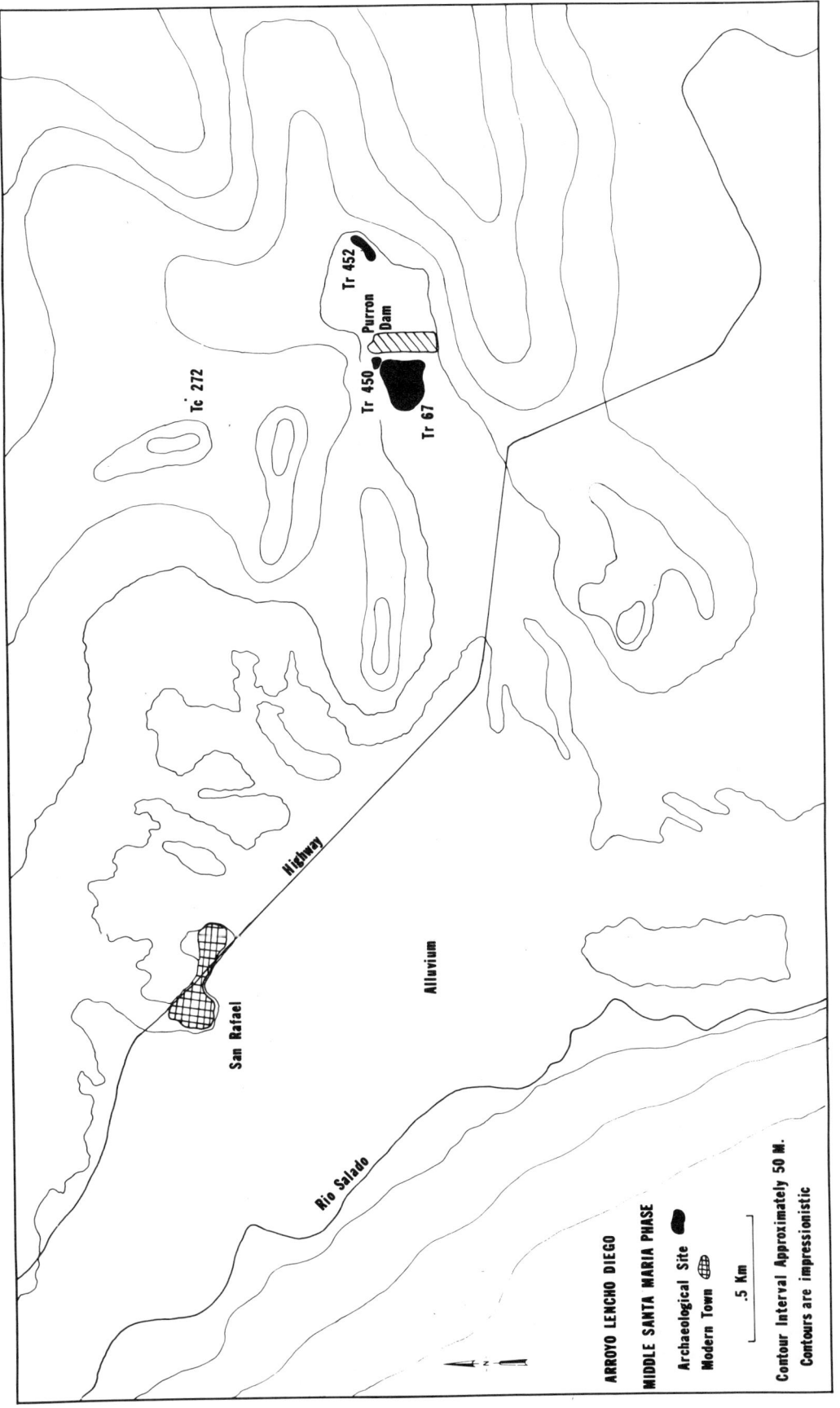

Fig. 2.5. Middle Santa María settlement in the Arroyo Lencho Diego.

TABLE 2.3

ARTIFACT DISTRIBUTIONS FOR MIDDLE AND LATE SANTA MARIA SITES

(Average number per square or average ratio)

Artifact category or ratio	Upstream					Downstream
	Ts67 N=3*	Ts450 N=1	Ts451 N=1	Ts452 N=4	All 4 sites	Ts131 N=20
Obsidian fragments	16.00	11	19	3.25		2.60
Chert fragments	0.67	0	0	0.00		2.90
Quartz fragments	13.30	1	0	0.00		5.15
Obsidian blades	5.67	9	16	2.00		1.15
Obs./Other ch. stn.	1.21	11.00	19/0	3.25/0	2.12	0.49
Obs. bl./All ch. stn.	0.19	0.75	0.84	0.71	0.37	0.12
Incense burner frags.	0.33	1	2	0.00	0.44	0.00

* N is number of squares collected.

Ts452 (Fig. 2.6) is situated at the edge of what would have been the lake impounded by the dam. There are five to seven households here, all with masonry foundations. One of the houses sits on a mound 2 m high with a stone staircase leading up to it. Ts67 (Fig. 2.7), on the other hand, contains 25 to 27 households, but only a couple have stone foundations. The differential distribution of obsidian was even more marked than before: whereas Ts67 yielded some obsidian and some other chipped stone, all 13 pieces of chipped stone collected at Ts452 were obsidian (Table 2.3). It seems reasonable to suggest that Ts452 was inhabited by descendents of the occupants of the two masonry structures at Ts449. These people appeared to have greatly increased their standing in society. They now lived physically separated from the rest of the community, in much more elaborately constructed houses and with even more exclusive access to scarce resources like obsidian. Furthermore, the residences within Ts452 appear to be ranked with respect to one another. The structures associated with collection squares 21 and 22 (Fig. 2.6) sit atop mounds with masonry staircases, and of these two the structure associated with square 22 is situated on the higher mound. The other structures at Ts452, though having stone foundations, are located on comparatively small rises.

Ts450 (Fig. 2.7) had no associated domestic debris, such as grinding stones, nor any evidence for house mounds or foundations. It did, however, have a relatively large number of obsidian blades (Table 2.3). It was argued in the previous section that obsidian blades may have functioned importantly in certain rituals. The abundance of obsidian blades and the absence of domestic debris would suggest that Ts450 was a public building. It is situated right at the exit point of the dam's spillway and perhaps

2. IRRIGATION, ADMINISTRATION, AND SOCIETY

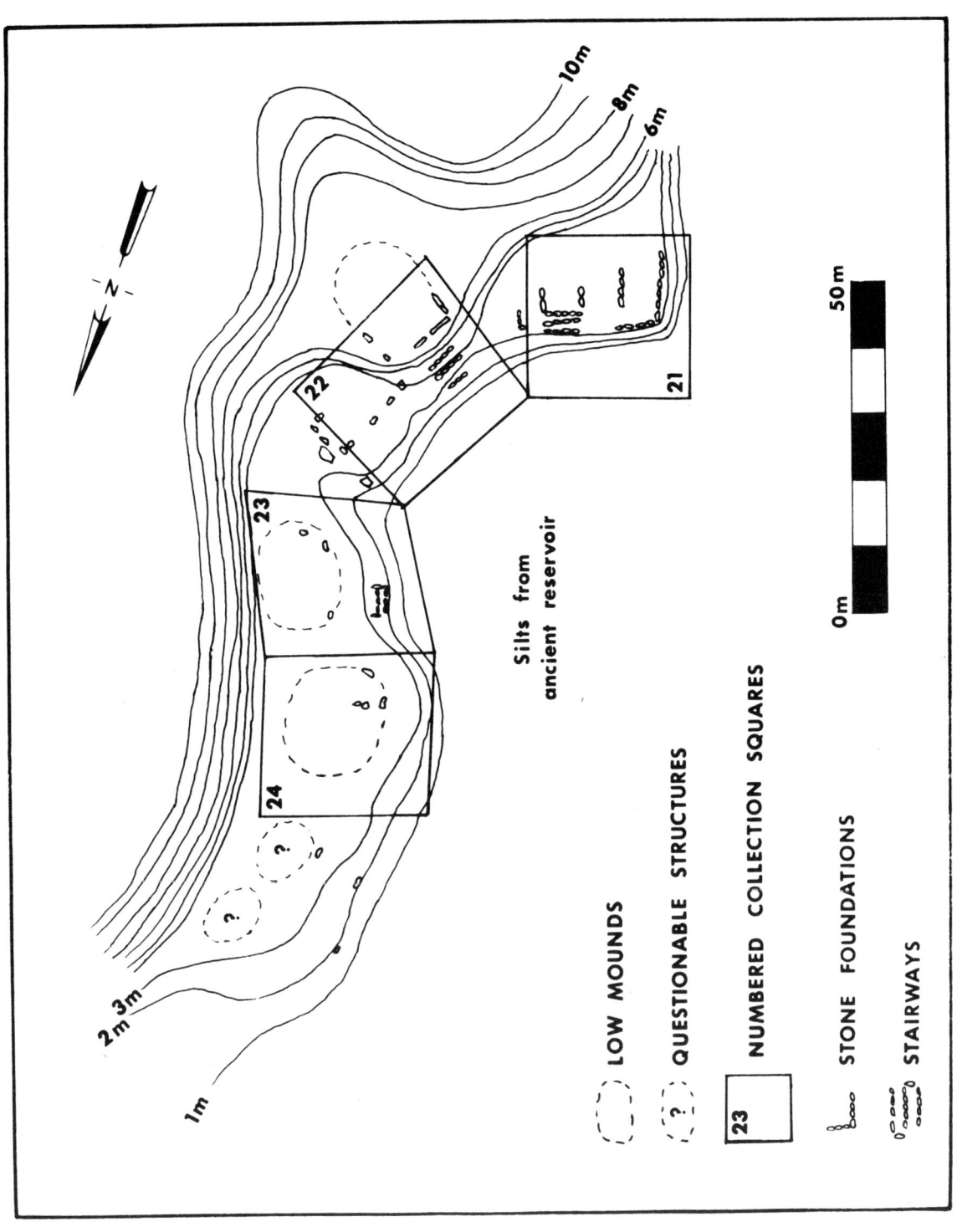

Fig. 2.6. Site map of Ts452.

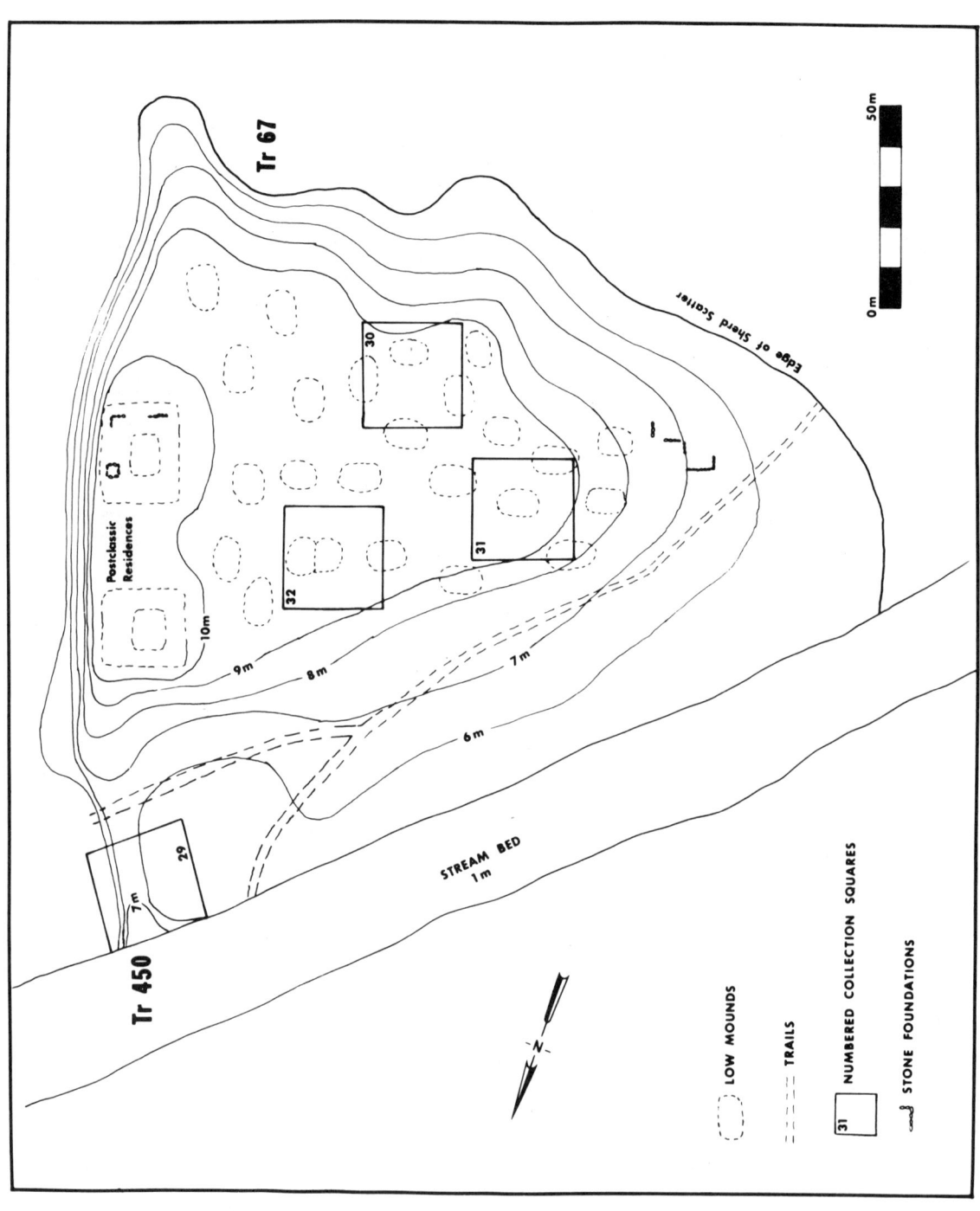

Fig. 2.7. Site map of Ts450 and Ts67.

TABLE 2.4

DISTRIBUTION OF MOUNDED RESIDENCES AND OBSIDIAN BLADES AT Ts452

Collection No.	Architectural Evidence	Ratio Obsidian blades/All ch. stone
21	Stone foundations on mound	1.0
22	Stone foundations on mound	1.0
23	Stone foundations not on mound	0.25
24	Stone foundations not on mound	0.6

served in some capacity related to water control and distribution.

The distribution of obsidian blades among the sites argues for more extreme differential participation in ritual than was the case in the previous phase: at Ts450 and Ts452, obsidian blades account for far more of the chipped stone than at Ts67 (Table 2.3). We can tentatively conclude that much or most of the ritual activity involving obsidian blades was occurring at the single public building (Ts450) and at the settlement component that appears to have represented the elite sector of society (Ts452). Perhaps Ts450 served as the ritual focus for the community as a whole, and the higher-status people continued to conduct some of the rituals involving obsidian blades at their own households.

The internal ranking we observed in the residential architecture of Ts452 is paralleled by the distribution of obsidian blades. Table 2.4 shows that, in the two collections associated with the mounded structures just discussed, obsidian blades comprised all the chipped stone recovered, while at the non-mounded structures other chipped stone was recovered as well. Thus, by the Middle Santa María phase, not only was the elite segment of society physically separated from the lower-status segment, but also a principle of ranking characterized the internal organization of that elite. It seems clear that the tendency toward social differentiation that we saw in the Early Santa María phase has now become rather developed social ranking (Fried 1967). Accompanying this was a continuation of the pattern of differential participation in rituals according to social status. And at the same time, there was a formalization of political and/or religious administrative organization, manifested by the construction of the first public building in the arroyo. In Johnson's (1978) terminology, we see in Middle Santa María the emergence of one order of vertical spcialization in the organization of decision making.

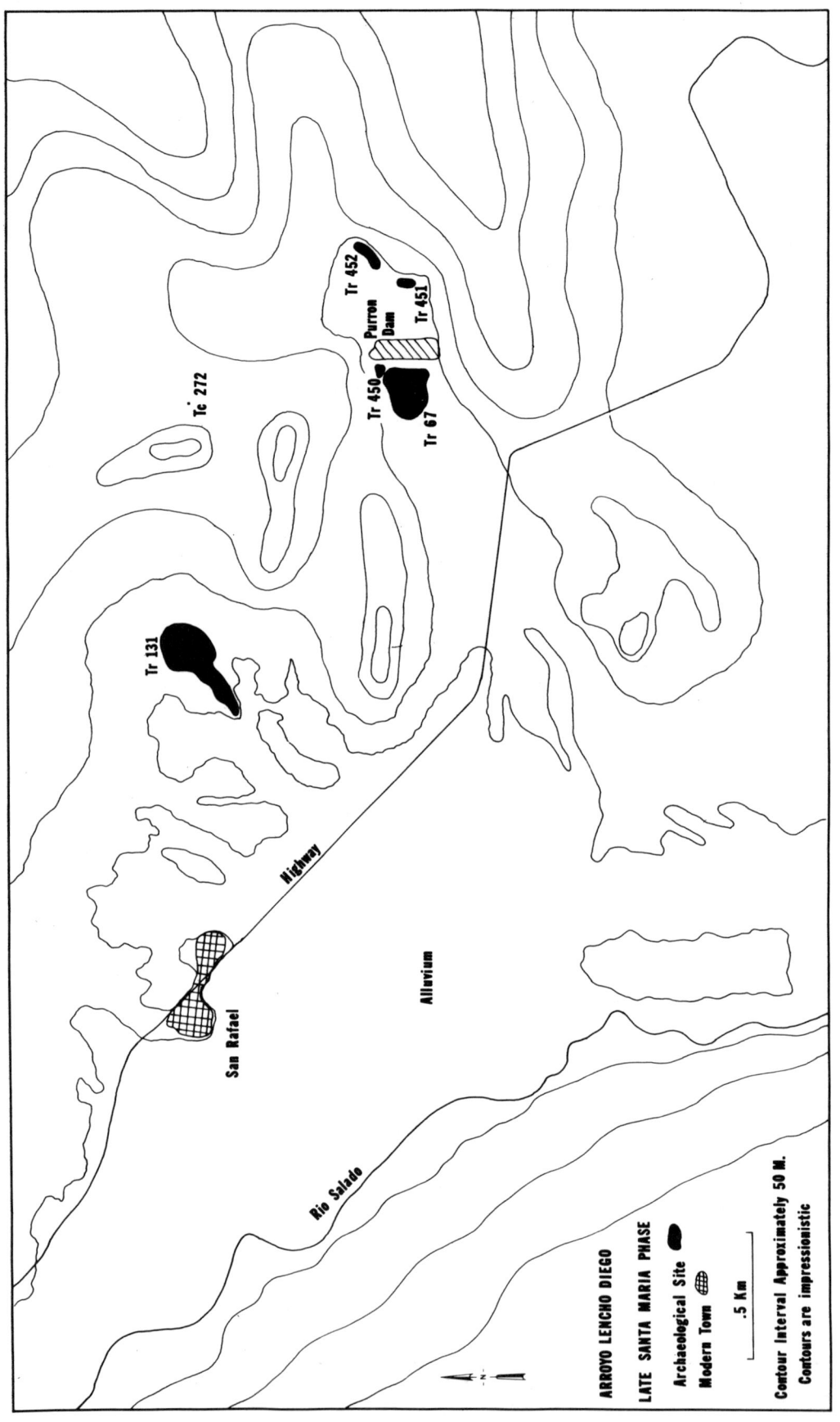

Fig. 2.8. Late Santa María settlement in the Arroyo Lencho Diego.

2. IRRIGATION, ADMINISTRATION, AND SOCIETY

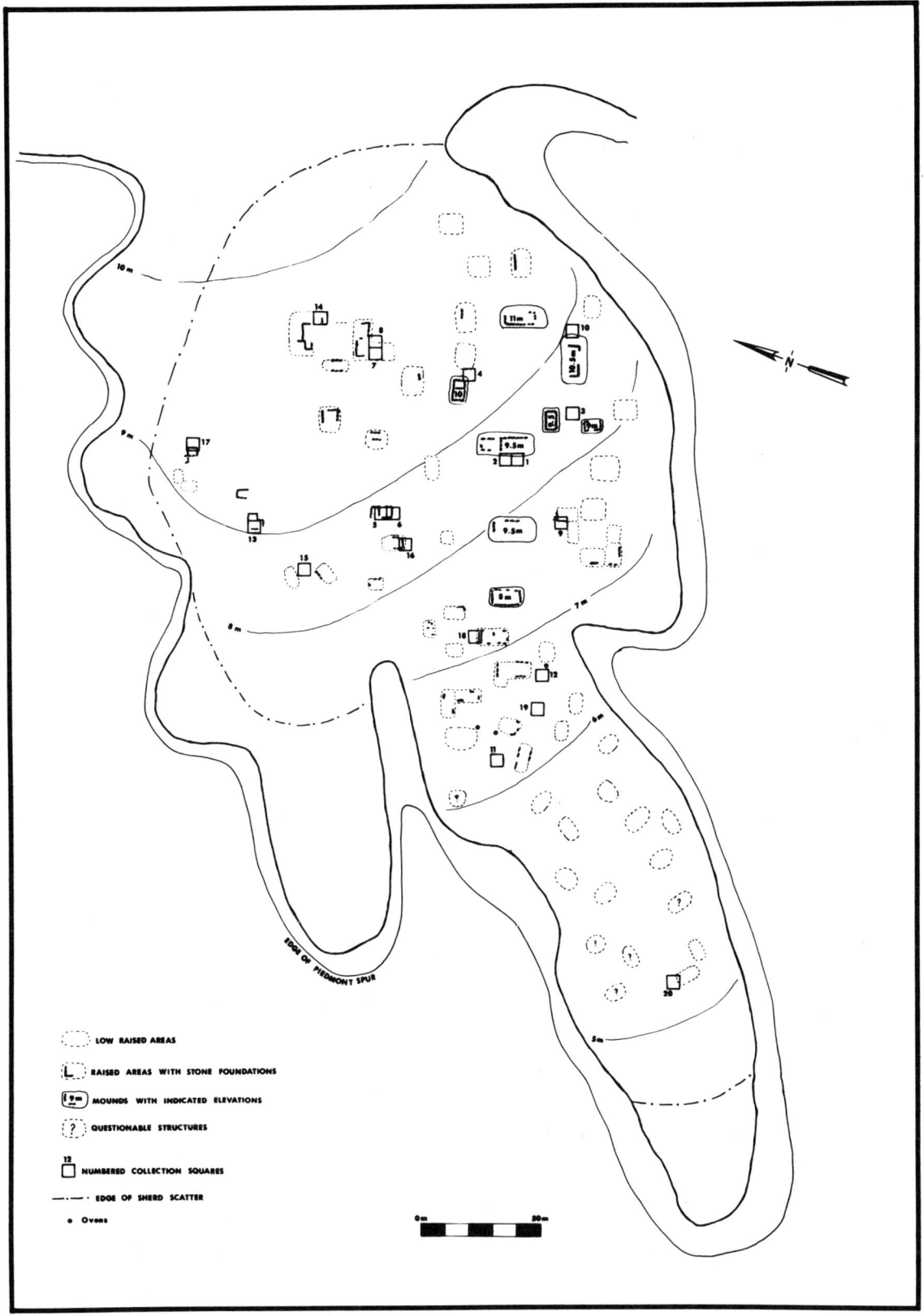

Fig. 2.9. Site map of Ts131.

Late Sata María Phase (450-150 B.C.)

No rebuilding or enlargement of the dam is evident until the very end of the Late Santa María phase. Occupation continued at Ts452, Ts450, and Ts67, but two new sites appeared at this time (Fig. 2.8). One of these is Ts131, a rather amorphous collection of 65 to 70 residences located about 2 km downstream from the dam (Fig. 2.9). The other, situated near Ts452, is Ts451, a modified natural rise 10 m high with a single large residence on top. Although Ts451 was reoccupied during the Postclassic, a looted Late Santa María tomb in the patio (Fig. 2.10) leads us to believe that the elaborate residence was first built and occupied during Late Santa María times.

The total area of settlement by the Late Santa María phase was 8.0 ha. The total number of households is estimated between 96 and 105. At five persons per house, this would be a total Late Santa María phase population of 480 to 525. The average estimated density for this phase is 62.8 persons per ha of occupation (Table 2.1).

Ts451 represents an even higher status component for the community at the dam. The large residence is well constructed of masonry blocks. The collection we made at Ts451 yielded no chert or quartzite but did produce 19 pieces of obsidian, 16 of which were obsidian blades (Table 2.3). Since Ts451 was reoccupied during the Postclassic, some of the collected blades may date from that period, but we have used the total count, lacking any certain way to distinguish earlier from later blades in a surface collection.

Downstream from the dam, the inhabitants of Ts131 seem to have had less access to obsidian than did the inhabitants of the dam community composed of Ts67, 450, 451, and 452, to judge from the surface collections (Table 2.3). Furthermore, the differentiation between elite and nonelite components of the two communities was more extreme at the upstream community than at Ts131. Although the higher-status residences at Ts131 did yield higher proportions of obsidian than the lower-status residences, the difference was not nearly so great as that between the elite and nonelite residential components of the dam community (Table 2.5). Ts450 continued to be the only structure at the dam community that could be termed a public building (aside from the dam itself); at Ts131 there was no evidence of any public buildings. The lower proportion of obsidian blades at Ts131 suggests a continuation of the pattern suggested above of status-based differences in participation in some rituals (Table 2.3). Parallel evidence resides in the recovery of four incense burner fragments at the dam community and none at Ts131.

It is at Ts131 that we get the first shreds of evidence for craft specialization in the arroyo. The survey found three features which appeared to be large ovens located near collection squares 11, 12, and 19 (Fig. 2.9). We also found (in squares 2, 16, 17, 19, and 20) a total of 27 grayware sherds that were reddish-pink due to over-firing. It is possible that the households associated with these ovens and over-fired sherds

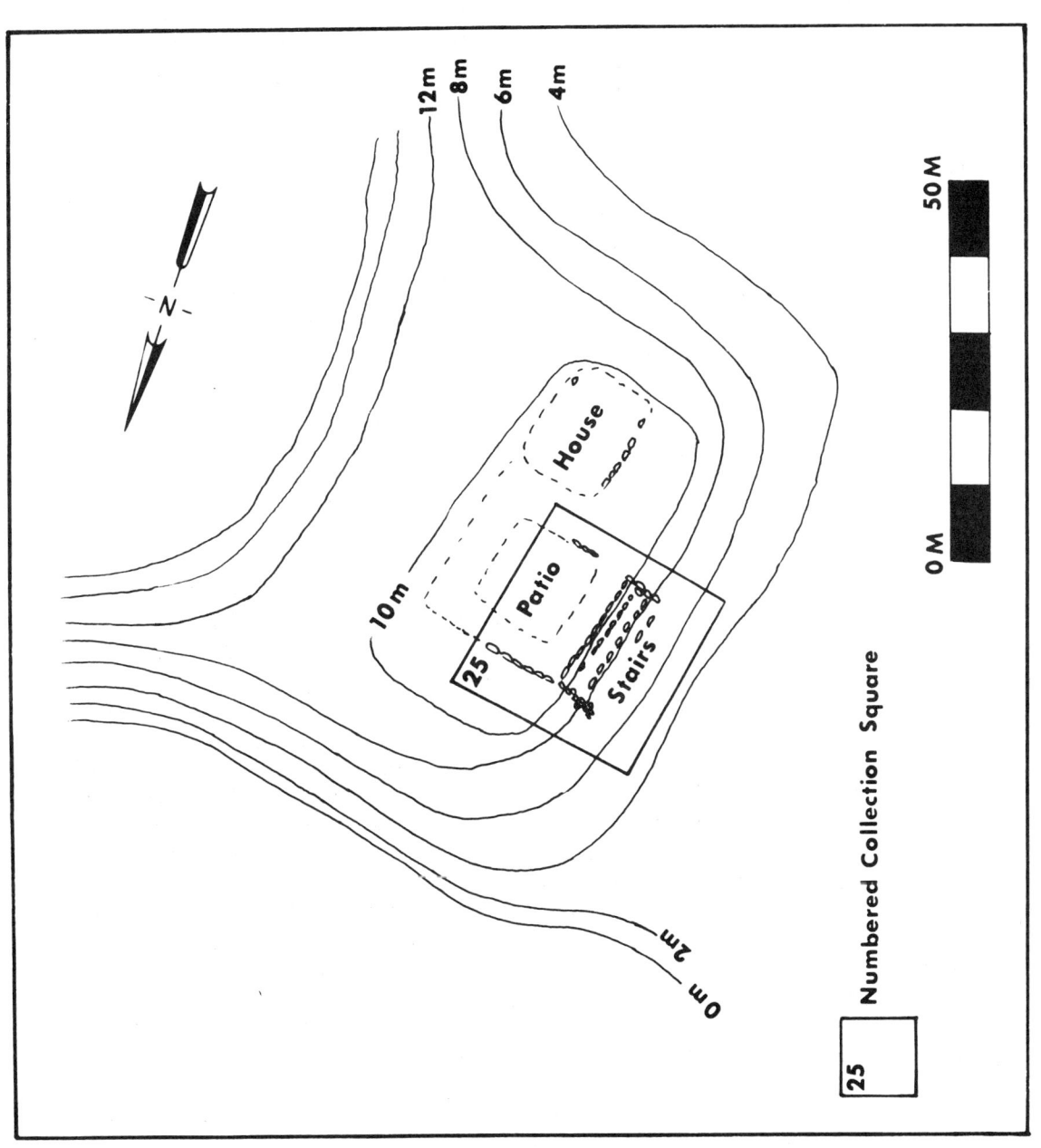

Fig. 2.10. Site map of Ts451.

TABLE 2.5

DISTRIBUTION OF OBSIDIAN IN LATE SANTA MARIA SITES

	Residential Sector	Average ratio Obsidian/Other chipped stone
Upstream community	Ts452 and Ts451 (elite sector) N=5*	6.4/0.0
	Ts67 (non-elite sector) N=3	1.21
Downstream community	Houses on mounds (higher-status sector?) N=6	0.13
	Houses not on mounds (lower-status sector?) N=14	0.12

* N is number of squares collected.

were involved in part-time ceramic production. Without excavated data it is difficult to determine exactly how many households at Ts131 might have been involved in ceramic production, but a reasonable estimate based on the distribution of the ovens and over-fired sherds would be about one-third of the 65 to 70 households which make up the site.

In sum, Late Santa María settlement in the arroyo was characterized by a 214% increase in population over the previous phase. The pattern of social ranking, expressed in terms of differential access to precious resources, became extremely pronounced, with one family in particular attaining a position of very high relative status. This social differentiation was also manifested, as in earlier phases, by differential participation in some ritual activities. Further, in the Late Santa María phase we first encounter evidence for household-level ceramic production of some of the pottery used in the arroyo. There was no apparent change, however, in the nature of formalized administrative organization, as Ts450 continued to be the only example of public architecture in the arroyo.

At the very end of the Late Santa María phase, possibly around 150 B.C., the dam underwent a third phase of construction. This level, composed of 51,870 m^3 of fill, represents a repair job according to Woodbury and Neely (1972:90-91). Continual silting-in and damage due to flash-flooding, of course, would have been constant problems, and there is evidence that both factors were important considerations in the decision to undertake the third construction effort. But in spite of this rebuilding, silting had brought the reservoir associated with this third level down to a capacity of 970,000 m^3, rather less than the 1,430,000 m^3 capacity after

2. IRRIGATION, ADMINISTRATION, AND SOCIETY

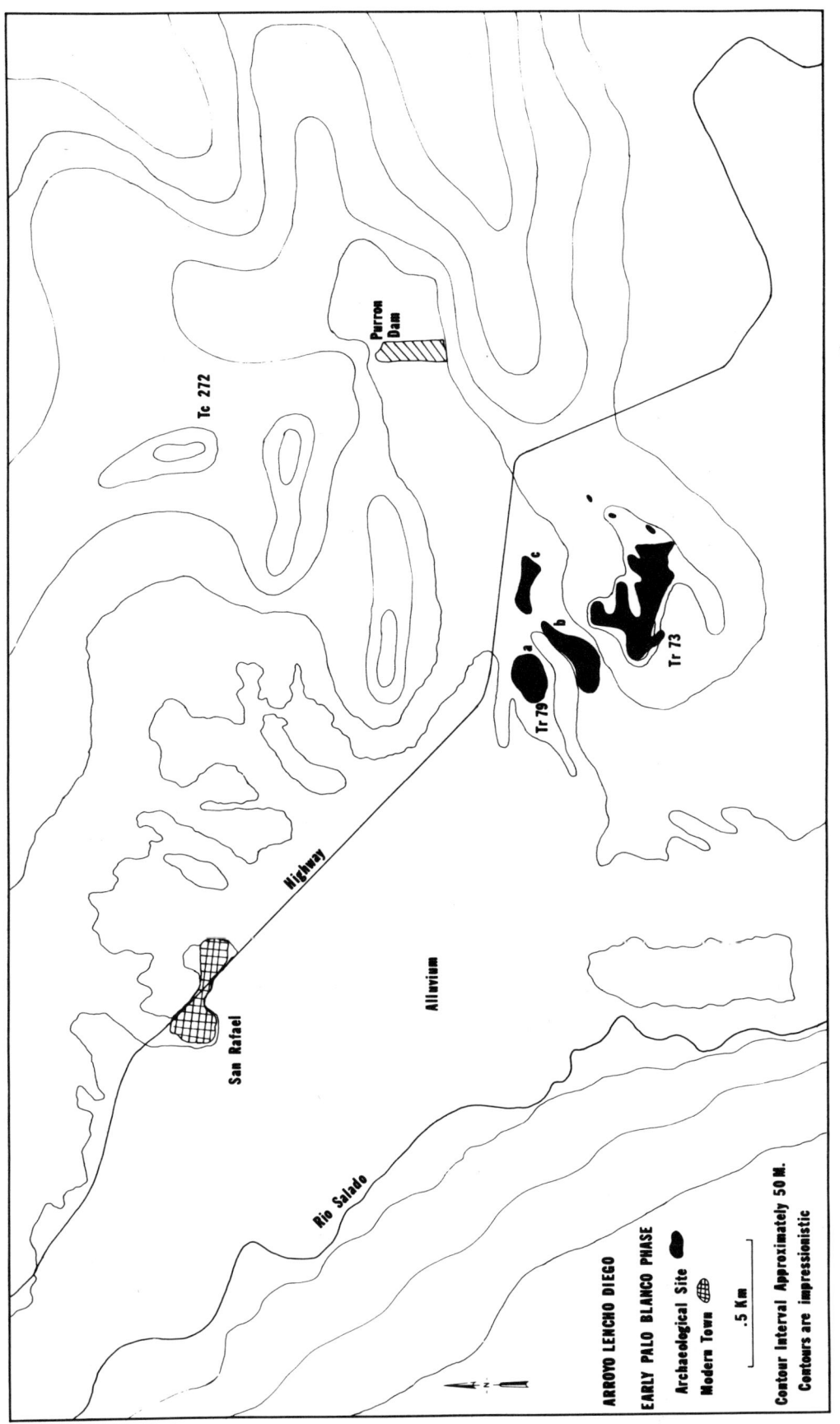

Fig. 2.11. Early Palo Blanco settlement in the Arroyo Lencho Diego.

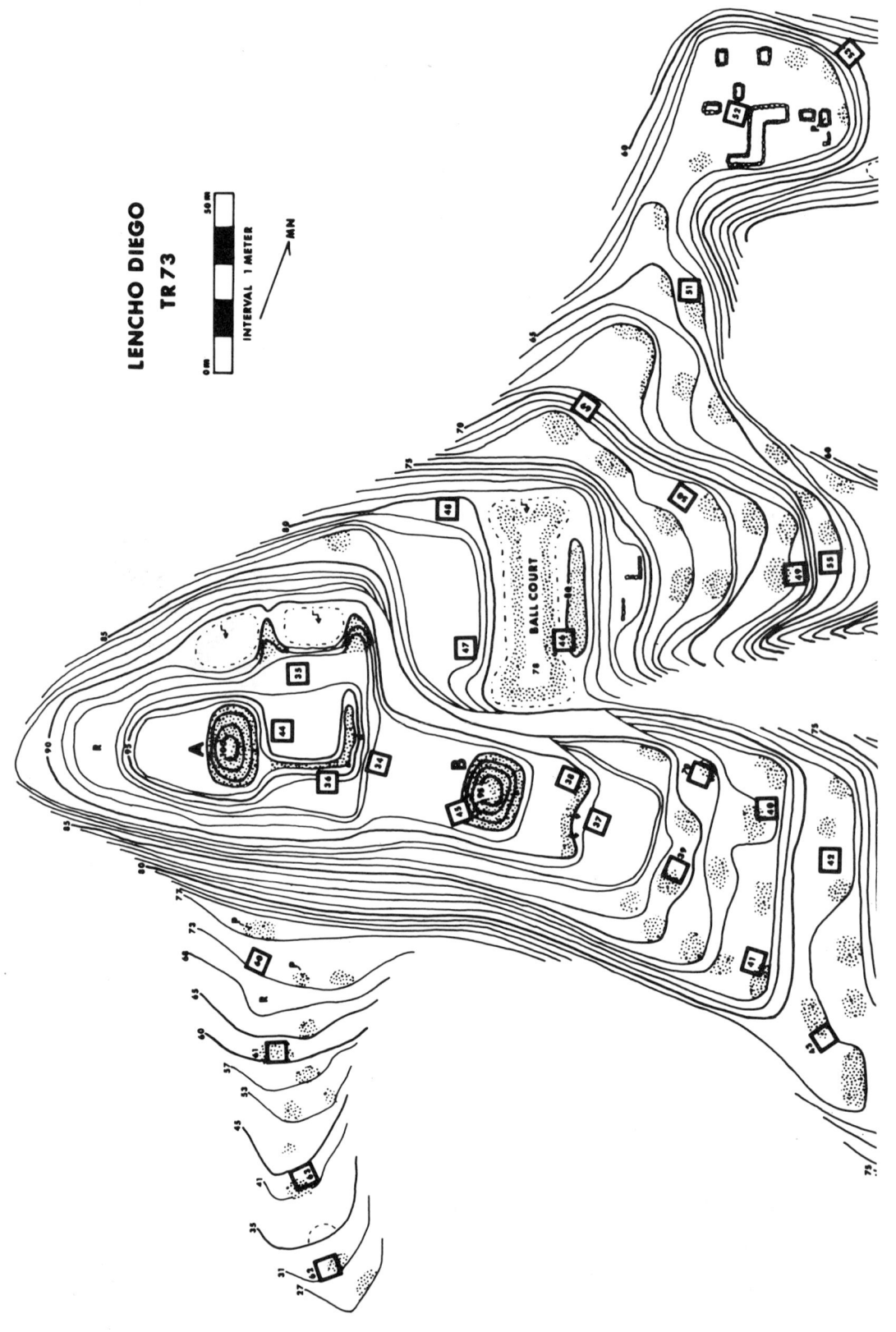

2. IRRIGATION, ADMINISTRATION, AND SOCIETY

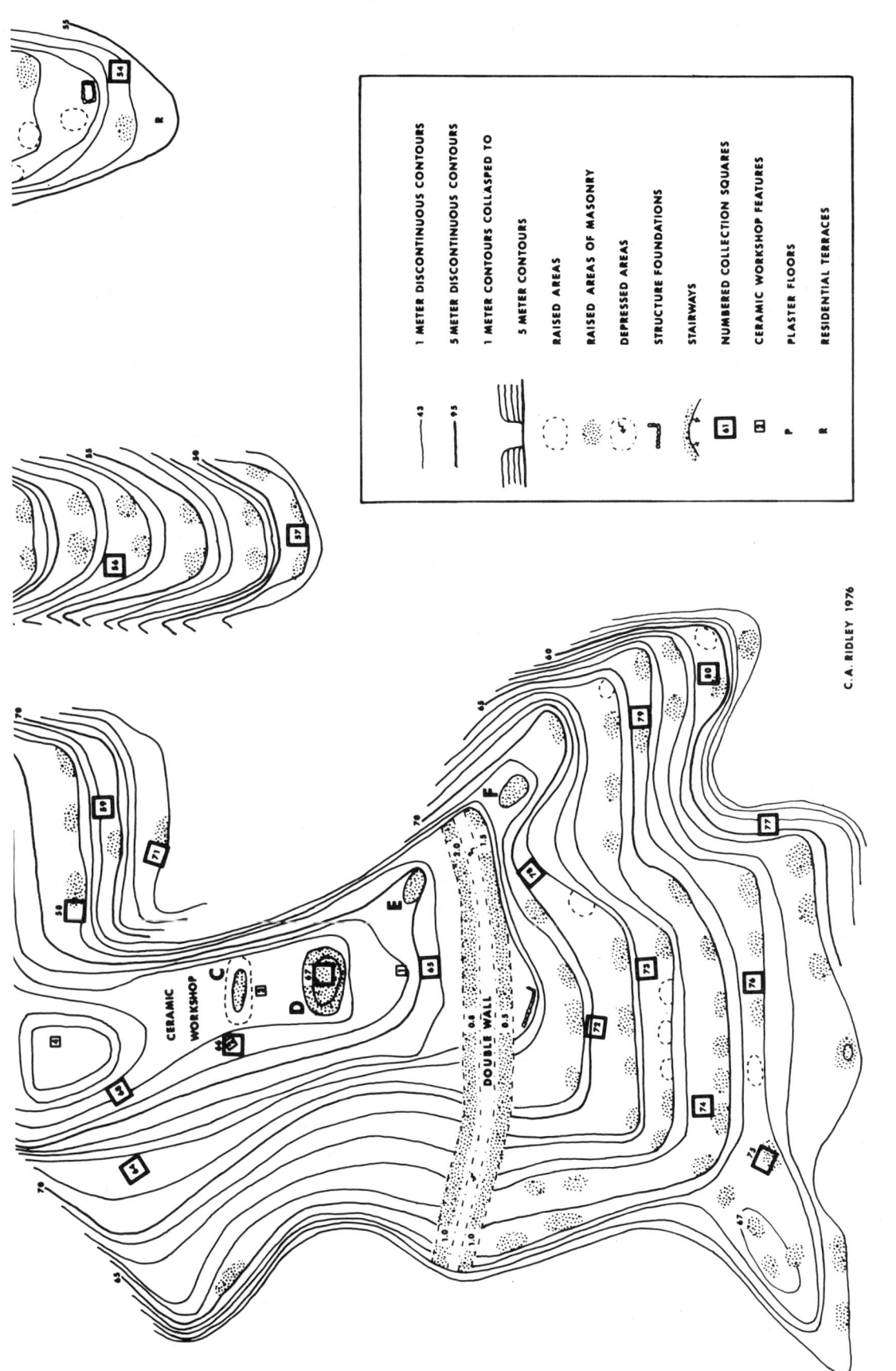

Fig. 2.12. Site map of Ts73.

42 PREHISTORIC DEVELOPMENT IN THE TEHUACAN VALLEY

Level 2 was built. Throughout the Middle and Late Santa María phases, therefore, the dam was not expanded appreciably, and the reservoir behind the dam was steadily shrinking.

Early Palo Blanco Phase (150 B.C.-A.D. 250)

In the first part of the Early Palo Blanco phase, probably between 150 B.C. and A.D. 1, a decision was made to enlarge the Purrón Dam. At this time Level 4 was built, bringing the structure to the size we see today: some 18 to 20 m high, 400 m long, and 100 m wide. Level 4, containing an estimated 192,000 m^3 of fill, was built in much the same manner as Level 2. The reservoir behind the dam was increased at this time to an estimated capacity of 2,640,000 m^3 (Woodbury and Neely 1972:82-99).

The settlement pattern for the Early Palo Blanco phase represents a significant departure from that of the previous phase. The sites around the dam and Ts131 were abandoned. A single large community was built on top of and around the base of a hill at the mouth of the arroyo, overlooking the irrigated alluvium (Fig. 2.11). The component atop the hill is called Ts73 by MacNeish (1972:413), and the component at the foot of the hill Ts79. The total area of settlement for this phase is 14.1 ha, and the total number of households is estimated between 195 and 238, 975 to 1190 persons altogether at five persons per house. This is an average population density of 76.8 persons per ha of occupation, a substantial increase over the density figures for Middle and Late Santa María, which were 59.3 and 62.8 respectively (Table 2.1). We made 47 collections in the settlement component termed Ts73 (Fig. 2.12). Ten of these collections were located in an area containing pyramids, plazas, a ballcourt, and large staircases, all constructed of large masonry blocks. Using architectural criteria, we classified this sector of the site as "Civic-ceremonial 1."

Adjacent to Civic-ceremonial 1 is an area containing 80 to 85 smaller structures that appeared to be domestic. 95% of these structures (Table 2.6) had masonry foundations. This sector of the site was designated "Residential 1"; we placed a total of 23 collection squares here.

TABLE 2.6
RESIDENTIAL AREAS OF Ts73/79 (EARLY PALO BLANCO PHASE)

Sector	No. of houses	No. of houses with masonry	Proportion with masonry	Est. population (5 persons/house)
Residential 1	80-85	76	.95	400-425
Residential 3	50-53	43	.86	250-265
Residential 3	65-100	35	.44	325-500
Total	195-238	154	.71	975-1190

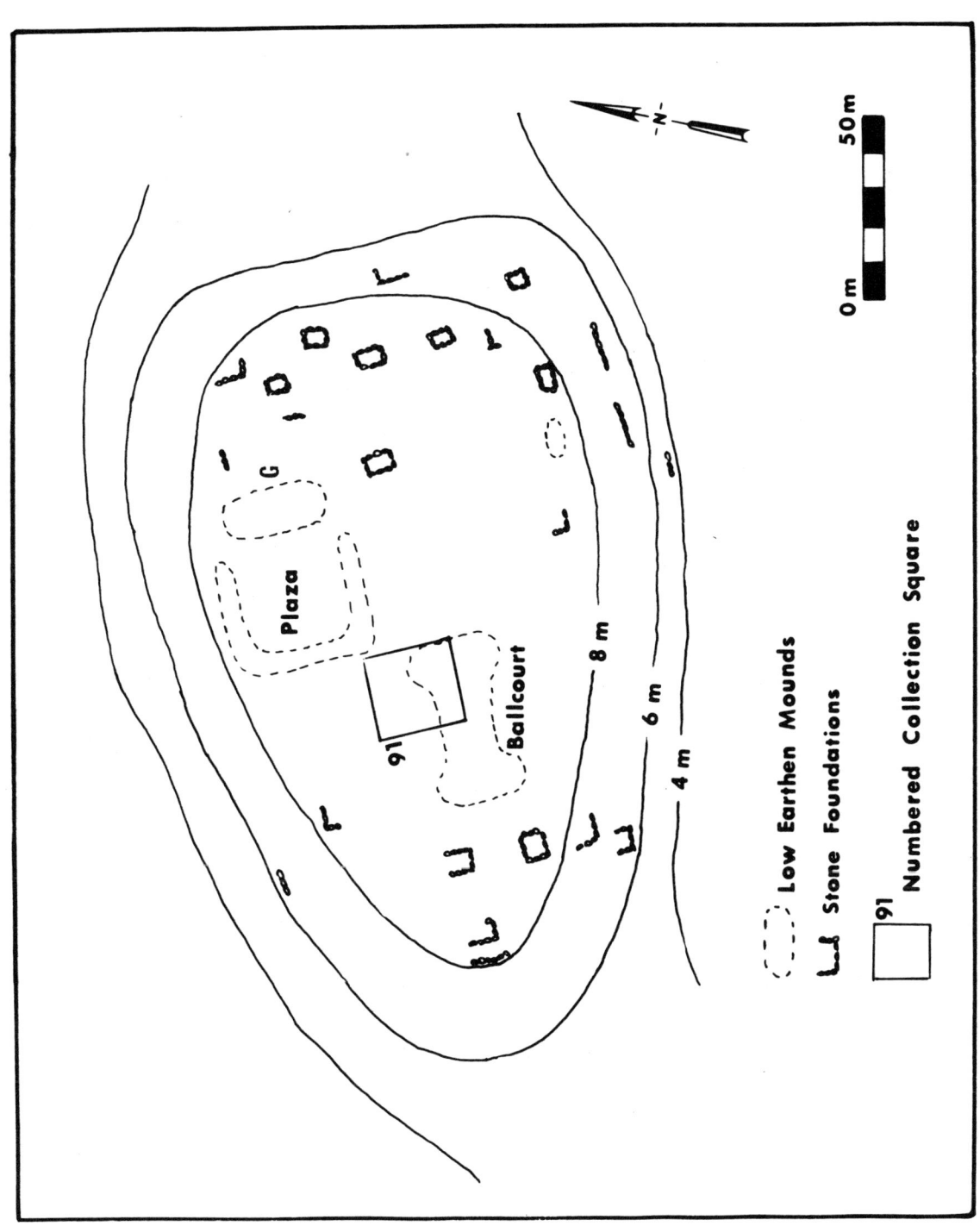

Fig. 2.13. Site map of Ts79a (after MacNeish et al. 1972:Fig. 166).

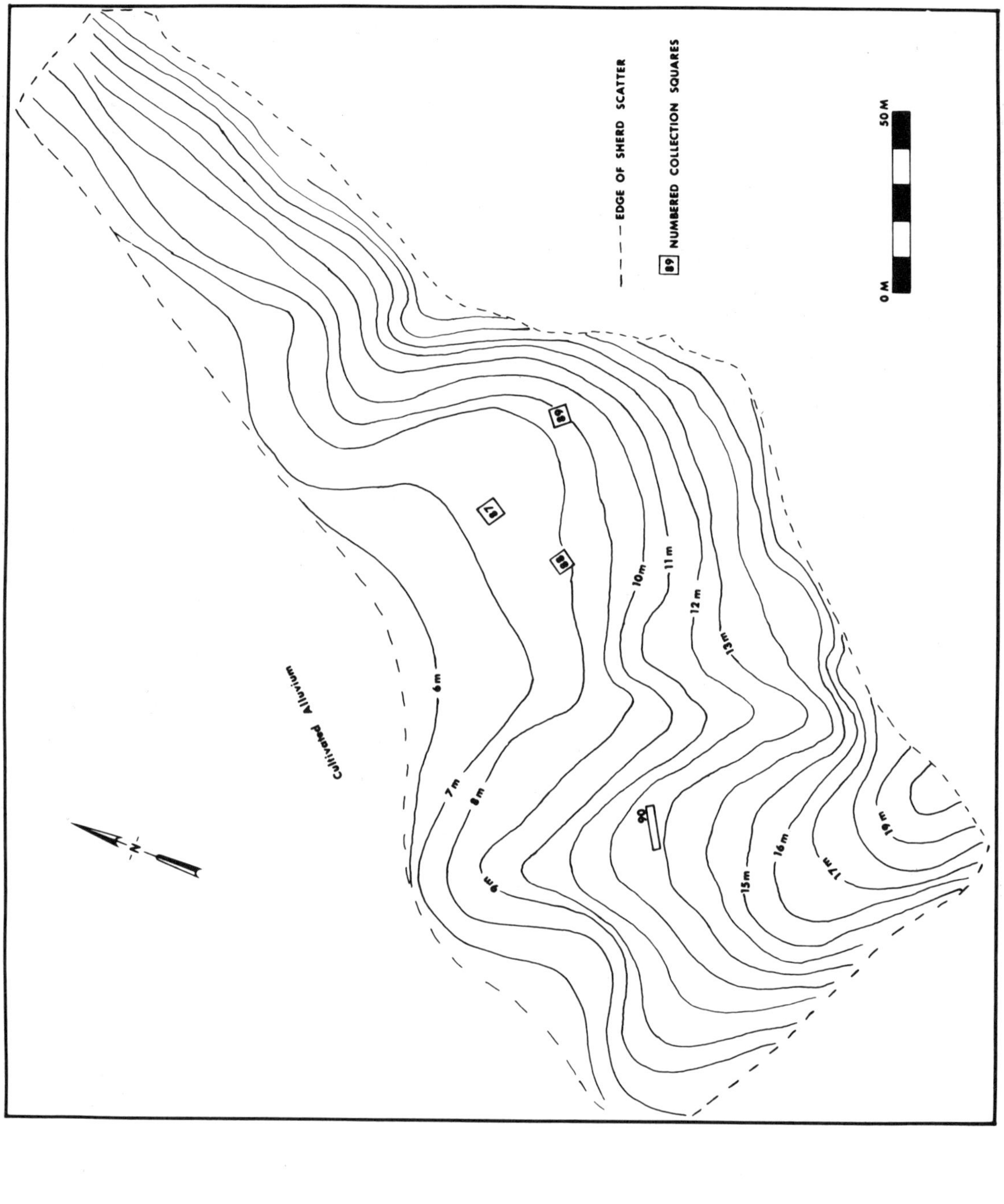

Fig. 2.14. Site map of Ts79b.

2. IRRIGATION, ADMINISTRATION, AND SOCIETY

We also found a ceramic production workshop at Ts73. This area, measuring 100 by 25 m, totally lacks residential architecture, but has several features with burned edges that are probably large ovens. Scores of very clear kiln wasters were also collected in this area. This sector of the site was designated "Workshop"; we collected five sample squares here, and the area is described in more detail in Chapter 3.

Just east of the ceramic workshop is a double wall sealing off the only slope gentle enough to climb without great difficulty. At what appears to have been the only point of access through the wall is a structure which may have been a sort of guard house. Entry to the main part of Ts73 seems to have been strictly regulated.

East of the double wall and separated by it from the center of Ts73 is another sector of residential structures. Here were found 50 to 53 structures; 86% of them had masonry foundations (Table 2.6). We designated this sector "Residential 2" and placed a total of nine collection squares here.

Ts79, the settlement component at the foot of the hill (Fig. 2.11), is actually comprised of three sections, labelled Ts79a (Fig. 2.13), Ts79b (Fig. 2.14), and Ts79c (Fig. 2.15). On Ts79a there is a small plaza and a ballcourt. Interestingly, this ballcourt is constructed of earth fill and rubble, not of masonry like the one in sector Civic-ceremonial 1. We designated this part of Ts79a "Civic-ceremonial 2" and made one 25 by 25 m collection (because of the low density of material). Ts79a also contained about 25 to 35 house mounds. We were unable to make further collections at Ts79a. We did, however, make a total of nine collections from Ts79b and Ts79c. At Ts79c (Fig. 2.15) we located 30 house mounds, 11 of which had masonry foundations. Because of extremely heavy brush, we were unable to cover all of Ts79c with equal intensity; we estimate that there may be as many as 20 more house mounds here. At Ts79b we were presented with an even more difficult situation regarding house mound preservation. This settlement component (Fig. 2.14) sits on a severely eroded hill slope. We located the remnants of two or three houses, but we cannot at this time make a confident estimate of the total number of households. We feel, however, that a figure of 10 to 20 would not be unreasonable. The residential areas at Ts79a, 79b, and 79c are collectively termed "Residential 3" in this analysis and together contain 65 to 100 houses, 44% of which have masonry foundations.

In summary, the site of Ts73-79 has been stratified into the following sectors employing <u>only</u> locational and architectural criteria:

1. Residential 1: those houses on top of the hill and inside the double wall; 95% have masonry foundations.
2. Residential 2: those houses on top of the hill but outside the double wall; 86% have masonry foundations.
3. Residential 3: those houses at the foot of the hill; 44% have masonry foundations.
4. Civic-ceremonial 1: the area of pyramids, plazas, and a ballcourt on top of the hill; these structures are all of masonry.
5. Civic-ceremonial 2: the area of a plaza and a ballcourt at

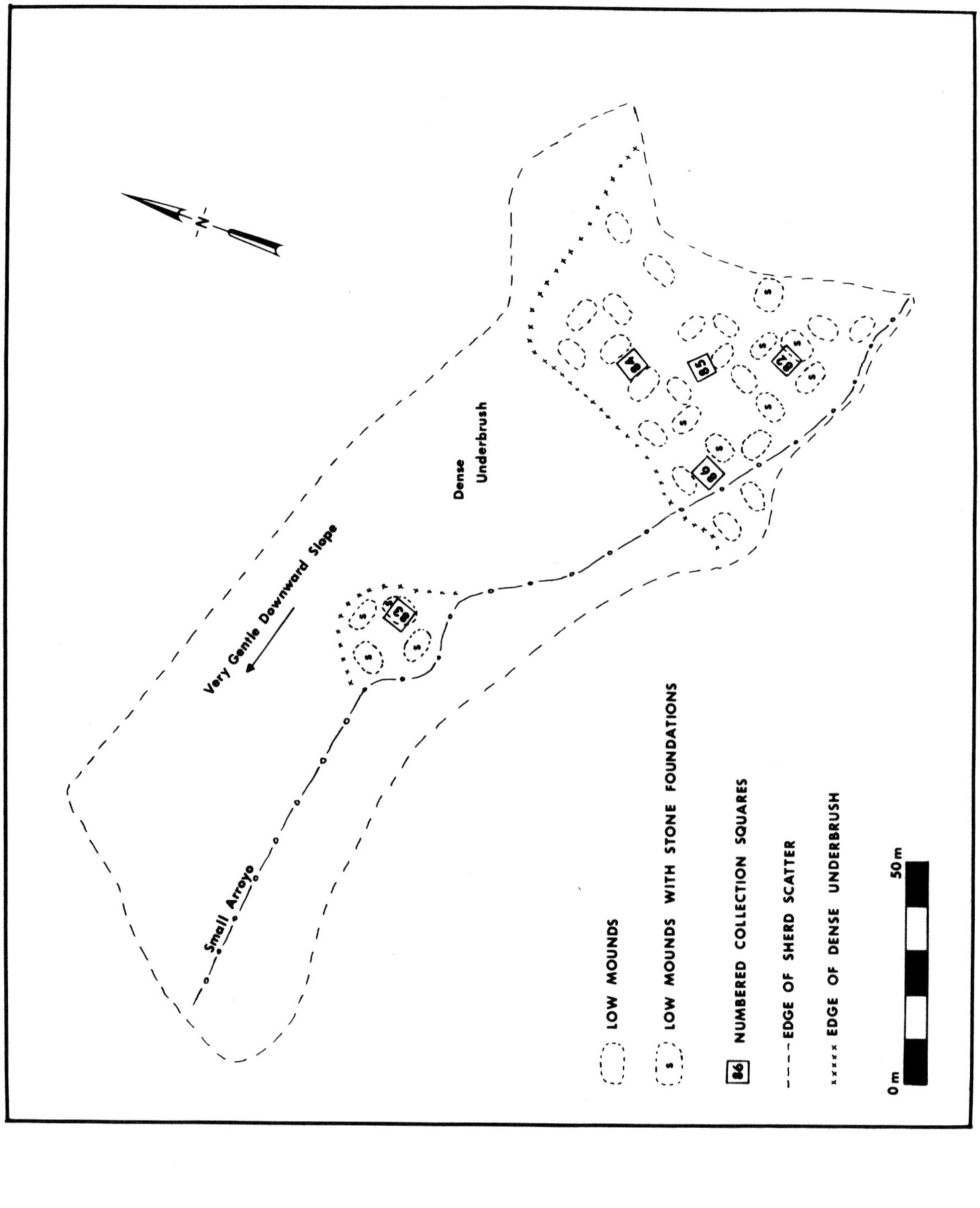

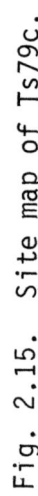

Fig. 2.15. Site map of Ts79c.

2. IRRIGATION, ADMINISTRATION, AND SOCIETY

the foot of the hill; these buildings are contructed of rubble and earth fill.

   6. Workshop: the area on top of the hill which lacks residential architecture but contains the remains of large ovens.

The architectural and locational criteria alone imply that Residential 1, Residential 2, and Residential 3 represent three social segments that are ranked with respect to one another, Residential 1 being of highest rank, Residential 2 of intermediate rank, and Residential 3 of lowest rank. Furthermore, the two civic-ceremonial areas would appear to be similarly differentiated; we suggest that Civic-ceremonial 1 occupied a more elevated position in the administrative hierarchy than Civic-ceremonial 2. We should now compare these sectors of the site on the basis of the artifact samples collected in each. If our interpretations of the site sectors are valid, we would expect to find corroborative patterning in the distributions of these artifacts.

As Table 2.7 shows, the distribution of grinding stones, one of the least equivocal items of domestic debris, closely parallels our stratification of the site into civic-ceremonial, residential, and workshop sectors.

TABLE 2.7

ARTIFACT DISTRIBUTIONS AT Ts73/79 (EARLY PALO BLANCO PHASE)

(Average number per square or average ratio)

Artifact category or ratio	Res. 1 N=23*	Res. 2 N=9	Res. 3 N=9	Civic-cer. 1 N=10	Civic-cer. 2 N=1	Workshop N=5
Ground stone frags.	1.17	1.55	1.78	0.00	0	0.20
Obsidian/Other ch. stn.	0.99	0.40	0.39	2.55	0.00	1.06
Gray jars/Plain jars (rims only)	2.37	1.17	1.32	1.67	0.00	1.94
Daub fragments	0.00	0.22	0.88	0.00	0	0.00
Kiln wasters	0.67	0.00	0.00	0.00	0	28.40
Obsidian angular debris/ All chipped stone	0.19	0.10	0.07	0.18	0.00	0.20
Incense burner frags.	0.52	0.00	0.00	0.50	0	0.00
Obsidian blades/All ch. stn.	0.29	0.05	0.12	0.36	0.00	0.10
Snapped ret. obs. blades/ All obs. blades	0.43	0.68	0.69	0.30	0.00	0.33

* N is number of squares collected.

The average number of grinding stone fragments per collection ranges from 1.2 to 1.8 in the residential sectors, while no grinding stone fragments at all were found in either of the civic-ceremonial sectors, and only 0.2 per collection in the workshop sector. The distribution of kiln wasters likewise supports our interpretation of the workshop sector as a non-residential, ceramic production area.

The distribution of obsidian among collections from Residential 1, Residential 2, and Residential 3 provides support for our interpretation of differential status among these three sectors. The collections made in Residential 1 have the highest proportion of obsidian; those from Residential 2 and 3 have less (Table 2.7). This distribution was analyzed with the KSAMPLE routine of the Michigan Interactive Data Analysis System (Fox and Guire 1976), a non-parametric analogue of analysis of variance. It compares the distribution of a continuous variable between specified strata, or groups of cases, to test the null dypothesis that the distribution of the variable is the same in each stratum. Two tests were conducted, the Kruskal-Wallis test (Gibbons 1971:198) and the median test (Gibbons 1971: 196). These tests do not demand the assumptions of normality and homogeneity of the variances required by a traditional analysis of variance. The former test assumes that the observations are independent random samples from populations with continuous distributions, while the latter test requires only independence among the samples. In our case the median test is clearly the more appropriate, but both statistics will be given for comparative purposes. In our first application, the distribution of the obsidian to other chipped stone ratio for Residential 1, 2, and 3 yielded a Kruskal-Wallis statistic of 14.661 (2 degrees of freedom; associated probability of .0007) and a median test statistic of 11.403 (2 degrees of freedom; associated probability of .003). Thus the higher proportion of obsidian in Residential 1 is not likely the result of chance alone.

A certain amount of additional corroboration is lent to our stratification of the residential sectors by the distribution of grayware and plainware jar rims. Although a fixed number of jars per household was probably necessary for normal domestic functioning, it is likely that higher-status households would tend to have had proportionately more of the finer grayware jars and fewer of the cruder plainware jars. Once again, it is Residential 1 which is assigned the position of highest status (Table 2.7).

Finally, note the distribution of daub fragments recovered in the three residential sectors (Table 2.7). These are preserved fragments of mud that was applied to the walls of wattle-and-daub houses, a form of contruction likely to be more prevalent by this time period among the lower-status members of society. For Residential 1, 95% of whose structures had masonry foundations, the average number of daub fragments per collection is 0. For Residential 2, which contained 86% masonry structures, the figure is .22. And for Residential 3, 44% of whose structures were masonry, the average number of daub fragments per collection is .89.

Taken together, the above lines of evidence support our stratification of the residential portion of Ts73/79 into three sectors of differing status or rank. Residential 1 clearly represents a social segment that had preferential access to high-quality building materials, scarce resources like obsidian, and finer pottery. Residential 2 appears to have been of slightly higher status than Residential 3, but this difference was not as great as that separating these two sectors from Residential 1.

The above analysis leads to an obvious question: were these three social segments all engaged in the same kinds of activities? The locational and artifactual data suggest that they were not. Many of the occupants of Residential 1, of course, were probably simply the elite members of society and their retainers. However, as we shall see shortly, it is likely that some of the inhabitants of this sector were involved in administrative activities; the proximity of Civic-ceremonial 1 to their houses certainly argues for this. Still other inhabitants of Residential 1 may have been rather heavily involved in obsidian working. An index of the intensity of obsidian working can be computed by taking the average number of obsidian fragments in each collection classified as angular debitage (that is, waste material, often with part of the cortex or striking platform still remaining) and dividing this by the average total number of pieces of chipped stone of all kinds in each collection. As Table 2.7 indicates, this index is much higher for the collections taken in Residential 1 (0.19) than it is for the collections made in Residential 2 (0.10) and Residential 3 (0.07). This implies that more obsidian working was occurring in Residential 1 than in the other two residential sectors. It should also be noted that the ratio for the collections in Civic-ceremonial 1 is nearly as high as that for Residential 1, suggesting that a good deal of obsidian working occurred here as well. It is, of course, no surprise to find obsidian working associated with civic-ceremonial architecture and high-status houses: we have repeatedly noted the role that obsidian blades probably played in certain self-sacrificial rituals, which in Mesoamerica were typically performed by priests and other high-status persons. In the Workshop collections, we also have a high ratio that may or may not imply obsidian working, as such angular debris is often used in ceramic manufacture for trimming and incising (Saunder Van der Leeuw 1977, personal communication).

The inhabitants of Residential 2 may have supplied the labor for the ceramic workshop. Although Residential 2 is located across the double wall from the ceramic workshop, these people could have filed in every day through the gate with the masonry guard house (Fig. 2.12). By contributing just one or two members per household, the inhabitants of Residential 2 could have mustered a force of 50 to 100 workers. Of course, it is possible that some of these people might have been involved in other tasks such as maintaining public buildings or working as servants for the elite. But the size and complexity of the workshop clearly argues for the existence of a full-time staff of ceramic producers. The workshop, as Redmond points out in Chapter 3, was producing <u>at least</u> all the gray pottery used at Ts73/79, and it may well have been producing all the pottery used in the community. This is a rather different situation from Late Santa María times when only part of the ceramic assemblage was being produced by some households, probably on a part-time basis.

The proximity of their houses to the irrigated alluvium suggests that the inhabitants of Residential 3 were a specialized agricultural labor force. Kirkby's (1973:Table 10) figures indicate that modern day Zapotecs in the Valley of Oaxaca using the traditional coa or digging stick can cultivate about 2 ha of land per farmer. If all 425 ha of alluvium in the Arroyo Lencho Diego locality had been under cultivation, a work force of about 213 farmers would have been required to cultivate the land. It will be remembered that the number of households in Residential 3 is estimated to be between 65 and 100 with a mean value of 82.5. If each household had contributed two or three members to the agricultural work force (a father and a son or two, for example), the entire force would have numbered between 165 and 247. The expected work force size of 213 falls within this range, suggesting that the inhabitants of Residential 3 would have constituted a sizeable enough group to keep all 425 ha of alluvium uder cultivation, should this have been necessary. But to do this they probably would have had to work full-time as farmers, at least during the agricultural season. These figures are therefore consistent with our interpretation of Residential 3 as a sector of specialized agricultural producers.

If Residential 1, Residential 2, and Residential 3 represent, respectively, sectors of elite families plus specialized administrators and obsidian-workers, specialized ceramic producers, and specialized farmers, how might the relationships among these groups have been regulated? There is substantial evidence that the structure of administrative decision making in the Early Palo Blanco phase was rather more complex than it had been in previous phases. We can assess the complexity of administration at Ts73/79 by examining the morphology and distribution of public buildings on the site (Flannery and Marcus 1976). First, let us examine the evidence for vertical specialization in decision making (Johnson 1978). To do this, we will assume that the large mounds on the site represent decision-making loci. We will further assume that the relative size of a mound reflects the position of the decision-making function that occurs there within the overall administrative hierarchy. There are six masonry mounds at Ts73 and one nonmasonry mound in the plaza of Ts79a that are used in the present analysis. These mounds are marked with letters A through G on the site maps. They are as follows:

Mound A: a mound 4 m high at the highest point of the site;
Mound B: another mound 4 m high on a platform just below and to the south of Mound A;
Mound C: a mound 1 m high in the ceramic workshop;
Mound D: a mound 2 m high in the ceramic workshop;
Mound E: a mound 1 m high just northeast of the ceramic workshop;
Mound F: a mound 1 m high near the north end of the double wall, on the Residential 2 side of that wall;
Mound G: a low (just under 1 m high) mound in the plaza of Civic-ceremonial 2 at Ts79a.

A simple histogram of these mounds according to their heights is presented in Fig. 2.16. The histogram manifests a fairly clear bimodality which suggests that the administrative structure at Ts73/79 was characterized by two orders of vertical specialization, that is, two levels of decision making above the level of the primary producers. The higher of these two

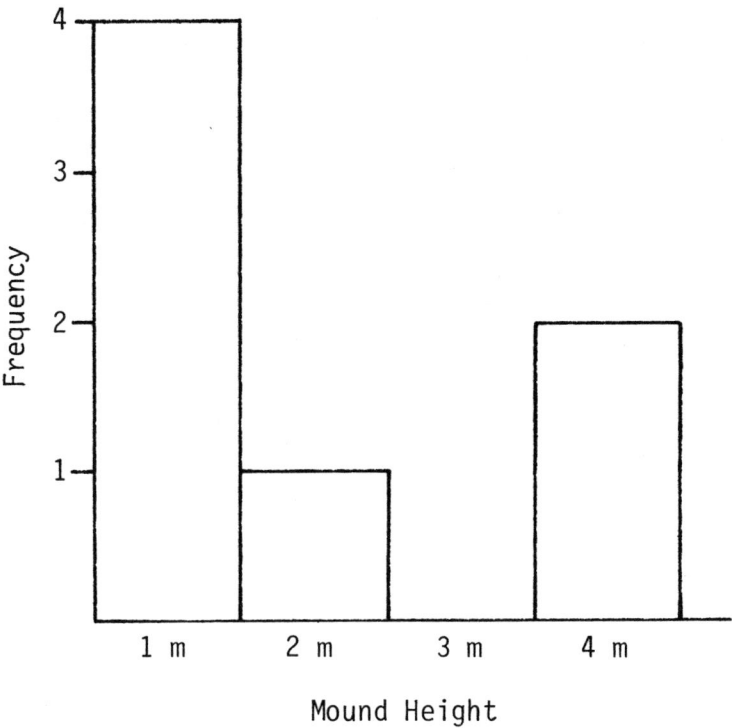

Fig. 2.16. Histogram of mound heights at Ts73/79.

levels, represented by Mounds A and B, undoubtedly pertained to general administration. Policy level decisions were made here, and lower order decision making was regulated. The lower of the two levels, represented by Mounds C through G, related to more specific administrative activities.

Now we must consider the evidence for horizontal specialization in the administrative structure at Ts73/79 (Johnson 1978). To do this we will use contextual data to infer the administrative functions of the public buildings just discussed. We will then estimate the number of decision-making units represented on each of the two administrative levels.

On the higher level, or second vertical order of decision making, we have two masonry mounds. One of these, Mound B, is located on a platform adjacent to the houses in Residential 1. The other, Mound A, faces a small plaza that forms a spatially discrete architectural unit (Fig. 2.12). Although we do not know precisely what kinds of decisions were made at these locales, the difference between the contexts of the two mounds implies that they had somewhat different administrative functions. This, in turn, suggests that the top level in the administrative hierarchy was horizontally specialized to the extent of two units of decision making.

On the lower level of administration we have five mounds. We will use the contexts of these mounds to suggest the possible administrative duties associated with them.

Mound C: Administrative duties almost certainly involved

managing activities in the ceramic workshop;

    Mound D: administrative duties, as above, probably involved managing the workshop;

    Mound E: administrative duties are not completely clear from the context, but possibly have to do with the double wall (that is, controlling access to the walled portion of the site);

    Mound F: administrative duties were probably related either to controlling access at the double wall, as above, or to managing the affairs of the inhabitants of Residential 2;

    Mound G: administrative dutes probably involved managing the affairs of Residential 3, the specialized farmers of the community.

The contextual analysis suggests that there were between two and four distinct units of decision making on the lower level of administration at Ts73/79.

    To sum up, an examination of the morphology and distribution of public architecture at Ts73/79 has led us to propose the following assessment of administrative complexity at the community: the structure of decision making was characterized by two orders of vertical specialization; the higher of these levels was horizontally specialized to the extent of two decision-making units, while the lower level was horizontally specialized to the extent of two to four units of decision making. Fig. 2.17 is a schematic rendering of the possible structure of the administrative hierarchy at Ts73/79.

    All the individuals involved in administration, of course, would have constituted the bureaucracy, which apparently grew to be quite large by the end of the Early Palo Blanco phase. As stated above, most of the

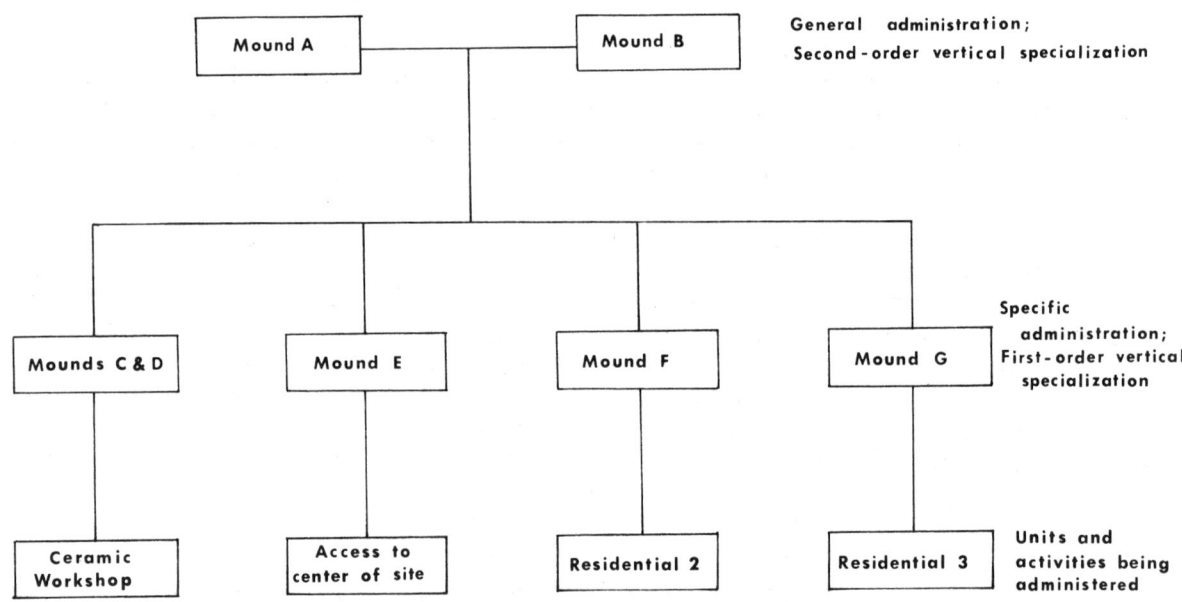

Fig. 2.17. Proposed administrative hierarchy at Ts73/79.

people involved in administration probably lived in Residential 1. By the end of the Early Palo Blanco phase, the total population of this sector had reached 80 to 85 households (Table 2.6) or one-third of the total population at Ts73/79. In order to support this growing bureaucracy, greater and greater demands would have been placed upon the productive base of the system, a point to which we shall return later.

The evidence for differential participation in ritual activities is presented in Table 2.7. All the incense burners, for instance are found either in Residential 1 or in Civic-ceremonial 1. Civic-ceremonial 1 has the highest proportion of obsidian blades, with Residential 1 not too far behind. Residential 2 and Residential 3, on the other hand, have much lower proportions of obsidian blades. This distribution yielded a Kruskal-Wallis statistic of 25.753 (3 degrees of freedom; associated probability less than .0001) and a median test statistic of 20.131 (3 degrees of freedom; associated probability of .0002). So we see a continuation of the by-now-familiar pattern of differential participation in ritual activities according to relative social status.

Table 2.7 also presents the distribution of a ratio computed by dividing the number of snapped, retouched obsidian blades by the total number of obsidian blades for each collection. An interesting comparison can be made by considering these ratios in conjunction with the overall distribution of obsidian blades. Although Civic-ceremonial 1 has the highest proportion of obsidian blades, it has the lowest proportion of obsidian blades that were snapped and retouched. The residential sectors as a group have higher average proportions of snapped and retouched blades, and Residential 2 and Residential 3 have the highest average proportions of snapped, retouched blades of all the sectors. The distribution of this ratio across the four sectors yielded a Kruskal-Wallis statistic of 8.1406 (3 degrees of freedom; associated probability of .043) and a median test statistic of 7.2967 (3 degrees of freedom; associated probability of .063). We suggest that obsidian blades had multiple functions: those in pristine condition were used extensively in self-sacrificial rituals which were practiced more frequently by the elite than by the nonelite. Once the blades became dull and/or broken, they were put to different uses in a domestic context. The frequency of their occurrence in such contexts, however, continued to be status-related, as any obsidian tool was still a scarce and highly valued item.

In summary, the Early Palo Blanco phase in the Arroyo Lencho Diego witnessed the following developments:

    1. a three-fold growth in the capacity of the reservoir;
    2. a 115% growth in population over the previous phase;
    3. more formalized social differentiation, with the appearance of three well-defined social strata that appear to have been ranked with respect to one another;
    4. an extreme social division of labor or economic specialization, with one of the above social strata involved in agricultural production, another in ceramic production, and the third in administrative activities and obsidian working;
    5. a great elaboration of the political/religious administrative

organization, which became highly centralized and complex, and was characterized by a decision-making hierarchy with two orders or vertical specialization, the higher of which had two units of horizontal specialization, and the lower, two to four units;

    6. a continuation of the pattern of differential participation in some ritual activities, with the elite members of society more active participants than the nonelite, and a substantial amount of ritual activity associated with public buildings.

    We have, then, examined four phases of human settlement in the Arroyo Lencho Diego. We have endeavored to deal systematically with the changes that occurred in dam size and reservoir capacity, population size and distribution, social differentiation, productive specialization, differential participation in ritual, and administrative centralization and complexity. Now let us shift to a more diachronic frame of reference and evaluate the four hypotheses presented earlier that proposed certain kinds of covariant relationships among some of these variables.

Evaluation of Hypothesis 1

    The first hypothesis postualated a positive covariant relationship between the physical size of an irrigation system and the degree of administrative complexity in the society which builds and uses it. This, of course, is a major element in the Wittfogelian formulation. It holds that the development of complex administration is a response to the problems of organizing mass labor for building and maintaining a large-scale irrigation system. Under this hypothesis, we would expect greater complexity in administrative structure to result when the organizational problems are most acute. Once again, remember that the degree to which administration in the arroyo was religious or secular in nature does not concern us here, for our focus will be more upon the administrative function than the ideological matrix of administration.

    The sequence of development in the Arroyo Lencho Diego manifests two points in time when marked change occurred in administrative structure, as measured by changes in the organization of public space. The first was at the Early Santa María/Middle Santa María juncture when the first public building appeared. The second was at the Late Santa María/Early Palo Blanco juncture, when a complex of public buildings was built atop Ts73/79 and at a few other places on the site. To the extent that administrative function can be attached to public architecture, we would suggest that the decision-making structure in Middle and Late Santa María times consisted of one order of vertical specialization, while the Early Palo Blanco decision-making hierarchy was comprised of two orders of vertical specialization, with two units of horizontal specialization on the top level of that hierarchy and two to four units on the lower. For the Early Santa María phase, we suggest that the political situation in the arroyo was similar to a "big-man" form of organization (Sahlins 1963), characterized by a small amount of centralized authority due to the charisma of an ambitious individual or small group of individuals but no formalized administrative decision making

2. IRRIGATION, ADMINISTRATION, AND SOCIETY 55

above the level of the heads of households.

Are the above two critical junctures of political change related to the problems of organizing mass labor for the construction of the irrigation works? We do, in fact, find that Ts15 and Level 2 of the dam were constructed concurrently with the establishment of one level of formalized administrative decision making above the household level, and Level 3 of the dam was constructed concurrently with the establishment of the two-level administrative hierarchy. Level 1 was constructed within a political context where, as mentioned above, there was no formalized administration above the heads of households, and Level 4 was constructed within the context of an established two-level administrative hierarchy.

Under the first hypothesis, we would expect the degree of administrative complexity, as measured by the degree of vertical and horizontal specialization in decision making, to vary positively with the degree of organizational difficulty presented by the task to the human group building each level of the dam. As a shorthand, the organizational difficulty involved in building each level of the dam will be called the "organizational stress" for that endeavor. But, how should we attempt to measure the severity of organizational stress involved in each construction effort? We suggest that a relative measure of such stress could be computed by estimating the manpower requirements of the task at hand and dividing this figure by the size of the available work force. This ratio would be a better measure of organizational stress than simply a figure based on the gross manpower requirements, as a large task can be accomplished by a very large group of workers with minimal supervision. It is only when the work force is limited relative to the task at hand that considerations of efficiency demand effective overall control and direction. The measures resulting from this ratio, of course, would have little absolute significance. But they would be useful in a relative sense for comparing the four construction levels of the dam in terms of the organizational problems each might have presented to the population doing the building. A high value for such a ratio, here called the Manpower Stress Index, would imply relatively more organizational stress, while a low value would suggest a relative lack of such stress. Under our first hypothesis, we would expect this index to vary positively with the degree of administrative complexity.

First, however, we must devise a way of calculating the manpower requirements for building each of the four construction levels. We derived figures from Erasmus's (1965) experiments at hiring Maya workmen in Yucatán to quarry and carry loads of rock and earth fill. He found that carrying was by far the more significant task for determining overall manpower requirements. His data include the weights and volumes of earth and stone that one person could move over various distances in a working day of varying length. Our figures are based on several assumptions: 1) that the limestones and sandstones of the Arroyo Lencho Diego were comparable to those of Yucatán; 2) that the dam fill, as shown in the profile drawings and pictures, contains a constant earth to stone ratio of 3 to 1; and 3) that construction activity would have taken place only in the dry season, some eight months long. There are two reasons for this last assumption: first, the dry season is the time when most people would have been freed from their rainy season agricultural chores; and second, it is the time when flash flooding, a constant worry in the arroyo during the rainy season, would not have disrupted construction or destroyed new work.

Tables 2.8 and 2.9 give figures on the manpower requirements for each stage of the dam's construction. Included are man-day estimates if the average length of carry varied between 50 and 100 m and between 50 and 200 m. Estimates are also given for 5-hour, 8-hour, and 10-hour working days. There are also estimates of the size of the work force required to complete the task at hand in one dry season of eight months or two or three dry seasons as the case warranted. Finally, there are two estimates of the work force available at the time of each construction effort. The first estimate assumes that each household contributed two of its members to the work force, while the second assumes that each contributed three members to the effort.

As Table 2.8 indicates, Level 1 of the dam could have been built in one dry season by a work force of between three and eight people. Two or three households probably could have supplied the labor necessary to complete the task. Just prior to the first construction, of course, the arroyo was occupied only only on a seasonal basis by people who spend the rest of the year elsewhere. They came here to hunt, collect wild plants, and plant a limited amount of maize during the wet season. The building of Level 1 probably represents an experimental venture by a small group of these people, perhaps only two families out of the four or five that MacNeish et al. (1972:67-127) estimated as having used the arroyo. Evidently the dividend in terms of increased agricultural productivity was so great that they decided to set up permanent residence. It is tempting to suggest that the two masonry structures at Ts449 represent the homes of these two enterprising families. The other structures may represent those of people attracted to the arroyo by the success of the venture, some of whom may have been part of the group that had originally visited the arroyo on a seasonal basis. At any rate, the Manpower Stress Index for Level 1 (computed by taking an average of the values for the required work force size and dividing this by an average of the values for the size of the available work force) is 0.61, which, as we shall see, is relatively low.

Level 2 of the dam is composed of a very large quantity of fill, and completing the job in one dry season would have far exceeded the organizational capabilities of the population at the beginning of the Middle Santa María phase, the time of its construction (Table 2.8). In this light, the function of Ts15, mentioned earlier as a vexing problem, becomes more comprehensible, since a project to build a dam across the arroyo would probably have been restricted to work in the dry season because of the danger of wash-outs in the rainy season. There are two ways to deal with this problem: a concerted effort could have been made to finish the job in one dry season, or a way devised to get rid of the water while working on the main dam. That is, a cofferdam or diversionary dam could have been built to keep the water away from the main structure until Level 2 had been completed. Our calculations suggest that while there would not have been

2. IRRIGATION, ADMINISTRATION, AND SOCIETY 57

TABLE 2.8

MANPOWER REQUIREMENTS OF DAM CONSTRUCTION

Dam Level	Fill (m³)	Work Day (hr)	Labor Required (total days) A**	Labor Required (total days) B**	1 dry season A**	1 dry season B**	2 dry seasons A**	2 dry seasons B**	3 dry seasons A**	3 dry seasons B**	Midpoint of Estimates*
1	2,940	5	1,424	1,831	6	8					5.5
		8	890	1,145	4	5					
		10	712	916	3	4					
Ts15	40,000	5	19,378	24,918	81	104					72.5
		8	21,112	15,574	51	65					
		10	9,688	12,459	41	52					
2	123,000	5	59,586	76,623	248	319	124	160	83	106	73.5
		8	37,244	47,889	155	199	77	100	52	66	
		10	29,793	38,312	124	160	62	80	41	53	
3	51,870	5	25,128	32,312	105	135					93.5
		8	15,706	20,195	65	84					
		10	12,564	16,156	52	67					
4	192,000	5	93,012	119,606	387	498	194	249	130	166	346
		8	58,138	74,753	242	311	121	156	81	104	
		10	46,506	59,804	194	249	97	124	65	83	

* Calculated on the assumption of construction during one dry season, except for Level 2 where construction during three dry seasons is assumed.

** Estimate A is based on the assumption that the distance material had to be carried for dam construction was 50 to 100 m; Estimate B, on the assumption of 50 to 200 m carries.

TABLE 2.9

AVAILABLE MANPOWER AND MANPOWER STRESS INDEX

Dam Level	Available Manpower			Workers Required	Manpower Stress Index*
	2 workers per household	3 workers per household	Midpoints of Estimates		
1	6-8	9-12	9	5.5	0.61
Ts15	18-24	27-36	27	72.5	2.69
2	18-24	27-36	27	73.5	2.72
3	192-210	288-315	253.5	93.5	0.37
4	228-260	342-390	309	346	1.12

* The Manpower Stress Index (MSI) is computed by dividing the midpoint of the estimates of the numbers of workers required (from Table 2.8) by the midpoint of the estimates of the available manpower. The higher the value of the MSI, the more stressful the relationship.

enough available manpower to construct Level 2 in one dry season, building Ts15 in one dry season would have required a labor foce much more commensurate with the amount of available manpower (Table 2.9). Ts15 could then have served as a diversionary structure or cofferdam, and Level 2 could have been constructed over a period of three or more dry seasons. Building Ts15, however, would still have presented an extremely complex organizational problem for those directing the construction effort: the Manpower Stress Index (MSI) for Ts15 is computed at 2.69. Dealing effectively with this stress would have involved, in the words of Marshall Sahlins (1972:82), "getting people to work more or more people to work." Possibly both strategies were employed. People from outside the arroyo might have been recruited to help in the construction effort, and the people already inhabiting the arroyo could have been exhorted to work harder. It was, of course, precisely at the time of the Level 2 dam that the first public building appeared, implying the establishment of one order of vertical specialization in the organization of decision making. This pattern would seem to be consistent with the hypothesized relationship between a high MSI value and an increase in administrative complexity, but we will have to examine the entire sequence before deciding on the validity of this hypothesis.

The first hypothesis would also predict a high MSI value for Level 3 of the dam, which was constructed at the Late Santa María/Early Palo Blanco interface, approximately concurrent with the establishment of Ts73/79. At this point in time, administrative organization in the arroyo underwent a marked elaboration with the construction of a large civic-ceremonial precinct and the establishment of a two-level administrative hierarchy. However, as Table 2.9 indicates, Level 3 could have been easily built by only a fraction of the population in the arroyo; the MSI value for Level 3 is only 0.37, indicating a relatively low level of organizational stress. This pattern is clearly inconsistent with our first

TABLE 2.10
MANPOWER STRESS AND ADMINISTRATIVE COMPLEXITY

Dam level	Manpower Stress Index	Administrative Complexity
1	0.61	No formalized administration; Household head decision making
Ts15	2.69	First public building; One-level administrative hierarchy; One order of vertical specialization in decision-making organization
2	2.72	One-level administrative hierarchy continues
3	0.37	Establishment of two-level administrative hierarchy; Two orders of vertical specialization with two units of horizontal specialization on the upper level and two to four units of horizontal specialization on the lower level
4	1.12	Two-level administrative hierarchy continues

hypothesis. It appears that the great increase in administrative complexity which occurred at this time was related to factors other than the organizational stresses entailed in building Level 3.

The construction of Level 4 of the dam has a moderate MSI value (1.12), but we should note that this building effort took place at least 50 to 100 years after the establishment of Ts73/79. The structure of Early Palo Blanco administrative decision making had probably been established well before the effort was undertaken.

Our first hypothesis postulated a positive covariant relationship between the degree of administrative complexity and the degree of organizational stress related to the various construction stages of the dam. As Table 2.10 indicates, there is no consistent overall relationship between the measure of organizational stress, the MSI, and the degree of administrative complexity. We must tentatively conclude that the long-term development of administrative complexity in the Arroyo Lencho Diego was not in response to the organizational demands of building the irrigation system per se.

This is not to say that the irrigation system had nothing to do with the development of administrative complexity in the arroyo. Administrative structures, after all, exist for certain reasons, and it is likely that allocating water among users in the arroyo was one important administrative task. The placement of the first public building near the spillway of the Level 2 dam would certainly argue for this (Fig. 2.1). At this time, a more complex decision-making apparatus for allocating water was probably required, probably because water was being distributed inequitably and some form of payment exacted for its use. As we shall see, water had become a commodity subject to political manipulation. Administrative structure in the arroyo developed during the Middle Santa María phase to carry out and regulate this manipulation.

The second important increase in administrative complexity, occurring at the time of the Level 3 dam (beginning of the Early Palo Blanco phase), seems related to factors other than water allocation. Distributing water, of course, probably continued to be an important activity, but by the Early Palo Blanco phase there were other, equally important, administrative functions. As we saw earlier, these apparently included regulating the relationships between specialized potters and specialized farmers, controlling access to the community, and managing the affairs of segregated residence groups. There is also evidence (to be discussed in detail later on) that defense was a major concern of the Early Palo Blanco community; directing the defensive actions of Ts73/79, then, would have been another important administrative activity.

Rather than emphasize any single factor, it seems more reasonable to suggest that near the beginning of the Early Palo Blanco phase a great increase occurred in the variety of managerial tasks that had to be performed to preserve the community's viability, and administrative structure in the arroyo became more complex in order to deal with this variety. This position is virtually identical to that taken by Johnson (1973 and 1978). He has proposed that administrative structures become more complex as the amount and variety of information they must process increase. We would further suggest that administrative development should be interpreted within the context of the power structure in society. It is important to ask which segment of society is likely to benefit from an increase in administrative complexity and how this factor affects the course of administrative development. As we shall see later on, administration probably became more complex during the Early Palo Blanco phase, not just because there was a greater variety of information available to be processed, but because a greater variety of information had to be processed in order to preserve the structure of power relationships within arroyo society.

Evaluation of Hypothesis 2

The second hypothesis argues that in a system where irrigation is essential for agricultural production and there is but one water source, an emergent elite can seize control over the distribution of water and use this power in an entrepreneurial fashion to regulate the surplus production of the rest of the population (Friedman 1974:463 and Adams 1966). As more and more households are incorporated into such an irrigation system, the amount of absolute surplus which the elite can manipulate for its own aggrandizement will increase accordingly. This hypothesis would therefore predict a positive covariant relationship between the number of households incorporated into the irrigation system and the degree to which society was characterized by differential access to power and valuable resources.

In the Arroyo Lencho Diego, irrigation is absolutely essential for

2. IRRIGATION, ADMINISTRATION, AND SOCIETY

TABLE 2.11

SOCIAL DIFFERENTIATION AND NUMBER OF HOUSEHOLDS
DEPENDENT UPON IRRIGATION SYSTEM

Phase	Nature of Social Differentiation	No. of Households
Early Santa María	Some social differentiation; Big-man organization(?)	9-12
Middle Santa María	Ranking	30-34
Late Santa María	More pronounced ranking	96-105
Early Palo Blanco	Social stratification	195-238

successul agriculture, and during the periods in question the water for irrigation probably came exclusively from one source, the Purrón Dam reservoir. The settlement pattern analysis revealed that while a certain degree of status differentiation existed in the Early Santa María phase, it was not until the Middle Santa María phase that a principle of ranking appeared to characterize social relationships. The higher-ranking members of Middle Santa María society were also living in direct physical association with the reservoir, suggesting that their elevated status was in some way related to their access to the stored water. Ranking became still more pronounced in the Late Santa María phase, with one family in particular attaining an extremely elevated position in society. In the Early Palo Blanco phase, we noted a change in the nature of social differentiation, with the ranking of earlier times supplanted by the establishment of three social strata.

Table 2.11 presents estimates of the number of households in the arroyo along with a characterization of the mode and degree of social differentiation for each phase. The Early Santa María phase was marked by a certain degree of social differentiation, what could be termed the social expression of a "big-man" form of political organization. The number of households involved in the irrigation system at this time was only 9 to 12. During Middle Santa María times, when ranking was the mode of social differentiation, 30 to 34 households were dependent upon the irrigation system. The even more pronounced ranking of the Late Santa María phase was associated with an increase to 96 to 105 in the number of households relying upon the Purrón Dam irrigation system. Finally, during the Early Palo Blanco phase, when social differentiation reached its most formal and extreme expression in the arroyo, the number of households supported by the irrigation system increased to 195 to 238. Table 2.11 thus shows a clear positive relationship between the nature and degree of social differentiation and the number of households incorporated into the irrigation system. Obviously, we are not able to reject the second hypothesis on the basis of these data.

Evaluation of Hypothesis 3

The third hypothesis states that in cases where two or more communities are using the same water source for irrigation, there is a certain potential for conflict between upstream and downstream users over water rights. This sort of conflict has been cited as a major selective agent in the development of administrative complexity and centralized authority (Sanders and Price 1968 and Lees 1973). This hypothesis would predict that the addition of downstream Ts131 in the Late Santa María phase greatly raised the probability of conflict over water rights, and in this way led to more complex administration and centralized authority in the system as a whole.

Ts131 appeared on the Lencho Diego scene around 450 B.C. It is not clear at this time whether Ts131 was a daughter community that budded off from the main dam community, or whether it represents an influx of outsiders attracted to the area by the success of the irrigation operation. But we found clear evidence for differences in access to scarce resources and ritual paraphernalia between the upstream dam community and downstream Ts131. This supports Lees's (1973) contention that such an upstream-downstream settlement configuration would foster a power differential stemming largely from inequitable access to the source of irrigation water. There would, in other words, have been a definite <u>potential</u> for conflict between the upstream and downstream communities in the Late Santa María phase.

But did this conflict potential figure importantly in the evolution of administrative complexity in the arroyo? To answer this, we should consider what changes occurred in the organization of decision making in the 300 years between the establishment of Ts131 and its abandonment at the end of the Late Santa María phase. It will be remembered that the public building erected in the Middle Santa María phase continued to be the only public structure throughout the Late Santa María phase as well. We used this evidence to suggest, for both Middle and Late Santa María, one order of vertical specialization in the organization of decision making. Not until the establishment of Ts73/79 at the beginning of the Early Palo Blanco phase did we see any major change in the nature of administrative organization, with the establishment of a two-level decision-making hierarchy and a proliferation of horizontal specialization on both levels of that hierarchy. What <u>did</u> happen during the Late Santa María phase is that the existing elite greatly augmented its status in society, and one family in particular came to occupy a very prestigious position, living atop a rise 10 m high and having preferential access to a great deal of imported obsidian.

It appears that the addition of a downstream community in the arroyo served largely to increase the power and prestige of the existing elite within the existing administrative framework. The new community contributed more households to the system, giving the elite control over greater amounts of absolute surplus. Furthermore, if there <u>had</u> been any conflict over water rights, it is likely that the established elite would have acted as arbitrators in such disputes. It already controlled, after all, the dam and reservoir. By engaging in such arbitration, the elite could have further increased its power and prestige by exacting payments, playing off one

2. IRRIGATION, ADMINISTRATION, AND SOCIETY

lower-status faction against another, and so forth. We conclude that the addition of a downstream community definitely fostered a power differential between it and the upstream community (Lees 1973). However, any conflict deriving from this power differential does not seem to have played a significant role in the development of administrative complexity in the arroyo.

Evaluation of Hypothesis 4

The fourth hypothesis is based on the assumption that people intensify production only when they are forced to by population pressure (Boserup 1965, Sanders and Price 1968, and many others). This hypothesis would predict that each decision to expand the reservoir was prompted by a stressful relationship between the productive potential of the mode of production and the nutritional requirements of the population.

An evaluation of the population pressure hypothesis obviously demands some reasonable way of computing the carrying capacity of the irrigation-based agricultural regime for each of the four phases under consideration. As agriculture without irrigation is impossible in the Arroyo Lencho Diego locality, we can use the volume estimates for the reservoir to estimate the area of land that could have been kept under irrigated cultivation during each phase. Estimates of maize yields appropriate for the times can then be taken into account, and a carrying capacity figure for all the irrigated land finally generated by considering the annual maize requirements for a typical Mesoamerican household.

First we must determine the area of land that could be kept under irrigation for each phase of the dam's construction. The exact number of irrigated hectares, of course, would depend greatly on the actual way the water was used. However, we can generate a series of maximum and minimum estimates that probably include in their ranges the true figures. Let us begin with the final stage of the reservoir and work backwards in time from that vantage point.

For a minimum estimate we can use the figure reported by Woodbury and Neely (1972:99) that derives from the water requirements of the sugar cane grown today in the Lencho Diego vicinity. This crop, they report, requires 10,000 m^3 of water per ha. Obviously, sugar cane was not grown in antiquity in the Arroyo Lencho Diego, and the water requirements of maize are somewhat less than those of the cane (cf. Woodbury and Neely 1972:99). Nevertheless, if we divide the 2,640,000 m^3 capacity of the Level 4 reservoir by this figure, we get 264 ha, which will serve us admirably as a minimum estimate for the area that could have been irrigated with water from the fourth reservoir.

Deriving a maximum estimate is rather more difficult, as maize is no longer grown in the Lencho Diego locality, and figures pertaining to the water requirements of maize here are consequently lacking. However, as a maximum estimate of irrigated land for the fourth and final reservoir, we could use the total amount of alluvium contained between the two places where the piedmont pinches in nearly to the banks of the river. (See, for example, Fig. 2.11.) This amounts to 425 ha.

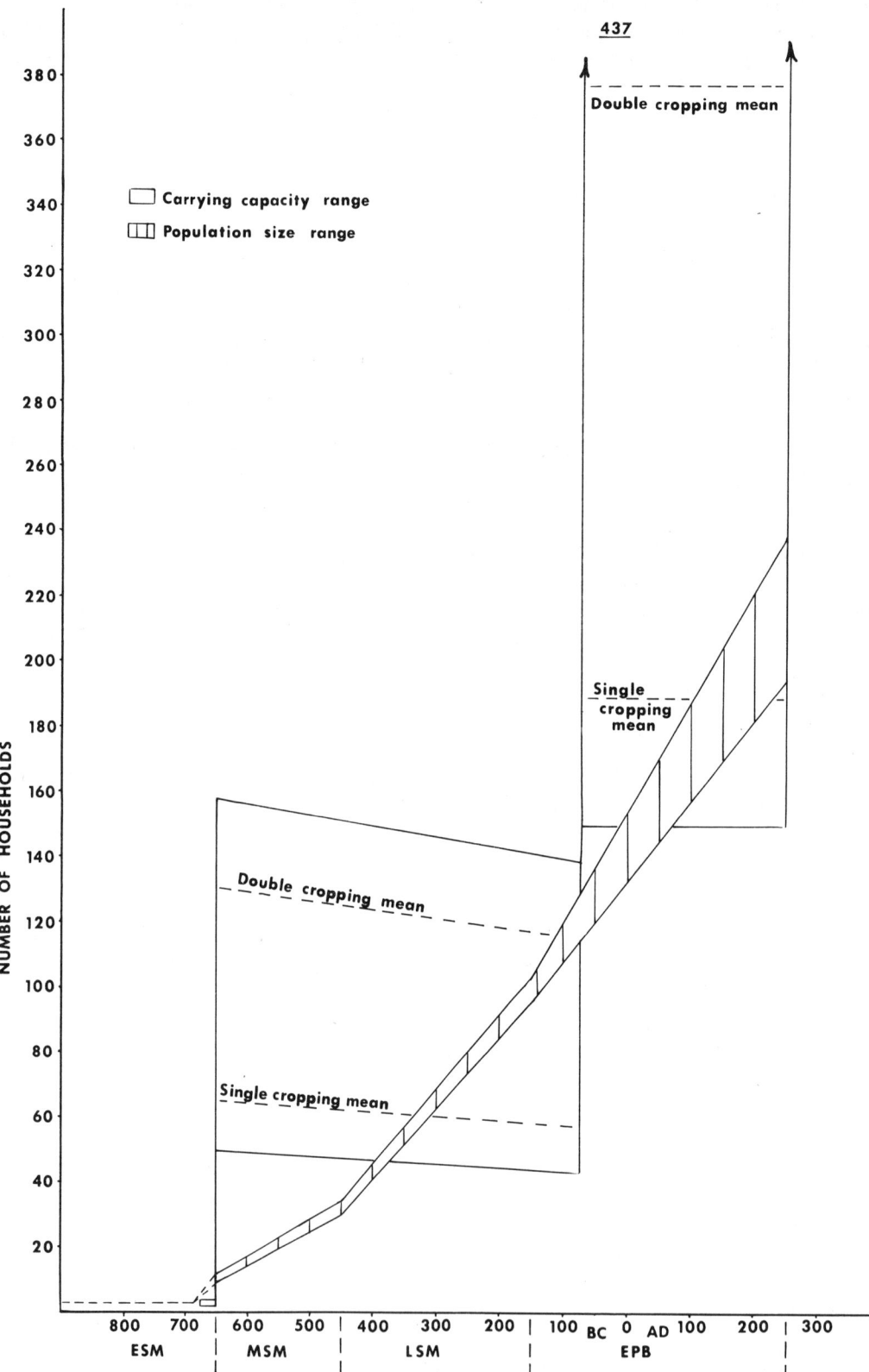

Fig. 2.18. Estimated population and predicted carrying capacity for 950 years of development in the Arroyo Lencho Diego.

2. IRRIGATION, ADMINISTRATION, AND SOCIETY

For the three earlier reservoirs, minimum estimates of the area of irrigated land are obtained as described above. The estimated volume of the reservoir is simply divided by 10,000 m^3 of water per ha, the figure that derives from the water requirements of sugar cane. The maximum estimate, on the other hand, is computed by reducing the irrigated area from its maximum of 425 ha by the same proportion that the reservoir itself is reduced. The reasoning for this is as follows: if the amount of land that can be irrigated with x m^3 of water is 100 ha, then (assuming the same techniques of water application) the amount of land that could be irrigated with .6x m^3 of water would be 60 ha, and so on. Table 2.13 presents the minimum and maximum estimates of irrigated land for each of the four construction stages of the dam.

Now we must calculate the number of households that could be supported by these differing amounts of irrigated land. This involves first estimating the yields in maize per ha. Only maize will be used in these determinations because it forms the key part of the traditional Mesoamerican diet. Consequently, the final carrying capacity estimates based on maize yields will necessarily be maximum ranges, as each hectare set aside for growing another crop would serve to reduce the total output of the central staple and thus the overall carrying capacity.

Two local residents questioned during the 1976 field season in the arroyo remembered when some maize had been grown on the alluvium. Each recalled independently average yields of 800 kg of shelled maize per ha per planting. These figures, however, cannot be used in our present analysis since, as Flannery (1973:297-300) and Kirkby (1973:124-127) have demonstrated, the productivity of maize has grown remarkably over the past several thousand years due to selective intervention by man. Kirkby (1973: Fig. 48) presented a set of graphs reconstructing the average productivity of maize for any prehistoric epoch. It is notable that for modern times her figures indicate average yields of 800 kg per ha per planting, corresponding exactly to the information given us by the two older men in the vicinity. This suggests that Kirkby's figures, although derived from Valley of Oaxaca data, can be applied to the Arroyo Lencho Diego as well. Table 2.12 gives the derived productivity estimates of maize for the four prehistoric phases which concern us here.

A number of recent studies have estimated carrying capacity in ancient Mesoamerica (Sanders 1976, Parsons 1976, and Flannery 1976b). All these studies agree that an average peasant household in Mesoamerica requires about 1 metric ton of shelled maize per year, regardless of whatever else the household consumes. I will follow this lead and use 1 metric ton per household per year as my estimate of maize consumption in the arroyo for the purpose of generating carrying capacity estimates. In Table 2.13 we have presented these estimates of carrying capacity for each of the four stages of the Purrón Dam's construction. Also included in this table is the actual estimated population (expressed in terms of households) for each of the four phases that together span the time when the dam was functioning. The relationship between population size and carrying capacity is presented in Fig. 2.18. In this figure, the population estimates for a phase are considered to be the total accumulated population by the _end_ of that phase.

TABLE 2.12
MAIZE PRODUCTIVITY

Phase	Cob Length (cm)	Yield (Metric tons/ha/crop)	Land Required (ha/household)	
			Single cropping	Double cropping
ESM	7.0	.35	2.86	1.43
MSM	7.0	.35	2.86	1.43
LSM	7.5	.45	2.22	1.11
EPB	8.0	.55	1.82	0.91

Source: Kirkby 1973:124-127.

TABLE 2.13
CARRYING CAPACITY ESTIMATES

Dam Level	Phase	Reservoir Capacity (m2)	Land Irrigated (ha)	Carrying Capacity (households)		Estimated Population (households)
				Single cropping	Double cropping	
1	ESM	37,000	3.7-6.0	1.3-2.1	2.6-4.2	9-12
2	MSM	1,430,000	143-230	50.0-80.4	100.1-160.8	30-34
3	LSM	970,000	97-156	43.7-70.3	87.4-140.5	96-105
4	EPB	2,640,000	264-425	145.0-233.5	290.0-467.0	195-238

TABLE 2.14
RECONSTRUCTED DIETS OF OCCUPANTS OF PURRON CAVE

Level	Phase	Season of Occupation	Domesticated Plants (%)	Wild Plants (%)	Animals (%)
Zone J	Purrón	wet	43	19	38
Zone I	ESM	dry (light occ.) & wet (heavy occ.)	52	17	31
Zone H	MSM	wet	48	09	43
Zone G	LSM	dry (light occ.) & wet (heavy occ.)	88	09	03
Zone F	LSM/EPB	dry (light occ.) & wet (heavy occ.)	67	23	10
Zone E	EPB	dry & wet	68	24	08
Zone D	EPB	dry & wet	72	27	01

Source: MacNeish et al. 1972:95-115.

The sudden increases in carrying capacity represent growths in the scale of the irrigation system brought about by enlargements of the reservoir.

Was population pressure a factor in the decision to build Level 1 of the Purrón Dam? Let us consider the evidence. Level 1 was a small structure that could easily have been built in one dry season by the members of two households. The enterprising individuals who constructed the first dam were probably among the group of four to five families who visited the Arroyo Lencho Diego on a seasonal basis to do some hunting, wild plant collecting, and a limited amount of maize cultivation in the moister parts of the arroyo. Apparently Purrón Cave was most frequently visited in the wet season. Zone J from Purrón Cave dates to the Purrón or Ajalpan phase, before the construction of the first dam. Three occupations were found in Zone J, all dating to the wet season. MacNeish et al. (1972:95) have analyzed the floral and faunal material from Zone J and estimate that the "diet" of the cave's occupants was composed of 43% domesticated plants, 19% wild plants, and 38% animals (Table 2.14). After the construction of the first dam (Level 1), the dietary remains in the cave (Zone I, Early Santa María phase) suggest that the people who were using the cave had not changed their resource procurement strategy appreciably. A light spring occupation was also found in Zone I, but the main occupation dated to the wet season, and the constitution of the "diet" of the cave's inhabitants remained essentially unchanged. The introduction of irrigation apparently had the effect of increasing the productive capabilities (and probably the predictability) of the existing mixed strategy of hunting, wild plant collecting, and farming, to the extent that the overall carrying capacity of the arroyo was increased and sedentary occupation became possible and desirable for the first time.

If population pressure prompted the initial decision to build the Purrón Dam, we would expect that the population all over the Tehuacán Valley by the Ajalpan/Early Santa María juncture had reached the carrying capacity of the existing mode of agricultural production. Although there are no carrying capacity estimates for the valley as a whole, Table 15 does give the population estimates for the valley made by MacNeish et al. (1972:378-432). A steady growth in valley-wide population occurred from the Abejas phase (300 to 600 people) to the Ajalpan phase (600 to 1200 people). In the Early Santa María phase the pace quickened, and there was about a tripling a population over the previous phase, to a total of 1800 to 3600. It was near the end of the Early Santa María phase that Level 1 of the Purrón Dam was constructed. Without data on the overall carrying capacity of the Tehuacán Valley under different productive modes, we cannot positively confirm or refute the hypothesis that the development of Middle Formative irrigation technology there (of which the Purrón Dam is but one example) was a response to population pressure. But we can take note of the fact that valley-wide population tripled during the phase in which Level 1 was built and leave this hypothesis untested but open as a possibility.

The estimated carrying capacity of the agricultural regime associated with Level 1 ranges between 1.3 and 2.1 households for single cropping and between 2.6 and 4.2 households for double cropping (Table 2.11). Had subsistence during the Early Santa María phase depended solely on irrigation agriculture, the estimated population of nine to twelve households would have exceeded the carrying capacity of the regime. As we have seen, however, the subsistence procurement strategy during the Early Santa María phase was not markedly different from that of earlier periods, according to the dietary evidence in Purrón Cave. It would appear that irrigation agriculture in this phase was a supplement to a varied resource procurement strategy that continued to exploit animals and wild plants along with irrigated crops.

The decision to build Level 2 represented the first truly drastic change in the economic policy of the arroyo's inhabitants. Level 2 is an immense structure whose construction would have placed heavy demands upon the existing labot supply. Ts15 would have been built in one dry season with the existing work force and Level 2 itself completed over the course of several dry seasons, although even Ts15 would have required a tremendous outlay of labor and a high degree of organization. Concurrent with the building of Ts15 and Level 2, the first public building in the arroyo was erected, and the elite of the community now had residences physically separated from lower-status ones as well as much greater access to scarce resources and, presumably, power. It was probably also at this time that subsistence economy in the arroyo became almost totally dependent upon irrigation agriculture. As Table 2.14 shows, the reconstructed wild plant contribution to the diet of the occupants of Purrón Cave drops markedly in Zone H (Middle Santa María phase), although the contribution of animals increases. Some members of the community were probably using Purrón Cave as a hunting camp. The total carrying capacity for the irrigation-based agricultural regime in the Middle Santa María phase is quite high: for single cropping the carrying capacity ranges between 50 and 80 households; for double cropping the range is from 100 to 161 households. The total

2. IRRIGATION, ADMINISTRATION, AND SOCIETY

TABLE 2.15

REGIONAL POPULATION ESTIMATES FOR THE TEHUACAN VALLEY

Phase	Total Estimated Population
Abejas	300-600
Purrón	?
Ajalpan	600-1200
Early Santa María	1800-3600
Late Santa María	5000-8000
Early Palo Blanco	20,000-30,000
Late Palo Blanco	15,000-25,000

Source: MacNeish et al. 1972:378-432

estimated population, on the other hand, is only 30 to 34 households for this phase (Fig. 2.18).

Why was the reservoir built so large? Could it be that the ancient engineers so grossly overestimated the needs of the population? Or were they using the surplus water for a purpose other than subsistence? A possible answer is suggested by the floral remains in Purrón Cave. In the Middle Santa María phase (Zone H), a variety of tropical plants which would have required extensive irrigation begin to appear in the Purrón Cave deposits (cf. Woodbury and Neely 1972:Table 12). These include cotton, ciruela, black zapote, and others—tropical plants which cannot be grown successfully at the higher elevations where the Tehuacán Valley's first sedentary communities are located (Ajalpan, Las Canoas, and Coatepec). We suggest that the Middle Santa María phase inhabitants of the Arroyo Lencho Diego were growing quantities of these tropical plants in addition to their usual subsistence crops for the purpose of exchanging these products with communities in higher parts of the Tehuacán Valley. One item they might have received in exchange is obsidian, which began to appear in large amounts at this time in the arroyo. It is notable, however, that the elite was receiving most of the obsidian, and this suggests that the elite was directing the production of the tropical plants. Since the elite controlled the water supply necessary for subsistence as well as surplus production, it could have stimulated tropical plant production by requiring such products as payments for water rights or as some other form of tribute. The Lencho Diego elite could then have exchanged the tropical fruits and cotton with other elites to the north for obsidian and other desired items.

Was the decision to build the greatly over-sized Level 2 motivated by a condition of population pressure? If so, we would have to ask why the reservoir was built so much larger than would have been necessary for purely subsistence purposes. It is difficult to see Level 2 as simply an overly zealous reaction to nutritional stress. Furthermore, while the productive potential of the irrigated land in the Early Santa María phase could not have supported all the people living in the arroyo at that time, we found that there is no reason to believe that it needed to. The building of Level 2 surely represents, not just the expansion of the irrigation system, but a far-reaching change in basic economic, social, and political organization in the arroyo, of which the enlarged reservoir was but a single manifestation. The autonomy of individual households would have been greatly diminished by this change from a generalized productive strategy to one that was highly specialized and totally dependent upon a single source of water controlled by the emergent elite. The potential for surplus production inherent in this new irrigation-based regime would have been available for mobilization by the elite through rent or tribute.

The expansion of the reservoir around 600 B.C. thus seems to have been fundamentally a political maneuver, part of a strategy by which the emergent elite sought to transform and control the basic means of agricultural production and use the power gained thereby to manipulate the surplus value of the rest of the producing population. The irrigation system served as an instrument for political gain and consolidation.

But why did lower-status people not just move away rather than endure such exploitation? It may well be that they had little choice. Population in the Tehuacán Valley as a whole was growing rapidly at this time, though for reasons not fully understood. MacNeish reconstructed nearly three-fold growth in population throughout the valley between the Early and Late Santa María phases (Table 2.15). Lower-status people may have stayed and "supported" the elite in their entrpreneurial scheme simply because they had no place else to go—at least no place where they could maintain themselves as sedentary agriculturalists. A developing condition of regional population pressure, therefore, would have provided a context amenable to an elite take-over and transformation of the productive system in Middle Santa María times.

The construction of Level 3 (essentially a repair job) occurred around the Late Santa María/Early Palo Blanco juncture. The effort did not result in greatly increased reservoir capacity, and because the total population of the community was still well below the mean of the double-cropping carrying capacity estimates (Fig. 2.18), it is likely that something other than population pressure was the stimulus for the repair operation. Woodbury and Neely (1972:87-88), in fact, cited evidence for damage to the main structure from flash floods which they felt had led to the construction of Level 3.

At about the time of the building of Level 3, great changes in settlement pattern occurred, heralding the Early Palo Blanco phase in the Arroyo Lencho Diego. All the existing settlements were abandoned and a new community, Ts73/79, was founded on a hill overlooking the irrigated alluvium. At this point it is useful to stress a few points made above in the detailed discussion of this community.

First, there was little increase in the rate of population growth

2. IRRIGATION, ADMINISTRATION, AND SOCIETY

between Late Santa María and Early Palo Blanco. (The slope of the population curve in Fig. 2.18 remains essentially the same.) Nevertheless, we do find an increase in the overall density of population within settlements: from 63 persons per ha to 77 persons per ha. Furthermore, the elite segment of this population and the primary civic-ceremonial area were protected by a double defensive wall that cuts across the only side of the hill with a gentle slope. The social segment represented by Residential 2 also lived on the defensible hilltop. Only the 65 to 100 households of specialized farmers in Residential 3 lived at the foot of the hill near the fields. All these aspects of settlement point toward a concern for defense of the community from attack. The presence in the surface collections from Ts73/79 of seven projectile points (ordinarily rare finds at Formative sites) would support the conclusion that warfare was prevalent at this time.

Another important development at Ts73/79 is the appearance of a specialized ceramic production area that was making most, if not all, of the pottery used by the community. This represents a real departure from the situation in Late Santa María times. At Ts131 we found evidence for ceramic production associated with some of the houses on the site. The occupants of these houses were apparently making pottery in addition to performing normal domestic tasks, and, significantly, they were producing just part of the entire ceramic assemblage used at this time in the arroyo. The remainder was evidently being imported into the arroyo. At Ts73/79, by contrast, we have no evidence for the importation of pottery from other Early Palo Blanco settlements. Though not definitive proof, this suggests that Ts73/79 was characterized by a greater degree of economic self-sufficiency than the Late Santa María community and in general was interacting less with other communities in the Tehuacán Valley at this time.

Why would the Early Palo Blanco phase in the arroyo see the establishment of a densely settled hilltop community preoccupied with defense and possibly less involved in intra-valley exchange than previous communities had been? We have no final answer to this question, but communities similar to Ts73/79 appear in various parts of the Tehuacán Valley at this time (Nowack 1977 and Drennan 1978:3). All seem to be found in defensible locations and some have defensive walls. On at least three of these sites, evidence was found for ceramic production, perhaps indicating that these communities were also becoming more self-sufficient. It seems not unreasonable to suggest that the Early Palo Blanco phase was generally a time of political "balkanization" and instability within the Tehuacán Valley.

One possible source of this instability may lie outside the Tehuacán Valley altogether. 150 km southeast of the Arroyo Lencho Diego is the site of Monte Albán, the capital of the ancient Zapotec state in the Valley of Oaxaca (Blanton 1978). On a building known as Mound J in the main plaza of Monte Albán is carved a series of inscriptions that Caso (1947) and Marcus (1976) have interpreted as a list of places subdued by Monte Albán by the Terminal Formative or Monte Albán II phase, which is contemporaneous with the Early Palo Blanco phase in the Tehuacán Valley. The militaristic activities of the Zapotec apparently carried them at least as far as the Cuicatlán Cañada, a narrow tropical canyon just south of the Arroyo Lencho Diego (Chapter 6 and Marcus 1976). While we do not believe that the

Arroyo Lencho Diego was ever placed under Zapotec subjugation, it may have been within the range of occasional Zapotec military campaigns. We must allow, therefore, for the possible role of Zapotec militarism in the creation of the unstable political climate of Early Palo Blanco times in the Tehuacán Valley.

To return to the evaluation of the population pressure hypothesis, we note that population continued to grow into the Early Palo Blanco phase, and by 100-50 B.C. a rather stressful relationship was developing between the carrying capacity of the irrigation agriculture regime and the number of people it supported (Fig. 2.18). It is quite likely that by the Early Palo Blanco phase more of this alluvium was given over to subsistence farming and far less to tropical fruit production than was the case in earlier times. Every hectare not planted in staple crops, of course, would only serve to intensify the population pressure problem.

Supporting evidence for the above interpretation of population pressure is lent by the subsistence data from Purrón Cave (Table 2.14). Two occupation zones (E and F) were laid down in Purrón Cave during the Late Santa María/ Early Palo Blanco juncture and the early part of the Early Palo Blanco phase. Both manifest a marked rise in the dietary contribution of wild plants. This contribution exceeds that of wild plants during the period _before_ the building of the dam transformed the subsistence economy of the arroyo into one based on irrigation agriculture. The data clearly suggest that _some_ people in the arroyo locality were feeling the need at this time to _go up_ into the piedmont and engage in wild plant collecting, likely as the result of increasing nutritional stress as the total population of the arroyo approached the carrying capacity of the irrigation-based agricultural regime.

As population pressure became an increasingly severe problem, the decision makers at Ts73/79 might have considered out-migration by a portion of the population as a possible solution. However, the condition of increased militarism just described would probably have placed a premium on community defense, and an effective defense may well have demanded that all able-bodied people remain members of the community, eliminating out-migration as an effective response to the population pressure problem. If the leaders of the community decided to maintain the large population and high-density settlement for the purpose of military defense, the only feasible solution to the population pressure dilemma would have been to rebuild the dam and greatly enlarge the reservoir. It was precisely at this time, probably between 150 B.C. and A.D. 1, that the last level of the Dam, Level 4, was constructed. This raised the carrying capacity of the regime to a much higher level (Fig. 2.18) and probably had the effect of temporarily reducing the pressure on the agricultural base.

In spite of this measure, by the end of the Early Palo Blanco phase the population in the arroyo had again grown over the mean estimated carrying capacity for single cropping (Fig. 2.18). If the presence of warfare made it difficult for the inhabitants of Ts73/79 to grow consistently two crops per year (or if marauders occasionally raided the crops before harvest), another population pressure problem would have existed by the end of the

2. IRRIGATION, ADMINISTRATION, AND SOCIETY 73

Early Palo Blanco phase, once again exacerbated by militaristic exigencies.

In addition to the above problems, underwriting the complex administrative apparatus at Ts73/79 would have absorbed much of the surplus generated by the productive regime. That the administration had grown in size is evidenced by the relatively large number of people living in Residential 1 by the end of the Early Palo Blanco phase. Many of them were probably specialized administrators, and they comprised over a third of the total population at Ts73/79 (Table 2.6). This almost certainly means that the bureaucracy was growing in size throughout the Early Palo Blanco phase; supporting it would have demanded greater and greater amounts of surplus production, further straining the productive base and thus contributing to the population pressure problem. The subsistence data from Purrón Cave (Table 2.12) show heavy reliance on wild plants for all of the Early Palo Blanco phase, perhaps as a continuation of the response suggested above to nutritional stress (for at least some members of the community) deriving from population pressure on the existing mode of agricultural production. In any event, something was definitely awry at Ts73/79, for at the end of the Early Palo Blanco phase all parts of the site were abandoned and the Purrón Dam ceased to function.

So what do we conclude regarding our last hypothesis? We are unable, for lack of data, to confirm or deny that population pressure was a factor in the decision to build the small first stage of the Purrón Dam, though indirect evidence appears to favor confirmation. However, we do conclude that the great expansion of the reservoir around 600 B.C. is best understood not simply as a reaction to population pressure, but rather as a political maneuver by an emergent elite to transform and then dominate the basic means of production for the purpose of regulating the surplus value of the rest of the producing population. We also note that increasing regional (valley-wide) population may have helped provide a context in which such a political maneuver could succeed. Obviously, this is not the same as saying that regional population pressure caused Level 2 of the dam to be built.

After the econmic transformation (a shift from a generalized to a specialized strategy greatly dependent on the single irrigation source), it would have been in the interest of the elite to encourage local population growth. Adding more primary production units (that is, households) to the system, either by recruitment or internal processes of population growth, would have served to increase the total amount of potential surplus available for political manipulation.

This policy of local population growth ultimately led to a contradiction between the nutritional needs of the population, the elite's demands for surplus production, and the carrying capacity of the productive base (cf. Friedman 1976). Contributing to this contradiction by the Early Palo Blanco phase was the militaristic climate of the times, which demanded a large and dense enough population for effective defensive action.

A condition of population pressure probably led to the construction of Level 4 of the Purrón Dam. But this pressure was brought about not by the uncontrollable fertility of Ts73/79's inhabitants per se, but rather by the established political/ideological superstructure which probably encouraged such growth. Like the irrigation system, population size was a variable acted upon and manipulated by the elite for political gain and, by Early Palo Blanco times, for political preservation. Population pressure in the arroyo was a by-product of the manipulation.

Conclusions

Does our study of the Arroyo Lencho Diego allow us to come to any <u>general</u> conclusions regarding the relationship between irrigation and human society? It is, after all, but one example of such an articulation. On the other hand, it does provide a case where several aspects of an irrigation-based community were investigated for nearly 1,000 years of development. Four hypotheses derived from what is generally known as "the hydraulic theory" were applied to these data with differing records of support and refutation. This study is by no means a definitive test of the hydraulic theory in all of its aspects. The way to resolve the controversy surrounding this theory, however, is through systematic, <u>diachronic</u> considerations of different kinds of irrigation systems in varying cultural and environmental contexts, and this study is one contribution to that end.

In this chapter we have examined a single irrigation-based community in an area where aridity demanded irrigation for viable agriculture, and all the water used in irrigation came from a single source. Furthermore, the human population at the time of the first dam was already marked by a certain amount of social differentiation, and this differentiation was codified or mapped into the extant religious system. Finally, regional (valley-wide) population was in a state of steady growth.

As a tentative general conclusion, the following developmental model is proposed: <u>in this particular socioenvironmental context</u>, irrigation's major significance lies in its potential for use as a political instrument by an emergent elite eager to increase its power and prestige. The elite could accomplish this by assuming control of the single water source and using this power to regulate the surplus production of the subordinate population, which would have little recourse but to accept such regulation in a pattern of regional demographic growth. Adding more households to the irrigation system would make greater amounts of absolute surplus available for political manipulation by the elite, and it is likely that a policy of local population growth would be encouraged.

The administrative structure of such a system would serve largely to implement the policies of the elite. Increases in the complexity of administration would be related, not to the organizational demands of building and enlarging the irrigation system per se, but more generally to 1) the elite's concern with managing and protecting its own interests and 2) the <u>variety</u> of tasks the administrative structure is called upon to perform. Thus, administration would become more complex in response to increases in the variety of information to be processed, but within the context of the power structure in society. The irrigation system, by greatly increasing the surplus potential of the agricultural base, would underwrite the

2. IRRIGATION, ADMINISTRATION, AND SOCIETY

administrative apparatus and contribute to the aggrandizement of the elite.

Supporting the growing administrative apparatus, however, would demand greater and greater amounts of surplus production from the primary producers. Ultimately, the elite's policy of promoting growth in population and surplus production might lead to a contradiction between this policy, the nutritional needs of the population, and the carrying capacity of the productive base. One manifestation of this contradiction would be population pressure, and if the administration were unable to deal effectively with the problem, collapse of the social formation could result.

In a different socioenvironmental context, irrigation and society might articulate in a rather different fashion. Irrigation in an egalitarian tribal society, for example, might be merely a technological innovation benefiting all producers more or less equally, especially if regional population were stable and if water sources were many and not readily susceptible to central control.

In sum, irrigation agriculture can be characterized as an especially productive kind of subsistence technology which may or may not be associated with sociopolitical complexity, depending upon a variety of contextual factors. But it is clear that in the appropriate context irrigation can become an important vehicle for social and political change.

2. IRRIGACION, ADMINISTRACION Y SOCIEDAD EN EL FORMATIVO DE TEHUACAN

por Charles S. Spencer

SUMARIO

Durante el verano de 1976 el autor condujo un reconocimiento de superficie en el Arroyo Lencho Diego (Fig. 1.2), donde se encuentra situada la presa Purrón, una estructura de irrigación bastante substancial, cuya construcción se comenzó cerca de 700 a.C. Ya que bastante información sobre la propia presa estaba al alcance de todos por medio del estudio de Woodbury y Neely (1972), el enfoque principal de este reconocimiento fue los sitios de ocupación humana en la vecindad. Información fue recogida para investigar la relación entre el desarrollo de este sistema de irrigación y el desarrollo socio-político de la región. Cuatro hipótesis fueron derivadas del continuo debate sobre la "teoría hidráulica" que fue propuesta por Wittfogel (1957) y modificada por muchos otros. Estas cuatro hipótesis que el reconocimiento trató de poner a prueba son explicadas y evaluadas después de un pequeño sumario del desarrollo socio-político de la región.

La primera ocupación sedentaria en al Arroyo Lencho Diego (Fig. 2.3) y la primera fase de construcción en la presa Purrón coinciden una con la otra y ocurrieron en la fase Santa María Temprana (850-650 a.C.). Durante este tiempo la presa era muy pequeña y la población del arroyo solamente de 45 a 60 personas. Todos los habitantes del arroyo vivían en una sola aldea (Ts449). No hay indicios de edificios públicos, pero dos de las casas pertenecen a una condición social más alta que las demás.

En la fase Santa María Media (650-450 a.C.) la presa fue ampliada en gran escala y la población aumentó a 150 ó 170 personas. Una comunidad (Ts452) situada en la vera del depósito de agua atrás de la presa consistía en cinco a siete casas de posición social alta. Otra comunidad (Ts67), situada abajo de la presa, consistía en 25 a 27 casas de posición social más baja. Un edificio público (Ts450) fue construído sobre una plataforma junto a la esclusa de la presa.

La única construcción en la presa durante la fase Santa María Tardía (450-150 a.C.) fue una pequeña reparación efectuada hacia el final de la fase. La población, sin embargo, creció hasta llegar a entre 480 a 525 personas. Cerca de la presa y reserva los sitios Ts67, 451, y 452, anteriormente fundados, llegaron a formar una comunidad grande de alta posición social. Ts452 es la sección de la comunidad donde residían las personas de posición social más alta que todas las demás. Otra comunidad, y ésta mucho más grande (Ts131) fue fundada casi dos kilómetros abajo de la presa por gente de posición social bastante más baja de la de la gente viviendo en la comunidad alrededor de la presa. Ts450 continuó funcionando como un edificio público al lado de la esclusa de la presa.

2. IRRIGATION, ADMINISTRATION, AND SOCIETY

Durante la primera parte de la fase Palo Blanco Temprana (150 a.C.-250 d.C.) la presa fue otra vez ampliada y los sitios previamente ocupados fueron abandonados. Todos los habitantes del arroyo pasaron a vivir en una sola comunidad (Ts73/79) en la cima y la base de una colina aislada que dominaba la tierra aluvial irrigada. En esta comunidad, dividida en seis sectores diferentes, vivían un total de 975 a 1190 personas. El sector llamado Cívico-ceremonial 1 consistía de un grupo de pirámides, plazas, escalinatas, y un juego de pelota y estaba situado en la parte más alta de la colina. A la par de este sector estaba situada Residencial 1, el área de habitación de las personas de posición social más alta. El Taller situado al este de Residencial 1 contenía evidencia de mucha producción de cerámica, pero ninguna residencia. Estos tres sectores, ocupando la cima de la colina, estaban separados del resto de la comunidad por medio de barrancas o lugares empinados, excepto en el este, donde una muralla doble cortaba el acceso en el único ascenso gradual a la cima. Residencial 2, un grupo de residencias de posición social más baja que las de Residencial 1, estaba situada justo afuera de la muralla, en las pendientes y terrazas. Una área residencial más grande en la base de la colina poseía la posición social más baja de la comunidad y se le llamó Residencial 3. Asociado con esta área había otro complejo menos grandioso de edificios públicos. Este complejo consistía de una plaza rodeada de montículos y de un juego de pelota. A este grupo de edificios públicos se le dió el nombre de Cívico-ceremonial 2. Las conclusiones concernientes a las distintas posiciones sociales de las áreas residenciales son apoyadas por los restos arquitectónicos, los cuales contienen la proporción más grande de residencias de piedra, bastante elaborada, en Residencial 1, y la proporción más grande de arcilla con paja quemada en los restos de las residencias más sencillas de Residencial 3. Evidencia adicional proviene de la distribución de artefactos. La gente en Residencial 1 poseían más obsidiana importada, mientras que los habitantes de Residenciales 2 y 3 usaban más piedra local. En Residencial 1 también había una proporción más alta de cerámica gris fina comparada con la cerámica ordinaria encontrada en las otras Residenciales.

Aparentemente los residentes de posición social más alta, los de Residencial 1, se dedicaban principalmente a actividades relacionadas con cuestiones de administración y liderazgo (incluyendo religión) así como en el área Cívico-ceremonial 1. Los residentes de posición social más baja, los de Residencial 2, probablemente aportaban la labor para el taller de cerámica, así como tal vez otras tareas relacionadas con las actividades de Cívico-ceremonial 1, tal como el mantenimiento de los edificios. Los habitantes de posición social aún más baja, los de Residencial 3, localizada al pie de la colina y a la par de la tierra aluvial irrigada, deben haber estado a cargo de casi toda la labor agrícola. Dos o tres trabajadores de cada casa en Residencial 3 hubieran constituído una fuerza laboral suficiente para trabajar las 425 ha de tierra irrigada situada en la boca del arroyo. La división de la población de la región en subgrupos especializados implica un mecanismo más complejo del que había existido durante períodos más tempranos. Los tipos y distribución de la arquitectura pública en Ts73/79 sugieren una jerarquía para hacer decisiones, de por lo menos dos niveles arriba de los trabajadores, con varias unidades en cada nivel (Fig. 2.17).

La información recogida hace posible la evaluación de cuatro hipótesis relacionadas con la "teoría hidráulica." La La primera hipótesis es que el desarrollo de estructuras administrativas complejas es principalmente una reacción a los problemas de organizar la mano de obra para la construcción y mantenimiento de sistemas de irrigación. Esta hipótesis implica una relación entre el tamaño y complejidad del sistema de irrigación y el grado de complejidad administrativa de la sociedad que lo utiliza. En la secuencia arqueológica del Arroyo Lencho Diego hay dos puntos donde cambios en la complejidad administrativa son indicados: al comienzo de la fase Santa María Media, cuando el primer edificio público hace su apariencia, y otra vez cuando los edificios públicos de Ts73/79 son construídos al comienzo de la fase Palo Blanco Temprana. Si la primera hipótesis es la correcta se espera que estos dos aumentos en la complejidad administrativa sean asociados con períodos particularmente difíciles de organizar la mano de obra para los trabajos en el sistema de irrigación. Sin embargo, de las dos fases de construcción en la presa que requirieron gran cantidad de trabajadores, una ocurrió durante el primer cambio en la estructura administrativa, pero la otra ocurrió durante un período en que ningún cambio en la estructura administrativa está indicado. El cambio mayúsculo administrativo al comienzo de la fase Palo Blanco fue acompañado por un pequeño esfuerzo en la presa. Aunque no se niega la relación entre irrigación y subsistencia en el arroyo, ni la relación entre irrigación y administración, sin embargo la primera hipótesis debe ser negada en este caso.

La segunda hipótesis es que un sistema de irrigación aporta a una naciente elite la oportunidad de ganar control sobre un recurso natural escaso (agua) y de usar este poder para regular la producción excedente del resto de la población. Ya que la cantidad de producción excedente que se puede producir y que se puede manipular depende del número de productores, esta hipótesis implica una relación entre la población local y el grado de poder y de diferencia de posición social. Ya que ambas población y diferencias en posición social aumentan en cada fase de la secuencia esta hipótesis es consistente con la información recogida.

La tercera hipótesis es que conflicto entre comunidades sobre acceso al agua, especialmente entre comunidades río arriba y río abajo hace necesaria una administración compleja y centralizada. La oportunidad para este tipo de conflicto aparece por primera vez en el Arroyo Lencho Diego con la fundación de Ts131 al comienzo de la fase Fanta María Tardía. Sin embargo, durante esta fase la elite aumentó su poder y prestigio adentro de la estructura que ya existía; no hubo ningún cambio en esta estructura. El cambio estructural de grandes proporciones que ocurrió en la fase Palo Blanco Temprana fué asociado, no con el aumento en comunidades río arriba y río abajo, sino más bien con la consolidación de todos los residentes del arroyo en una sola comunidad. Mientras conflicto entre comunidades puede haber contribuído tanto a las diferencias de poder como de posición social, parece no haber tenido mayor significado en el desarrollo de la complejidad administrativa.

La cuarta hipótesis es que agricultura con irrigación, siendo más productiva, pero también necesitando más labor que agricultura sin irrigación, se desarrolla solamente cuando un aumento en población requiere que otros

2. IRRIGATION, ADMINISTRATION, AND SOCIETY

medios se usen para aumentar producción. Esta hipótesis propone que cada una de las cuatro decisiones a ampliar la presa fue asociada con un aumento en población más grande del que podía ser acomodado por el sistema de irrigación que ya existía. Contrario a esta expectativa, la construcción de grandes dimensiones de la fase 2 parece haber creado un sistema de irrigación cuyo tamaño era considerablemente más grande del necesario para satisfacer las necesidades de la población. La apariencia, en este tiempo, en los restos vegetales de la cueva Purrón de plantas tropicales tales como algodón, ciruela, y zapote negro sugiere que el ímpetus para este aumento en el tamaño de la presa fue el deseo de cultivar estas plantas para usarlas en el comercio, tal vez con la Cuenca de Puebla, cuyas altitudes no permiten su cultivo. El cambio de proporciones mayores que ocurrió al comienzo de la fase Palo Blanco Temprana no fué asociado con un marcado aumento de población. En efecto, la única etapa de construcción en la presa que aparece en respuesta a un aumento en población fué la última, que sucedió más tarde en la fase Palo Blanco Temprana (Fig. 2.12). La cuarta hipótesis debe ser entonces negada.

Una prueba general de la "teoría hidráulica" requiere una cantidad de estudios en una variedad de contextos culturales y ambientales. Los resultados de este estudio pueden contribuir a esa prueba. Por esta razón es importante sugerir un modelo que parece explicar correctamente la secuencia del desarrollo observado en el Arroyo Lencho Diego. En este caso el mayor significado de la irrigación parece residir en su potencial para uso como un instrumento político por una elite naciente con ambiciones de aumentar su poder y prestigio. Al asumir control sobre la única fuente de agua, esta elite podría ganar el poder para regular la producción excedente de una población subordinada. Aumento en la complejidad de la administración puede estar relacionada, no con las demandas de organizar la construcción y el ampliamiento del sistema de irrigación, sino con 1) el interés de la elite en manejar y proteger sus intereses, y 2) la variedad de las tareas que la estructura administrativa tuvo que satisfacer. Irrigación y estructura social pueden articularse en varias maneras distintas, dependiendo del contexto socio-ambiental. Aunque está claro que en este contexto irrigación no fue la causa principal del cambio social y político, no cabe duda que fue un vehículo muy importante para este cambio.

APPENDIX TO CHAPTER 2

The following tables present all the recorded data for each sample square collected during the 1976 Lencho Diego Survey. Each column represents one of the 91 collection squares. The rows give the values of the variables recorded for the squares and the collections they yielded. There are 252 variables in all, although the variable numbering goes as high as 343 because some gaps were left in the numbering system during the analysis for methodological purposes. These gaps have been preserved in the numbering of variables here to insure consistency between the final, published variable numbers and those used in the original anlaysis and on the permanent magnetic storage tape.

A variable directory describing each variable precedes the tables. In the directory, "diagnostic sherds" means all rim sherds, decorated body sherds, and sherds with special form features. Most of the type distinctions in the directory follow the ceramic typology developed by MacNeish, Peterson and Flannery (1970), but two exceptions should be noted. First, the ware called "Gray" in the variable directory is a composite of what MacNeish, Peterson, and Flannery (1970) call Río Salado Gray, Quachilco Gray, Quachilco Brown, and El Riego Gray. The gray pottery was coded this way because we felt that the most valuable chronological indicators were attributes of vessel form and decoration, rather than those relating to paste (cf. Drennan 1977a:9). Consequently, our coding scheme pays considerable attention to vessel morphology and decoration and less attention to paste variability within this general ware category. There is, however, a set of variables relating to the coarseness of the paste, analogous to the differences between Río Salado Gray on the one hand and Quachilco Gray, Quachilco Brown and El Riego Gray on the other. In a similar fasion, the ware "Plain" in our variable category is a composite of what MacNeish, Peterson, and Flannery (1970) call Río Salado Coarse, Quachilco Mica, and El Riego Plain. The rationale for this coding method is the same as that for the Gray ware. Although Drennan (1977a:12) has pointed out several paste variables of Plain ware that show useful chronolgical variation through time, we decided that the time involved in coding these variables would not have been warranted by the increase in chronological information that would result, because the Gray ware vessel morphology and decoration variables were already such excellent providers of this information. For the Plain ware, therefore, we decided to concentrate more on variables that would reveal "functional" and other kinds of non-chronological information.

In the tables, the ceramic and chipped stone data are recorded, not in terms of the individual artifact, but according to the frequencies of occurrence of certain attributes and combinations of attributes per collection square. This method obviously sacrifices some information about how attributes go together on individual artifacts. Nevertheless, since we were primarily interested in comparing the artifact inventories of various collection squares and not in comparing the artifacts themselves, it was a procedure appropriate to our goals. Moreover, recording combinations of attributes by provenience is much more efficient than recording these same attributes by individual artifact. This method of recording data is borrowed from Drennan; a fuller explanation of the rationale supporting it can be found in Drennan (1976b:290-291).

Most of the original variable categories were defined on the basis of MacNeish, Peterson, and Flannery (1970), and Drennan (1977a). But as we began coding the material, we were forced to add more variables to the scheme in order to deal with variability not accounted for by the system derived from these volumes. These added variables are usually not frequent and probably relate to geographical variability in style between the artifact samples of these authors and those of the present survey. The converse to this effect, of course, is that some of our original variables (that is, certain combinations of ceramic or stone tool attributes) never occurred in the Lencho Diego collections. These variables, in other words, have a value of zero for all cases. Although these variables are not included in the tables, they are noted in the variable directory since they represent examples of attributes and attribute combinations that were found elsewhere in the Tehuacán Valley but not in the Arroyo Lencho Diego. Since printing tables with numerous columns composed primarily of zeros is not efficient use of space, those variables with five or fewer non-zero values have been omitted from the tables. The non-zero values of these variables have been indicated in the variable directory instead by lists of the numbers of the squares with non-zero values followed by the corresponding non-zero values in parentheses.

Variables 1 through 11 concern the collection square itself and associated features. Variables 80 through 87 give counts of assorted artifacts. Variables 91 through 96 give weights of major ceramic and chipped stone categories. Variables 101 through 157 enumerate the ceramics by type and vessel form. Variables 158 through 184 give more detailed information on Coatepec White sherds, and variables 185 through 285 on Gray sherds. And Variables 301 through 343 enumerate chipped stone by material and artifact type.

Two irregularities regarding the collection squares should be noted. There is no information concerning square 33 because it yielded only Postclassic material and was thus omitted from the analysis. Square 81 from Ts73 is not indicated on the map in Fig. 2.12 because it was located along the trail leading up to the site, just east of the area depicted in the site map.

Square Information

1. SQUARE   The collection square number (91 in all). These appear in the tables as column headings.
2. SITE   The Tehuacán Valley site number. Code: 1=Ts449; 2=Ts67; 3=Ts450; 4=Ts452; 5=Ts131; 7=Ts451; 8=Ts73; 9=Ts79.
3. SAMPAREA   The area of the collection square. Code: 1=25 m^2; 2=625 m^2.
4. SECTOR   The sector of the site in which the sample square is located (only for Ts73/79). Code: 1=Residential 1 (inside the wall

APPENDIX TO CHAPTER 2　　　　　　　　　　　　　　　　　　83

at Ts73); 2=Residential 2 (outside the wall at Ts73); 3=Residential 3 (residential part of Ts79); 4=Civic-ceremonial 1 (Ts73); 5=Civic-ceremonial 2 (Ts79); 6=Ceramic workshop (Ts73); 7=Not applicable.

5. FEATURE   The architectural feature associated with the collection square. Code: 1=Residence; 2=Pyramidal structure ("public building"); 3=Plaza or platform; 4=Ballcourt; 5=Sherd scatter with no associated architecture.
6. ARCHEVID   The nature of the architectual evidence associated with the collection square. Code: 1=Masonry (with or without mound); 2=Earthen rise; 3=None.
7. LOCSAMP   Location of the collection square with respect to the associated feature. Code: 1=On feature; 2=Adjacent to feature; 3=Less than 10 m from feature; 4=Not applicable.
8. SLOPE   Subjective ranking of the degree of slope where the collection square was placed. Code: 1=Gentle; 2=Gentle to moderate; 3=Moderate; 4=Moderate to steep; 5=Steep.
9. EROSION   Subjective ranking of the degree of erosion where the collection square was placed. Code: 1=Light; 2=Light to moderate; 3=Moderate; 4=Moderate to heavy; 5=Heavy.
10. DISTURB   Degree of disturbance where the collection square was placed. Code: 1=None; 2=Minor; 3=Major.
11. VEGETATN   Subjective ranking of the amount of vegetation covering the ground in the collection square. Code: 1=None; 2=Light; 3=Light to moderate; 4=Moderate; 5=Moderate to dense; 6=Dense.

Miscellaneous Artifacts

81. GRNDSTN   The number of grinding stone pieces, including both manos and metates.
82. OTHART   The number of artifacts not recorded under any other categories. A list can be obtained by writing to the author.
83. EXOTIC   The number of "exotic" artifacts, such as shell, mica, alabaster, etc. A list can be obtained by writing to the author.
84. CRAFT   The number of craft-related artifacts, such as polishing stones, sherd disks, etc. A list can be obtained by writing to the author. These occurred only in the following squares: 19(1), 28(1), and 64(2).
85. DAUB   The number of preserved daub fragments. These occurred only in the following squares: 23(2), 77(2), 86(2), 87(4), and 88(2).
86. FIGURINE   The number of figurine fragments. These occurred only in square 26(1).
87. INCENSE   The number of incense burner fragments in addition to those listed below under Variable No. 141. These occurred only in square 37(1).

Artifact Weight

91. WTDIAGS   The weight (in grams) of all diagnostic sherds (rims, decorated bodies, and special form features).
92. WTGRAY   The weight (in grams) of all Gray diagnostic sherds. Gray includes Río Salado Gray, Quachilco Gray, Quachilco Brown, and El Riego Gray (MacNeish, Peterson, and Flannery 1970).
93. WTPLAIN   The weight (in grams) of all Plain diagnostic sherds. Plain includes Río Salado Coarse, Quachilco Mica, and El Riego Plain (MacNeish, Peterson, and Flannery 1970).
94. WTQUARTZ   The weight (in grams) of all quartzite fragments.
95. WTCHERT   The weight (in grams) of all chert fragments.
96. WTOBSID   The weight (in grams) of all obsidian fragments.

Ceramic Types

101. TOTDIAGS   The total number of diagnostic sherds (all rims, decorated bodies, and special form features).
102. TOTCANW   The total number of Canoas White diagnostic sherds (MacNeish, Peterson, and Flannery 1970:59-68). These occurred only in the following squares: 26(6) and 27(3).
103. CANWCYL   The number of Canoas White cylinder rims (MacNeish, Peterson, and Flannery 1970:Fig. 35, rows 4-5). These occurred only in square 26(2).
104. CANWCWB   The number of Canoas White convex-wall bowl rims (MacNeish, Peterson, and Flannery 1970:Fig. 35, row 1). These occurred only in square 26(1).
105. CANWOTR   The number of other kinds of Canoas White rims. These did not occur.
106. CANWDBS   The number of Canoas White decorated body sherds and sherds with special form features. These occurred only in squares 26(2) and 27(3).
107. CANWUND   The number of Canoas White undecorated body sherds. These occurred only in squares 26(2) and 27(1).
108. TOTCANOB   The total number of Canoas Orange-Brown diagnostic sherds (MacNeish, Peterson, and Flannery 1970:69-71). These occurred only in square 26(2).
109. CANOBOWB   The number of Canoas Orange-Brown outleaned-wall bowl rims (MacNeish, Peterson, and Flannery 1970:Fig. 39, row 1). These did not occur.
110. CANOBCWB   The number of Canoas Orange-Brown convex-wall bowl rims (MacNeish, Peterson, and Flannery 1970:Fig. 38, row 1). These occurred only in square 26(2).
111. CANOBOTR   The number of Canoas Orange-Brown other rims. These did not occur.
112. CANOBDBS   The number of Canoas Orange-Brown decorated body sherds and sherds with special form features. These did not occur.
113. CANOBUND   The number of Canoas Orange-Brown undecorated body sherds. These occurred only in squares 26(13), 27(8), and 28(4).
114. TOTCOAT   The total number of Coatepec White diagnostic sherds

APPENDIX TO CHAPTER 2

(MacNeish, Peterson, and Flannery 1970:103-107).

115. COATOWB   The number of Coatepec White outleaned-wall bowl rims (MacNeish, Peterson, and Flannery 1970:Fig. 62, row 3). These occurred only in the following squares: 26(3), 27(2), 31(1), and 32(4).
116. COATCWB   The number of Coatepec White convex-wall bowl rims (MacNeish, Peterson, and Flannery 1970:Fig. 62, rows 1-2).
117. COATCYL   The number of Coatepec White cylinder rims (MacNeish, Peterson, and Flannery 1970:Fig. 62, row 4).
118. COATOLLA   The number of Coatepec White olla rims (MacNeish, Peterson, and Flannery:Fig. 64, row 6, fourth from left). These occurred only in square 32(2).
119. COATOTR   The number of Coatepec White other rims. These occurred only in square 25(1).
120. COATDBS   The number of Coatepec White decorated body sherds and sherds with special form features.
121. COATUND   The number of Coatepec White undecorated body sherds.
122. TOTQR   The total number of Quachilco Red diagnostic sherds (MacNeish, Peterson, and Flannery 1970:155-157). These occurred only in the following squares: 13(3), 14(1), 16(1), 34(2), and 71(1).
123. QROLLA   The number of Quachilco Red olla rims (MacNeish, Peterson, and Flannery 1970:Fig. 95, rows 1-2). These occurred only in the following squares: 13(3), 14(1), 16(1), 34(1), and 71(1).
124. QROTR   The number of Quachilco Red other rims. These occurred only in square 34(1).
125. TOTGRAY   The total number of Gray diagnostic sherds. Gray includes Río Salado Gray, Quachilco Gray, Quachilco Brown, and El Riego Gray (MacNeish, Peterson, and Flannery 1970:78-83, 120-134, and 146-155).
126. GROWB   The number of Gray outleaned-wall bowl rims (MacNeish, Peterson, and Flannery 1970:Fig. 75).
127. GRCWB   The number of Gray convex-wall bowl rims (MacNeish, Peterson, and Flannery 1970:Fig. 74).
128. GRCYL   The number of Gray cylinder rims (MacNeish, Peterson, and Flannery 1970:Fig. 76, row 1).
129. GRINCURV   The number of Gray incurved-rim bowl rims (MacNeish, Peterson, and Flannery 1970:Fig. 76, row 5).
130. GROLLA   The number of Gray olla rims (MacNeish, Peterson, and Flannery 1970:Fig. 78).
131. GRMNOLLA   The number of gray "mini-olla" rims. Miniature versions of Gray ollas whose sizes were assessed subjectively.
132. GRTECOM   The number of Gray tecomate (neckless jar) rims.
133. GRCRDCYL   The number of Gray "crude cylinder" rims. These unburnished Gray cylindrical bowls with bolstered rims are very similar to that illustrated in MacNeish, Peterson, and Flannery (1970:Fig. 92, row 3, first on left).
134. GROTR   The number of Gray other rims, including kiln wasters not classifiable under another heading.
135. GRDBS   The number of Gray decorated body sherds and sherds with special form features.
136. GRUND   The number of Gray undecorated body sherds.

137.	TOTPL	The total number of Plain diagnostic sherds. Plain includes Río Salado Coarse, Quachilco Mica, and El Riego Plain (MacNeish, Peterson, and Flannery 1970:76-78, 110-119, and 168-170).
138.	PLOLLA	The number of Plain olla rims (MacNeish, Peterson, and Flannery 1970:Fig. 65, rows 1-5, and elsewhere).
139.	PLCWB	The number of Plain convex-wall bowl rims (MacNeish, Peterson, and Flannery 1970:Fig. 65, row 6, first on left).
140.	PLCOMAL	The number of Plain comal rims, including various examples of what MacNeish, Peterson, and Flannery (1970:Fig. 66, rows 1-5) call "shallow plate-like vessels."
141.	PLINCENS	The number of Plain incense burner fragments, including a variety of forms, most of which are illustrated by MacNeish, Peterson, and Flannery (1970:Fig. 66, rows 7-8, and Fig. 67, rows 5-6).
142.	PLOTR	The number of Plain other rims. These occurred only in the following squares: 55(1), 59(1), and 80(1).
143.	PLSTRHAN	The number of Plain strap handle fragments (MacNeish, Peterson, and Flannery 1970:Fig. 67, rows 1-3).
144.	PLLUGHAN	The number of Plain lug handle fragments (MacNeish, Peterson, and Flannery 1970:Fig. 67, row 4, third from left).
145.	PLDBS	The number of Plain decorated body sherds and sherds with special form features.
146.	PLUND	The number of Plain undecorated body sherds.
147.	TOTERO	The total number of El Riego Orange diagnostic sherds (MacNeish, Peterson, and Flannery 1970:164-168).
148.	EROOWB	The number of El Riego Orange outleaned-wall bowl rims (MacNeish, Peterson, and Flannery 1970:Fig. 99, rows 2 and 4). These occurred only in the following squares: 41(2), 43(1), 52(1), 53(1), 70(1).
149.	EROOTR	The number of El Riego Orange other rims. These occurred only in square 63(1).
150.	TOTTHO	The total number of Thin Orange diagnostic sherds (MacNeish, Peterson, and Flannery 1970:170-174).
151.	THOOWB	The number of Thin Orange outleaned-wall bowl rims (MacNeish, Peterson, and Flannery 1970:Fig. 103, row 2, third and fourth from left).
152.	THOCWB	The number of Thin Orange convex-wall bowl rims (MacNeish, Peterson, and Flannery 1970:Fig. 103, rows 1 and 3).
153.	THOOTR	The number of Thin Orange other rims. These did not occur.
154.	THORNBS	The number of Thin Orange ring base fragments (MacNeish, Peterson, and Flannery 1970:Fig. 103, rows 3-4). These occurred only in the following squares: 87(1) and 88(1).
155.	THODBS	The number of Thin Orange decorated body sherds and sherds with special form features.
156.	THOUND	The number of Thin Orange undecorated body sherds.
157.	OTHWARES	The number of diagnostic sherds that do not belong in any of the above categories. A list can be obtained by writing the author.

APPENDIX TO CHAPTER 2   87

Coatepec White Attributes

158. COATUNIF   The number of Coatepec White sherds with uniform white surface color.
159. COATYW   The number of Coatepec White sherds with yellowish-white surface color. These occurred only in the following squares: 25(2), 27(2), and 32(1).
160. COATWRB   The number of Coatepec White sherds with white vessel walls but black rims. These did not occur.
161. COATFRCL   The number of Coatepec White sherds with surfaces marked by firing clouds. These occurred only in the following squares: 13(2), 25(2), 26(1), 28(1), and 32(2).
162. COATOTSR   The number of Coatepec White sherds with surfaces that do not fit into one of the above categories. These occurred only in the following squares: 22(1), 26(18), 27(3), and 32(8).
163. COATDEC   The total number of decorated Coatepec White sherds.
164. COATINC   The number of Coatepec White sherds with incising.
165. COATRASP   The number of Coatepec White sherds with raspada decoration. These occurred only in square 25(1).
166. COATOTDC   The number of Coatepec White sherds with other forms of decoration. These did not occur.
167. COATMO1   The number of Coatepec White sherds with incised motif No. 1: a single horizontal line on the interior rim. These did not occur.
168. COATMO2   The number of Coatepec White sherds with incised motif No. 2: a single horizontal line on the exterior rim. These occurred only in square 32(1).
169. COATMO3   The number of Coatepec White sherds with incised motif No. 3: two horizontal lines on the interior rim.
170. COATMO4   The number of Coatepec White sherds with incised motif No. 4: two horizontal lines on the exterior rim. These occurred only in the following squares: 23(1), 27(2), and 30(1).
171. COATMO5   The number of Coatepec White sherds with incised motif No. 5: three or more horizontal lines on the interior rim. These occurred only in the following squares: 22(1), 31(2), and 32(2).
172. COATMO6   The number of Coatepec White sherds with incised motif No. 6: three or more horizontal lines on the exterior rim.
173. COATMO7   The number of Coatepec White sherds with incised motif No. 7: "line break" motif on the interior rim (MacNeish, Peterson, and Flannery 1970:Fig. 62, row 3, third from left). These occurred only in square 25(1).
174. COATMO8   The number of Coatepec White sherds with incised motif No. 8: "line break" motif on the exterior rim. This did not occur.
175. COATMO9   The number of Coatepec White sherds with incised motif No. 9: vertical lines on the exterior wall.
176. COATMO10   The number of Coatepec White sherds with incised motif No. 10: large rectangles (MacNeish, Peterson, and Flannery 1970:Fig. 63, row 1, third from left).
177. COATMO11   The number of Coatepec White sherds with incised motif No. 11: small rectangles, or a checkerboard-like pattern

178. COATMO12 The number of Coatepec White sherds with incised motif No. 12: hachure. These occurred only in the following squares: 29(1) and 32(2).
179. COATMO13 The number of Coatepec White sherds with incised motif No. 13: cross-hachure. These occurred only in the following squares: 23(1), 26(1), and 28(1).
180. COATMO14 The number of Coatepec White sherds with incised motif No. 14: triangles (MacNeish, Peterson, and Flannery 1970: Fig. 62, row 1, fifth from left). These did not occur.
181. COATMO15 The number of Coatepec White sherds with incised motif No. 15: pointed triangles (MacNeish, Peterson, and Flannery 1970:Fig. 62, row 4 second from left). These occurred only in the following squares: 26(2), 30(1), and 32(1).
182. COATMO16 The number of Coatepec White sherds with incised motif No. 16: half-moons (MacNeish, Peterson, and Flannery 1970: Fig. 63, row 2, first on right). These did not occur.
183. COATMO17 The number of Coatepec White sherds with incised motif No. 17: indeterminate motif. These occurred only in the following squares: 26(7), 28(1), 30(2), and 32(1).
184. COATINMO The number of Coatepec White sherds with motifs not classifiable according to the above categories. These did not occur.

Gray Atttributes

185. GRSF1 The number of Gray sherds with special form No. 1: basal flanges (MacNeish, Peterson, and Flannery 1970:Fig. 92, row 1).
186. GRSF2 The number of Gray sherds with special form No. 2: strap handles (MacNeish, Peterson, and Flannery 1970:Fig. 94, row 2, first on left).
187. GRSF3 The number of Gray sherds with special form No. 3: other kinds of handles.
188. GRSF4 The number of Gray sherds with special form No. 4: ring bases.
189. GRSF5 The number of Gray sherds with special form No. 5: bridge spouts (MacNeish, Peterson, and Flannery 1970:Fig. 73, bottom row, first on left).
190. GRSF6 The number of Gray sherds with special form No. 6: hollow nubbin feet (MacNeish, Peterson, and Flannery 1970:Fig. 92, row 5, first on left).
191. GRSF7 The number of Gray sherds with special form No. 7: mammiform feet. These did not occur.
192. GRSF8 The number of Gray sherds with special form No. 8: hollow bulb feet (MacNeish, Peterson, and Flannery 1970:Fig. 92, row 5, second and third from left).
193. GRSF9 The number of Gray sherds with special form No. 9: solid nubbin feet (MacNeish, Peterson, and Flannery 1970:Fig. 92, row 5, fourth from left).

APPENDIX TO CHAPTER 2

194. GRSF10   The number of Gray sherds with special form No. 10: other kinds of feet.
195. GROTHSF   The number of Gray sherds with other special forms.
196. GRSF12   The number of Gray sherds with special form No. 12: potstands.
197. RIOSALGR The number of Gray sherds having a coarse paste of the type MacNeish, Peterson, and Flannery (1970:78-83) called Río Salado Gray.
198. ERQACHGR The number of Gray sherds having a fine paste of the type MacNeish, Peterson, and Flannery (1970:120-134 and 146-155) called El Riego Gray and Quachilco Gray.
199. INDGRPST The number of Gray sherds with a paste not classifiable into one of the two above types.
200. GRSURF1   The number of Gray sherds with surface color No. 1: gray.
201. GRSURF2   The number of Gray sherds with surface color No. 2: brown.
202. GRSURF3   The number of Gray sherds with surface color No. 3: gray and brown mottled.
203. GRSURF4   The number of Gray sherds with surface color No. 4: orange.
204. GRSURF5   The number of Gray sherds with surface color No. 5: orange and brown mottled.
205. GRSURF6   The number of Gray sherds with surface color No. 6: red and/or pink.
206. GRSURF7   The number of Gray sherds with surface color No. 7: light green.
207. GROTHSUR The number of Gray sherds with a surface color not classifiable according to the above categories. These did not occur.
208. GRKLNWST The number of Gray sherds which are classified as kiln wasters. See Chapter 3 for a description of these items.
209. GROLLAFL The number of Gray olla rims with flaring necks: (MacNeish, Peterson, and Flannery 1970:Fig. 78, row 1, first on left, and row 2, fourth and fifth from left).
210. GROLLASL The number of Gray olla rims with straight, long necks (MacNeish, Peterson, and Flannery 1970:Fig. 93, row 2).
211. GROLLASS The number of Gray olla rims with straight, short necks (MacNeish, Peterson, and Flannery 1970:Fig. 93, row 5, first and second from left).
212. GROLLAOT The number of Gray olla rims with necks not classifiable according to the above categories. These occurred only in square 56(1).
213. GRECCNTR The number of Gray bowl sherds with eccentric rims (MacNeish, Peterson, and Flannery 1970:Fig. 70, row 4, first on left, and row 5, first on left). These occurred only in the following squares: 17(1) and 20(1).
214. GRRIM1   The number of Gray bowl rims of rim form No. 1: direct rim with round lip (MacNeish, Peterson, and Flannery 1970:Fig. 91, row 4, third from left).
215. GRRIM2   The number of Gray bowl rims of rim form No. 2: direct rim with a squared-off lip (MacNeish, Peterson, and Flannery 1970:Fig. 91, row 2, third from left).
216. GRRIM3   The number of Gray bowl rims of rim form No. 3: direct rim with a grooved lip (MacNeish, Peterson, and Flannery 1970: Fig. 91, row 4, fifth from left).

217.	GRRIM4	The number of Gray bowl rims of rim form No. 4: a sharply flaring rim (MacNeish, Peterson, and Flannery 1970:Fig. 75, row 1, first through fourth from left, and row 2).
218.	GRRIM5	The number of Gray bowl rims of rim from No. 5: a gradually flaring or outcurving rim (MacNeish, Peterson, and Flannery 1970:Fig. 75, row 3).
219.	GRRIM6	The number of Gray bowl rims of rim form No. 6: an everted rim (MacNeish, Peterson, and Flannery 1970:Fig. 75, rows 5 and 6).
220.	GRRIM7	The number of Gray bowl rims of rim form No. 7: a rim with a small tab on the exterior (MacNeish, Peterson, and Flannery 1970:Fig. 91, row 1, third from left).
221.	GRRIM8	The number of Gray bowl rims of rim form No. 8: a rim with a rounded exterior flange (Drennan 1977a:Fig. 3j).
222.	GRRIM9	The number of Gray bowl rims of rim form No. 9: a rim with an exterior "rabbet" (Drennan 1977a:Fig. 3l).
223.	GRRIM10	The number of Gray bowl rims of rim form No. 10: a rim with a sharp exterior flange, that is, one that is triangular in profile.
224.	GRRIM11	The number of Gray bowl rims of rim form No. 11: a rim with with a long exterior flange. These are like rim form No. 12, except that they are over 1.5 cm in length. These did not occur.
225.	GRRIM12	The number of Gray bowl rims of rim form No. 12: a rim with a short exterior flange (MacNeish, Peterson, and Flannery 1970:Fig. 92, row 2, first and second on left).
226.	GROTHRIM	The number of Gray bowl rims of rim forms not classifiable into any of the other categories. These did not occur.
227.	GRINDRIM	The number of Gray bowl rims that have indeterminate rim forms. These occurred only in the following squares: 1(2), 2(1), and 23(1).
228.	GRRIM15	The number of Gray bowl rims of rim form No. 15: a direct rim with the interior lip beveled to the exterior (MacNeish, Peterson, and Flannery 1970:Fig. 91, row 5, fourth from left).
229.	GRRIM16	The number of Gray bowl rims of rim form No. 16: an exterior thickened, grooved rim (MacNeish, Peterson, and Flannery 1970:Fig. 92, row 3, first on left).
230.	TOTGRDEC	The total number of decorated Gray sherds.
231.	GRDECOWB	The number of decorated Gray outleaned-wall bowl rims.
232.	GRDECCWB	The number of decorated Gray convex-wall bowl rims.
233.	GRDECCYL	The number of decorated Gray cylinder rims.
234.	GRDECINC	The number of decorated Gray incurving rim bowl rims.
235.	GRDECOTR	The number of decorated Gray other kinds of rims.
236.	GRDCBWLB	The number of decorated Gray bowl body sherds.
237.	GRDCJARB	The number of decorated Gray jar body sherds.
238.	GRDCINDB	The number of decorated Gray body sherds of indeterminate form.
239.	GRDECOTH	The number of decorated Gray sherds of other kinds of forms. These occurred only in the following squares: 39(1), 54(1), 64(2), and 82(1).
240.	GRNODEC	The number of Gray sherds with no decoration.
241.	GRINCISD	The number of incised Gray sherds.

APPENDIX TO CHAPTER 2

242. GRSLSHRM   The number of Gray sherds with slashes on the interior rim. These occurred only in the following squares: 72(2) and 19(1).
243. GRCARV   The number of Gray sherds with grooving or carving.
244. GRRASP   The number of Gray sherds with raspada decoration.
245. GRREDPGM   The number of Gray sherds with red pigment. These occurred only in the following squares: 64(1) and 65(1).
246. GRPUNCT   The number of Gray sherds with punctations.
247. GRDRHOLE   The number of Gray sherds with drilled holes. These did not occur.
248. GRAPDOT   The number of Gray sherds with applique dots.
249. GRAPPBUT   The number of Gray sherds with applique buttons. These did not occur.
250. GROTHAPP   The number of Gray sherds with other kinds of applique decoration. These occurred only in the following squares: 11(1) and 64(3).
251. GRZNDTNG   The number of Gray sherds with zoned toning. These did not occur.
252. GRWEDGE   The number of Gray sherds with wedge-type engraving (MacNeish, Peterson, and Flannery 1970:Fig. 70, bottom row, second from left). These occurred only in square 51(3).
253. GRSLSHBF   The number of Gray sherds with slashes or notches on a basal flange. These occurred only in the following squares: 39(1), 45(1), 64(1), and 87(1).
254. GRMODLNG   The number of Gray sherds with modeling. These occurred only in the following squares: 9(1), 43(1), and 78(1).
255. GRDECOTM   The number of Gray sherds with other decorative techniques.
256. GRNTCHRF   The number of Gray sherds with notches on a rim flange. These occurred only in the following squares: 7(1), 64(1), and 68(1).
257. GRMOT1   The number of Gray sherds with incised motif No. 1: zigzags on the interior rim (MacNeish, Peterson, and Flannery 1970:Fig. 70, row 1, first on left).
258. GRMOT2   The number of Gray sherds with incised motif No. 2: zigzags on the body of the vessel.
259. GRMOT3   The number of Gray sherds with incised motif No. 3: wavy lines on the interior rim (MacNeish, Peterson, and Flannery 1970:Fig. 70, row 1, second and third from left).
260. GRMOT4   The number of Gray sherds with incised motif No. 4: wavy lines on the body of the vessel.
261. GRMOT5   The number of Gray sherds with incised motif No. 5: "line break" (MacNeish, Peterson, and Flannery 1970:Fig. 70, column 2, fifth from bottom).
262. GRMOT6   The number of Gray sherds with incised motif No. 6: a single horizontal line on the interior or exterior rim.
263. GRMOT7   The number of Gray sherds with incised motif No. 7: two horizontal lines on the interior or exterior rim.
264. GRMOT8   The number of Gray sherds with incised motif No. 8: three or more horizontal lines on the interior or exterior rim.
265. GRMOT9   The number of Gray sherds with incised motif No. 9: widely spaced diagonal lines on the rim (MacNeish, Peterson, and Flannery 1970:Fig. 71, row 4, fourth from left).

266. GRMOT10   The number of Gray sherds with incised motif No. 10: bands consisting of horizontal lines and dots (MacNeish, Peterson, and Flannery 1970:Fig. 70, row 4, second and third from left).

267. GRMOT11   The number of Gray sherds with incised motif No. 11: "scallop" (MacNeish, Peterson, and Flannery:Fig. 72, row 2, second from left).

268. GRMOT12   The number of Gray sherds with incised motif No. 12: hachure.

269. GRMOT13   The number of Gray sherds with incised motif No. 13: cross-hachure.

270. GRMOT14   The number of Gray sherds with incised motif No. 14: opposed hachure (MacNeish, Peterson, and Flannery 1970:Fig. 72, row 2, second from left).

271. GRMOT15   The number of Gray sherds with incised motif No. 15: small semi-circles on the interior rim (MacNeish, Peterson, and Flannery 1970:Fig. 70, column 2, fourth from bottom).

272. GRMOT16   The number of Gray sherds with incised motif No. 16: small semi-circles on the body of the vessel. These occurred only in square 77(1).

273. GRMOT17   The number of Gray sherds with incised motif No. 17: triangle (MacNeish, Peterson, and Flannery 1970:Fig. 71, row 5, second from left).

274. GRMOT18   The number of Gray sherds with incised motif No. 18: double triangles joined at the pointed end (MacNeish, Peterson, and Flannery 1970:Fig. 71, row 5, third from left). These did not occur.

275. GRMOT19   The number of Gray sherds with incised motif No. 19: pointed triangle (MacNeish, Peterson, and Flannery 1970: Fig. 71, row 4, second from left).

276. GRMOT20   The number of Gray sherds with incised motif No. 20: miscellaneous curvilinear motifs.

277. GRMOT21   The number of Gray sherds with incised motif No. 21: steps (MacNeish, Peterson, and Flannery 1970:Fig. 71, row 1, second from left).

278. GRMOT22   The number of Gray sherds with incised motif No. 22: parallel vertical lines on the interior rim. These did not occur.

279. GRMOT23   The number of Gray sherds with incised motif No. 23: parallel vertical lines on the vessel body.

280. GRMOT24   The number of Gray sherds with incised motif No. 24: miscellaneous rectilinear motifs.

281. GRMOT25   The number of Gray sherds with incised motif No. 25: "pennant" (MacNeish, Peterson, and Flannery 1970:Fig. 71, row 6, second and third from left).

282. GRMOT26   The number of Gray sherds with incised motif No. 26: very large zig-zags on the body of the vessel (MacNeish, Peterson, and Flannery 1970:Fig. 94, row 1, fifth from left).

283. GRMOT27   The number of Gray sherds with incised motif No. 27: "flame eyebrow" (MacNeish, Peterson, and Flannery 1970:Fig. 72, row 1, third from left). These did not occur.

284. GRINDMOT The number of Gray sherds with incised motifs that are indeterminate.

285. GROTHMOT The number of Gray sherds with other kinds of incised motifs.

APPENDIX TO CHAPTER 2

Chipped Stone

301. TOTQRTZ   The total number of quartzite fragments.
302. TOTCHERT   The total number of chert fragments.
303. TOTOBSID   The total number of obsidian fragments.
304. QRTCHNKS   The number of quartzite chunks with no evidence of striking or utilization.
305. QRTSTRK   The number of quartzite fragments that appear to have been struck. A few of these also show evidence for retouching
306. CHCORES   The number of chert cores.
307. CHANGDEB   The number of pieces of chert angular debitage: waste pieces of all sizes, usually with part of the striking platform or cortex still remaining.
308. CHUNUTFL   The number of chert unutilized flakes: flakes and flake fragments with no sign of use or retouch.
309. CHUTILFL   The number of chert utilized flakes: flakes and flake fragments with evidence of use such as fine serrations or nicks along edges.
310. CHRETUNI   The number of chert retouched unifaces: flakes and flake fragments with unifacial retouch.
311. CHSDSCR   The number of chert sidescrapers (showing lateral retouch). These are also included in the counts under variable 310.
312. CHENDSCR   The number of chert endscrapers (showing end retouch). These are also included in the counts under variable 310. These occurred only in the following squares: 3(1), 55(1), 71(1), and 88(1).
313. CHOTHUNI   The number of other kinds of chert unifaces.
314. CHBIFACE   The number of chert bifaces.
315. CHTHOVBF   The number of whole or fragmentary chert thick ovoid bifaces. MacNeish, Nelken-Terner, and Johnson (1967:89-90) call these "thin, crude, ovoid bifaces." These occurred only in the following squares: 76(1) and 82(1).
316. CHTHKBF   The number of whole or fragmentary chert thin bifaces (MacNeish, Nelken-Terner, and Johnson 1967:91-92). These did not occur.
317. CHPROJPT   The number of whole or fragmentary chert projectile points. These occurred only in the following squares: 41(1), 42(1), 49(1), and 60(1).
318. CHCHOPPR   The number of chert choppers: percussion-flaked bifacial tools with battered edges.
319. CHOTHBF   The number of chert bifaces that do not fit any of the above categories. These occurred only in the following squares: 52(1) and 86(1).
320. OBCORES   The number of obsidian cores. These occurred only in the following squares: 28(1), 29(1), and 36(1).
321. OBANGDEB   The number of pieces of obsidian angular debitage: waste pieces of all sizes, usually with part of the striking platform or cortex still remaining.
322. OBUNUTFL   The number of obsidian unutilized flakes: flakes and flake fragments with no sign of use or retouch.

323. OBUTILFL   The number of obsidian utilized flakes: flakes and flake fragments with evidence of use such as fine serrations or nicks along edges.
324. OBRETANG   The number of pieces of obsidian angular debitage which was later re-used or retouched.
325. OBRETFLK   The number of obsidian retouched flakes: flakes and flake fragments which have been retouched unifacially (usually to form a scraper of some sort).
326. OBSDSCR   The number of sidescrapers: flakes and flake fragments with lateral retouch. These are also included in the counts under variable 325.
327. OBENDSCR   The number of obsidian endscrapers: flakes and flake fragments with end retouch. These are also included in the counts under variable 325.
328. OBOTHUNI   The number of other kinds of obsidian unifaces. These occurred only in the following squares: 28(1), 30(1), and 42(2).
329. OBBIFACE   The number of obsidian bifaces. These occurred only in the following squares: 55(1), 56(1), 59(1), 74(2), and 84(1).
330. OBTHNBF   The number of whole or fragmentary obsidian thin bifaces (MacNeish, Nelken-Terner, and Johnson 1967:91-92). These occurred only in the following squares: 56(1) and 59(1).
331. OBPROLPT   The number of whole or fragmentary obsidian projectile points. These occurred only in the following squares: 74(2) and 84(1).
332. OBOTHBF   The number of other kinds of obsidian bifaces. These occurred only in square 55(1).
333. OBBLADES   The number of whole or fragmentary obsidian blades.
334. OBBLDS1   The number of obsidian blades or blade fragments less than 2 cm long.
335. OBBLDS2   The number of obsidian blades or blade fragments between 2 and 3.5 cm long.
336. OBBLDS3   The number of obsidian blades longer than 3.5 cm.
337. OBBLPNTD   The number of obsidian blades with pointed striking platforms (MacNeish, Nelken-Terner, and Johnson 1967:23).
338. OBBLGRND   The number of obsidian blades with ground striking platforms (MacNeish, Nelken-Terner, and Johnson 1967:25).
339. OBBL1DOR   The number of obsidian blades with one dorsal ridge.
340. OBBL2DOR   The number of obsidian blades with two dorsal ridges.
341. OBBLSNP1   The number of snapped and laterally retouched obsidian blades (MacNeish, Nelken-Terner, and Johnson 1967:23-25).
342. OBBLSNP2   The number of snapped and end-retouched obsidian blades (MacNeish, Nelken-Terner, and Johnson 1967:41-42).
343. CHBLADES   The number of chert blades. These occurred only in the following squares: 40(1) and 55(1).

LENCHO DIEGO SURVEY DATA -- VARIABLES 1-121

	VAR. NO.	SQ. 1	SQ. 2	SQ. 3	SQ. 4	SQ. 5	SQ. 6	SQ. 7	SQ. 8	SQ. 9	SQ. 10	SQ. 11	SQ. 12	SQ. 13	SQ. 14	SQ. 15
SITE	2	5	5	5	5	5	5	5	5	5	5	5	5	5	5	5
SAMPAREA	3	1	1	1	1	1	1	1	1	1	1	1	1	1	1	1
SECTOR	4	7	7	7	7	7	7	7	7	7	7	7	7	7	7	7
FEATURE	5	1	1	1	1	1	1	1	1	1	1	1	1	1	1	1
ARCHEVID	6	1	1	1	1	1	1	1	1	1	1	1	1	1	1	1
LOCSAMP	7	1	1	3	3	1	1	3	3	1	1	3	3	1	1	3
SLOPE	8	1	1	1	1	1	1	1	1	1	1	1	1	1	1	1
EROSION	9	1	1	2	2	1	1	2	2	2	1	2	1	1	1	1
DISTURB	10	1	1	1	1	1	1	2	2	2	1	1	1	1	2	1
VEGETATN	11	2	2	1	1	2	2	1	1	2	2	2	2	2	1	2
GRNDSTN	81	2	1	2	1	1	2	0	1	0	0	2	1	1	0	1
OTHART	82	0	0	0	0	0	0	0	0	0	0	0	0	0	0	0
EXOTIC	83	0	0	0	0	0	0	0	0	0	0	0	0	0	0	0
WTDIAGS	91	350	230	1050	120	275	240	150	165	140	405	355	255	320	1100	140
WTGRAY	92	315	230	995	115	265	140	150	140	105	345	290	230	175	925	140
WTPLAIN	93	35	0	55	0	10	25	0	25	35	55	65	25	60	150	0
WTQUARTZ	94	60	65	1	50	45	175	30	26	70	4	70	65	50	20	65
WTCHERT	95	70	28	34	40	80	6	12	33	0	11	90	1	15	45	9
WTOBSID	96	5	3	19	2	5	0	0	4	3	5	1	1	22	8	0
TOTDIAGS	101	36	20	80	13	24	33	15	29	10	30	47	28	34	75	11
TOTCOAT	114	0	0	0	1	0	0	0	0	0	0	0	0	0	0	0
COATCWB	116	0	0	0	0	0	0	0	0	0	0	0	0	0	0	0
COATCYL	117	0	0	0	0	0	0	0	0	0	0	0	0	0	0	0
COATOBS	120	0	0	0	1	0	0	0	0	0	0	0	0	0	0	0
COATUND	121	0	0	0	0	0	0	0	0	0	0	0	0	0	0	0

	VAR. NO.	SQ. 16	SQ. 17	SQ. 18	SQ. 19	SQ. 20	SQ. 21	SQ. 22	SQ. 23	SQ. 24	SQ. 25	SQ. 26	SQ. 27	SQ. 28	SQ. 29	SQ. 30
SITE	2	5	5	5	5	5	4	4	4	4	7	1	1	1	3	2
SAMPAREA	3	1	1	1	1	1	2	2	2	2	2	2	2	2	2	2
SECTOR	4	7	7	7	7	7	7	7	7	7	7	7	7	7	7	7
FEATURE	5	1	1	1	1	1	1	1	1	1	1	1	1	1	2	1
ARCHEVID	6	1	1	1	1	2	1	1	1	1	1	1	2	2	2	2
LOCSAMP	7	1	1	1	3	2	1	1	1	1	1	1	1	1	1	1
SLOPE	8	1	1	1	1	1	4	5	4	4	5	5	5	5	1	3
EROSION	9	1	2	1	1	2	5	5	5	5	5	5	5	5	3	4
DISTURB	10	2	2	2	1	1	1	2	1	1	3	1	1	1	3	1
VEGETATN	11	1	1	2	2	3	6	5	5	5	5	5	4	4	2	4
GRNDSTN	81	0	2	1	0	0	0	0	0	0	3	2	3	1	0	0
OTHART	82	0	0	0	0	1	0	2	0	2	0	1	1	0	1	0
EXOTIC	83	0	0	0	0	0	2	0	0	0	1	0	0	0	0	0
WTDIAGS	91	569	865	320	590	450	345	330	490	340	5075	960	535	375	545	445
WTGRAY	92	495	795	80	590	410	45	165	95	100	660	245	240	185	370	85
WTPLAIN	93	15	70	240	0	40	50	20	340	35	690	85	20	40	75	15
WTQUARTZ	94	21	0	13	45	55	0	0	0	0	0	5	60	60	2	121
WTCHERT	95	0	70	10	26	125	0	0	0	0	0	70	21	20	0	16
WTOBSID	96	9	5	6	4	4	5	1	10	4	45	50	18	20	26	24
TOTDIAGS	101	21	106	16	71	46	8	20	18	21	139	66	40	19	15	21
TOTCOAT	114	0	0	0	0	0	2	4	4	4	11	34	15	5	5	8
COATCWB	116	0	0	0	0	0	2	2	1	0	3	14	8	2	3	2
COATCYL	117	0	0	0	0	0	0	2	2	3	6	10	4	0	2	2
COATOBS	120	0	0	0	0	0	0	0	1	1	1	6	1	2	0	3
COATUND	121	0	0	0	0	0	1	0	3	6	0	18	7	0	0	2

	VAR. NO.	SQ. 31	SQ. 32	SQ. 34	SQ. 35	SQ. 36	SQ. 37	SQ. 38	SQ. 39	SQ. 40	SQ. 41	SQ. 42	SQ. 43	SQ. 44	SQ. 45	SQ. 46
SITE	2	2	2	8	8	8	8	8	8	8	8	8	8	8	8	8
SAMPAREA	3	2	2	1	1	1	1	1	1	1	1	1	1	1	1	1
SECTOR	4	7	7	4	4	4	4	4	1	1	1	1	1	4	4	4
FEATURE	5	1	1	3	3	3	3	3	1	1	1	1	1	3	2	4
ARCHEVID	6	2	2	1	3	1	1	1	1	1	1	1	1	3	1	1
LOCSAMP	7	1	1	1	1	1	1	1	1	2	2	3	2	1	1	1
SLOPE	8	2	2	4	3	4	2	1	3	3	3	3	1	1	5	5
EROSION	9	4	4	3	3	3	3	3	3	3	3	3	3	1	5	5
DISTURB	10	2	2	2	1	1	1	1	1	1	1	1	1	1	3	1
VEGETATN	11	4	4	2	3	4	2	4	2	4	2	2	3	6	4	6
GRNDSTN	81	1	1	0	0	0	0	0	1	1	2	5	0	0	0	0
OTHART	82	0	2	1	1	0	1	0	1	0	1	1	0	0	0	0
EXOTIC	83	0	2	1	0	0	0	0	1	0	0	1	0	0	0	0
WTDIAGS	91	300	935	1025	1325	850	1566	1030	1395	1760	3200	5790	2310	590	320	400
WTGRAY	92	75	180	895	1300	810	1451	980	1798	1550	3045	5735	2070	555	280	330
WTPLAIN	93	125	230	5	20	20	105	30	87	210	135	150	145	35	40	15
WTQUARTZ	94	55	65	0	0	0	0	0	0	0	0	0	0	0	2	0
WTCHERT	95	0	2	65	45	14	30	25	50	230	305	198	126	9	9	11
WTOBSID	96	7	31	11	15	21	10	6	15	19	32	33	17	4	7	2
TOTDIAGS	101	16	49	96	107	50	183	104	224	175	391	487	282	36	25	42
TOTCOAT	114	4	18	0	0	0	0	0	0	0	0	0	0	0	0	0
COATCWB	116	3	6	0	0	0	0	0	0	0	0	0	0	0	0	0
COATCYL	117	0	4	0	0	0	0	0	0	0	0	0	0	0	0	0
COATOBS	120	0	2	0	0	0	0	0	0	0	0	0	0	0	0	0
COATUND	121	1	6	0	0	0	0	0	0	0	0	0	0	0	0	0

APPENDIX TO CHAPTER 2

LENCHO DIEGO SURVEY DATA -- VARIABLES 1-121

	VAR. NO.	SQ. 47	SQ. 48	SQ. 49	SQ. 50	SQ. 51	SQ. 52	SQ. 53	SQ. 54	SQ. 55	SQ. 56	SQ. 57	SQ. 58	SQ. 59	SQ. 60	SQ. 61
SITE	2	8	8	8	8	8	8	8	8	8	8	8	8	8	8	8
SAMPAREA	3	1	1	1	1	1	1	1	1	1	1	1	1	1	1	1
SECTOR	4	4	4	1	1	1	1	1	1	1	1	1	1	1	1	1
FEATURE	5	4	3	1	1	1	1	1	1	1	1	1	1	1	1	1
ARCHEVID	6	1	3	1	1	1	1	1	1	1	1	1	1	1	1	1
LOCSAMP	7	2	1	2	3	3	3	3	3	3	3	3	2	3	3	1
SLOPE	8	1	1	3	3	3	1	3	3	3	3	1	1	4	3	5
EROSION	9	3	3	3	3	3	1	3	3	3	3	3	1	3	3	4
DISTURB	10	2	1	2	1	1	1	2	2	1	1	1	1	1	1	1
VEGETATN	11	4	4	2	6	2	3	4	3	2	2	2	5	5	2	2
GRNDSTN	81	0	0	3	2	2	0	0	0	1	0	1	3	1	1	1
OTHART	82	0	0	2	0	1	0	0	1	0	0	0	0	0	0	0
EXOTIC	83	0	0	0	0	0	0	0	1	0	0	0	0	0	0	0
WTDIAGS	91	845	1780	1810	875	1360	690	1195	1285	2920	3325	795	5975	1520	2175	1660
WTGRAY	92	715	1630	1595	830	1215	610	1140	1085	2810	3115	770	6105	1495	2180	1475
WTPLAIN	93	120	130	210	45	125	60	47	200	105	205	25	1870	25	195	170
WTQUARTZ	94	0	0	20	9	0	1	0	0	0	1	4	0	9	2	1
WTCHERT	95	21	14	360	10	145	35	9	70	295	260	40	250	50	92	55
WTOBSID	96	11	7	45	8	11	3	2	8	54	21	1	10	14	23	2
TOTDIAGS	101	78	187	210	100	137	98	82	127	344	287	78	330	82	240	142
TOTCOAT	114	0	0	0	0	0	0	0	0	0	0	0	0	0	0	0
COATCWB	116	0	0	0	0	0	0	0	0	0	0	0	0	0	0	0
COATCYL	117	0	0	0	0	0	0	0	0	0	0	0	0	0	0	0
COATDBS	120	0	0	0	0	0	0	0	0	0	0	0	0	0	0	0
COATUND	121	0	0	0	0	0	0	0	0	0	0	0	0	0	0	0

	VAR. NO.	SQ. 77	SQ. 78	SQ. 79	SQ. 80	SQ. 81	SQ. 82	SQ. 83	SQ. 84	SQ. 85	SQ. 86	SQ. 87	SQ. 88	SQ. 89	SQ. 90	SQ. 91
SITE	2	8	8	8	8	8	9	9	9	9	9	9	9	9	9	9
SAMPAREA	3	1	1	1	1	1	1	1	1	1	1	1	1	1	1	2
SECTOR	4	2	2	2	2	2	7	3	3	3	3	3	3	3	3	5
FEATURE	5	1	1	1	1	1	3	1	1	1	1	1	1	5	5	5	4
ARCHEVID	6	1	1	1	1	1	3	1	1	2	2	2	1	3	3	3	2
LOCSAMP	7	3	3	2	2	3	1	1	2	2	3	3	4	4	4	1
SLOPE	8	5	2	3	2	4	1	1	1	1	1	3	3	3	4	4
EROSION	9	4	3	3	3	4	1	2	2	2	2	4	4	4	4	5
DISTURB	10	3	2	1	1	3	1	2	2	2	1	1	1	1	1	3
VEGETATN	11	6	4	5	2	2	3	2	2	2	2	3	4	4	4	6
GRNDSTN	81	1	4	0	0	2	1	2	3	0	2	6	1	1	0	0
OTHART	82	2	0	0	0	0	0	0	0	0	2	4	2	0	0	0
EXOTIC	83	0	0	0	0	0	0	0	0	0	0	0	0	0	0	0
WTDIAGS	91	3115	2355	1760	1215	2445	1195	1030	985	970	1095	1970	1995	995	165	145
WTGRAY	92	2890	2275	1740	1160	2250	1095	935	910	905	1020	1940	1900	930	140	130
WTPLAIN	93	185	75	15	60	195	100	95	75	65	65	85	85	65	15	15
WTQUARTZ	94	5	31	4	37	25	55	300	0	9	0	0	130	80	0	55
WTCHERT	95	150	295	125	72	65	135	140	60	155	100	400	40	140	3	0
WTOBSID	96	3	15	3	4	2	5	1	9	8	7	5	2	1	0	0
TOTDIAGS	101	179	225	166	138	132	113	35	82	87	71	172	184	120	23	13
TOTCOAT	114	0	0	0	0	0	0	0	0	0	0	0	0	0	0	0
COATCWB	116	0	0	0	0	0	0	0	0	0	0	0	0	0	0	0
COATCYL	117	0	0	0	0	0	0	0	0	0	0	0	0	0	0	0
COATDBS	120	0	0	0	0	0	0	0	0	0	0	0	0	0	0	0
COATUND	121	0	0	0	0	0	0	0	0	0	0	0	0	0	0	0

	VAR. NO.	SQ. 62	SQ. 63	SQ. 64	SQ. 65	SQ. 66	SQ. 67	SQ. 68	SQ. 69	SQ. 70	SQ. 71	SQ. 72	SQ. 73	SQ. 74	SQ. 75	SQ. 76
SITE	2	8	8	8	8	8	8	8	8	8	8	8	8	8	8	8
SAMPAREA	3	1	1	1	1	1	1	1	1	1	1	1	1	1	1	1
SECTOR	4	1	1	6	6	6	6	6	1	1	1	2	2	2	2	2
FEATURE	5	1	1	5	5	5	2	5	1	1	1	1	1	1	1	1
ARCHEVID	6	1	1	3	3	3	1	3	1	1	1	1	1	1	1	1
LOCSAMP	7	1	1	4	4	4	1	4	3	1	2	2	3	2	1	3
SLOPE	8	5	5	5	3	1	1	3	3	1	4	3	1	2	1	1
EROSION	9	4	5	5	3	2	2	3	3	2	3	3	3	3	1	3
DISTURB	10	1	1	1	1	1	2	2	1	1	1	1	1	1	1	1
VEGETATN	11	2	2	2	4	2	3	2	5	2	4	2	2	2	3	2
GRNDSTN	81	1	0	0	3	0	1	0	1	0	1	3	3	1	1	1
OTHART	82	0	0	2	0	2	0	0	0	0	0	0	0	0	0	0
EXOTIC	83	0	0	0	0	0	0	0	0	0	0	0	0	0	0	0
WTDIAGS	91	1285	425	12360	2800	2395	845	3900	1905	1090	4855	2580	4020	2390	1520	4135
WTGRAY	92	1100	335	11900	2705	2275	770	3770	1520	1060	4785	2290	3705	2285	1515	3920
WTPLAIN	93	185	70	460	95	115	75	125	175	30	40	290	310	70	105	150
WTQUARTZ	94	16	0	0	0	0	4	0	0	2	7	50	105	135	16	150
WTCHERT	95	122	35	220	175	46	22	65	47	14	152	180	864	215	139	250
WTOBSID	96	3	1	27	26	27	16	16	2	6	19	7	32	22	10	17
TOTDIAGS	101	73	27	1177	308	272	52	256	165	87	397	186	501	261	146	342
TOTCOAT	114	0	0	0	0	0	0	0	0	0	0	0	0	0	0	0
COATCWB	116	0	0	0	0	0	0	0	0	0	0	0	0	0	0	0
COATCYL	117	0	0	0	0	0	0	0	0	0	0	0	0	0	0	0
COATDBS	120	0	0	0	0	0	0	0	0	0	0	0	0	0	0	0
COATUND	121	0	0	0	0	0	0	0	0	0	0	0	0	0	0	0

LENCHO DIEGO SURVEY DATA -- VARIABLES 122-152

	VAR. NO.	SQ. 1	SQ. 2	SQ. 3	SQ. 4	SQ. 5	SQ. 6	SQ. 7	SQ. 8	SQ. 9	SQ. 10	SQ. 11	SQ. 12	SQ. 13	SQ. 14	SQ. 15
TOTGRAY	125	34	20	75	12	23	28	15	17	8	24	41	27	19	63	11
GROWB	126	22	6	49	5	14	8	9	7	3	13	25	15	9	30	7
GRCWB	127	0	3	4	3	0	1	0	2	0	1	0	2	0	2	1
GRCYL	128	0	0	1	0	0	7	0	2	0	1	0	1	0	10	0
GRINCURV	129	0	0	0	0	0	0	0	0	0	0	0	0	0	0	0
GROLLA	130	3	6	6	2	1	4	1	0	0	1	6	0	4	5	0
GRMNOLLA	131	0	0	0	0	0	0	0	0	0	0	0	0	0	0	0
GRTECOM	132	0	0	1	0	0	0	0	0	0	0	0	0	0	0	0
GRCRDCYL	133	0	0	0	0	0	0	0	0	0	0	0	0	0	0	0
GROTR	134	0	1	0	0	0	0	0	0	0	0	0	1	0	0	0
GRDBS	135	7	4	14	0	8	8	5	6	5	8	10	8	6	16	3
GRUND	136	106	98	445	0	62	85	87	111	28	138	277	160	75	204	19
TOTPL	137	2	0	5	0	1	2	0	2	2	5	5	1	10	10	0
PLOLLA	138	1	0	5	0	1	1	0	2	2	5	5	1	0	10	0
PLCWB	139	0	0	0	0	0	0	0	0	0	0	0	0	0	0	0
PLCOMAL	140	0	0	0	0	0	0	0	0	0	0	0	0	0	0	0
PLINCENS	141	0	0	0	0	0	0	0	0	0	0	0	0	0	0	0
PLSTRHAN	143	1	0	0	0	0	1	0	0	0	0	0	0	0	0	0
PLLUGHAN	144	0	0	0	0	0	0	0	0	0	0	0	0	0	0	0
PLDBS	145	0	0	0	0	0	0	0	0	0	0	0	0	0	0	0
PLUND	146	15	0	15	11	110	89	10	9	26	25	63	25	203	197	5
TOTERO	147	0	0	0	0	0	0	0	0	0	0	0	0	0	0	0
TOTHO	150	0	0	0	0	0	0	0	0	0	0	0	0	0	0	0
THOOWB	151	0	0	0	0	0	0	0	0	0	0	0	0	0	0	0
THOCWB	152	0	0	0	0	0	0	0	0	0	0	0	0	0	0	0

	VAR. NO.	SQ. 16	SQ. 17	SQ. 18	SQ. 19	SQ. 20	SQ. 21	SQ. 22	SQ. 23	SQ. 24	SQ. 25	SQ. 26	SQ. 27	SQ. 28	SQ. 29	SQ. 30
TOTGRAY	125	18	97	11	71	42	2	14	7	3	28	19	20	9	9	3
GROWB	126	9	39	7	47	30	0	5	4	2	5	9	3	1	3	0
GRCWB	127	1	3	0	3	2	0	3	0	0	12	1	2	0	2	1
GRCYL	128	4	2	0	1	0	0	0	0	1	1	3	5	0	0	0
GRINCURV	129	0	0	0	0	1	0	0	1	0	0	0	0	1	0	0
GROLLA	130	1	6	0	4	4	0	4	1	0	2	3	8	4	3	1
GRMNOLLA	131	0	1	0	0	0	0	0	0	0	0	0	0	0	0	0
GRTECOM	132	0	0	0	0	0	0	0	0	0	0	0	0	1	0	0
GRCRDCYL	133	0	0	0	0	0	0	0	0	0	0	0	0	0	0	0
GROTR	134	0	0	0	0	0	0	0	0	0	0	0	0	0	0	0
GRDBS	135	3	46	4	16	5	2	0	1	0	8	3	2	2	1	1
GRUND	136	76	435	130	298	165	47	44	32	46	0	115	132	61	18	13
TOTPL	137	1	9	5	0	4	3	2	6	2	15	5	1	2	1	2
PLOLLA	138	0	9	4	0	3	3	1	5	1	8	2	1	2	0	1
PLCWB	139	0	0	0	0	0	0	1	0	0	1	2	0	0	0	0
PLCOMAL	140	0	0	0	0	0	0	0	0	0	1	0	0	0	0	0
PLINCENS	141	0	0	0	0	0	0	0	0	0	2	1	0	0	1	0
PLSTRHAN	143	1	0	0	0	0	0	0	0	0	3	0	0	0	0	0
PLLUGHAN	144	0	0	1	0	0	0	0	1	1	1	0	0	0	0	1
PLDBS	145	0	0	0	0	1	0	0	0	0	0	0	0	0	0	0
PLUND	146	13	92	105	86	50	52	11	122	23	0	59	60	22	33	64
TOTERO	147	0	0	0	0	0	0	0	0	0	0	0	0	0	0	0
TOTHO	150	0	0	0	0	0	0	0	0	0	0	0	0	0	0	0
THOOWB	151	0	0	0	0	0	0	0	0	0	0	0	0	0	0	0
THOCWB	152	0	0	0	0	0	0	0	0	0	0	0	0	0	0	0

	VAR. NO.	SQ. 31	SQ. 32	SQ. 34	SQ. 35	SQ. 36	SQ. 37	SQ. 38	SQ. 39	SQ. 40	SQ. 41	SQ. 42	SQ. 43	SQ. 44	SQ. 45	SQ. 46
TOTGRAY	125	5	11	92	103	46	169	96	209	152	369	467	252	33	23	40
GROWB	126	1	4	24	44	18	84	33	78	76	87	203	92	13	6	10
GRCWB	127	1	0	36	28	13	48	28	54	23	112	99	52	14	6	14
GRCYL	128	0	0	8	4	1	11	9	9	6	18	9	8	4	1	5
GRINCURV	129	0	0	1	4	1	3	6	10	5	17	25	34	0	2	0
GROLLA	130	0	2	6	9	3	11	8	29	18	81	59	30	0	3	1
GRMNOLLA	131	0	0	1	0	0	0	0	0	1	0	0	0	0	0	0
GRTECOM	132	0	0	1	0	0	0	0	0	0	0	0	0	0	0	0
GRCRDCYL	133	0	0	0	0	0	4	0	5	6	0	6	2	0	0	1
GROTR	134	0	0	0	0	0	0	0	0	0	0	0	0	0	0	0
GRDBS	135	3	5	15	15	9	8	12	24	17	54	66	34	2	5	9
GRUND	136	23	40	437	418	126	656	466	1262	677	1526	1389	1175	114	181	230
TOTPL	137	5	13	1	3	1	11	7	14	23	19	19	21	3	2	1
PLOLLA	138	2	8	0	3	1	7	5	10	20	14	15	15	2	1	1
PLCWB	139	0	1	0	0	0	0	0	0	1	0	0	1	0	0	0
PLCOMAL	140	0	0	0	0	0	2	1	0	0	1	3	4	0	0	0
PLINCENS	141	1	0	1	0	0	1	0	4	0	1	1	0	1	1	0
PLSTRHAN	143	0	2	0	0	0	0	1	0	2	1	0	1	0	0	0
PLLUGHAN	144	1	0	0	0	0	0	0	0	0	2	0	0	0	0	0
PLDBS	145	1	2	0	0	0	0	1	0	0	0	0	0	0	0	0
PLUND	146	38	100	50	105	21	128	153	276	250	233	209	182	32	17	37
TOTERO	147	0	0	0	0	0	0	0	0	0	2	0	1	0	0	0
TOTHO	150	0	0	1	0	2	1	1	1	0	0	1	6	0	0	1
THOOWB	151	0	0	0	0	1	0	0	0	0	0	0	2	0	0	0
THOCWB	152	0	0	1	0	1	0	0	1	0	0	1	4	0	0	1

APPENDIX TO CHAPTER 2   99

LENCHO DIEGO SURVEY DATA -- VARIABLES 122-152

	VAR. NO.	SQ. 47	SQ. 48	SQ. 49	SQ. 50	SQ. 51	SQ. 52	SQ. 53	SQ. 54	SQ. 55	SQ. 56	SQ. 57	SQ. 58	SQ. 59	SQ. 60	SQ. 61
TOTGRAY	125	70	156	193	96	125	90	76	112	301	263	74	305	80	215	122
GROWB	126	27	64	79	38	50	46	34	50	164	138	24	140	37	101	66
GRCWB	127	14	25	51	13	32	19	20	21	64	47	15	50	15	56	20
GRCYL	128	6	1	10	2	5	3	1	3	11	19	3	24	6	7	4
GRINCURV	129	2	13	6	13	2	0	1	2	10	6	4	12	1	8	5
GROLLA	130	8	12	14	10	14	5	8	14	27	17	8	35	9	19	12
GRMNOLLA	131	1	0	0	0	0	0	0	1	1	0	0	0	0	0	1
GRTECOM	132	0	1	0	0	0	0	0	0	0	0	0	2	0	0	0
GRCRDCYL	133	3	3	4	0	1	2	2	3	11	1	5	1	1	3	0
GROTR	134	1	0	1	0	0	0	0	0	0	1	0	0	0	0	0
GRDBS	135	8	38	28	20	21	15	10	18	40	34	15	41	11	21	14
GRUND	136	390	485	895	389	589	429	244	514	1614	972	283	1271	273	363	675
TOTPL	137	7	25	14	4	10	6	2	15	13	23	4	25	2	25	17
PLOLLA	138	7	23	13	4	10	5	1	13	11	17	4	24	0	22	10
PLCWB	139	0	0	0	0	0	0	0	0	0	0	0	0	0	0	0
PLCOMAL	140	0	2	1	0	0	0	1	2	0	3	0	1	0	1	3
PLINCENS	141	0	0	0	0	0	1	0	0	0	1	0	0	2	1	0
PLSTRHAN	143	0	0	0	0	0	0	0	0	0	1	0	0	0	1	2
PLLUGHAN	144	0	0	0	0	0	0	0	0	0	0	0	0	0	0	1
PLDBS	145	0	0	0	0	0	0	0	0	1	1	0	0	1	0	1
PLUND	146	175	230	303	235	161	271	84	201	222	349	72	202	70	162	330
TOTERO	147	0	0	0	0	0	1	1	0	0	0	0	0	0	0	0
TOTHO	150	1	5	2	0	2	0	2	0	3	0	0	0	0	0	3
THOOWB	151	0	2	1	0	0	0	0	0	0	1	0	0	0	0	0
THOCWB	152	1	2	1	0	1	0	2	0	1	0	0	0	0	0	2

	VAR. NO.	SQ. 62	SQ. 63	SQ. 64	SQ. 65	SQ. 66	SQ. 67	SQ. 68	SQ. 69	SQ. 70	SQ. 71	SQ. 72	SQ. 73	SQ. 74	SQ. 75	SQ. 76
TOTGRAY	125	63	20	1121	296	259	49	246	147	81	386	157	461	242	139	320
GROWB	126	31	12	511	164	141	22	117	70	40	221	109	290	130	78	199
GRCWB	127	12	2	246	59	39	10	39	23	8	43	17	40	22	19	30
GRCYL	128	5	0	47	6	10	7	13	9	3	24	6	38	16	3	29
GRINCURV	129	4	1	38	10	3	1	2	8	0	11	0	2	3	3	0
GROLLA	130	3	2	102	7	18	3	22	9	15	43	12	18	11	7	22
GRMNOLLA	131	0	0	1	1	1	1	3	0	0	1	1	0	0	0	0
GRTECOM	132	0	0	2	0	0	0	0	0	0	2	0	0	0	0	0
GRCRDCYL	133	1	1	25	3	4	0	2	2	0	3	0	0	1	0	3
GROTR	134	0	0	35	4	14	0	30	0	0	1	0	2	0	0	0
GRDBS	135	7	2	114	43	29	5	18	26	15	37	12	71	59	29	37
GRUND	136	160	103	5497	2044	1146	243	921	674	259	1527	1000	3166	1884	1153	2222
TOTPL	137	10	6	55	12	11	3	8	15	5	7	28	38	13	7	20
PLOLLA	138	8	6	49	11	10	3	7	12	5	6	23	31	12	7	20
PLCWB	139	0	0	1	0	0	0	1	0	0	1	0	2	0	0	0
PLCOMAL	140	1	0	3	0	1	0	0	3	0	0	4	5	0	0	0
PLINCENS	141	1	0	0	0	0	0	0	0	0	0	0	0	0	0	0
PLSTRHAN	143	0	0	1	0	0	0	0	0	0	0	0	0	0	0	0
PLLUGHAN	144	0	0	1	0	0	0	0	0	0	0	0	0	0	0	0
PLDBS	145	0	0	0	0	0	0	0	0	0	0	1	0	1	0	0
PLUND	146	303	181	529	162	235	86	108	413	48	271	331	914	290	198	394
TOTERO	147	0	1	0	0	0	0	0	0	1	0	0	0	0	0	0
TOTHO	150	0	0	0	0	0	0	1	2	0	2	0	2	3	0	2
THOOWB	151	0	0	0	0	0	0	0	0	0	2	0	0	0	0	0
THOCWB	152	0	0	0	0	0	0	1	2	0	0	0	2	2	0	2

	VAR. NO.	SQ. 77	SQ. 78	SQ. 79	SQ. 80	SQ. 81	SQ. 82	SQ. 83	SQ. 84	SQ. 85	SQ. 86	SQ. 87	SQ. 88	SQ. 89	SQ. 90	SQ. 91
TOTGRAY	125	151	211	163	127	113	101	29	75	77	65	159	168	111	20	11
GROWB	126	100	112	93	82	64	66	14	40	38	33	68	76	52	9	5
GRCWB	127	10	25	14	6	8	9	5	14	14	7	16	15	19	3	2
GRCYL	128	8	20	15	10	7	0	2	3	2	4	8	9	5	4	0
GRINCURV	129	1	1	1	1	0	2	0	1	0	1	4	2	4	0	0
GROLLA	130	9	15	12	8	7	4	5	3	6	5	29	38	11	1	0
GRMNOLLA	131	0	0	0	0	0	0	0	0	0	0	0	0	0	0	0
GRTECOM	132	0	0	0	0	0	0	0	0	0	0	0	0	0	0	0
GRCRDCYL	133	1	0	0	0	0	3	1	2	3	4	8	6	2	1	1
GROTR	134	1	1	0	1	0	0	0	0	0	0	0	0	1	0	0
GRDBS	135	21	37	28	19	25	17	2	12	14	11	26	22	17	2	3
GRUND	136	756	972	809	887	839	558	119	474	424	358	678	932	803	120	9
TOTPL	137	26	14	3	11	19	12	6	7	10	5	11	13	8	2	2
PLOLLA	138	26	13	3	9	18	11	5	3	7	5	11	12	8	2	2
PLCWB	139	0	0	0	0	0	0	0	1	1	0	0	0	0	0	0
PLCOMAL	140	0	0	0	0	1	0	0	1	1	0	0	1	0	0	0
PLINCENS	141	0	0	0	0	0	0	0	0	0	0	0	0	0	0	0
PLSTRHAN	143	0	0	0	0	0	0	0	0	1	0	0	0	0	0	0
PLLUGHAN	144	0	0	0	1	0	0	0	1	2	0	0	0	0	0	0
PLDBS	145	0	1	0	0	0	1	0	0	0	0	0	0	0	0	0
PLUND	146	175	215	183	190	191	95	19	213	175	63	162	164	109	25	19
TOTERO	147	0	0	0	0	0	0	0	0	0	0	0	0	0	0	0
TOTHO	150	0	0	0	0	0	0	0	0	0	1	2	3	0	1	0
THOOWB	151	0	0	0	0	0	0	0	0	0	0	0	0	0	0	0
THOCWB	152	0	0	0	0	0	0	0	0	0	0	1	2	0	1	0

LENCHO DIEGO SURVEY DATA -- VARIABLES 153-200

	VAR. NO.	SQ. 1	SQ. 2	SQ. 3	SQ. 4	SQ. 5	SQ. 6	SQ. 7	SQ. 8	SQ. 9	SQ. 10	SQ. 11	SQ. 12	SQ. 13	SQ. 14	SQ. 15
THODBS	155	0	0	0	0	0	0	0	0	0	0	0	0	0	0	0
THOUND	156	0	0	0	0	0	0	0	0	0	0	0	0	0	0	0
OTHWARES	157	0	0	0	0	0	3	0	0	0	1	0	0	0	1	0
COATUNIF	158	0	0	0	1	0	0	0	0	0	0	0	0	0	0	0
COATDEC	163	0	0	0	1	0	0	0	0	0	0	0	0	0	0	0
COATINC	164	0	0	0	1	0	0	0	0	0	0	0	0	0	0	0
COATMO3	169	0	0	0	0	0	0	0	0	0	0	0	0	0	0	0
COATMO6	172	0	0	0	0	0	0	0	0	0	0	0	0	0	0	0
COATMO9	175	0	0	0	1	0	0	0	0	0	0	0	0	0	0	0
COATMO10	176	0	0	0	1	0	0	0	0	0	0	0	0	0	0	0
GRSF1	185	0	0	0	0	0	0	0	0	0	0	0	0	0	0	0
GRSF2	186	0	0	0	0	0	0	0	0	0	0	0	0	0	0	0
GRSF3	187	0	0	0	0	0	0	0	0	0	0	0	0	0	0	0
GRSF4	188	1	0	1	0	0	0	0	0	1	0	0	1	2	1	0
GRSF5	189	0	0	0	0	0	0	0	0	0	0	0	0	0	0	0
GRSF6	190	0	0	0	0	0	0	0	0	0	0	0	0	0	0	0
GRSF8	192	0	0	0	0	0	0	0	0	0	0	0	0	0	0	0
GRSF9	193	0	0	0	0	0	0	0	0	0	0	0	0	0	0	0
GRSF10	194	0	0	0	0	1	0	0	0	0	1	0	1	0	0	0
GROTHSF	195	0	0	0	0	0	0	0	0	0	0	0	0	0	0	0
GRSF12	196	0	0	2	0	0	1	0	1	0	0	3	1	0	1	0
RIOSALGR	197	0	0	1	2	1	0	0	4	0	3	1	0	0	3	1
ERQACHGR	198	34	20	74	10	22	28	15	13	8	21	40	27	19	60	10
INDGRPST	199	0	0	0	0	0	0	0	0	0	0	0	0	0	0	0
GRSURF1	200	27	15	71	11	21	27	12	13	5	18	32	25	17	57	10

	VAR. NO.	SQ. 31	SQ. 32	SQ. 34	SQ. 35	SQ. 36	SQ. 37	SQ. 38	SQ. 39	SQ. 40	SQ. 41	SQ. 42	SQ. 43	SQ. 44	SQ. 45	SQ. 46
THODBS	155	0	0	0	0	0	0	1	0	0	0	0	0	0	0	0
THOUND	156	0	0	0	3	0	8	9	6	1	19	5	13	0	1	0
OTHWARES	157	2	0	1	1	1	2	0	0	0	1	0	2	0	0	0
COATUNIF	158	4	7	0	0	0	0	0	0	0	0	0	0	0	0	0
COATDEC	163	4	14	0	0	0	0	0	0	0	0	0	0	0	0	0
COATINC	164	4	14	0	0	0	0	0	0	0	0	0	0	0	0	0
COATMO3	169	2	5	0	0	0	0	0	0	0	0	0	0	0	0	0
COATMO6	172	0	4	0	0	0	0	0	0	0	0	0	0	0	0	0
COATMO9	175	0	2	0	0	0	0	0	0	0	0	0	0	0	0	0
COATMO10	176	0	1	0	0	0	0	0	0	0	0	0	0	0	0	0
GRSF1	185	0	0	6	4	1	3	3	11	2	17	20	6	0	1	0
GRSF2	186	2	3	0	2	0	0	0	2	4	4	12	8	0	0	2
GRSF3	187	0	0	0	0	1	1	0	0	0	1	0	0	0	1	0
GRSF4	188	0	0	0	0	1	0	0	0	1	3	2	0	0	0	0
GRSF5	189	0	0	0	1	0	0	3	1	0	3	3	1	0	0	1
GRSF6	190	0	0	0	3	0	0	3	1	5	2	7	3	0	0	0
GRSF8	192	0	0	0	0	0	0	0	1	0	3	1	2	1	0	0
GRSF9	193	0	0	0	0	0	0	1	0	0	0	0	0	0	0	0
GRSF10	194	0	0	0	0	1	0	0	0	2	5	8	4	1	0	0
GROTHSF	195	0	0	0	0	0	0	0	0	1	0	1	1	0	0	2
GRSF12	196	0	1	0	0	0	0	0	0	0	0	1	0	0	1	0
RIOSALGR	197	0	1	0	1	0	2	1	0	0	0	0	0	0	0	0
ERQACHGR	198	5	10	92	0	46	167	95	209	152	369	467	252	33	0	40
INDGRPST	199	0	0	0	0	0	0	0	0	0	0	0	0	0	0	0
GRSURF1	200	5	11	89	4	36	165	89	195	145	346	445	236	32	0	36

	VAR. NO.	SQ. 16	SQ. 17	SQ. 18	SQ. 19	SQ. 20	SQ. 21	SQ. 22	SQ. 23	SQ. 24	SQ. 25	SQ. 26	SQ. 27	SQ. 28	SQ. 29	SQ. 30
THODBS	155	0	0	0	0	0	0	0	0	0	0	0	0	0	0	0
THOUND	156	0	0	0	0	0	0	0	0	0	0	0	0	0	0	0
OTHWARES	157	1	0	0	0	0	1	0	1	11	84	0	1	3	0	8
COATUNIF	158	0	0	0	0	0	2	3	4	4	7	15	10	4	5	7
COATDEC	163	0	0	0	0	0	2	4	4	4	10	29	11	4	4	6
COATINC	164	0	0	0	0	0	2	4	4	4	10	29	11	4	4	6
COATMO3	169	0	0	0	0	0	2	1	1	0	2	13	6	2	2	1
COATMO6	172	0	0	0	0	0	0	2	1	2	4	2	1	0	0	1
COATMO9	175	0	0	0	0	0	0	0	1	2	4	1	1	0	1	0
COATMO10	176	0	0	0	0	0	0	0	1	2	1	5	2	0	1	0
GRSF1	185	0	0	0	0	0	0	0	0	0	0	0	0	0	0	0
GRSF2	186	0	0	0	0	0	0	0	0	0	4	0	0	0	0	0
GRSF3	187	0	0	0	0	0	0	0	0	0	0	0	0	0	0	0
GRSF4	188	0	3	0	1	1	1	0	0	0	0	0	0	0	0	0
GRSF5	189	0	0	0	0	0	0	0	0	0	0	0	0	0	0	0
GRSF6	190	0	0	0	0	0	0	0	0	0	0	0	0	0	0	0
GRSF8	192	0	0	0	0	0	0	0	0	0	0	0	0	0	0	0
GRSF9	193	0	0	0	0	0	0	0	0	0	0	0	0	0	0	0
GRSF10	194	1	0	0	3	0	0	0	0	0	0	0	0	0	0	0
GROTHSF	195	0	2	0	0	0	0	0	0	0	0	0	0	0	0	0
GRSF12	196	0	0	0	0	0	0	0	0	0	0	0	0	0	0	0
RIOSALGR	197	2	0	0	1	1	1	1	2	2	1	13	12	5	2	1
ERQACHGR	198	16	97	11	70	41	1	13	5	1	27	6	8	4	7	2
INDGRPST	199	0	0	0	0	0	0	0	0	0	0	0	0	0	0	0
GRSURF1	200	15	55	8	59	37	2	11	6	3	27	18	17	6	6	2

APPENDIX TO CHAPTER 2   101

LENCHO DIEGO SURVEY DATA -- VARIABLES 153-200

	VAR. NO.	SQ. 47	SQ. 48	SQ. 49	SQ. 50	SQ. 51	SQ. 52	SQ. 53	SQ. 54	SQ. 55	SQ. 56	SQ. 57	SQ. 58	SQ. 59	SQ. 60	SQ. 61
THODBS	155	0	1	0	0	1	0	0	0	2	0	0	0	0	0	1
THOUND	156	5	12	12	2	3	0	5	4	20	11	6	14	1	9	5
OTHWARES	157	0	1	1	0	0	1	0	0	0	0	0	0	0	0	0
COATUNIF	158	0	0	0	0	0	0	0	0	0	0	0	0	0	0	0
COATDEC	163	0	0	0	0	0	0	0	0	0	0	0	0	0	0	0
COATINC	164	0	0	0	0	0	0	0	0	0	0	0	0	0	0	0
COATM03	169	0	0	0	0	0	0	0	0	0	0	0	0	0	0	0
COATM06	172	0	0	0	0	0	0	0	0	0	0	0	0	0	0	0
COATM09	175	0	0	0	0	0	0	0	0	0	0	0	0	0	0	0
COATM010	176	0	0	0	0	0	0	0	0	0	0	0	0	0	0	0
GRSF1	185	2	16	10	5	11	4	6	2	3	11	7	7	3	3	5
GRSF2	186	1	3	2	5	0	0	0	4	6	5	1	10	2	1	0
GRSF3	187	0	1	0	0	0	0	0	0	0	0	0	0	0	1	0
GRSF4	188	0	0	0	1	1	3	0	0	2	1	0	1	0	1	0
GRSF5	189	0	4	1	0	0	1	0	2	0	5	1	1	0	0	0
GRSF6	190	1	1	6	4	2	0	0	3	8	6	0	7	3	2	1
GRSF8	192	0	1	0	1	0	0	0	1	0	1	0	0	0	0	0
GRSF9	193	2	2	0	0	1	0	0	0	2	0	0	1	0	1	0
GRSF10	194	0	3	0	4	3	0	4	1	2	5	1	6	1	3	3
GROTHSF	195	0	0	0	0	0	1	0	0	1	0	0	0	1	0	1
GRSF12	196	0	0	0	0	0	1	0	0	0	0	0	0	0	0	0
RIOSALGR	197	0	0	0	0	0	0	0	0	0	0	0	0	0	0	0
ERQACHGR	198	70	156	193	96	125	90	76	111	302	263	0	305	80	215	122
INDGRPST	199	0	0	0	0	0	0	0	1	0	0	0	0	0	0	0
GRSURF1	200	65	141	182	88	113	84	72	102	292	253	70	295	74	192	116

	VAR. NO.	SQ. 62	SQ. 63	SQ. 64	SQ. 65	SQ. 66	SQ. 67	SQ. 68	SQ. 69	SQ. 70	SQ. 71	SQ. 72	SQ. 73	SQ. 74	SQ. 75	SQ. 76
THODBS	155	0	0	0	0	0	0	0	0	0	0	0	0	1	0	0
THOUND	156	1	0	10	0	21	0	3	2	0	2	2	10	2	1	1
OTHWARES	157	0	0	1	0	2	0	1	1	0	1	0	0	3	0	0
COATUNIF	158	0	0	0	0	0	0	0	0	0	0	0	0	0	0	0
COATDEC	163	0	0	0	0	0	0	0	0	0	0	0	0	0	0	0
COATINC	164	0	0	0	0	0	0	0	0	0	0	0	0	0	0	0
COATM03	169	0	0	0	0	0	0	0	0	0	0	0	0	0	0	0
COATM06	172	0	0	0	0	0	0	0	0	0	0	0	0	0	0	0
COATM09	175	0	0	0	0	0	0	0	0	0	0	0	0	0	0	0
COATM010	176	0	0	0	0	0	0	0	0	0	0	0	0	0	0	0
GRSF1	185	4	1	20	4	6	0	3	12	4	4	1	1	0	0	1
GRSF2	186	0	0	23	5	9	1	1	1	4	11	3	14	6	4	13
GRSF3	187	0	0	0	0	0	0	0	0	0	0	0	1	0	0	0
GRSF4	188	1	0	2	0	0	0	1	0	0	0	0	0	0	0	0
GRSF5	189	0	0	5	1	0	1	0	1	0	2	1	5	3	1	0
GRSF6	190	3	1	12	1	5	0	2	1	1	4	0	0	0	0	0
GRSF8	192	0	0	1	0	3	0	0	0	0	0	0	1	0	0	0
GRSF9	193	0	0	2	0	0	0	0	3	0	0	0	0	0	0	0
GRSF10	194	1	0	9	1	0	0	1	3	3	7	0	2	8	3	4
GROTHSF	195	0	0	5	1	0	0	0	0	0	1	1	3	0	0	1
GRSF12	196	0	0	0	0	0	0	0	0	0	0	0	0	0	0	0
RIOSALGR	197	0	0	0	0	0	2	0	1	0	0	0	0	0	0	0
ERQACHGR	198	63	20	1121	296	252	49	242	147	81	386	186	461	242	139	320
INDGRPST	199	0	0	0	0	5	0	3	0	0	0	0	0	0	0	0
GRSURF1	200	60	18	1011	271	236	42	176	138	0	365	171	436	225	0	307

	VAR. NO.	SQ. 77	SQ. 78	SQ. 79	SQ. 80	SQ. 81	SQ. 82	SQ. 83	SQ. 84	SQ. 85	SQ. 86	SQ. 87	SQ. 88	SQ. 89	SQ. 90	SQ. 91
THODBS	155	0	0	0	0	0	0	0	0	0	0	0	0	0	0	0
THOUND	156	0	2	1	2	0	3	0	1	0	0	7	3	2	0	0
OTHWARES	157	0	0	0	0	0	0	0	0	0	0	0	0	1	0	0
COATUNIF	158	0	0	0	0	0	0	0	0	0	0	0	0	0	0	0
COATDEC	163	0	0	0	0	0	0	0	0	0	0	0	0	0	0	0
COATINC	164	0	0	0	0	0	0	0	0	0	0	0	0	0	0	0
COATM03	169	0	0	0	0	0	0	0	0	0	0	0	0	0	0	0
COATM06	172	0	0	0	0	0	0	0	0	0	0	0	0	0	0	0
COATM09	175	2	0	0	0	0	0	0	0	0	0	0	0	0	0	0
COATM010	176	0	0	0	0	0	0	0	0	0	0	0	0	0	0	0
GRSF1	185	0	0	2	1	0	0	4	0	0	3	6	3	1	6	0
GRSF2	186	7	4	2	3	10	1	1	2	2	1	4	3	4	0	0
GRSF3	187	0	0	0	0	0	0	0	0	0	0	0	0	0	0	0
GRSF4	188	0	0	0	0	0	0	0	0	0	0	1	0	0	0	0
GRSF5	189	4	0	2	2	3	1	0	0	1	0	2	5	0	0	0
GRSF6	190	2	2	0	1	1	0	0	1	2	2	2	7	1	0	1
GRSF8	192	1	1	0	0	0	0	0	0	0	0	0	0	0	0	0
GRSF9	193	0	1	0	0	0	1	0	0	0	0	0	0	1	0	0
GRSF10	194	0	3	2	0	2	3	0	1	1	1	4	1	2	0	0
GROTHSF	195	0	1	1	1	1	2	0	1	0	0	0	1	0	0	0
GRSF12	196	0	0	0	0	0	0	0	0	0	0	0	0	0	0	0
RIOSALGR	197	0	0	0	0	0	0	0	0	0	0	0	0	0	0	0
ERQACHGR	198	150	211	163	125	113	101	29	75	77	65	158	168	110	20	11
INDGRPST	199	1	0	0	2	0	0	0	0	0	0	1	0	1	0	0
GRSURF1	200	135	0	145	108	89	99	26	65	71	62	149	149	105	19	10

LENCHO DIEGO SURVEY DATA -- VARIABLES 201-231

	VAR. NO.	SQ. 1	SQ. 2	SQ. 3	SQ. 4	SQ. 5	SQ. 6	SQ. 7	SQ. 8	SQ. 9	SQ. 10	SQ. 11	SQ. 12	SQ. 13	SQ. 14	SQ. 15
GRSURF2	201	5	1	2	1	2	1	2	3	2	5	7	1	2	3	1
GRSURF3	202	1	0	1	0	0	0	1	0	0	0	1	1	0	2	0
GRSURF4	203	0	0	0	0	0	0	0	1	1	0	0	0	0	0	0
GRSURF5	204	1	0	0	0	0	0	0	0	0	1	1	0	0	1	0
GRSURF6	205	0	3	0	0	0	0	0	0	0	0	0	0	0	0	0
GRSURF7	206	0	1	1	0	0	0	0	0	0	0	0	0	0	0	0
GRKLNWST	208	0	0	0	0	0	0	0	0	0	0	0	0	0	0	0
GROLLAFL	209	3	6	6	2	1	4	1	0	0	0	6	0	1	5	0
GROLLASL	210	0	0	0	0	0	0	0	0	0	0	0	0	3	0	0
GROLLASS	211	0	0	0	0	0	0	0	0	0	0	0	0	0	0	0
GRRIM1	214	1	3	5	3	1	1	0	0	0	1	0	2	0	3	0
GRRIM2	215	1	0	0	1	0	0	0	0	0	0	0	0	0	0	0
GRRIM3	216	0	0	0	0	0	0	0	0	0	0	0	0	0	0	0
GRRIM4	217	0	0	3	0	1	7	1	0	0	2	3	3	1	12	0
GRRIM5	218	19	5	45	6	12	8	6	3	3	12	22	14	8	21	7
GRRIM6	219	1	0	0	0	0	0	1	0	0	0	0	0	0	5	0
GRRIM7	220	0	0	1	0	0	0	0	0	0	0	0	0	0	1	0
GRRIM8	221	0	0	0	0	0	0	0	0	0	0	0	0	0	0	0
GRRIM9	222	0	0	0	0	0	0	0	0	0	0	0	0	0	0	0
GRRIM10	223	0	0	0	0	0	0	0	0	0	0	0	0	0	0	0
GRRIM12	225	0	0	0	0	0	0	1	0	0	0	0	0	0	0	0
GRRIM15	228	0	0	0	0	0	0	0	0	0	0	0	0	0	0	1
GRRIM16	229	0	0	0	0	0	0	0	0	0	0	0	0	0	0	0
TOTGRDEC	230	18	12	44	1	13	16	10	9	7	17	25	21	11	51	10
GRDECOWB	231	11	6	32	1	6	1	5	2	3	8	18	12	7	27	7

	VAR. NO.	SQ. 16	SQ. 17	SQ. 18	SQ. 19	SQ. 20	SQ. 21	SQ. 22	SQ. 23	SQ. 24	SQ. 25	SQ. 26	SQ. 27	SQ. 28	SQ. 29	SQ. 30
GRSURF2	201	1	23	1	6	3	0	2	1	0	1	1	2	3	1	1
GRSURF3	202	1	0	2	2	0	0	0	0	0	0	0	0	0	1	0
GRSURF4	203	0	0	0	0	0	0	0	0	0	0	0	0	0	1	0
GRSURF5	204	0	0	0	0	0	0	0	0	0	0	0	1	0	0	0
GRSURF6	205	1	19	0	2	2	0	1	0	0	0	0	0	0	0	0
GRSURF7	206	0	0	0	2	0	0	0	0	0	0	0	0	0	0	0
GRKLNWST	208	0	0	0	0	0	0	0	0	0	0	0	0	0	0	0
GROLLAFL	209	1	7	0	4	1	0	2	0	0	1	3	8	3	1	0
GROLLASL	210	0	0	0	0	0	0	0	0	0	0	0	0	0	0	0
GROLLASS	211	0	0	0	0	0	0	2	1	0	1	0	0	1	2	1
GRRIM1	214	1	5	0	1	2	0	3	2	1	5	2	5	1	0	0
GRRIM2	215	0	0	0	0	0	0	0	0	0	0	0	1	0	0	0
GRRIM3	216	0	0	0	0	0	0	0	0	0	0	0	0	0	0	0
GRRIM4	217	4	3	0	7	2	0	0	1	0	3	3	2	0	1	0
GRRIM5	218	9	31	7	42	27	0	5	0	0	0	5	1	0	2	0
GRRIM6	219	0	5	0	0	0	0	0	0	2	0	0	0	0	0	0
GRRIM7	220	0	0	0	0	0	0	0	0	0	5	1	0	0	0	0
GRRIM8	221	0	0	0	0	0	0	0	0	0	0	0	0	0	0	0
GRRIM9	222	0	0	0	0	0	0	0	0	0	0	0	0	0	0	0
GRRIM10	223	0	0	0	0	0	0	0	0	0	0	0	0	0	0	0
GRRIM12	225	0	0	0	0	0	0	0	0	0	0	0	0	0	0	0
GRRIM15	228	0	0	0	1	1	0	0	0	0	5	1	1	0	2	1
GRRIM16	229	0	0	0	0	0	0	0	0	0	0	0	0	0	0	0
TOTGRDEC	230	8	72	8	40	29	1	8	2	2	6	8	7	2	3	1
GRDECOWB	231	3	28	4	26	23	0	5	0	1	2	3	0	0	2	0

	VAR. NO.	SQ. 31	SQ. 32	SQ. 34	SQ. 35	SQ. 36	SQ. 37	SQ. 38	SQ. 39	SQ. 40	SQ. 41	SQ. 42	SQ. 43	SQ. 44	SQ. 45	SQ. 46
GRSURF2	201	0	0	2	0	5	3	3	8	4	5	11	5	1	0	1
GRSURF3	202	0	0	0	1	0	0	2	2	0	4	5	3	0	0	1
GRSURF4	203	0	0	1	3	4	0	1	2	3	10	4	2	0	0	1
GRSURF5	204	0	0	0	0	1	1	1	0	0	1	0	2	0	0	0
GRSURF6	205	0	0	0	1	0	0	0	1	0	2	1	2	0	0	1
GRSURF7	206	0	0	0	0	0	0	0	1	0	1	1	2	0	0	0
GRKLNWST	208	0	0	0	0	0	0	0	1	0	0	0	0	0	0	0
GROLLAFL	209	0	2	4	8	2	5	3	8	8	22	25	12	0	1	1
GROLLASL	210	0	0	0	0	0	2	1	4	2	23	6	0	0	2	0
GROLLASS	211	0	0	3	1	1	4	4	17	8	36	28	18	0	0	0
GRRIM1	214	1	1	40	28	15	71	43	74	58	119	138	73	19	9	23
GRRIM2	215	0	0	1	2	1	5	2	4	2	3	7	4	2	0	0
GRRIM3	216	0	0	0	2	0	1	3	3	1	5	0	1	0	0	0
GRRIM4	217	0	1	25	37	14	58	20	51	42	78	151	65	8	3	6
GRRIM5	218	0	1	0	0	0	0	0	0	0	0	0	0	0	0	0
GRRIM6	219	1	1	0	1	1	1	0	0	0	2	0	5	0	0	0
GRRIM7	220	0	0	0	2	1	6	0	5	2	1	6	3	0	1	0
GRRIM8	221	0	0	0	0	0	1	0	2	0	0	2	0	1	0	0
GRRIM9	222	0	0	0	0	0	0	0	0	0	0	0	0	0	0	0
GRRIM10	223	0	0	0	0	0	0	0	1	0	0	0	0	0	0	0
GRRIM12	225	0	0	1	1	0	0	1	0	0	4	2	1	1	0	0
GRRIM15	228	0	0	1	2	0	1	1	2	1	4	3	0	0	0	0
GRRIM16	229	0	0	0	1	0	3	0	4	5	1	8	2	0	0	1
TOTGRDEC	230	1	2	15	7	6	6	4	12	8	25	26	16	3	3	5
GRDECOWB	231	0	0	0	0	0	1	0	0	1	0	0	2	0	1	0

APPENDIX TO CHAPTER 2

LENCHO DIEGO SURVEY DATA -- VARIABLES 201-231

	VAR. NO.	SQ. 47	SQ. 48	SQ. 49	SQ. 50	SQ. 51	SQ. 52	SQ. 53	SQ. 54	SQ. 55	SQ. 56	SQ. 57	SQ. 58	SQ. 59	SQ. 60	SQ. 61
GRSURF2	201	3	4	5	1	6	6	0	4	7	9	4	7	3	17	2
GRSURF3	202	1	0	3	3	3	0	0	2	0	0	0	1	3	2	0
GRSURF4	203	1	7	0	4	2	0	2	3	2	1	0	1	0	1	1
GRSURF5	204	0	1	0	0	0	0	0	0	0	0	0	0	0	1	2
GRSURF6	205	0	3	3	0	1	0	1	1	1	0	0	0	0	1	1
GRSURF7	206	0	0	0	0	0	0	1	0	0	0	0	1	0	1	0
GRKLNWST	208	0	0	0	0	0	0	0	3	0	0	0	0	0	0	0
GROLLAFL	209	3	3	7	6	2	3	0	4	8	2	3	8	6	6	4
GROLLASL	210	1	3	2	0	0	0	1	6	4	0	1	0	0	2	5
GROLLASS	211	6	6	5	4	12	2	7	4	15	14	4	27	3	11	4
GRRIM1	214	21	32	71	26	37	44	28	43	145	130	26	146	41	102	39
GRRIM2	215	1	3	0	0	2	1	0	1	7	2	0	0	1	2	2
GRRIM3	216	0	0	3	0	0	0	0	2	5	1	4	1	1	3	1
GRRIM4	217	22	47	63	27	42	21	25	25	79	65	12	62	13	51	45
GRRIM5	218	0	0	0	0	0	0	0	0	0	0	0	0	0	0	0
GRRIM6	219	0	1	1	0	1	0	2	1	0	0	0	0	0	0	2
GRRIM7	220	1	4	2	0	2	0	0	1	2	5	0	3	1	3	0
GRRIM8	221	0	0	0	0	1	0	0	0	0	1	2	0	0	1	0
GRRIM9	222	0	0	0	0	0	0	0	0	0	0	0	0	0	0	0
GRRIM10	223	0	0	0	0	0	0	0	0	0	0	0	0	0	1	0
GRRIM12	225	1	0	0	0	0	0	0	0	1	0	0	2	1	1	0
GRRIM15	228	1	3	1	0	2	2	0	1	0	1	0	1	0	1	1
GRRIM16	229	3	3	5	0	1	2	2	3	11	0	3	0	1	2	0
TOTGRDEC	230	2	11	10	3	11	4	6	8	18	10	10	20	6	18	7
GRDECOWB	231	0	0	0	0	0	0	0	0	0	0	0	1	1	2	1

	VAR. NO.	SQ. 62	SQ. 63	SQ. 64	SQ. 65	SQ. 66	SQ. 67	SQ. 68	SQ. 69	SQ. 70	SQ. 71	SQ. 72	SQ. 73	SQ. 74	SQ. 75	SQ. 76
GRSURF2	201	3	2	27	6	17	3	19	5	0	7	5	8	5	2	10
GRSURF3	202	0	0	17	6	2	3	12	0	1	2	4	6	4	4	0
GRSURF4	203	0	0	9	2	2	0	3	3	0	0	0	0	0	0	1
GRSURF5	204	0	0	8	0	0	1	6	1	1	4	3	5	3	1	1
GRSURF6	205	0	0	39	10	1	0	13	0	1	5	3	6	5	2	1
GRSURF7	206	0	0	10	1	1	0	17	0	0	3	0	0	0	0	0
GRKLNWST	208	0	0	60	4	15	0	63	0	0	1	0	0	0	0	0
GROLLAFL	209	2	0	39	4	12	2	15	4	7	15	11	15	9	6	19
GROLLASL	210	0	0	7	0	0	0	0	0	1	3	1	2	2	1	3
GROLLASS	211	1	2	54	4	6	1	7	5	7	26	0	1	0	0	0
GRRIM1	214	30	8	471	129	139	21	48	65	18	180	90	224	90	59	164
GRRIM2	215	1	0	32	18	2	3	24	3	1	7	4	1	2	1	0
GRRIM3	216	0	0	16	6	2	2	25	0	4	0	4	33	13	13	23
GRRIM4	217	17	6	265	71	43	8	58	31	27	94	32	82	46	25	47
GRRIM5	218	0	0	0	0	0	0	0	0	0	0	0	0	0	0	0
GRRIM6	219	0	0	4	2	0	0	6	0	1	0	0	0	3	0	0
GRRIM7	220	0	0	4	0	0	1	2	1	0	3	0	0	1	0	0
GRRIM8	221	1	0	6	1	2	0	2	0	0	1	0	6	4	0	4
GRRIM9	222	0	0	3	0	0	2	1	0	0	0	0	4	1	2	3
GRRIM10	223	0	0	2	0	1	0	0	0	0	1	0	3	0	0	2
GRRIM12	225	0	0	1	1	1	1	1	1	0	2	2	15	9	0	14
GRRIM15	228	0	0	5	2	0	1	2	1	0	0	0	0	0	0	1
GRRIM16	229	0	1	20	3	3	0	2	2	0	3	0	0	0	0	3
TOTGRDEC	230	0	1	77	44	9	6	23	16	5	20	9	64	49	28	19
GRDECOWB	231	0	1	3	3	0	0	4	1	0	1	0	2	1	1	1

	VAR. NO.	SQ. 77	SQ. 78	SQ. 79	SQ. 80	SQ. 81	SQ. 82	SQ. 83	SQ. 84	SQ. 85	SQ. 86	SQ. 87	SQ. 88	SQ. 89	SQ. 90	SQ. 91
GRSURF2	201	6	11	11	9	3	1	1	3	2	2	4	8	2	1	1
GRSURF3	202	4	3	2	4	9	1	0	3	2	0	3	3	0	0	0
GRSURF4	203	0	0	1	0	0	0	0	0	0	1	1	2	1	0	0
GRSURF5	204	2	0	2	1	6	0	2	0	2	0	0	3	1	0	0
GRSURF6	205	4	2	2	5	6	0	0	4	0	0	2	2	2	0	0
GRSURF7	206	0	0	0	0	0	0	0	0	0	0	0	1	0	0	0
GRKLNWST	208	0	0	0	0	0	0	0	0	0	0	0	0	0	0	0
GROLLAFL	209	8	14	11	7	7	3	5	1	2	5	18	29	5	1	0
GROLLASL	210	1	1	1	1	0	0	0	1	0	0	4	0	0	0	0
GROLLASS	211	0	0	0	0	0	1	0	1	4	0	7	9	6	0	0
GRRIM1	214	67	104	75	64	54	42	11	34	29	34	60	63	47	14	3
GRRIM2	215	1	4	2	2	3	2	0	1	3	2	4	2	0	0	1
GRRIM3	216	14	16	10	4	6	8	1	4	8	0	4	5	1	0	0
GRRIM4	217	30	23	29	25	12	22	5	14	29	8	23	29	27	2	2
GRRIM5	218	0	0	0	0	0	0	0	0	0	0	0	0	0	0	0
GRRIM6	219	0	0	0	0	0	0	0	0	0	0	0	0	0	0	0
GRRIM7	220	0	0	0	0	0	0	1	0	0	0	0	0	1	0	0
GRRIM8	221	1	3	1	0	1	0	0	0	0	0	0	0	0	1	0
GRRIM9	222	2	0	1	0	1	0	1	0	1	0	0	0	0	0	0
GRRIM10	223	0	3	1	2	0	0	1	0	1	0	0	0	0	0	0
GRRIM12	225	3	4	2	1	4	0	1	2	0	0	0	0	0	0	0
GRRIM15	228	1	0	1	0	0	0	0	2	2	0	1	1	0	0	1
GRRIM16	229	0	0	0	0	0	3	1	2	3	4	8	6	2	0	0
TOTGRDEC	230	10	32	29	16	7	7	2	9	8	7	18	9	9	2	2
GRDECOWB	231	1	2	1	0	0	0	1	1	0	1	2	0	1	0	0

LENCHO DIEGO SURVEY DATA -- VARIABLES 232-267

	VAR. NO.	SQ. 1	SQ. 2	SQ. 3	SQ. 4	SQ. 5	SQ. 6	SQ. 7	SQ. 8	SQ. 9	SQ. 10	SQ. 11	SQ. 12	SQ. 13	SQ. 14	SQ. 15
GRDECCWB	232	1	2	0	0	0	1	0	0	0	1	0	2	0	0	0
GRDECCYL	233	0	0	1	0	0	7	0	2	0	1	0	1	0	10	0
GRDECINC	234	0	0	0	0	0	0	0	0	0	0	0	0	0	0	0
GRDECOTR	235	0	0	0	0	0	0	0	0	0	0	0	1	0	0	0
GRDCBWLB	236	0	2	5	0	3	0	0	0	3	6	1	5	3	5	2
GRDCJARB	237	4	0	0	0	2	0	0	0	0	1	1	0	1	2	1
GRDCINDB	238	2	2	6	0	2	7	5	5	1	0	5	0	0	7	0
GRNODEC	240	16	8	31	11	10	12	5	8	1	7	16	6	8	12	1
GRINCISD	241	18	12	44	1	13	16	9	9	6	17	24	20	11	51	10
GRCARV	243	0	0	0	0	0	0	0	0	0	0	0	0	0	0	0
GRRASP	244	0	0	0	0	0	0	0	0	0	0	0	0	0	0	0
GRPUNCT	246	2	2	2	0	0	0	1	0	0	0	3	2	4	11	1
GRAPPDOT	248	0	0	0	0	0	0	0	0	0	0	0	0	0	0	0
GRDECOTM	255	0	0	0	0	0	0	0	0	0	0	0	1	0	0	0
GRMOT1	257	0	0	0	0	0	0	0	0	0	0	0	0	0	0	0
GRMOT2	258	0	0	0	0	0	0	0	0	0	0	0	0	0	0	0
GRMOT3	259	6	1	5	0	1	1	0	1	3	2	4	7	0	5	1
GRMOT4	260	0	0	0	0	1	0	1	0	1	0	0	0	0	0	0
GRMOT5	261	1	1	0	0	1	0	2	0	0	0	0	1	0	1	0
GRMOT6	262	0	1	0	0	1	0	0	0	0	1	0	0	0	0	0
GRMOT7	263	1	0	2	1	0	1	1	0	0	2	3	0	0	3	1
GRMOT8	264	0	0	0	0	0	0	0	0	0	0	0	0	0	1	0
GRMOT9	265	1	2	1	0	0	0	0	0	0	0	0	0	0	0	0
GRMOT10	266	2	2	2	0	0	0	0	0	0	0	3	3	4	11	2
GRMOT11	267	0	0	2	0	1	0	0	1	0	2	0	0	0	2	1

	VAR. NO.	SQ. 16	SQ. 17	SQ. 18	SQ. 19	SQ. 20	SQ. 21	SQ. 22	SQ. 23	SQ. 24	SQ. 25	SQ. 26	SQ. 27	SQ. 28	SQ. 29	SQ. 30
GRDECCWB	232	0	0	0	1	1	0	1	0	0	0	1	1	0	0	0
GRDECCYL	233	3	2	0	1	0	0	0	0	1	0	1	4	0	0	0
GRDECINC	234	0	0	0	0	0	0	0	0	0	0	0	0	0	0	0
GRDECOTR	235	0	0	0	0	1	0	0	1	0	0	0	0	0	0	0
GRDCBWLB	236	0	15	3	7	2	1	0	1	0	1	1	0	0	1	1
GRDCJARB	237	2	5	1	0	2	0	0	0	0	3	2	1	0	0	0
GRDCINDB	238	0	21	0	4	0	0	2	0	0	0	0	1	2	0	0
GRNODEC	240	10	25	3	31	13	1	6	5	1	22	11	13	17	6	2
GRINCISD	241	8	72	8	38	29	1	6	2	2	4	8	7	1	3	1
GRCARV	243	0	0	0	0	0	0	0	0	0	2	0	0	0	0	0
GRRASP	244	0	0	0	0	0	0	0	0	0	0	0	0	0	0	0
GRPUNCT	246	1	2	0	4	3	0	0	0	0	0	0	0	0	0	0
GRAPPDOT	248	0	0	0	0	0	0	0	0	0	0	0	0	0	0	0
GRDECOTM	255	0	0	0	2	0	0	0	0	0	0	0	0	1	0	0
GRMOT1	257	0	0	0	0	0	0	0	0	0	0	0	0	0	0	0
GRMOT2	258	0	0	0	0	0	0	0	0	0	0	0	0	0	0	0
GRMOT3	259	1	16	3	8	8	0	3	0	0	0	1	0	0	0	0
GRMOT4	260	1	0	0	0	0	0	0	0	0	0	0	0	0	0	0
GRMOT5	261	1	1	0	0	1	0	0	0	0	0	0	0	0	0	0
GRMOT6	262	0	1	2	3	0	0	0	1	0	0	0	0	0	0	0
GRMOT7	263	0	4	0	1	0	0	0	0	0	1	3	2	0	0	0
GRMOT8	264	0	0	0	0	0	0	0	0	2	1	1	1	0	1	0
GRMOT9	265	0	9	0	0	4	0	0	0	0	0	0	0	0	0	0
GRMOT10	266	1	1	0	4	3	0	0	0	0	0	0	0	0	0	0
GRMOT11	267	0	0	0	1	0	0	0	0	0	0	0	0	0	0	0

	VAR. NO.	SQ. 31	SQ. 32	SQ. 34	SQ. 35	SQ. 36	SQ. 37	SQ. 38	SQ. 39	SQ. 40	SQ. 41	SQ. 42	SQ. 43	SQ. 44	SQ. 45	SQ. 46
GRDECCWB	232	0	0	1	0	0	0	0	0	1	0	2	0	1	0	0
GRDECCYL	233	0	0	4	2	1	0	0	1	0	6	1	1	1	0	1
GRDECINC	234	0	1	0	0	0	0	1	0	3	2	5	4	0	0	1
GRDECOTR	235	0	0	0	0	0	0	0	0	0	0	1	0	0	0	0
GRDCBWLB	236	1	0	6	2	3	3	2	8	3	16	14	0	1	2	4
GRDCJARB	237	0	0	2	2	0	1	0	1	0	1	1	0	0	0	0
GRDCINDB	238	0	1	2	1	2	1	1	1	0	0	2	0	0	0	0
GRNODEC	240	4	9	77	97	40	163	92	197	144	344	440	232	30	20	35
GRINCISD	241	1	1	13	6	5	6	3	11	8	22	27	15	3	2	5
GRCARV	243	0	0	2	2	1	0	1	0	0	3	0	0	0	1	0
GRRASP	244	0	0	0	1	0	0	0	1	0	0	1	1	0	0	0
GRPUNCT	246	0	0	0	0	0	0	0	0	0	0	0	0	0	0	0
GRAPPDOT	248	0	1	0	1	0	0	0	0	0	0	0	0	0	0	0
GRDECOTM	255	0	0	0	0	0	0	0	0	0	0	0	0	0	0	0
GRMOT1	257	0	0	0	0	0	1	0	0	1	0	0	0	1	0	0
GRMOT2	258	0	0	3	0	0	0	0	0	0	0	1	0	1	0	0
GRMOT3	259	0	0	0	0	0	0	0	0	0	0	0	1	0	0	0
GRMOT4	260	0	0	0	0	0	0	0	0	2	4	5	2	0	0	0
GRMOT5	261	0	0	0	0	0	0	0	0	0	0	0	0	0	0	0
GRMOT6	262	0	0	2	0	0	0	0	0	0	1	0	1	0	0	1
GRMOT7	263	0	0	2	1	0	0	0	0	0	0	0	0	0	1	0
GRMOT8	264	0	0	0	0	0	0	0	0	0	2	0	0	0	0	0
GRMOT9	265	0	0	0	0	0	0	0	0	0	0	0	0	0	0	0
GRMOT10	266	0	0	0	0	0	0	0	0	0	0	0	0	0	0	0
GRMOT11	267	0	0	0	0	0	1	0	0	0	0	0	0	0	0	0

APPENDIX TO CHAPTER 2   105

LENCHO DIEGO SURVEY DATA -- VARIABLES 232-267

	VAR. NO.	SQ. 47	SQ. 48	SQ. 49	SQ. 50	SQ. 51	SQ. 52	SQ. 53	SQ. 54	SQ. 55	SQ. 56	SQ. 57	SQ. 58	SQ. 59	SQ. 60	SQ. 61
GRDECCWB	232	0	1	1	0	3	0	0	1	0	1	0	0	1	1	0
GPDECCYL	233	0	0	0	0	2	0	1	1	2	2	2	3	0	2	0
GRDECINC	234	0	1	0	2	0	0	0	1	1	0	2	3	0	2	0
GRDECOTR	235	0	0	0	0	0	0	0	0	0	1	0	0	0	0	0
GPDCBWLB	236	2	8	8	1	5	3	3	3	11	4	5	8	3	7	6
GRDCJARB	237	0	1	1	0	0	1	1	0	1	0	0	5	0	1	0
GRDCINDB	238	0	0	0	0	1	0	1	1	3	1	1	0	1	3	0
GPNODEC	240	68	145	183	93	114	86	70	104	284	253	64	285	74	197	115
GRINCISD	241	2	10	10	3	7	3	6	7	16	8	7	18	5	18	6
GRCARV	243	0	1	0	0	0	1	1	1	1	1	3	3	1	0	0
GRRASP	244	0	0	0	0	1	0	0	0	1	0	0	1	0	1	1
GRPUNCT	246	0	0	0	0	0	0	0	0	0	0	0	0	0	0	0
GRAPPDOT	248	0	0	0	0	0	0	0	0	0	1	0	1	0	0	0
GPDECOTM	255	0	0	0	0	0	0	0	0	1	0	0	0	0	0	0
GRMOT1	257	0	0	0	0	0	0	0	0	0	0	0	0	0	3	1
GRMOT2	258	0	0	0	0	0	0	0	0	0	0	0	0	0	1	0
GRMOT3	259	0	0	0	0	0	0	0	0	0	0	0	0	0	0	0
GRMOT4	260	0	3	0	2	0	0	1	1	0	0	2	4	1	4	0
GRMOT5	261	0	0	0	0	0	0	0	0	0	0	0	0	0	0	0
GPMOT6	262	0	0	0	0	0	0	0	0	0	0	0	0	0	0	0
GPMOT7	263	0	0	0	0	0	0	0	0	0	0	0	0	0	0	0
GRMOT8	264	0	0	0	0	0	0	0	1	0	0	0	0	0	0	0
GPMOT9	265	0	0	0	0	0	0	0	0	0	0	0	0	0	0	0
GRMOT10	266	0	0	0	0	0	0	0	0	0	0	0	0	0	0	0
GRMOT11	267	0	0	1	0	0	0	0	0	0	0	1	0	0	0	0

	VAR. NO.	SQ. 62	SQ. 63	SQ. 64	SQ. 65	SQ. 66	SQ. 67	SQ. 68	SQ. 69	SQ. 70	SQ. 71	SQ. 72	SQ. 73	SQ. 74	SQ. 75	SQ. 76
GRDECCWB	232	0	0	12	5	1	1	2	0	0	1	1	1	1	0	0
GPDECCYL	233	0	0	13	4	1	2	3	2	0	7	2	17	4	5	0
GRDECINC	234	0	0	6	1	0	0	2	3	0	1	0	0	0	1	0
GRDECOTR	235	0	0	1	0	0	0	0	0	0	0	0	0	0	0	0
GRDCBWLB	236	0	0	38	37	7	3	10	6	5	2	0	44	22	12	5
GRDCJARB	237	0	0	3	0	0	0	0	1	0	2	5	0	6	4	1
GRDCINDB	238	0	0	0	0	0	0	1	4	0	6	1	0	15	5	12
GRNODEC	240	0	19	1044	252	235	43	223	129	0	366	148	397	193	111	301
GRINCISD	241	0	1	68	44	8	6	21	13	5	19	8	63	49	26	19
GPCARV	243	0	0	6	2	1	0	1	2	0	4	1	1	0	2	0
GRRASP	244	0	0	4	2	0	0	0	0	1	0	0	8	3	1	2
GRPUNCT	246	0	0	0	0	0	0	0	0	0	0	0	0	0	0	0
GRAPPDOT	248	0	0	0	0	0	0	0	0	0	0	0	0	2	0	0
GRDECOTM	255	0	0	0	0	0	0	0	1	0	0	0	0	0	0	0
GPMOT1	257	0	0	2	0	0	0	1	1	0	0	0	0	0	0	0
GRMOT2	258	0	0	1	0	0	1	3	0	0	1	0	1	2	0	1
GRMOT3	259	0	0	0	0	0	0	1	0	0	0	0	0	0	0	0
GPMOT4	260	0	0	5	5	0	0	1	1	1	0	0	0	0	0	2
GRMOT5	261	0	0	0	0	0	0	0	0	0	0	0	0	0	0	0
GRMOT6	262	0	0	1	1	0	0	0	0	0	2	0	0	1	0	0
GRMOT7	263	0	0	2	2	0	0	0	0	0	0	1	2	1	0	0
GRMOT8	264	0	0	0	0	0	0	0	0	0	0	0	0	0	0	0
GRMOT9	265	0	0	0	1	0	0	0	0	0	0	0	0	0	0	0
GRMOT10	266	0	0	0	0	0	0	0	0	0	0	0	0	0	0	0
GRMOT11	267	0	0	0	0	0	0	0	0	0	0	0	0	0	0	0

	VAR. NO.	SQ. 77	SQ. 78	SQ. 79	SQ. 80	SQ. 81	SQ. 82	SQ. 83	SQ. 84	SQ. 85	SQ. 86	SQ. 87	SQ. 88	SQ. 89	SQ. 90	SQ. 91
GRDECCWB	232	0	2	1	0	0	1	0	0	1	0	1	2	1	0	0
GRDECCYL	233	2	4	7	4	0	0	0	1	0	2	1	2	0	0	0
GRDECINC	234	0	0	1	0	0	0	0	0	0	0	0	0	0	3	0
GRDECOTR	235	0	0	0	0	0	0	0	0	0	0	0	0	0	0	0
GRDCBWLB	236	6	20	12	9	7	5	1	7	7	3	12	3	4	1	2
GRDCJARB	237	0	0	1	0	0	0	0	0	0	0	2	0	1	0	0
GRDCINDB	238	1	4	6	3	0	0	0	0	0	1	0	2	2	1	0
GRNODEC	240	141	179	134	111	106	94	27	0	69	58	141	159	102	2	9
GRINCISD	241	10	31	25	16	7	7	2	7	8	6	0	9	9	0	2
GRCARV	243	0	0	4	0	0	0	0	0	0	1	1	0	0	0	0
GRRASP	244	0	2	1	0	1	0	0	1	0	0	0	0	0	0	0
GRPUNCT	246	0	0	0	0	0	0	0	0	0	0	0	0	0	0	0
GRAPPDOT	248	0	0	0	0	1	0	0	0	0	0	0	0	0	0	0
GRDECOTM	255	0	2	0	0	0	0	0	0	0	0	1	0	0	0	0
GRMOT1	257	0	0	0	0	0	0	0	0	0	1	0	0	1	0	0
GRMOT2	258	0	3	2	1	0	0	0	1	0	0	1	0	3	0	1
GRMOT3	259	0	0	0	0	0	0	0	0	0	0	0	0	0	0	0
GRMOT4	260	0	4	0	0	0	1	1	0	1	0	2	2	0	0	0
GRMOT5	261	0	0	0	0	0	0	0	0	0	0	0	0	0	0	0
GRMOT6	262	0	0	0	0	0	0	0	0	0	0	0	0	1	0	0
GPMOT7	263	0	2	0	2	0	0	0	0	0	0	3	0	0	0	0
GPMOT8	264	0	0	0	0	0	0	0	0	0	0	0	0	0	0	0
GRMOT9	265	0	0	0	0	0	0	0	0	0	0	0	0	0	0	0
GRMOT10	266	0	0	0	0	0	0	0	0	0	0	0	0	0	0	0
GRMOT11	267	0	0	0	0	0	0	0	0	0	0	0	0	0	0	0

LENCHO DIEGO SURVEY DATA -- VARIABLES 268-311

	VAR. NO.	SQ. 1	SQ. 2	SQ. 3	SQ. 4	SQ. 5	SQ. 6	SQ. 7	SQ. 8	SQ. 9	SQ. 10	SQ. 11	SQ. 12	SQ. 13	SQ. 14	SQ. 15
GRMOT12	268	0	0	0	0	1	1	1	1	0	0	0	0	0	3	0
GRMOT13	269	0	3	8	0	2	9	3	2	1	3	1	1	2	2	3
GRMOT14	270	0	0	0	0	0	0	0	0	0	0	0	0	0	0	0
GRMOT15	271	3	1	15	0	0	0	1	0	0	2	7	5	2	14	1
GRMOT17	273	0	0	1	0	0	0	0	0	0	0	0	0	0	0	0
GRMOT19	275	0	0	0	0	0	0	0	0	0	0	0	0	0	0	0
GRMOT20	276	0	0	0	0	0	0	0	0	0	0	0	0	0	0	0
GRMOT21	277	0	0	0	0	0	0	0	0	0	0	0	0	0	1	0
GRMOT23	279	0	0	0	0	0	0	0	0	0	0	0	0	0	0	0
GRMOT24	280	0	0	0	1	1	4	0	0	2	2	1	0	0	9	2
GRMOT25	281	0	0	0	0	0	0	0	0	0	0	0	0	0	0	0
GRMOT26	282	0	0	0	0	0	0	0	0	0	0	0	0	0	0	0
GRINDMOT	284	3	1	11	0	3	3	1	4	1	4	8	5	3	10	2
GROTHMOT	285	1	0	0	0	0	0	1	0	0	0	0	0	1	0	0
TOTQRTZ	301	15	19	1	7	5	6	6	4	3	1	8	4	3	4	3
TOTCHERT	302	2	3	3	3	1	1	1	4	0	2	5	1	2	3	2
TOTOBSID	303	2	2	6	2	1	0	0	1	1	5	2	1	6	6	0
QRTCHNKS	304	13	19	0	4	5	6	6	0	3	0	6	1	0	2	2
QRTSTRK	305	2	0	1	3	0	0	0	0	0	1	2	3	3	2	1
CHCORES	306	0	0	0	0	0	0	0	0	0	0	0	0	0	0	0
CHANGDEB	307	1	1	0	1	1	0	0	2	0	1	2	0	2	0	0
CHUNUTFL	308	1	1	2	2	0	0	0	0	0	1	2	1	0	0	0
CHUTILFL	309	0	1	1	0	0	1	1	1	0	0	1	0	0	0	1
CHRETUN1	310	0	0	1	0	0	0	0	1	0	0	0	0	0	3	1
CHSDSCR	311	0	0	0	0	0	0	0	1	0	0	0	0	0	2	1

	VAR. NO.	SQ. 16	SQ. 17	SQ. 18	SQ. 19	SQ. 20	SQ. 21	SQ. 22	SQ. 23	SQ. 24	SQ. 25	SQ. 26	SQ. 27	SQ. 28	SQ. 29	SQ. 30
GRMOT12	268	1	4	0	1	2	0	0	0	0	1	0	0	0	0	0
GRMOT13	269	0	25	2	7	4	0	0	0	0	0	1	0	0	1	0
GRMOT14	270	0	0	0	0	0	0	0	0	0	0	1	0	0	0	0
GRMOT15	271	1	2	0	6	4	0	1	0	0	0	0	0	0	0	0
GRMOT17	273	0	0	0	0	0	0	0	0	0	0	0	0	0	0	0
GRMOT19	275	0	0	0	0	1	0	0	0	0	0	0	0	0	0	0
GRMOT20	276	0	0	0	0	0	0	0	0	0	0	0	0	0	0	0
GRMOT21	277	0	0	0	1	0	0	0	0	0	2	0	0	0	0	0
GRMOT23	279	0	0	0	0	0	0	0	1	0	0	0	0	0	0	0
GRMOT24	280	1	2	2	1	0	0	0	0	0	0	0	0	0	0	0
GRMOT25	281	0	0	0	0	0	0	0	0	0	0	0	0	0	0	0
GRMOT26	282	0	0	0	0	0	0	0	0	0	0	0	0	0	0	0
GRINDMOT	284	1	9	1	7	3	0	3	0	0	2	1	4	1	1	0
GROTHMOT	285	0	0	0	2	1	1	0	1	0	1	1	0	0	0	1
TOTQRTZ	301	2	0	1	5	6	0	0	0	0	0	1	4	4	1	18
TOTCHERT	302	0	4	1	7	13	0	0	0	0	0	8	7	11	0	1
TOTOBSID	303	2	4	1	7	3	3	1	4	5	19	29	15	7	11	14
QRTCHNKS	304	2	0	0	1	4	0	0	0	0	0	1	4	4	0	17
QRTSTRK	305	0	0	0	1	2	0	0	0	0	0	0	0	0	1	1
CHCORES	306	0	0	0	0	0	0	0	0	0	0	1	0	0	0	0
CHANGDEB	307	0	2	0	0	8	0	0	0	0	0	0	5	1	0	0
CHUNUTFL	308	0	1	1	5	5	0	0	0	0	0	4	1	6	0	0
CHUTILFL	309	0	0	0	2	0	0	0	0	0	0	1	1	1	0	0
CHRETUN1	310	0	1	0	0	0	0	0	0	0	0	2	0	3	0	0
CHSDSCR	311	0	0	0	0	0	0	0	0	0	0	2	0	2	0	0

	VAR. NO.	SQ. 31	SQ. 32	SQ. 34	SQ. 35	SQ. 36	SQ. 37	SQ. 38	SQ. 39	SQ. 40	SQ. 41	SQ. 42	SQ. 43	SQ. 44	SQ. 45	SQ. 46
GRMOT12	268	0	1	1	1	1	2	1	1	2	2	10	0	1	0	1
GRMOT13	269	0	0	1	0	0	0	0	1	0	4	0	1	0	0	0
GRMOT14	270	0	0	1	1	2	0	0	1	0	0	3	0	1	0	0
GRMOT15	271	0	0	0	0	0	0	0	0	0	0	0	0	0	0	0
GRMOT17	273	0	0	0	1	0	0	0	0	0	0	3	0	0	0	0
GRMOT19	275	0	0	0	0	0	0	0	0	0	1	0	0	0	0	0
GRMOT20	276	0	0	0	0	0	0	1	0	0	2	0	1	0	0	0
GRMOT21	277	1	0	0	0	0	1	1	0	0	1	1	0	0	0	1
GRMOT23	279	0	0	0	0	0	0	1	1	0	2	0	0	1	0	0
GRMOT24	280	0	1	1	0	1	0	0	0	0	2	2	0	0	0	1
GRMOT25	281	0	0	0	0	0	0	0	0	0	0	0	0	0	0	0
GRMOT26	282	0	0	0	0	0	0	0	0	1	0	4	1	0	0	0
GRINDMOT	284	0	0	4	2	2	3	2	7	3	7	7	8	0	1	1
GROTHMOT	285	0	0	0	2	1	0	1	0	1	1	0	1	0	0	0
TOTQRTZ	301	11	11	0	0	0	0	0	0	0	0	0	0	0	1	0
TOTCHERT	302	0	1	5	3	3	4	7	11	24	36	24	26	2	1	4
TOTOBSID	303	8	26	8	12	5	10	9	19	24	45	29	14	2	7	2
QRTCHNKS	304	8	7	0	0	0	0	0	0	0	0	0	0	0	0	0
QRTSTRK	305	3	4	0	0	0	0	0	0	0	0	0	0	0	1	0
CHCORES	306	0	0	0	0	0	0	0	0	0	0	0	0	0	0	0
CHANGDEB	307	0	0	3	0	3	0	3	3	10	17	15	11	1	0	0
CHUNUTFL	308	0	1	1	3	0	1	2	3	6	13	4	14	1	0	3
CHUTILFL	309	0	0	1	0	0	2	1	2	3	2	2	1	0	1	1
CHRETUN1	310	0	0	0	0	0	1	1	3	3	2	2	0	0	0	0
CHSDSCR	311	0	0	0	0	0	1	0	2	1	1	2	0	0	0	0

APPENDIX TO CHAPTER 2   107

LENCHO DIEGO SURVEY DATA -- VARIABLES 268-311

	VAR. NO.	SQ. 47	SQ. 48	SQ. 49	SQ. 50	SQ. 51	SQ. 52	SQ. 53	SQ. 54	SQ. 55	SQ. 56	SQ. 57	SQ. 58	SQ. 59	SQ. 60	SQ. 61
GRMOT12	268	0	2	0	1	0	0	0	0	4	2	1	1	1	5	0
GRMOT13	269	0	0	0	0	2	0	0	0	0	2	0	0	0	0	0
GRMOT14	270	0	0	0	0	0	0	0	0	1	0	0	1	0	1	0
GRMOT15	271	0	0	0	0	0	0	0	0	0	0	0	0	0	0	0
GRMOT17	273	0	1	1	0	0	0	0	0	0	1	0	0	0	2	0
GRMOT19	275	0	0	0	0	0	0	0	0	0	1	0	0	0	1	0
GRMOT20	276	0	0	0	0	0	0	0	1	1	0	0	0	1	1	0
GRMOT21	277	0	2	0	0	0	0	1	0	0	0	0	0	0	0	0
GRMOT23	279	0	0	0	0	0	0	0	0	1	0	0	0	0	0	0
GRMOT24	280	0	1	1	0	1	0	2	0	3	0	1	2	0	0	1
GRMOT25	281	0	0	0	0	0	0	0	0	0	0	0	0	0	0	0
GRMOT26	282	0	0	0	1	0	0	0	0	1	0	0	0	0	0	0
GRINDMOT	284	2	4	5	0	4	4	3	5	8	2	3	10	1	5	5
GROTHMOT	285	0	0	0	0	0	0	0	0	0	0	0	1	1	0	0
TOTQRTZ	301	0	0	2	1	0	1	0	0	0	1	1	0	1	1	1
TOTCHERT	302	3	2	24	3	4	8	2	9	29	31	5	13	9	15	9
TOTOBSID	303	12	11	24	11	7	5	2	7	41	22	2	12	3	21	4
QRTCHNKS	304	0	0	2	1	0	0	0	0	0	0	1	0	1	0	0
QRTSTRK	305	0	0	0	0	0	1	0	0	0	1	0	0	0	1	1
CHCORES	306	0	0	1	0	0	0	0	0	0	1	0	0	0	0	0
CHANGDEB	307	1	1	9	1	2	3	1	3	15	16	2	5	3	7	7
CHUNUTFL	308	1	0	8	2	2	0	1	4	5	6	2	6	3	3	0
CHUTILFL	309	1	1	3	0	0	4	0	2	5	6	1	2	3	3	2
CHRETUNI	310	0	0	2	0	0	0	0	0	2	2	0	0	0	1	0
CHSDSCR	311	0	0	2	0	0	0	0	0	1	1	0	0	0	1	0

	VAR. NO.	SQ. 62	SQ. 63	SQ. 64	SQ. 65	SQ. 66	SQ. 67	SQ. 68	SQ. 69	SQ. 70	SQ. 71	SQ. 72	SQ. 73	SQ. 74	SQ. 75	SQ. 76
GRMOT12	268	0	0	23	11	4	4	10	4	0	4	3	11	4	2	0
GRMOT13	269	0	0	1	3	0	1	2	2	0	0	0	0	2	0	2
GRMOT14	270	0	0	2	1	0	0	1	1	0	0	1	2	0	0	3
GRMOT15	271	0	0	0	0	0	0	0	0	0	0	0	0	0	0	0
GRMOT17	273	0	0	8	3	3	0	1	3	1	5	2	6	3	0	0
GRMOT19	275	0	0	6	4	0	0	0	0	0	0	0	0	0	0	0
GRMOT20	276	0	0	0	1	0	0	1	0	0	0	1	0	0	0	0
GRMOT21	277	0	0	8	0	0	2	0	0	0	0	0	6	2	2	2
GRMOT23	279	0	0	3	0	0	0	1	0	0	0	0	2	2	0	0
GRMOT24	280	0	0	6	4	0	3	3	1	0	2	0	9	6	7	2
GRMOT25	281	0	0	0	0	0	0	0	0	0	0	0	0	0	0	0
GRMOT26	282	0	0	3	2	0	1	6	1	1	0	0	0	0	0	0
GRINDMOT	284	0	1	19	14	1	1	4	3	2	5	2	32	25	13	7
GROTHMOT	285	0	0	8	4	1	1	1	1	1	5	2	6	4	4	2
TOTQRTZ	301	2	0	0	0	0	1	0	0	1	1	4	14	4	5	20
TOTCHERT	302	3	3	38	23	10	5	9	5	3	18	23	66	22	18	35
TOTOBSID	303	4	1	26	27	13	7	9	3	5	18	9	27	28	10	24
QRTCHNKS	304	1	0	0	0	0	1	0	0	1	1	2	3	2	1	2
QRTSTRK	305	1	0	0	0	0	0	0	0	0	0	2	11	2	4	18
CHCORES	306	0	0	0	0	0	0	0	0	0	0	0	2	0	0	0
CHANGDEB	307	1	2	25	14	6	2	5	3	2	10	10	37	11	11	13
CHUNUTFL	308	0	0	5	6	1	3	2	1	0	2	7	7	2	3	14
CHUTILFL	309	1	1	7	2	3	0	1	0	0	4	6	14	6	3	6
CHRETUNI	310	0	0	1	1	0	0	1	1	1	2	0	4	3	0	1
CHSDSCR	311	0	0	1	1	0	0	1	1	0	1	0	4	2	0	1

	VAR. NO.	SQ. 77	SQ. 78	SQ. 79	SQ. 80	SQ. 81	SQ. 82	SQ. 83	SQ. 84	SQ. 85	SQ. 86	SQ. 87	SQ. 88	SQ. 89	SQ. 90	SQ. 91
GRMOT12	268	0	10	8	1	1	1	1	3	3	2	2	5	2	0	2
GRMOT13	269	1	1	2	0	0	1	0	0	0	0	1	1	0	0	0
GRMOT14	270	0	4	2	0	1	1	0	1	1	0	0	0	0	0	0
GRMOT15	271	0	0	0	0	0	0	0	0	0	0	0	0	0	0	0
GRMOT17	273	0	1	4	1	0	1	0	1	1	2	0	1	0	0	1
GRMOT19	275	1	3	1	0	0	0	0	0	0	0	0	0	0	0	0
GRMOT20	276	0	0	0	1	0	0	0	0	0	1	0	0	0	0	0
GRMOT21	277	0	2	1	4	0	0	0	2	0	0	0	0	0	0	0
GRMOT23	279	1	1	0	0	0	0	0	0	0	0	1	0	1	0	0
GRMOT24	280	1	5	5	0	2	0	0	1	1	2	0	1	1	0	0
GRMOT25	281	0	0	0	0	0	0	0	0	0	0	0	0	0	0	0
GRMOT26	282	0	5	2	0	0	0	1	0	1	1	1	2	2	0	0
GRINDMOT	284	2	7	8	7	4	3	0	2	3	2	3	1	1	2	0
GROTHMOT	285	4	2	2	1	2	0	0	0	0	1	3	2	1	0	0
TOTQRTZ	301	3	2	1	3	1	6	1	0	2	0	0	1	1	0	2
TOTCHERT	302	15	30	12	5	4	8	2	14	12	9	13	6	6	1	0
TOTOBSID	303	4	14	1	2	2	8	1	8	9	4	7	2	1	0	0
QRTCHNKS	304	0	2	1	1	1	2	1	0	1	0	0	0	0	0	1
QRTSTRK	305	3	0	0	0	2	0	4	0	1	0	0	1	1	0	1
CHCORES	306	1	1	0	0	0	0	0	0	0	0	0	0	1	1	0
CHANGDEB	307	4	13	5	0	3	3	1	8	6	4	6	2	1	1	0
CHUNUTFL	308	6	8	3	2	1	1	0	1	1	3	1	3	2	0	0
CHUTILFL	309	2	7	3	2	0	3	0	5	4	0	4	0	2	0	0
CHRETUNI	310	2	1	0	0	0	0	0	0	0	1	1	1	0	0	0
CHSDSCR	311	1	1	0	0	0	0	0	0	0	1	1	0	0	0	0

LENCHO DIEGO SURVEY DATA -- VARIABLES 312-342

	VAR. NO.	SQ. 1	SQ. 2	SQ. 3	SQ. 4	SQ. 5	SQ. 6	SQ. 7	SQ. 8	SQ. 9	SQ. 10	SQ. 11	SQ. 12	SQ. 13	SQ. 14	SQ. 15
CHOTHUN1	313	0	0	0	0	0	0	0	0	0	0	0	0	0	1	0
CHBIFACE	314	0	0	0	0	0	0	0	0	0	0	0	0	0	0	0
CHCHOPPR	318	0	0	0	0	0	0	0	0	0	0	0	0	0	0	0
OBANGDEB	321	1	1	0	2	0	0	0	0	0	0	0	0	0	1	0
OBUNUTFL	322	0	0	1	0	0	0	0	0	0	3	1	1	0	2	0
OBUTILFL	323	0	0	0	0	0	0	0	0	0	1	0	0	0	0	0
OBRETANG	324	1	0	0	0	0	0	0	0	0	0	0	0	0	1	0
OBRETFLK	325	0	0	2	0	0	0	0	1	0	0	0	0	0	0	0
OBSDSCR	326	0	0	1	0	0	0	0	0	0	0	0	0	0	0	0
OBENDSCR	327	0	0	1	0	0	0	0	1	0	0	0	0	0	0	0
OBBLADES	333	1	1	3	0	1	0	0	0	1	1	1	0	6	3	0
OBBLDS1	334	0	1	1	0	0	0	0	0	0	1	1	0	0	3	0
OBBLDS2	335	1	0	1	0	0	0	0	0	1	0	0	0	5	0	0
OBBLDS3	336	0	0	1	0	1	0	0	0	0	0	0	0	1	0	0
OBBLPNTD	337	0	0	0	0	0	0	0	0	0	0	0	0	1	0	0
OBBLGRND	338	0	0	0	0	0	0	0	0	0	1	0	0	0	0	0
OBBL1DOR	339	1	0	3	0	0	0	0	0	0	0	1	0	0	2	0
OBBL2DOR	340	0	0	0	0	1	0	0	0	1	1	0	0	6	1	0
OBBLSNP1	341	0	1	1	0	0	0	0	0	1	1	0	0	0	0	0
OBBLSNP2	342	1	0	0	0	0	0	0	0	0	0	1	0	1	1	0

	VAR. NO.	SQ. 16	SQ. 17	SQ. 18	SQ. 19	SQ. 20	SQ. 21	SQ. 22	SQ. 23	SQ. 24	SQ. 25	SQ. 26	SQ. 27	SQ. 28	SQ. 29	SQ. 30
CHOTHUN1	313	0	1	0	0	0	0	0	0	0	0	0	0	1	0	0
CHBIFACE	314	0	0	0	0	0	0	0	0	0	0	0	0	0	0	0
CHCHOPPR	318	0	0	0	0	0	0	0	0	0	0	0	0	0	0	0
OBANGDEB	321	0	0	0	2	1	0	0	2	1	3	10	6	2	0	4
OBUNUTFL	322	0	1	0	3	1	0	0	1	1	0	4	5	0	0	2
OBUTILFL	323	0	0	0	1	0	0	0	0	0	0	1	0	1	0	1
OBRETANG	324	0	0	0	0	1	0	0	0	1	0	1	0	1	0	0
OBRETFLK	325	2	1	0	0	0	0	0	0	0	0	3	1	2	1	2
OBSDSCR	326	1	0	0	0	0	0	0	0	0	0	1	1	0	1	1
OBENDSCR	327	1	1	0	0	0	0	0	0	0	0	2	0	1	0	0
OBBLADES	333	0	2	1	1	1	3	1	1	3	16	11	3	1	9	5
OBBLDS1	334	0	0	0	0	1	1	1	0	2	7	6	2	0	2	4
OBBLDS2	335	0	2	0	1	0	0	0	0	1	8	5	1	1	5	1
OBBLDS3	336	0	0	1	0	0	2	0	1	0	1	0	0	0	2	0
OBBLPNTD	337	0	0	0	0	0	0	0	0	1	0	1	0	0	1	1
OBBLGRND	338	0	0	0	0	0	0	0	0	0	3	0	0	0	3	0
OBBL1DOR	339	0	1	1	1	0	2	0	0	1	1	4	2	0	2	0
OBBL2DOR	340	0	1	0	0	1	1	1	1	2	15	6	1	1	6	4
OBBLSNP1	341	0	2	0	0	0	1	0	0	0	3	1	1	0	3	2
OBBLSNP2	342	0	0	0	0	1	0	0	0	0	2	0	0	0	2	0

	VAR. NO.	SQ. 31	SQ. 32	SQ. 34	SQ. 35	SQ. 36	SQ. 37	SQ. 38	SQ. 39	SQ. 40	SQ. 41	SQ. 42	SQ. 43	SQ. 44	SQ. 45	SQ. 46
CHOTHUN1	313	0	0	0	0	0	0	1	1	1	1	0	0	0	0	0
CHBIFACE	314	0	0	0	0	0	0	0	0	1	1	1	0	0	0	0
CHCHOPPR	318	0	0	0	0	0	0	0	0	1	0	0	0	0	0	0
OBANGDEB	321	3	10	4	3	1	3	1	4	7	5	5	3	1	3	0
OBUNUTFL	322	1	3	2	1	0	2	0	5	4	8	5	0	0	0	2
OBUTILFL	323	0	2	0	0	0	0	0	0	1	1	1	0	0	0	0
OBRETANG	324	0	2	1	0	0	0	0	0	0	1	0	0	0	0	0
OBRETFLK	325	0	3	0	0	0	0	0	1	0	1	4	0	0	0	0
OBSDSCR	326	0	2	1	0	0	0	0	0	0	0	0	0	0	0	0
OBENDSCR	327	0	1	0	0	0	0	0	0	0	1	2	0	0	0	0
OBBLADES	333	4	8	2	7	3	5	8	9	12	30	14	11	1	4	0
OBBLDS1	334	2	8	2	5	2	5	4	6	9	22	7	6	0	3	0
OBBLDS2	335	2	0	0	2	1	0	4	2	2	8	6	5	1	1	0
OBBLDS3	336	0	0	0	0	0	0	0	1	1	0	1	0	0	0	0
OBBLPNTD	337	1	1	0	0	0	0	0	0	2	0	0	1	1	0	0
OBBLGRND	338	0	0	1	3	0	1	1	0	3	3	1	4	0	0	0
OBBL1DOR	339	0	1	0	0	0	1	2	0	2	4	1	2	1	1	0
OBBL2DOR	340	4	2	1	5	2	2	6	9	7	20	12	7	0	2	0
OBBLSNP1	341	3	4	1	1	0	3	0	6	4	8	2	2	0	1	0
OBBLSNP2	342	0	0	0	1	0	0	0	0	0	0	0	1	0	1	0

APPENDIX TO CHAPTER 2   109

LENCHO DIEGO SURVEY DATA -- VARIABLES 312-342

	VAR. NO.	SQ. 47	SQ. 48	SQ. 49	SQ. 50	SQ. 51	SQ. 52	SQ. 53	SQ. 54	SQ. 55	SQ. 56	SQ. 57	SQ. 58	SQ. 59	SQ. 60	SQ. 61
CHOTHUNI	313	0	0	0	0	0	0	0	0	0	0	0	0	0	0	0
CHBIFACE	314	0	0	1	0	0	1	0	0	1	0	0	0	0	1	0
CHCHOPPR	319	0	0	0	0	0	0	0	0	1	0	0	0	0	0	0
OBANGDEB	321	4	0	11	3	3	1	0	0	10	3	0	1	1	3	0
OBUNUTFL	322	0	4	1	0	1	1	0	1	6	7	0	0	0	3	0
OBUTILFL	323	0	0	2	0	1	0	0	1	3	1	0	0	0	2	0
OBRETANG	324	1	0	1	0	0	0	0	0	0	1	0	0	1	0	0
OBRETFLK	325	0	0	0	0	0	0	0	0	1	0	0	0	0	0	0
OBSDSCR	326	0	0	0	0	0	0	0	0	1	0	0	0	0	0	0
OBENDSCR	327	0	0	0	0	0	0	0	0	0	0	0	0	0	0	0
OBBLADES	333	8	7	9	8	2	3	2	5	20	10	2	11	1	13	4
OBBLDS1	334	7	6	5	8	2	3	1	4	15	7	2	7	0	7	4
OBBLDS2	335	1	1	3	0	0	0	1	1	3	2	0	4	1	6	0
OBBLDS3	336	0	0	0	0	0	0	0	0	2	1	0	0	0	0	0
OBBLPNTD	337	0	0	0	0	0	0	0	0	0	0	0	0	0	0	0
OBBLGRND	338	0	0	0	1	1	0	0	1	1	1	1	2	0	0	0
OBBL1DOR	339	0	1	1	0	0	0	0	1	6	0	0	1	0	1	0
OBBL2DOR	340	7	6	7	6	2	3	2	4	12	8	2	6	1	12	4
OBBLSNP1	341	3	3	5	3	0	1	1	2	9	4	1	3	0	8	4
OBBLSNP2	342	0	0	1	1	0	0	0	0	0	0	0	0	0	0	0

	VAR. NO.	SQ. 62	SQ. 63	SQ. 64	SQ. 65	SQ. 66	SQ. 67	SQ. 68	SQ. 69	SQ. 70	SQ. 71	SQ. 72	SQ. 73	SQ. 74	SQ. 75	SQ. 76
CHOTHUNI	313	0	0	0	0	0	0	0	0	1	0	0	0	1	0	0
CHBIFACE	314	1	0	0	0	0	0	0	0	0	0	0	2	0	1	1
CHCHOPPR	318	1	0	0	0	0	0	0	0	0	0	0	2	0	1	0
OBANGDEB	321	0	0	8	15	4	3	4	0	0	2	4	13	8	3	6
OBUNUTFL	322	0	0	4	6	5	1	2	0	0	2	3	4	6	2	5
OBUTILFL	323	0	0	1	1	1	2	1	0	2	3	1	4	3	3	5
OBRETANG	324	0	0	1	0	0	0	0	0	0	0	0	1	0	1	0
OBRETFLK	325	1	0	1	0	0	0	2	0	0	2	0	4	1	0	2
OBSDSCR	326	0	0	1	0	0	0	1	0	0	0	0	2	0	0	0
OBENDSCR	327	0	0	0	0	0	0	1	0	0	1	0	2	1	0	1
OBBLADES	333	3	1	12	5	3	1	0	0	3	9	1	2	8	2	6
OBBLDS1	334	2	1	10	5	2	1	0	3	2	8	1	1	4	2	6
OBBLDS2	335	1	0	2	0	1	0	0	0	1	1	0	0	3	0	0
OBBLDS3	336	0	0	0	0	0	0	0	0	0	0	0	1	1	0	0
OBBLPNTD	337	0	0	0	0	0	0	0	0	0	0	0	1	1	1	1
OBBLGRND	338	1	0	0	0	0	0	0	0	0	0	0	0	3	0	0
OBBL1DOR	339	1	0	1	0	0	0	0	0	0	2	0	1	3	0	1
OBBL2DOR	340	2	1	8	3	2	0	0	2	3	5	0	1	5	2	2
OBBLSNP1	341	1	0	6	0	1	0	0	3	2	6	1	1	2	1	3
OBBLSNP2	342	0	0	1	2	0	0	0	0	0	0	0	0	0	0	0

	VAR. NO.	SQ. 77	SQ. 78	SQ. 79	SQ. 80	SQ. 81	SQ. 82	SQ. 83	SQ. 84	SQ. 85	SQ. 86	SQ. 87	SQ. 88	SQ. 89	SQ. 90	SQ. 91
CHOTHUNI	313	0	0	0	0	0	0	0	0	0	0	0	0	0	0	0
CHBIFACE	314	0	0	1	1	0	1	1	0	1	1	1	0	0	0	0
CHCHOPPR	318	0	0	1	1	0	0	1	0	1	0	1	0	0	0	0
OBANGDEB	321	2	4	0	0	0	0	0	4	2	1	1	1	0	0	0
OBUNUTFL	322	0	5	0	0	0	1	0	0	1	0	0	0	0	0	0
OBUTILFL	323	2	3	1	1	0	3	0	1	1	0	1	1	0	0	0
OBRETANG	324	0	1	0	0	0	0	0	0	0	0	0	0	0	0	0
OBRETFLK	325	0	1	0	0	0	0	0	0	0	3	0	0	0	0	0
OBSDSCR	326	0	1	0	0	0	0	0	0	0	2	0	0	0	0	0
OBENDSCR	327	0	0	0	0	0	0	0	0	0	0	0	0	0	0	0
OBBLADES	333	0	1	0	1	2	4	1	2	5	0	5	0	1	0	0
OBBLDS1	334	0	1	0	1	1	4	0	1	5	0	5	0	0	0	0
OBBLDS2	335	0	0	0	0	1	0	0	1	0	0	0	0	1	0	0
OBBLDS3	336	0	0	0	0	0	0	1	0	0	0	0	0	0	0	0
OBBLPNTD	337	0	0	0	0	0	0	0	0	0	0	1	0	0	0	0
OBBLGRND	338	0	0	0	0	0	0	0	0	1	0	1	0	0	0	0
OBBL1DOR	339	0	0	0	0	0	1	0	0	2	0	0	0	1	0	0
OBBL2DOR	340	0	1	0	0	2	2	1	1	3	0	4	0	0	0	0
OBBLSNP1	341	0	1	0	0	0	3	1	2	4	0	3	0	0	0	0
OBBLSNP2	342	0	0	0	1	0	0	0	0	0	0	0	0	0	0	0

3. A TERMINAL FORMATIVE CERAMIC WORKSHOP IN THE TEHUACAN VALLEY

by Elsa M. Redmond

A Terminal Formative ceramic workshop was discovered during the intensive surface survey of the Arroyo Lencho Diego in the Tehuacán Valley (Chapter 2). The workshop was found in the Early Palo Blanco phase hilltop site designated Ts73 (Fig. 2.12), a densely settled community that was internally differentiated into four broad sectors. As described by Spencer in Chapter 2, the single public sector contained plazas delimited by large masonry platforms, pyramids, staircases, and a ballcourt. The two residential sectors of Ts73 are characterized by the presence of masonry foundations of domestic structures. One of these residential sectors lay well inside the site's double defensive wall. The second residential area was situated just outside the wall. The fourth sector of Ts73, the ceramic workshop, is the subject of this chapter. We will examine in turn the surface characteristics of this workshop, the organization of ceramic production manifested here, and the broader implications of the study of ceramic production at Ts73.

Surface Characteristics of the Ceramic Workshop

The ceramic workshop is located on the easternmost arm of the hilltop site, just inside the confines of the defensive wall. It is isolated from other parts of the community, and together with the wall it forms a gap between the two residential sectors of Ts73. The workshop occupies an area of about 100 by 25 m. The workshop debris extends over a large modified natural rise and down onto an adjacent long and broad terrace.

The architectural remains here are few and found only in the eastern half of the workshop. A masonry pyramid 2 m high and a smaller platform face one another across an open courtyard. To the east of this pair of structures and overlooking the defensive wall sits a third masonry structure. These three mounded structures are the only buildings of this kind outside the civic-ceremonial sector of the hilltop community. There are no house foundations or house mounds in the workshop sector of the site.

Within this workshop area there are several kinds of features and artifact distributions that are associated with the production of ceramics. They include features resembling the fire boxes of kilns, fire-cracked rock, lumps of fired clay, and high densities of broken pottery and kiln wasters. We will deal with each of these characteristics of the ceramic workshop separately and in some detail.

112 PREHISTORIC DEVELOPMENT IN THE TEHUACAN VALLEY

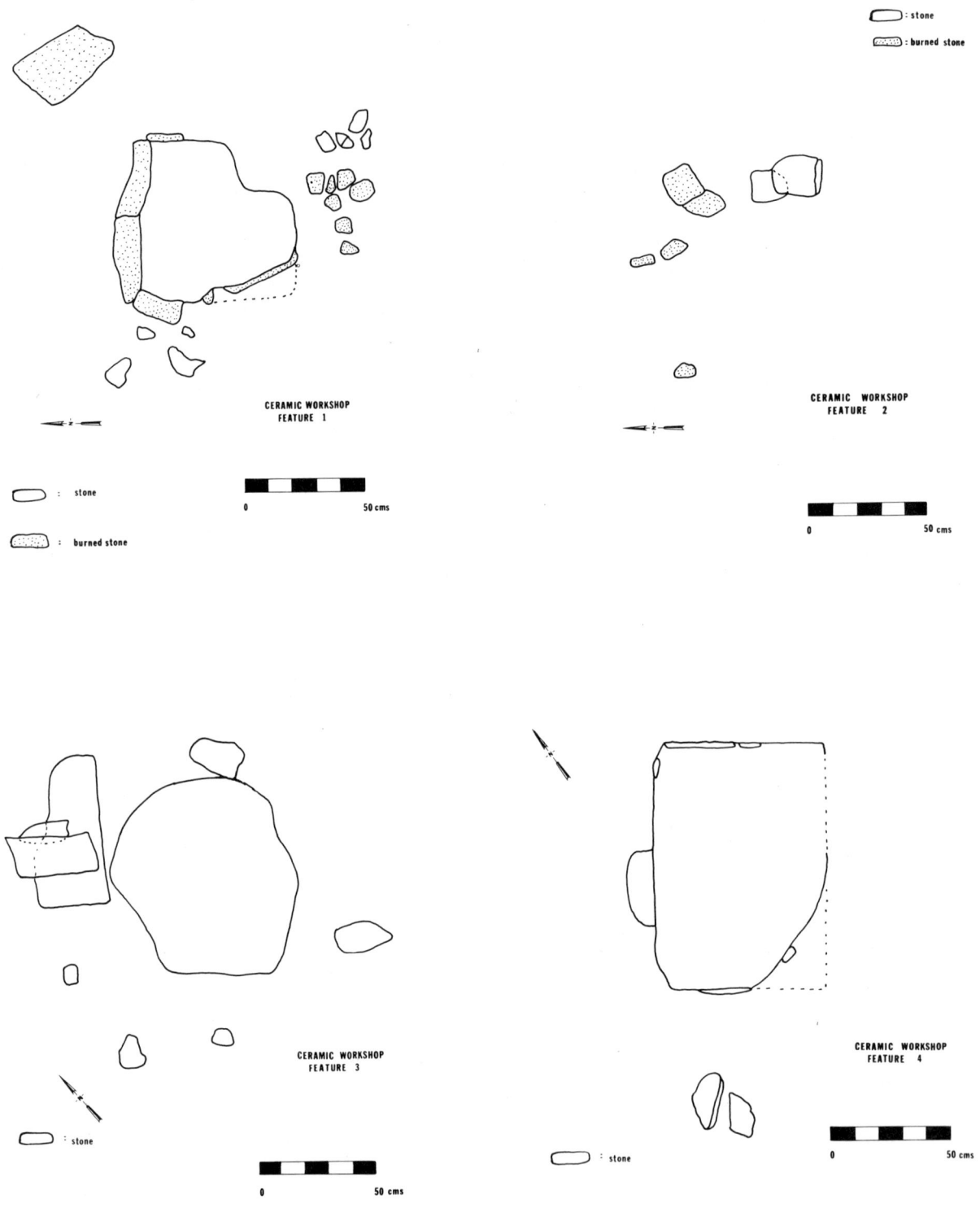

Fig. 3.1. Plans of ceramic workshop features. A pile of fire-cracked rocks was 2 m north of the corner of Feature 4.

3. TERMINAL FORMATIVE CERAMIC WORKSHOP

TABLE 3.1

FIRE-CRACKED ROCK AT Ts73

Collection Square	Count	Weight (kg)
64	69	5.385
65	88	4.250
66	54	3.700
68	27	3.725

Features

The surface outlines of four subterranean features were found within the workshop. These features are not concentrated in one particular locale but are distributed throughout the area of ceramic production (Fig. 2.12). They consist of rectangular, stone-lined boxes measuring approximately .7 to 1.0 m long and .7 m wide (Fig. 3.1). Features 1 and 3 both have a single lateral extension from the basic rectangular outline. Many of the stone slabs lining these features are reddened, friable, and fractured in a manner characteristic of exposure to intense heat.

The most complete description of a ceramic workshop from Mesoamerica to date comes from Bordaz's excavations at the Postclassic site of Peñitas in Nayarit. The three ceramic kilns in the workshop at Peñitas were horizontal pit kilns consisting of underground fire boxes where the fuel was burned connecting with roughly circular firing chambers where the pottery to be fired was placed (Bordaz 1964:48). The fire boxes of the Peñitas kilns are decribed as compartments with parallel walls, and their dimensions (70 by 45 cm, 55 by 35 cm, and 60 by 50 cm) are remarkably similar to the features at Ts73. We therefore conclude that the four rectangular, stone-lined features in the workshop sector of Ts73 are the underground fire boxes of four ceramic kilns. The lateral extensions observed for Features 1 and 3 are probably the surface traces of adjoining firing chambers. Our four surface collection squares in the workshop were placed near these ceramic kilns.

Fire-cracked rock

Our surface collection squares located in the ceramic workshop contained a significant amount of rock exhibiting angular fracture patterns resulting from intense heating, and much of it was fire-reddened (Table 3.1). There are no significant differences between the four collection squares in the weight of fire-cracked rock.

Similar fire-exposed stones line the kilns described above, and concentrations of fire-cracked rock lie in the immediate vicinity of these features. For example, a large pile of fire-cracked rock lay just 2 m from the edge of Feature 4. Fire-cracked rock, which must originally have formed part of the construction or fill of the ceramic kilns, appears to be a diagnostic surface characteristic of the ceramic workshop.

Fired lumps of clay

The four collection squares in the workshop area of Ts73 yielded a total of 13 lumps of fired clay (Fig. 3.2). These amorphous lumps of slag appeared only within the workshop area of Ts73. Some are gray and highly porous, while others are bright red and pink with many inclusions. Both kinds resemble the paste of misfired gray sherds, and the differences in their colors and pastes probably represent only differences in the degree of their firing. Bordaz (1964:107 and 117) found similar lumps of unfired and fired clay in the area of ceramic kilns at Peñitas.

Fired lumps of clay, a by-product of ceramic making, are another distinctive characteristic of the ceramic workshop. They may be accidentally fired pieces of unshaped clay either awaiting vessel construction or remaining after it.

Ceramic densities

The density of ceramics in the workshop area is astoundingly high compared to the usual density of ceramics at Ts73 (Table 3.2). Prior to the identification of this area as a ceramic workshop, we found the high sherd density intriguing in view of the absence of any recognizable houses or house mounds.

The majority of these pottery fragments probably resulted from vessels that simply broke apart during the firing process without exhibiting more specific attributes of misfiring. A smaller number probably represent fragments of ceramic vessels used in the production of ceramics. These

Fig. 3.2. Lumps of fired clay. Scale = 5 cm.

3. TERMINAL FORMATIVE CERAMIC WORKSHOP

TABLE 3.2

DENSITY OF SHERDS IN CERAMIC WORKSHOP

Collection Square	Sherd Density (per m^2)	Gray		Plain		Gray/Plain Ratio
		Rims & Dec. Bodies	Undec. Bodies	Rims & Dec. Bodies	Undec. Bodies	
64	288.12	1121	5497	55	529	11.3
65	100.56	296	2044	12	162	13.4
66	66.12	259	1146	11	235	5.7
68	51.40	246	921	8	108	10.1
Avg. for Workshop Squares	126.55					10.1
Avg. for other Squares	43.40					4.9

would include containers for storing water, clay, temper, pigment, and assorted utensils.

Within the workshop the number of fine gray ceramics far exceeds the number of coarse plain ceramics (Table 3.2). Whether the greater density of gray ceramics means that this ware alone was produced in the ceramic workshop is a question we will return to later.

Kiln wasters

A distinctive attribute of the ceramic workshop at Ts73 is the 135 kiln wasters or misfired sherds recovered in our four collection squares. All these were of the El Riego Gray paste (MacNeish, Peterson, and Flannery 1970). In examining these sherds we found evidence for at least 12 distinctive kinds of firing accidents that occurred during different stages of the firing process. They involve the responses of the clay constituents to the dehydration, oxidation, and vitrification stages of firing (Shepard 1956:20-23). I will first describe these different kinds of firing accidents manifested by the 135 kiln wasters from the four collection squares of the workshop, then turn to their co-occurrence with other ceramic attributes such as vessel form and surface color. It should be kept in mind that several manifestations of misfiring may be found on a single kiln waster.

1. *Angular fracture patterns.* A total of 64 sherds are fractured in a peculiar torn manner, different from normal fracture patterns (Fig. 3.3). Structurally weak points of a vessel's construction, such as the neck joint of a jar or the basal angle of a bowl, will give way to any

Fig. 3.3. Angular fracture patterns on misfired jar rims (left) and bowl rims (right). Scale = 5 cm.

trapped air in the clay that expands on heating. Some other inclusions in the clay will also escape when they are heated and will cause such cracking of the vessel walls (Shepard 1956:91). The angular fracture patterns seen on these sherds represent the most common firing accident in the ceramic workshop.

2. Spalled surfaces. There are 62 spalled sherds which exhibit a laminated or pitted surface caused by the removal of small convex flakes or spalls from the vessel walls during the period of firing (Fig. 3.4). Bordaz found a large number of spalled sherds at Peñitas and remarked that all these sherds were made from a fine paste with low thermal shock resistance

Fig. 3.4. Spalled surfaces. Scale = 5 cm.

3. TERMINAL FORMATIVE CERAMIC WORKSHOP   117

(Bordaz 1964:77). Apparently this is also the case with the Early Palo Blanco phase fine paste gray sherds found at Ts73.

3. <u>Highly oxidized sherds</u>. There are 33 sherds with highly oxidized surfaces, some of which also exhibit local discoloration and fire clouding due to differing degrees of oxidation (Shepard 1956:371). Characteristically, these sherds are bright red or pink. Several have spalled surfaces and suffered further exposure to fire after their surfaces had spalled.

4. <u>Marbled surfaces</u>. A single body sherd was marbled. One surface was white and gray, while the other was blue and pink and marbled in appearance.

5. <u>Mineral inclusions</u>. There are 29 sherds that still have fairly large mineral particles in their paste (Fig. 3.5). Particles such as quartz chips and tiny pebbles present in the clay during firing can result in cracked vessel walls and spalled vessel surfaces. Usually care is taken to remove all large mineral particles from the paste before using it to construct vessels; often smaller mineral particles simply pop out of the paste during the oxidation stage of firing (Shepard 1956:21).

6. <u>Bubbled surfaces</u>. Six sherds have surfaces with bumps or bubbles (Fig. 3.6), some of which remain unruptured. They are caused by trapped air or vegetable or mineral inclusions that usually escape from the paste during the oxidation stage of firing. Clearly, all the impurities in the clay had not been removed before the vitrification stage began (Shepard 1956:21). Most of the sherds with bubbled surfaces are also warped and green-yellow in surface color.

7. <u>Porous surfaces</u>. There are nine sherds whose surfaces have a peculiar sponginess, looking like an addition or a secretion that has vitrified (Fig. 3.6). These examples seem to represent a continuation of the process that resulted in the bubbled surfaces just described. An excessively

Fig. 3.5. Mineral inclusions. Scale = 5 cm.

Fig. 3.6. Bubbled surface (left) and porous surfaces (right). Scale = 5 cm.

high firing temperature, especially for a prolonged period, can cause the clay to vitrify before full oxidation is reached. Most of these examples are also warped or markedly deformed.

  8. <u>Porous cores</u>. Fourteen sherds have an exaggeratedly porous paste, much like a sponge (Fig. 3.7). Most of the examples lack any inclusions, and they tend to be warped or deformed. These examples of over firing are related to those with the bubbled and porous surfaces. The porous cores are formed by gases that are trapped in the paste due to incomplete oxidation prior to vitrification. Shepard (1956:21) states that "if carbonaceous matter is not fully removed before vitrification commences, gases will be trapped by the dense impervious surface that forms, the interior will become black and vesicular and the wall bloated."

  9. <u>Pocketed cores</u>. Ten sherds have what I would call a pocketed

Fig. 3.7. Porous core (left) and pocketed cores (right). Scale = 5 cm.

Fig. 3.8. Deformed sherds. Scale = 5 cm.

core (Fig. 3.7). In contrast to the sponge-like quality of the porous cores, the pocketed core examples exhibit large air pockets or horizontal slits in the paste. The expansion of trapped gases and other substances when the clay is heated produces these air pockets in the paste. Correspondingly, the walls expand and bloat. Similar firing accidents produce both pocketed and porous cores, and a few sherds combine the features of both types.

10. Warped sherds. A total of 21 sherds are warped. The thickening of the walls and warping caused by misfiring slightly alter the original shape of a vessel. Many of the warped sherds manifest heat ripples or stress marks indicative of such alteration.

11. Deformed sherds. There are six markedly deformed sherds (Fig. 3.8). Deformation can result when material has vitrified rapidly. Clays high in carbonaceous and calcareous impurities are more likely to deform during firing because these impurities will affect the temperature of vitrification and thus the rate of vitrification. In this light it is interesting to note that most of these sherds are also dark olive green or light green, colorations which Shepard (1956:23-24) attributes to vitrified calcareous clays.

12. Sherds with a hard-burned loam cover. A single body sherd from a jar resembles Bordaz's (1964:73) description of sherds with a hard-burned loam cover. One surface of this sherd is streaked with crusts of organic matter similar to what Bordaz interprets as parallel veined grass imprints (Fig. 3.9). In addition to such sherds, Bordaz also recovered pieces of hard-burned loam with grass imprints from his kilns at Peñitas. These baked pieces of loam having grass imprints formed part of the temporary covers placed over the kilns (Bordaz 1964:67-73). The single sherd from Ts73 might then have had something to do with the cover placed over the

kiln during firing.

Let us conclude the discussion of the kinds of firing accidents that occurred in the production of ceramics in this workshop with an examination of the co-occurrence of the different firing accidents with particular vessel forms and vessel surface colors. Most of the firing accidents occur on both bowls and jars, though there are some differences between the two (Table 3.3). A high degree of oxidation, angular fracture patterns, spalled surfaces and mineral inclusions are firing accidents that are more commonly found on bowls. On the other hand, significantly more jars have porous surfaces, porous cores, pocketed cores, or warped or markedly deformed shapes. These different sets of firing accidents on bowls and jars may correspond to differences in the paste, temper, vessel construction, and firing conditions in the production of the two vessel forms.

Table 3.4 lists the proportions of firing accidents that exhibit particular surface colors. Aside from the highly oxidized sherds which are defined on the basis of their bright red and pink surface colors, surface color turns out to be only a marginal indicator of the various firing accidents. Only a few general remarks can be made about the correspondences. The misfired sherds having bubbled surfaces tended to be green-yellow in surface color. This is probably due to calcareous impurities in the clay that produced both the green-yellow surface color and the associated bubbled surfaces (Shepard 1956:21-22). Also, jars that had porous surfaces, porous cores, pocketed cores, or warped or deformed shapes tended to be either dark gray or green-yellow in color. Perhaps jars were made from calcareous clays that Shepard(1956:23-24) suggests have a tendency to turn green when vitrified. The impurities in these clays would affect the temperature of vitrification and would therefore produce the related firing accidents.

Organization of Ceramic Production

A re-examination of the surface characteristics of the ceramic workshop may generate some suggestions concerning the organization of ceramic production at Ts73; and by analyzing the social and political aspects of

Fig. 3.9. Sherd with a hard-burned loam cover. Scale = 5 cm.

TABLE 3.3

DISTRIBUTION OF FIRING ACCIDENTS AMONG VESSEL FORMS

Firing Accident	Total Number	Bowls (%)	Jars (%)	Indeterminate forms (%)
Highly oxidized	33	73	15	12
Angular fracture	63	63	30	7
Spalled surface	62	66	26	8
Inclusions	29	62	38	0
Bubbled surface	6	50	50	0
Porous surface	9	11	22	66
Porous core	14	14	64	22
Pocketed core	10	40	50	10
Warped	21	33	57	10
Deformed	6	0	50	50

TABLE 3.4

RELATION BETWEEN FIRING ACCIDENTS AND SURFACE COLORS

Firing Accident	Gray (%)	Brown (%)	Brown-gray (%)	Brown-orange (%)	Red-pink (%)	Green-yellow (%)
Highly oxidized	0	0	9	12	79	0
Angular fracture	24	3	17	9	17	28
Spalled surface	27	3	31	5	22	10
Inclusions	27	3	17	7	14	31
Bubbled surface	17	0	0	0	0	83
Porous surface	11	0	0	0	33	22
Porous core	50	0	7	0	0	42
Pocketed core	10	10	20	0	10	40
Warped	28	0	5	0	5	57
Deformed	83	0	0	0	0	17

Total counts of firing accidents are the same as shown in Table 3.3.

ceramic production at Ts73, the spatial organization of the ceramic workshop, and the degree of specialization evident in the production of ceramics in this workshop, we hope to answer the following questions. First, who administered the production of ceramics, and who were the producers? Second, what were the units of production? And third, what were the finished products?

All the evidence of ceramic production at Ts73 comes from one isolated sector of the Early Palo Blanco community. The workshop is bounded on the east by a double wall and on the west by an elite residential sector. The only structures located inside the workshop are three masonry structures on top of platforms. Although smaller in size than any of the public buildings in the major civic-ceremonial sector of Ts73, these three structures comprise the only mound group outside the civic-ceremonial sector.

The complete absence of residences in the workshop sector is paralleled by the paucity of domestic items such as manos and metates. Thus the production of ceramics at Ts73 was a highly specialized activity, localized in one sector of the community where it was performed by individual workshop laborers drawn from many households in the community. In discussing the different sectors of Ts73 and their relative socio-economic statuses, Spencer (Chapter 2) proposes that the workshop was staffed by day laborers drawn from a lower-status residential sector, but not the one of lowest status. The presence of a mound group at the eastern end of the ceramic workshop suggests that specialized administrators supervised this group of full-time laborers. The degree of supervision exerted by these specialized administrators over the ceramic workshop laborers should be reflected in the spatial organization of the workshop and in the variety of ceramics produced there.

Inside the workshop there were at least four separate loci of ceramic production, corresponding to the four ceramic kilns. These kilns are distributed throughout the workshop area, not concentrated in one particular place. Since there was no single area in the workshop for firing ceramics, then by extension we might reason that there was no single area where pastes were prepared, no single area where vessels were shaped, and so on. Consequently, it does not appear that the workshop laborers were organized into teams, each engaged in a separate stage of ceramic making.

Do the four kilns then represent comparable work units in the manufacture of ceramics? Let us examine the associated dumps of fire-cracked rock, fired clay, broken pottery, and kiln wasters. If we compare the weights of fire-cracked rock in the four collection squares, we find that they are similar (Table 3.1). We have seen how fire-cracked rock is associated with the construction and fill of the firing kilns. Fire-cracked rock is a by-product of the firing stage of ceramic production. But lumps of fired clay were also recovered from all collection squares, and, unlike the fire-cracked rock, they do not belong solely to the firing stage of ceramic production. These unshaped lumps of clay that were accidentally fired originate from an earlier stage of vessel construction. If fire-cracked rock and lumps of fired clay are associated with different stages of the ceramic-making process, then their co-occurrence in the four collection squares located in the vicinity of the ceramic kilns would suggest the presence of four comparable work units or teams of laborers centered around the four separate firing locales. Each work unit would have been involved with the entire process of ceramic production, from the earliest stages of a vessel's construction to the final stages of its firing.

Further support for this interpretation emerges from a consideration of the ceramic densities in the nearby dumps. Besides containing ceramics produced in the workshop, the dumps also hold smaller quantities of plain ware, discussed below, which probably represent containers used to store water and other materials employed in the production of ceramics. Like the fire-cracked rock and lumps of fired clay, the numerous fragments of broken pottery associated with the four firing locales derive from both the primary and the final stages of ceramic manufacture. Consequently, the work unit centered at each of the four areas was probably involved in all the stages of ceramic making.

We can refine our working model for the organization of ceramic production at Ts73 by turning to the question of what kinds of ceramics were actually manufactured in the workshop. This entails first an analysis of the variety of ceramics found in the workshop dumps. Once we have established what kinds of pottery were produced in the workshop, we can turn to the smaller set of known kiln wasters for more specific information on the degree of specialization evident in the organization of ceramic production at Ts73.

The two major Early Palo Blanco phase ceramic types found in the four surface collection squares from the ceramic workshop were El Riego Gray and El Riego Plain. El Riego Gray (MacNeish, Peterson, and Flannery 1970:146-155) is characterized by a fine, compact gray paste and gray surface color. While the predominant El Riego Gray vessel form is the outleaned wall bowl, a full range of bowl forms and jars are fashioned from this paste. A small proportion of El Riego Gray ceramics exhibit geometric incised decorative motifs. El Riego Plain (MacNeish, Peterson, and Flannery 1970:168-170), on the other hand, is distinguished by a coarse, heavily tempered paste and reddish brown surface color. The predominant El Riego Plain vessel form is the jar or olla, a fact which led the original investigators to characterize this pottery type as utilitarian.

Of these two major Terminal Formative ceramic types, El Riego Gray is much more common than El Riego Plain in the four collections from the workshop at Ts73 (Table 3.2). While this is true of the site as a whole, the proportion of El Riego Gray in the workshop area is especially high. The ratio of El Riego Gray to El Riego Plain ranges from 5.7 to 13.4 in the workshop collections, with an average of 10.1, but the average ratio in collections outside the workshop is only 4.9.

There are two possible interpretations of the differences in these ratios. One deals with the non-residential character of the ceramic workshop. If El Riego Plain is a purely utilitarian type serving domestic needs, then its low frequency in the workshop collections simply relates to the absence of residences and associated domestic debris in the workshop. Another interpretation would treat the varying frequencies of

El Riego Gray and El Riego Plain in the workshop as a measure of the amounts of the different types produced there. Thus the higher frequencies of El Riego Gray would reflect a specialization in the making of this type. Both factors may be involved in producing the distribution of El Riego Gray and El Riego Plain observed at Ts73.

Perhaps the clearest evidence for the kind of ceramics produced in the workshop are those sherds showing obvious firing defects, the kiln wasters. All 135 kiln wasters are made from El Riego Gray paste. The fired lumps of clay also appear to have originated from El Riego Gray paste. This, together with the frequencies of El Riego Gray and El Riego Plain, suggests that the ceramic workshop specialized in the production of El Riego Gray ceramics alone. Although the possibility that El Riego Plain was made at Ts73 cannot be ruled out, there is no evidence favoring it except the smaller number of El Riego Plain sherds found. These may, of course, represent storage containers for water, materials, and tools used in making El Riego Gray ceramics.

Since the kiln wasters most clearly represent the ceramics produced in the workshop, we can use them to investigate possible specialization of production by vessel form as well. The wasters from the four kilns include from 59 to 72% bowls and from 28 to 41% jars (Table 3.5). If the proportions of vessel forms among the kiln wasters are related to the proportions of vessel forms manufactured, then we can conclude that the four teams in this specialized El Riego ceramic workshop each produced various vessel forms and in similar proportions.

In sum, our view of the organization of ceramic production at a Terminal Formative hilltop community in the Tehuacán Valley is one of a highly specialized operation. The production of gray ceramics was carried out in a workshop by a group of full-time laborers under the direct supervision of specialized administrators. The potters were organized into at least four separate units of production centered at the four kilns. Each work unit was responsible for all stages of the ceramic-making process, from the shaping of vessels to their firing. Each work unit produced the full range of vessel forms instead of specializing in a particular kind of vessel. Bowls were produced in higher quantities than jars, but these two general vessel forms were supplied by each of the workshop units in

TABLE 3.5

PROPORTIONS OF MISFIRED BOWLS AND JARS IN CERAMIC WORKSHOP COLLECTION SQUARES

Collection Square	Number of Kiln Wasters	Bowls (%)	Jars (%)
64	47	72	28
65	9	67	33
66	8	63	37
68	56	59	41

comparable proportions.

Broader Implications

The Terminal Formative ceramic workshop discovered at Ts73 provided us with an exceptionally complete surface plan of such a workshop, together with a set of distinctive surface characteristics which should provide other investigators with a means of detecting places where ceramics were produced. By knowing what to look for, we should be able to locate centers of ceramic production without relying so heavily upon the distributions of ceramics and their stylistic attributes as indicators of production loci.

The study of the organization of ceramic production at this Early Palo Blanco phase hilltop community should be examined in its local historical context. There is evidence for the production of ceramics at another community in the Arroyo Lencho Diego, the site of Ts131 (see Chapter 2). Ts131 is one of five Late Santa María phase settlements in the Arroyo Lencho Diego—an "amorphous collection of 65 to 70 residences" without any public architecture. In contrast to the localized evidence for ceramic production at Ts73 in the form of a workshop, the evidence for ceramic production at Ts131 is widespread throughout the community. The outlines of three, roughly circular features resembling kilns were discovered in association with several house foundations, and a total of 27 overfired gray sherds were recovered from collections made in all parts of the site. Ceramic production at Ts131 appears to have been a part-time activity organized at the level of individual households in the community. Seen in its local context, then, the Early Palo Blanco phase ceramic workshop at Ts73 represents a major change in the organization of ceramic production, from a part-time household activity to a full-time workshop activity.

The study of the ceramic workshop at Ts73 and of the degree of specialization evident in the production of ceramics here during Palo Blanco times should finally be placed in a regional context. Our present evidence suggests that the ceramic workshop at Ts73 was producing the full range of El Riego Gray ceramics. There are other Palo Blanco phase hilltop centers in the Tehuacán Valley, and they share many of the same elements of public architecture and internal organization seen at Ts73. Three of these, Ts281, Ts41/356, Ts364) have also yielded misfired El Riego Gray sherds (Nowack 1977). Ts73 was not alone, therefore, in producing El Riego Gray ceramics in the Tehuacán Valley. No regional system existed wherein individual centers specialized in particular ceramics and then exchanged their products for those specialized goods of other centers; each community evidently produced the same full range of El Riego Gray ceramics. In this sense, these Palo Blanco phase centers seem economically self-sufficient. From the point of view of ceramic production and distribution alone, the Tehuacán Valley appears to have lacked an integrated system for the exchange of craft products. The degree of specialization evident in the production of ceramics at Ts73 and probably also at other Palo Blanco phase hilltop centers is an important factor in our understanding of the economic and political organization of the Tehuacán Valley during Palo Blanco times.

3. UN TALLER DE CERAMICA DEL FORMATIVO TERMINAL EN EL VALLE DE TEHUACAN

por Elsa M. Redmond

SUMARIO

Durante el reconocimiento de superficie del Arroyo Lencho Diego descrito en el Capítulo 2, fue descubierta una área de producción de cerámica en el sitio Ts73 de la fase Palo Blanco Temprana (Fig. 2.12). Esta área ocupaba una superficie de más o menos 100 por 25 m en el espinazo que queda justo adentro de la muralla defensiva. El taller de cerámica contenía tres montículos pequeños, pero ninguna evidencia de arquitectura residencial, que es tan común en el resto del sitio. En el área del taller, cuatro elementos rectangulares forrados en piedra, visibles en la superficie, fueron interpretados como hornos de cerámica (Fig. 3.1). Se hicieron cuatro colecciones de superficie controladas, asociadas con cada uno de estos elementos. Estas colecciones contienen gran cantidad de piedra quebrada por fuego, sin duda un producto de la horneada de cerámicas. Además, 13 pedazos de arcilla amorfos horneados parecen ser el resultado de un cocimiento accidental del material del cual se manufacturaban las cerámicas. La densidad de tepalcates en las colecciones hechas en el área del taller eran más o menos tres veces mayor que la de las otras colecciones hechas en el sitio.

Un total de 135 restos cerámicos mal cocidos fueron recuperados en los cuatro cuadros de colección en el taller. Estos muestran por lo menos doce accidentes de cocimiento: 1) fracturas angulares en tepalcate ocurridas durante el cocimiento por la expansión de aire u otras inclusiones en la arcilla (Fig. 3.3); 2) superficies agrietadas que resultaron por la extracción de pequeñas escamas convexas de las paredes de las vasijas durante cocimiento (Fig. 3.4); 3) superficies altamente oxidadas que resultan en un color rojo o rosado; 4) superficies con apariencia de mármol en azul y rosado o blanco y gris; 5) inclusiones grandes de minerales (Fig. 3.5); 6) superficies burbujeadas que son el resultado de aire y partículas vegetales o minerales atrapadas (Fig. 3.6); 7) superficies porosas, resultado del reventamiento de burbujas (Fig. 3.6); 8) núcleos porosos, resultado de gases atrapados, producidos posiblemente cuando material carbonífero no fue completamente oxidado, antes de empezar el estado de vitrificación (Fig. 3.7); 9) núcleos con cavidades, resultado del mismo proceso que en 8 (Fig. 3.7); 10) tepalcates torcidos durante cocimiento; 11) tepalcates deformados por vitrificación rápida (Fig. 3.8); y 12) tepalcates cubiertos con una capa de material duro orgánico quemado (Fig. 3.9). De estos accidentes de cocimiento, los de los números 1, 2, 3 y 5 son más comunes en cajetes, mientras que los de los números 7, 8, 9, 10 y 11 se encuentran más a menudo en ollas.

No se encontró ninguna evidencia de producción de cerámica en otras partes de Ts73. La falta de estructuras domésticas y la escasez de

3. TERMINAL FORMATIVE CERAMIC WORKSHOP

artefactos domésticos tales como manos y metates sugiere que el taller de cerámica era una área donde especialistas que trabajaban solamente en cerámica ejercían su ocupación. El local del taller, junto a una área de residencias de posición social baja (aunque no la más baja del sitio) sugiere que los que trabajaban la cerámica venían de este sector. Las tres estructuras en los montículos bajos probablemente servían en la organización y administración de la producción de cerámica. La distribución de los cuatro hornos de cerámica en el área del taller sugiere que por lo menos cuatro grupos trabajaban en las varias etapas de producción. La proporción muy alta de cerámicas del tipo El Riego Gris en el taller, y el hecho de que todos los restos de cerámica mal cocida tenían barro de tipo El Riego Gris, sugieren que el taller se especializaba en la producción de cerámica de este tipo. Los restos de cerámica mal cocida incluyen ollas y cajetes y estas dos formas de vasijas ocurrieron en proporciónes similares en las cuatro colecciones asociadas con los hornos cerámicos, sugiriendo que los cuatro grupos de trabajadores manufacturaban varios tipos de vasijas.

Esta organización de la producción de cerámica es muy diferente de la que está indicada para la fase anterior, Santa María Tardía, en la cual en un sitio (Ts131) tepalcates sobrecocidos y tres posibles hornos de cerámica estaban distribuídos en una área residencial bastante grande. Esta evidencia sugiere que la producción de cerámica era una actividad que ocupaba solo parte del tiempo de las familias en esta fase, en contraste a la especialización y producción continua de la cual se tiene evidencia en Ts73 durante la fase Palo Blanco Temprana. Otros de los "lugares centrales" de esta fase también han producido evidencia de la producción de cerámicas del tipo El Riego Gris (Nowack 1977). Estos centros parecen haber producido toda la que necesitaban, en vez de estar integrados en un sistema de intercambio de producción especializada.

4. SYSTEMATIC SURFACE SURVEY AT QUACHILCO (Ts218)

by John R. Alden

In the summer of 1975, as part of the research of the Palo Blanco Project, surface materials were systematically collected at the site of Quachilco (Ts218) in the Tehuacán Valley. These collections were made to help answer the following questions:

1. Where are the borders of the site?
2. How did the site grow through time, and how are the earlier and later occupations of the site related?
3. How can the site be divided into areas or types of surface deposits (here called strata) which will reflect differences in artifact distribution across the site?
4. How can these strata be interpreted in functional or chronological terms?

Each of these problems is treated below.

The site of Quachilco, the earliest "town" in the Tehuacán Valley, was located on survey in 1961 and test excavated in 1962 as part of the Tehuacán Archaeological-Botanical Project (MacNeish et al. 1972:205-216 and 397). As an initial step toward the realization of the general goals of the Palo Blanco Project, further study of Quachilco took place in 1975 (described in preliminary form in Alden 1977 and Drennan 1977b). The surface survey described here was a part of this 1975 work, and it helped to guide excavations conducted at the site in 1977 (described in preliminary form in Drennan 1978).

This chapter first reports the details of the survey technique, then deals with the four questions presented above. A brief final section presents conclusions derived from the survey data, elaborates on their implications as they relate to the goals of the project, and reviews tests of these implications which might be made in future work.

The 1975 season of the Palo Blanco Project was sponsored and financed by the Robert S. Peabody Foundation for Archaeology and directed by Robert D. Drennan. The project was staffed by the author of this report, J. Nowack, E. Redmond, and C. Spencer. All participated in the collection and recording of the data presented in this chapter, but the analysis was performed by the author. While this chapter has benefited materially from comments and criticisms from Drennan, any mistakes or misinterpretations remain the sole responsibility of the author.

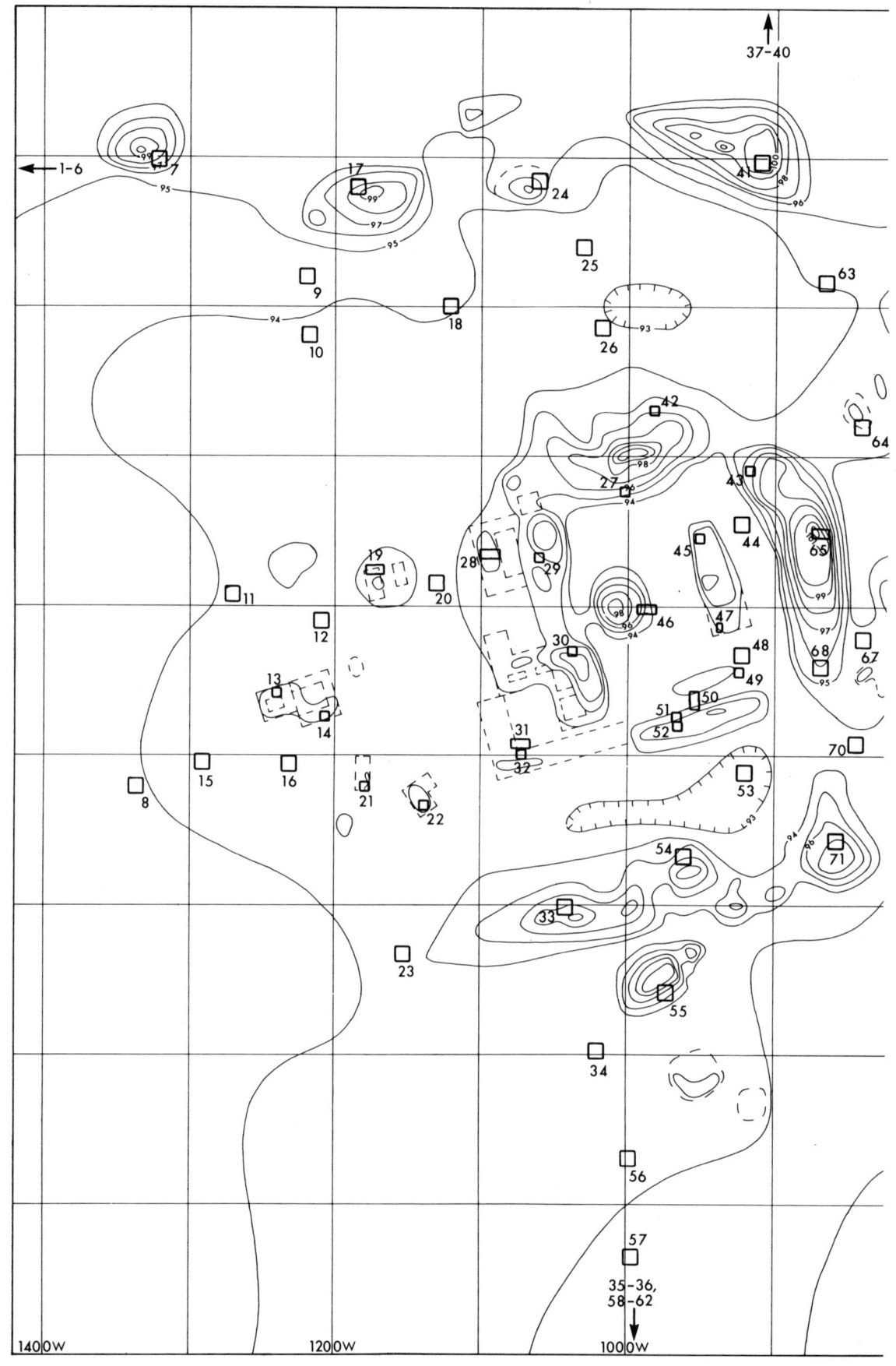

4. SYSTEMATIC SURFACE SURVEY AT QUACHILCO 131

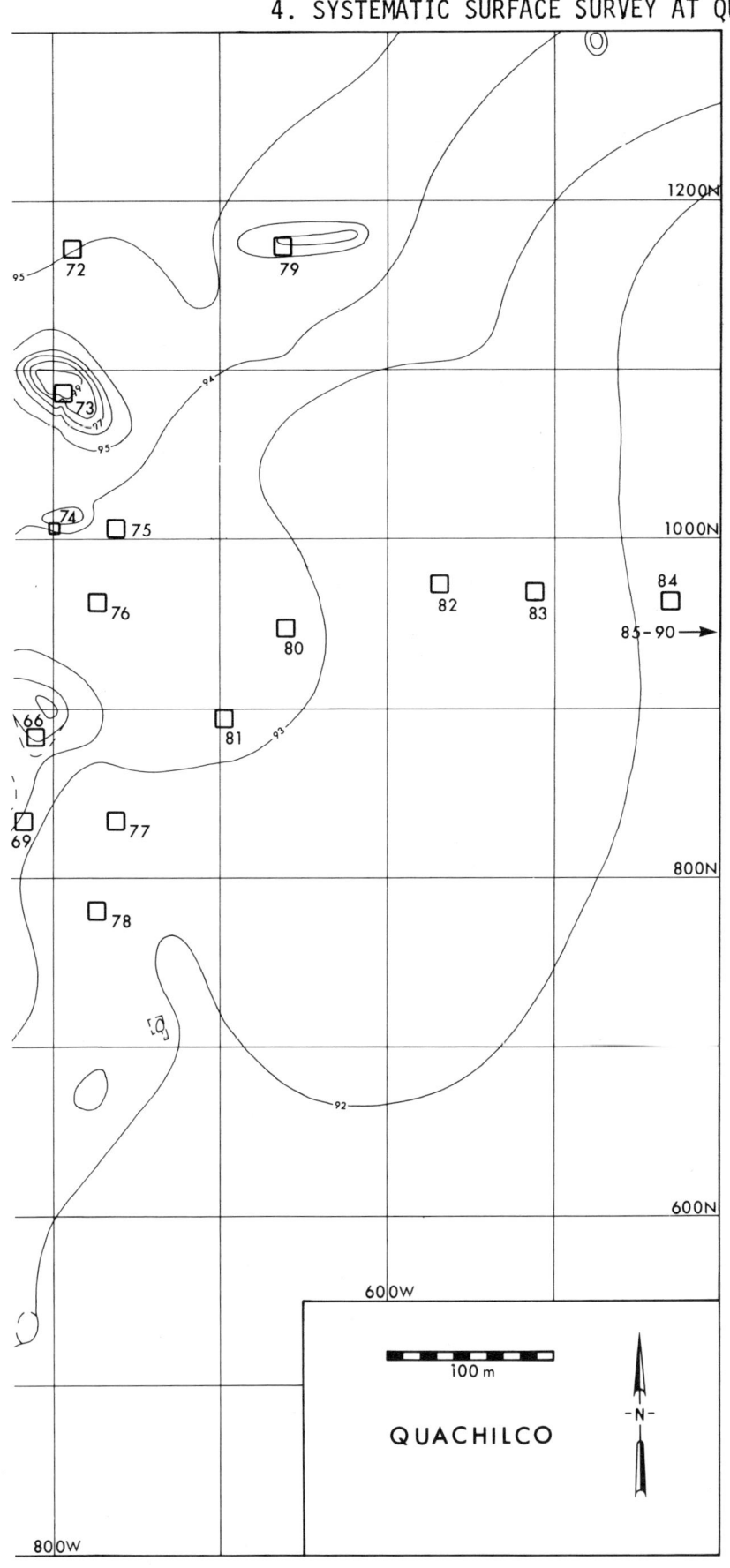

Fig. 4.1. Contour map of the central area of Quachilco, showing the locations of the surface collection squares.

Survey Techniques

As the first step of the survey, the central area of the site was mapped with alidade and plane table (see also Drennan 1978:16). All mounds were outlined, and visible features of archeological interest were located. Non-archeological features do not appear on this map (Fig. 4.1) unless they were more than 1 m high. The top of the northern mound in the central plaza group was assigned an arbitrary altitude of 100 m and the location 1000 North, 1000 West (100N1000W). All other points on the site were located relative to this origin. The map in Fig. 4.1 is gridded into 1 ha squares, and collection units are numbered sequentially from north to south in each 100 m strip, beginning at the west.

Surface collection units were selected to satisfy several different criteria. North-south and east-west transects of the site were sampled at intervals of 50 to 200 m in order to define the site borders. Collection squares in these transects were all located in fallow fields so that the sample would consist of comparable units. Each mound on the site was sampled by at least one square to allow the total population of mounds to be examined in the analysis. Finally, as many squares as time permitted were surface collected from the area surrounding the central plaza of the site, so that the chronology of occupation could be discovered.

```
┌─────────────────────────────────────────────────────────────────────┐
│       PALO BLANCO PROJECT   -   SURFACE PICK-UP DATA                │
│  Site____218_____  Location__819 N 961 W__  Lot #_0275_          │
│  Area_5_ X _5_ m., 1 of ___1___ adjacent squares                    │
│                                                                     │
│          IF MOUND:                    IF NOT MOUND:                 │
│                                                                     │
│  a) height __3.0__ m.          a) present land use _____          │
│  b) area __2,000__ m²          b) path/ditch/qanat                  │
│  c) ~~salt~~/construction/~~other~~   c) erosion? _____           │
│  Comments  light ground cover    top of mound (see 0274)            │
│            no disturbance                                           │
│  wt large stone  82.0          # glazed sherds —                    │
│  wt chipped ground stone       # plastic fragments —                │
│  wt ceramics                   # glass fragments —                  │
│                                # metal fragments —                  │
│     Date Collected 18/VI/75       By  JRA                           │
└─────────────────────────────────────────────────────────────────────┘
```

Fig. 4.2. A typical lot card, showing the data collected in the field during the surface survey.

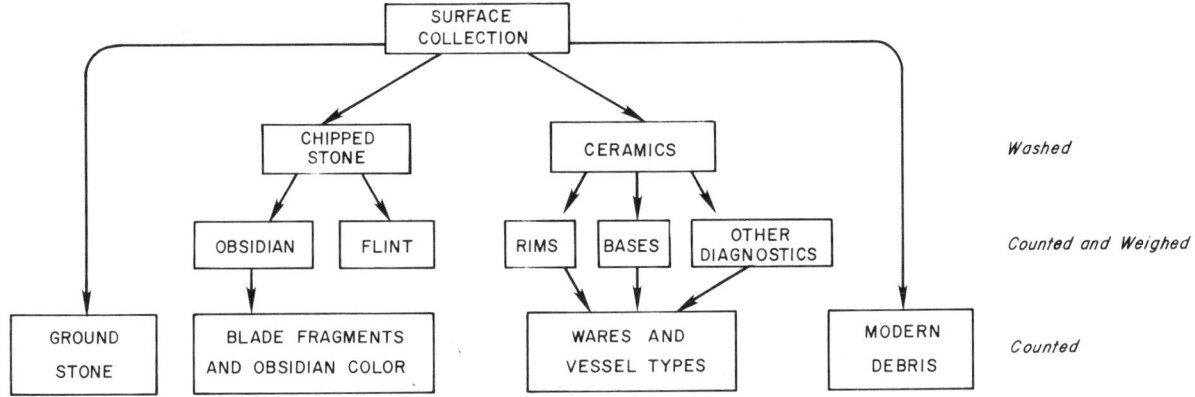

Fig. 4.3. The procedure followed in recording data from the surface collections.

Each square was assigned to one of five surface types: "salt" mounds, "construction" mounds, fallow fields, plowed fields, and areas that showed no indication of ever having been farmed. Thus the collection squares form a purposive (that is, neither random nor systematic) sample of surface deposits on the site, stratified by surface type.

Each collection unit was oriented along the cardinal axes of the compass, and each was located by the coordinates of its southeast corner in the site grid system. Squares were positioned by selecting areas where collections were desired and placing in each a small stake, located with the alidade and taken as the southeast sorner of the collection square. When possible, squares were laid out to exclude areas of recent disturbance or those presenting physical obstacles such as dense, thorny vegetation or hills of biting ants.

In collecting the squares, all sherds, chipped stone, small artifacts, and modern debris were removed for analysis. All fist-sized or larger stones scattered in the square were weighed, and fragments of manos and metates were counted and left in pace. Fig. 4.2 shows a lot card for a typical collection unit with the data recorded in the field for each surface collection. The collected artifacts were washed, divided into categories, weighed, and counted. Fig. 4.3 illustrates the general procedure followed, and the Appendix to this chapter summarizes the data acquired.

The collection technique used here presented a drawback others may wish to avoid. At Quachilco, both 5 by 5 m and 10 by 10 m squares were collected in order to decrease the sherd sample in areas with dense sherd cover or to limit the time spent weighing stones where they predominated. In some cases, adjacent 5 by 5 m squares were collected to get adequate ceramic samples and minimize the weighing of stones. But for analysis, these irregularities had to be resolved by adjusting each collection unit to a standard 10 by 10 m size. While this multiplication was not difficult, it was apparent that very localized irregularities in artifacte density which had been smoothed over in the larger collection units could

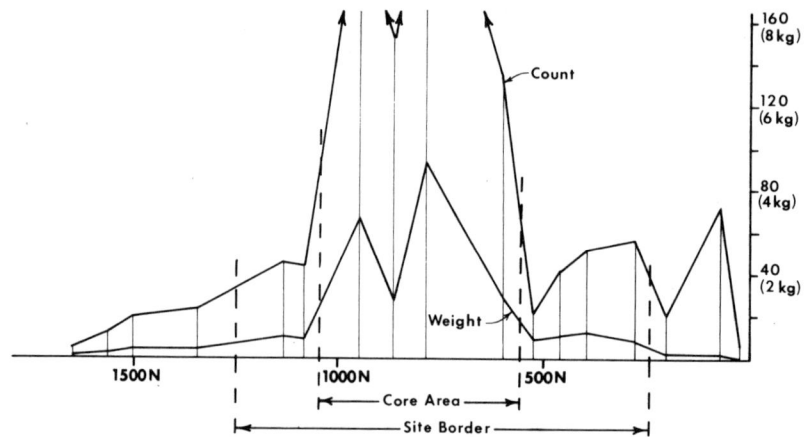

Fig. 4.4. Sherd counts and weights for the north-south transect samples.

affect the artifact proportions in smaller units. This problem could have been avoided by using only the larger sample units; they seemed to be on a scale more commensurate with the scale of variability being examined. Circular units or squares of odd sizes (for example, 7.07 by 7.07 m for an area of 50 m) could be used, but if at all possible all collections should be taken using a single sized unit.

Defining the Site Boundaries

The limits of prehistoric occupation at Quachilco were determined from an examination of the transect sample collections. Total counts and weights of prehistoric ceramics in each square were plotted against the north and west coordinates of the square (Figs. 4.4 and 4.5). These plots showed two apparent breaks in sherd density as measured by weight: areas with less than 0.3 kg per 100 m² were treated as outside the borders of the site, and areas with over 1.0 kg per 100 m² were considered the core, or area of densest occupation, of the site. These levels of sherd density are

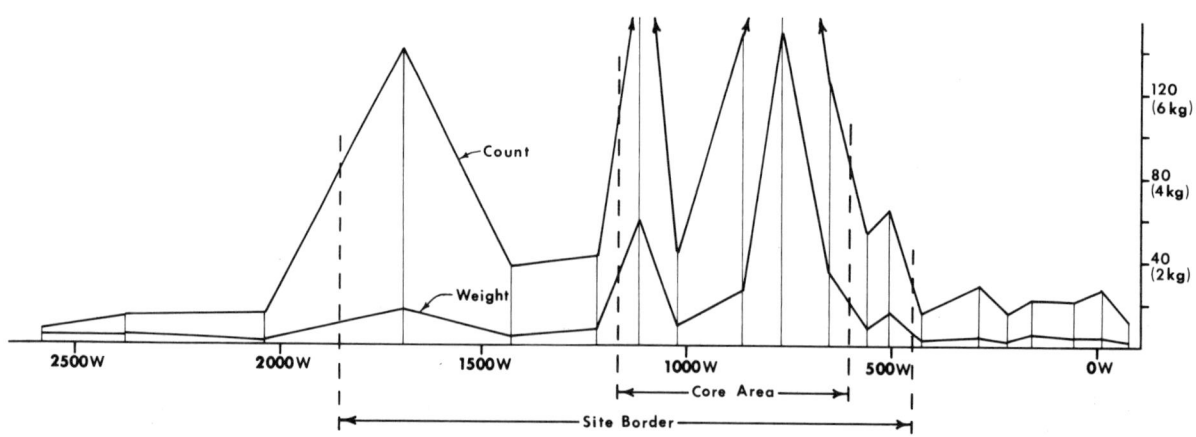

Fig. 4.5. Sherd counts and weights for the east-west transect samples.

4. SYSTEMATIC SURFACE SURVEY AT QUACHILCO 135

only empirical; while they seem to work at Quachilco, they cannot be directly applied to any other site.

The area of the site was calculated by connecting the points along each transect where these breaks occurred and measuring the enclosed area (Fig. 4.6). The area of the central plaza is about 4 ha, the core of the site covers about 16 ha, and the peripheral area of dispersed sherd scatter measures about 80 ha, giving a total site area of about 100 ha. Beyond these limits, there is an area about four times as large with a very light (less than 0.3 kg per 100 m^2) sherd cover.

These figures delimit the area to be studied as a "site" in this chapter, but note that Drennan (1978) has taken a broader definition. Because this site is composed of several distinct chronological periods of occupation, it will be necessary to use more detailed techniques to determine the areas occupied during each period and to estimate the period by period population at the site.

Chronological Patterns of Site Occupation

To estimate the population of Quachilco during the Late Santa María/ Early Palo Blanco, Late Palo Blanco, and Venta Salada phases it is first necessary to establish the site size during each of these periods (see chronological chart in Fig. 1.1). Unfortunately, the relationship between surface and subsurface material in the same location is often tenuous. When there have been multiple stratified occupations and only limited mixing (an ideal situation for excavation), surface materials tend to reflect only the latest occupation. A collection taken from a lower area of the site can be distorted by materials which have eroded from nearby higher areas. Further, use of earlier debris as fill or raw material for adobe construction during later occupations can make the area of the earlier occupation seem much larger than it actually was. These problems make distinguishing between occupied areas of short chronological periods almost impossible unless very good chronological markers are common. It is possible, however, to consider longer periods with greater confidence, especially when the corpus of ceramics defining each period is distinctive. Fortunately, this is the situation at Quachilco, as will be shown below.

Dating the occupied area of the site involves the following assumptions:

    1. Each collection unit represents an unbiased sample of the surface materials from immediately surrounding areas with the same surface type designation.
    2. Collection samples are large enough to predict accurately the relative proportions of various ceramic types from the immediately surrounding area.
    3. There has been significant mixing between superimposed occupations by cultural or natural processes, and as a result sherds from all phases of occupation can be found on the surface of an area with multiple occupations.
    4. Downslope migration of cultural materials through erosion has

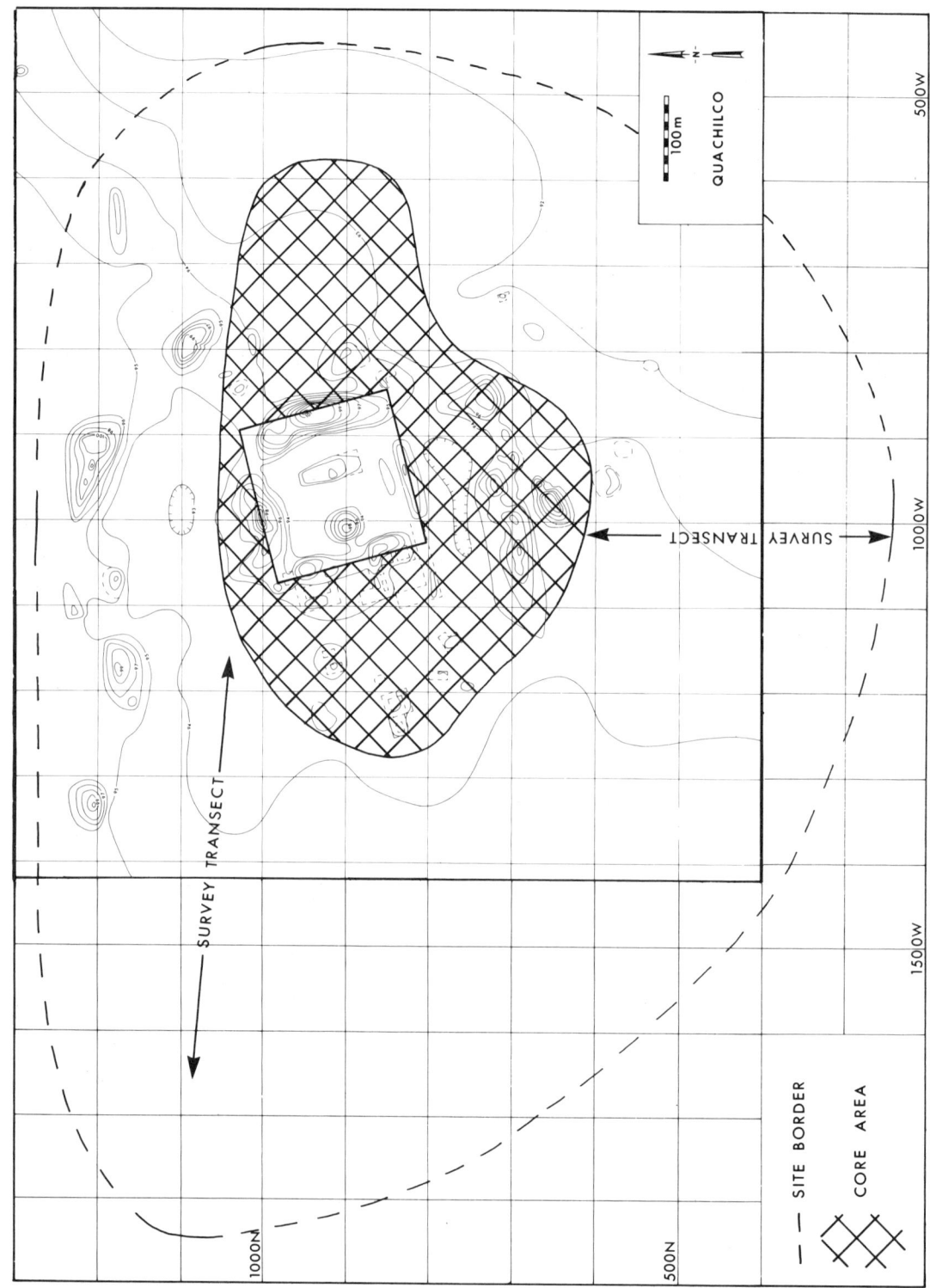

Fig. 4.6. Approximate boundaries of the site and its core area as defined by the transect samples.

4. SYSTEMATIC SURFACE SURVEY AT QUACHILCO 137

TABLE 4.1
DEFINITIONS OF CERAMIC TYPE GROUPS USED IN THIS REPORT

Ceramic Type Group	Ceramic Types Included (MacNeish, Peterson, and Flannery 1970)
Venta Salada	Teotitlán Incised, Coxcatlán Brushed, Coxcatlán Polychrome, Coxcatlán Red-on-Orange, Coxcatlán Black-on-Orange
Orange	El Riego Orange, Thin Orange
Gray	Río Salado Gray, Quachilco Gray, Quachilco Brown, El Riego Gray

been insignificant.

5. Transferral of earlier material into distant later occupation areas by cultural activity has been minimal.

6. Alluviation on the site has been insignificant, and therefore no areas of occupation have been hidden by geological processes.

Two techniques are used to date the collection units; they show varying sensitivity to the different assumptions above. The first technique examines the proportions of different ceramic types in the diagnostic sherds (defined here as rims, bases, decorated body sherds, and other unusual sherds such as handles, spouts, or feet) from each square. A square is considered to show occupation during a phase if a certain percentage of the diagnostic sherds found there can be definitely dated to that phase. This dating technique will require relatively large samples (Assumption 2) and will not identify an occupation if it has a superimposed occupation with relatively little mixing between the stratified layers (Assumption 3). The second dating technique uses absolute counts of chronologically specific ceramic types. If there is a certain minimum number of diagnostic sherds from a particular phase in a collection, then occupation during that phase is indicated. Mixing between superimposed occupations (Assumption 3) does not have to be as thorough as in the first dating technique for earlier occupations to be distinguished, but this method will be much more sensitive to transferred materials (Assumption 5). In practice, the second technique would be expected to indicate slightly larger areas of occupation per phase than the first technique, and after the collections have been dated I will briefly discuss how the validity of the above assumptions may affect the results obtained.

The frequencies of ceramic types defined by MacNeish, Peterson, and Flannery (1970) can be used to date surface collections. The approach here groups similar types together (Table 4.1). Table 4.2 gives the percentages of these type groups in the excavation units reported by MacNeish, Peterson, and Flannery (1970:Table 6), showing clear differences between the ceramics of the three periods of occupation at Quachilco. Late Santa María/Early Palo Blanco excavation units had negligible amounts of the Orange and Venta Salada groups. The total sherd assemblage studied by MacNeish, Peterson, and Flannery (1970) for the Late Santa María and Early Palo Blanco phases

TABLE 4.2

FREQUENCIES OF TYPE GROUPS FROM EXCAVATION UNITS

Type Group	Late Santa María/ Early Palo Blanco		Late Palo Blanco		Venta Salada	
	No.	%	No.	%	No.	%
Venta Salada	4	0.0	55	1.6	30,290	58.0
Orange	39	0.0	903	25.5	506	1.0
Gray	54,731	69.7	602	17.0	611	1.2
Total	78,476	100.0	3,543	100.0	52,252	100.0

Source: MacNeish, Peterson, and Flannery (1970:Table 6).

contained over 50% sherds from the Gray group. The Late Palo Blanco excavation units, when totalled contained 17% from the Gray group and 25% from the Orange group, with less than 2% Venta Salada types. The Venta Salada units, when totalled, had about 1% each from the Gray and Orange groups, but 58% Venta Salada types. It is possible to distinguish the chronological associations of the surface collections from Quachilco with these criteria.

Any significant percentage of Venta Salada types in a collection indicates that Venta Salada phase populations used that area of the site. Any significant percentage of types from the Orange group indicates a Late Palo Blanco use of the area, and any percentage of Gray types higher than the percentage of Orange types in a collection indicates a Late Santa María/ Early Palo Blanco occupation. In practice, the following percentages are taken to indicate occupations of the sampled area:
   Venta Salada phase—10% or more Venta Salada types;
   Late Palo Blanco phase—6% or more Orange types;
   Late Santa María/Early Palo Blanco phase—25% or more Gray types.
Thus, a single collection can indicate that an area was used during all three phases of occupation. Furthermore, any collection with the appropriate percentage of any one of these wares has to represent remains from that particular period (although it must be emphasized that those remains are not necessarily in situ).

Only collections with more than ten diagnostic sherds are considered in this percentage dating procedure, because small samples would not provide reliable estimate of the proportions of wares in the area sampled by the collection square (Assumption 2). This is not, of course, a conservative estimate of the reliability of a proportion derived from a small sample. It does, however, allow me to date 62 of the 90 collection squares. Had I used a more conservative number of diagnostic sherds as a lower limit (30, for example), I would have been able to date only 47 our of 90 squares.

For the second dating procedure, any square with five or more Orange or Venta Salada diagnostic sherds is considered to have been occupied during

4. SYSTEMATIC SURFACE SURVEY AT QUACHILCO

the Late Palo Blanco or Venta Salada phase, respectively. Any square having at least five more Gray sherds than Orange sherds is considered to have had a Late Santa María/Early Palo Blanco phase occupation. The choice of five diagnostics for identifying an occupation is also arbitrary. It reflects my belief that a few sherds may be scattered over very wide areas by subsequent cultural activity, but probably not more than one or two in any 10 by 10 m square. To avoid this problem, I chose five as a reasonable number of sherds for defining an occupation by this method.

Interestingly, only one square which was not datable to some phase by the first technique was dated by the second; conversely three squares not dated by the second technique were dated by the first. The main difference between the two methods is that the second (absolute counts) method identified five Venta Salada phase occupations on construction mounds where they had been disguised by very dense deposits of Late Santa María/Early Palo Blanco materials and four Late Santa María/Early Palo Blanco occupations which had been obscured by Venta Salada phase overburden. In general, however, the results of the two dating techniques are closer than might have been expected. Neither method is clearly superior in dating the Quachilco surface collections; the counts reveal light later occupations which have been numerically swamped by materials from earlier phases, but they also indicate early occupations in situations where the earlier materials may be derived from distant earlier deposits moved by later cultural activity.

One additional piece of evidence may be useful in evaluating the two dating techniques. A small excavation near collection square 79 revealed only Venta Salada phase deposits (Drennan 1977b:26 and Drennan 1978:60-62). It is possible that there are Late Santa María/Early Palo Blanco phase deposits under some portion of this mound, but none was found even though a small area was excavated to sterile soil. Both dating techniques correctly indicate a Venta Salada phase occupation, but only the counts technique indicates a Late Santa María/Early Palo Blanco phase occupation. Thus, the proportion technique (which is less sensitive to low sherd counts in large collections) may be more accurate in predicting when early occupations are actually not present under later deposits even though some early material occurs on the surface. That is, the proportion technique may not be as easily fooled by transportation of earlier debris into areas of later accupation. The results of both dating procedures are shown in Figs. 4.7-4.9.

In summation, a large number of the sample squares show clear evidence of a Late Santa María/Early Palo Blanco phase occupation substantially larger than that estimated by MacNeish et al. (1972:401). Only three of the collections indicate any occupation for the Late Palo Blanco phase. The conclusion that there was no significant occupation during this phase was also reached by MacNeish et al. (1972:205-216) on the basis of a non-systematic survey and several test excavations. But they seem to have underestimated the extent of the Venta Salada phase occupation of the site (1972:492); the systematic survey allows this later occupation to be delineated and permits the estimation of site populations during all phases of occupation.

Fig. 4.7. Sherd density across the Late Santa María/Early Palo Blanco occupation at Quachilco. Symbols identify collection squares showing Late Santa María/Early Palo Blanco occupations: stars, by the percentage method; open circles by the count method; and stars within circles, by both methods.

Estimating Site Population

Population estimates for the prehistoric occupations at Quachilco were derived by measuring the utilized area for each phase and then multiplying this area by a population density estimate based on surface sherd density. Density categories were defined by plotting sherd densities from

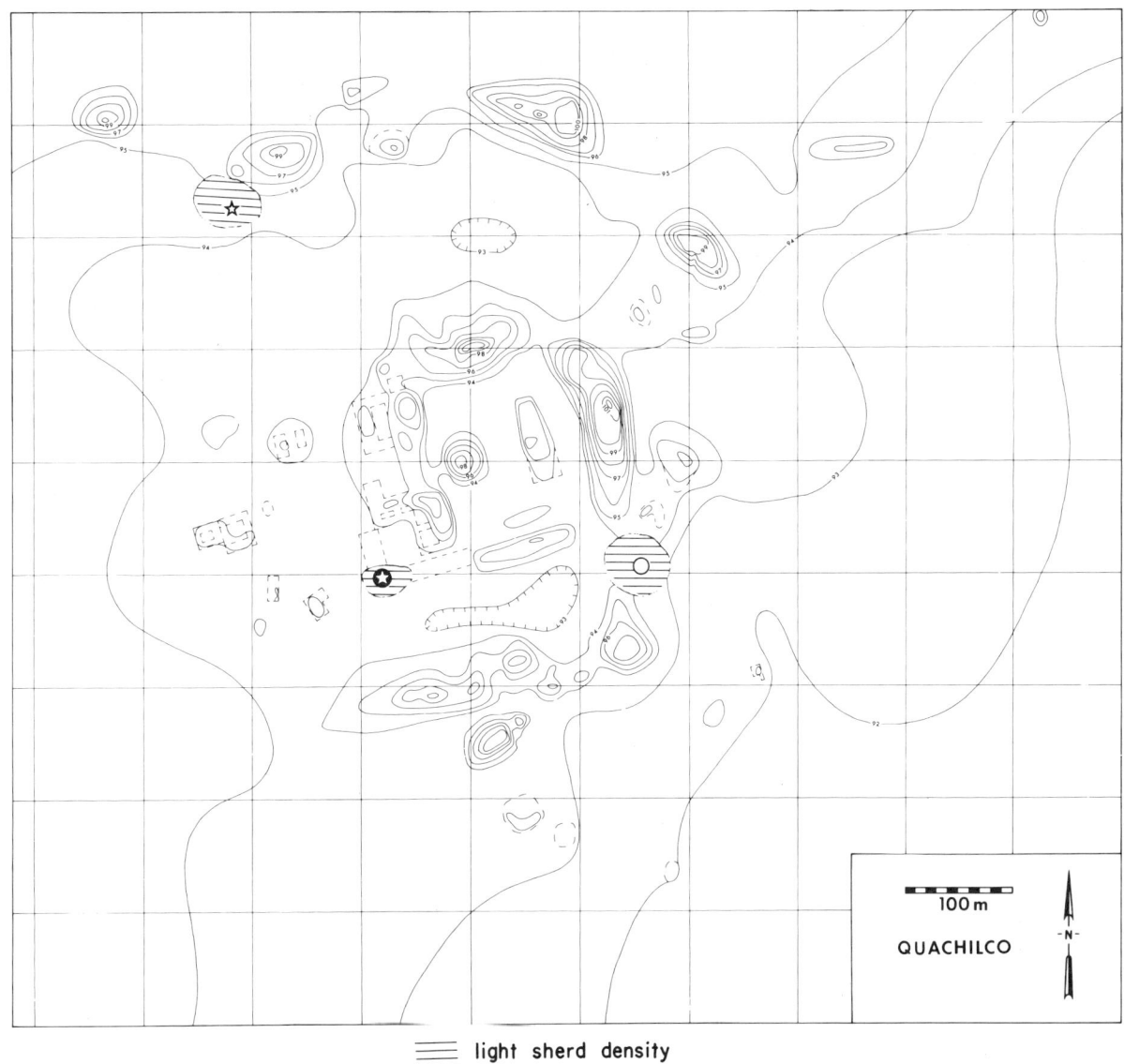

Fig. 4.8. Sherd density across the Late Palo Blanco occupation at Quachilco. Symbols are the same as in Fig. 4.7.

all dated squares by phase and dividing the collections into light, light to moderate, and moderate categories. Fig. 4.10 shows the frequency distributions of sherd density by phase and the limits of the density categories defined here.

For the sake of simplicity, the same categories were used for all phases of occupation, even though problems of overburden and erosion would tend to increase the numbers of surface sherds from the latest phase. As a result, the Venta Salada population is probably slightly overestimated relative to the Late Santa María/Early Palo Blanco population. Surface sherd density maps were drawn for each phase of occupation, and the total areas in each density category were measured. These areas were converted into population estimates by multiplying by the same figures used by Parsons (1971:23) in his Texcoco region survey; the results are shown in Table 4.3. The Late Santa María/Early Palo Blanco population is estimated between 300 and 650, approximately three times the estimated Venta Salada phase population.

These figures are of course only the simplest of estimates. Continuing excavations in the Tehuacán Valley should eventually allow more rigorous determinations of site populations, as presented by Tolstoy and Fish (1975:102-104). But the analysis of site area and sherd density presented

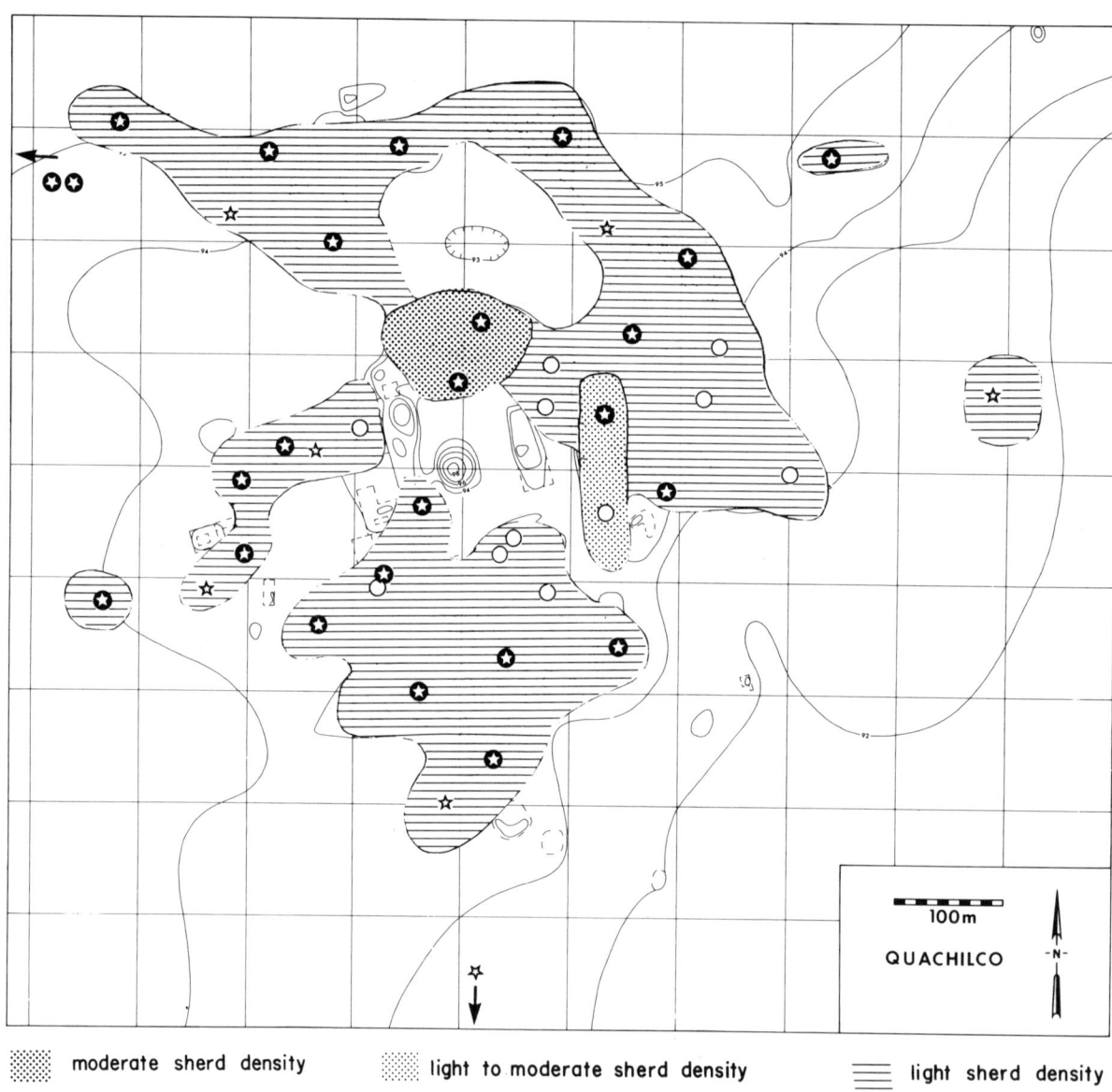

Fig. 4.9. Sherd density across the Venta Salada occupation at Quachilco. Symbols are the same as in Fig. 4.7.

4. SYSTEMATIC SURFACE SURVEY AT QUACHILCO   143

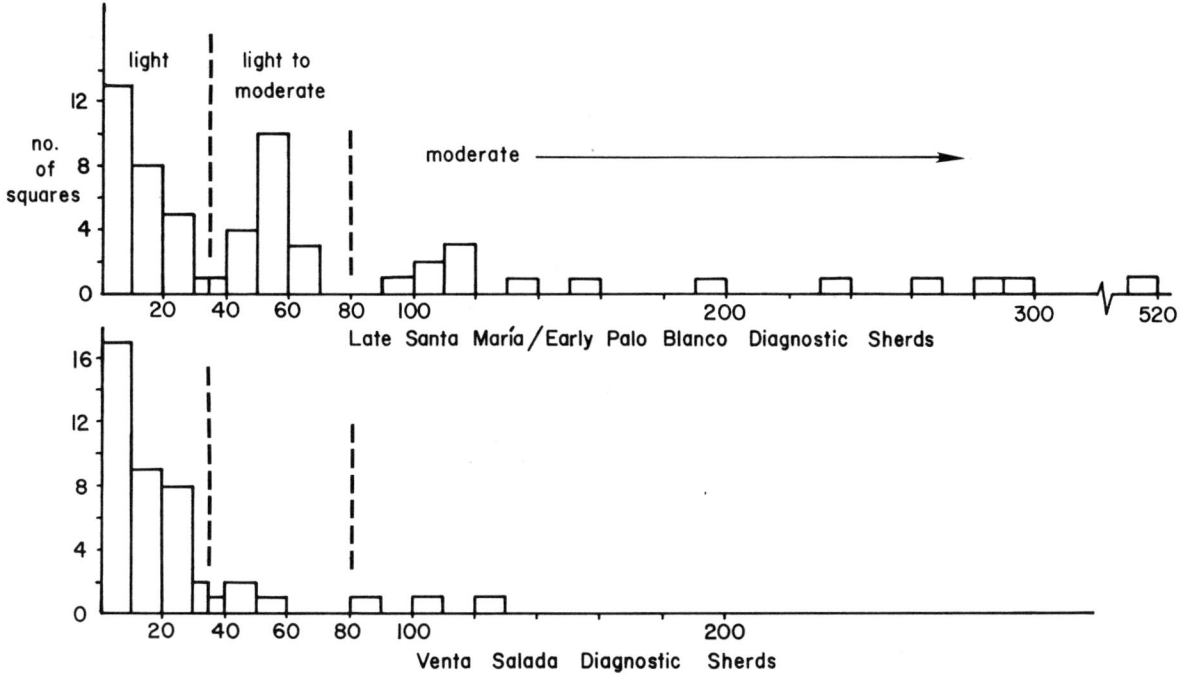

Fig. 4.10. Histograms of diagnostic sherd count in each collection square. The upper histogram shows counts of Late Santa María/Early Palo Blanco diagnostic sherds, and the lower histogram shows the Venta Salada ceramic counts (see Table 4.2). Divisions into density classes are shown by the heavy vertical dotted lines.

here should be useful in structuring research programs in the region which will eventually allow this analysis to be superseded.

Determining and Interpreting Strata within the Site

As was mentioned previously, surface squares were classified into five types in the course of the survey: "salt" and "construction" mounds, fallow and plowed fields, and areas with no indications of ever having been farmed. The only types requiring further definition are the two mound types. "Construction" mounds have numbers of fist-sized or large stones on their surfaces and are thought to represent the ruins of stone and plaster-faced architecture.

"Salt" mounds have few stones on their surfaces and also support very little vegetation; MacNeish et al. (1970:205) suggested that these mounds had resulted in some way from the process of salt production. It is not clear from the reports what criteria were used to distinguish salt production features from other mounds, basins, and terraces. In several places, MacNeish et al. (1972:443 and 447) mentioned that associated pottery, presumably Texcoco Fabric-Marked (Tolstoy 1958:51-53) suggested that mounds were used in salt production. Only one of the 13 salt mound collections at Quachilco contained any fabric-marked rims. Moreover, test excavations near collection squares 54, 73, and 79 (Drennan 1977b:26 and Drennan 1978:60-62) revealed that these three "salt" mounds were constructed of adobes. Neither of these facts is consistent with the identification of the "salt" mounds at Quachilco as locations of salt extraction.

Data were collected so that the five arbitrary surface types could be grouped together or distinguished on the basis of explicity quantitative measures. A histogram of the weights of large stones on the surface of the collection squares (Fig. 4.11) shows that the 13 salt mound squares are thereby easily distinguished from the 23 construction mound squares. No salt mound had more than 50 kg of large stones per 100 m^2, and no construction mound had less than 320 kg. No mound squares were misclassified in the field.

Field collection units could not be separated into categories on the basis of the large stone data. The four squares that showed no indications of ever having been farmed had more stone than most of the 50 farmed squares, but this is at least in part a result of farmers' tossing rocks into uncultivated areas. It was also impossible to subdivide the construction mound squares into two or more groups on the basis of weight of large stones on the surface. Future surface collecting on Palo Blanco phase sites, therefore, need not include weighing of large stones in each collection unit—the distinction between construction and salt mounds can be made accurately by eye, and a great deal of time and effort saved.

At this point, the plowed field and never farmed collection squares (five cases in all) were dropped from the sample because there were so few collections in each category. They were not lumped with the fallow field squares because the additional information they might have provided seemed less desirable than the advantage of having a clearly comparable set of collection units.

Next, the data were examined for patterns which could be related to

TABLE 4.3

POPULATION ESTIMATES FOR THE THREE OCCUPATIONS AT QUACHILCO

Sherd Density	Late Santa María/ Early Palo Blanco		Late Palo Blanco		Venta Salada	
	ha	pop.	ha	pop.	ha	pop.
Light	19.1	95-191	0.6	3-6	17.6	88-176
Light to Moderate	8.0	80-200			0.7	7- 17
Moderate	5.2	130-260			1.0	25- 50
Total Population		305-651		3-6		120-243

4. SYSTEMATIC SURFACE SURVEY AT QUACHILCO

the three remaining strata. Means and standard deviations of all ceramic and chipped stone variables were compared for all three strata. Scatter plots were drawn when these statistics for a variable differed greatly between strata. The most suggestive results were revealed by plots of counts versus weights of rim sherds and obsidian fragments.

Differences between Strata: Average Rim Sherd Size

The scatter plot of rim sherd counts versus weights by collection unit (Fig. 4.12) shows that construction mounds have the largest rim sherds and salt mounds the smallest. The possibility exists that the construction

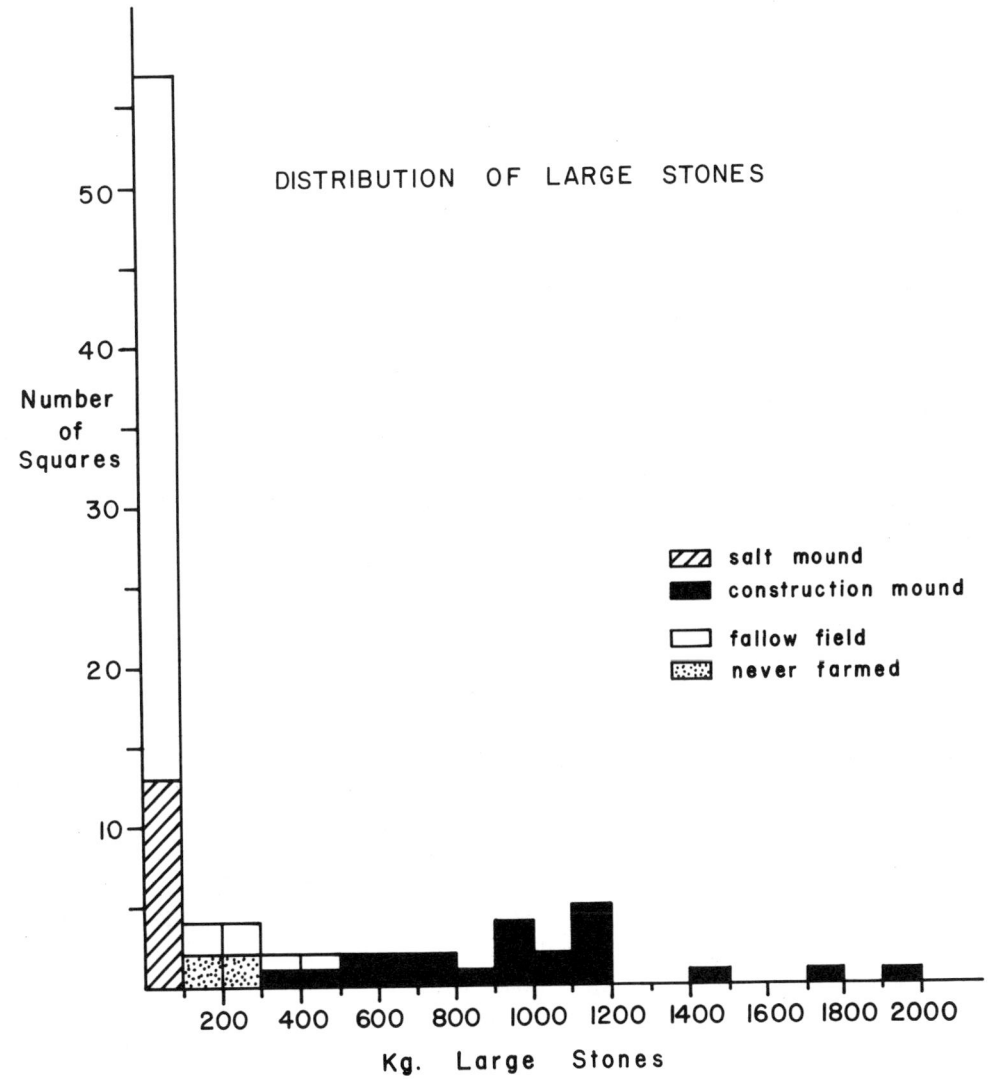

Fig. 4.11. Histogram of weights of fist-sized or larger stones from the collection squares. Surface types are distinguished by dots, parallel lines, and solid colors.

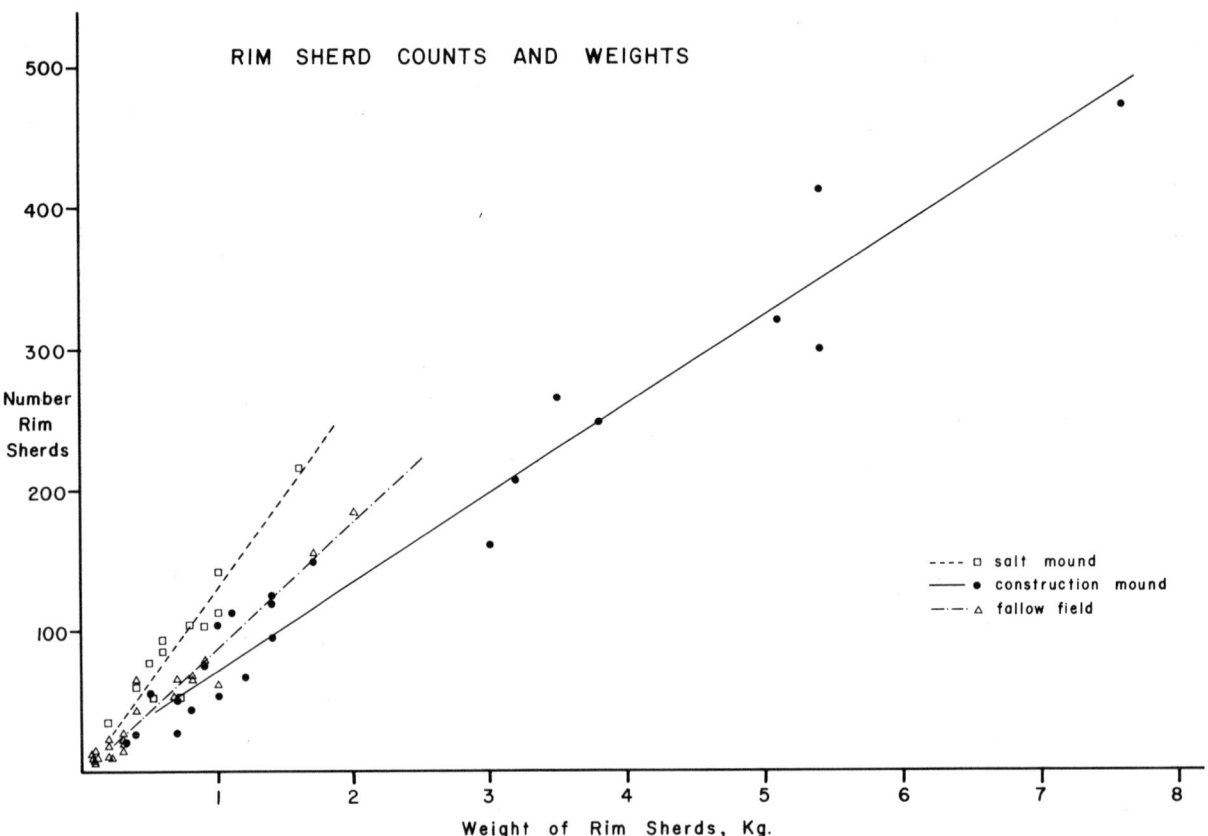

Fig. 4.12. Scatter plot of rim sherd counts and weights. The average rim sherd weight for each of the three surface types is indicated by the best-fit line drawn through each group of collections. Construction mound squares have the heaviest sherds, fallow field squares show a medium average weight, and salt mound collections have the lightest rim sherds.

mound collections represent two populations with respectively larger and smaller rim sherds, but all in all the average rim sherd size seems consistent within a stratum and clearly different between strata.

The non-parametric Mann-Whitney U test (Siegel 1956:116-127 was applied to the rim sherd weight data to determine if the rim sherds from construction mounds were significantly larger than fallow field rims, and if fallow field rims were significantly larger than salt mound rims. The average rim weights for all squares with 20 rims or more formed the basis of the calculations. For the comparison between construction mounds and fallow fields, $n_1 = 14$, $n_2 = 23$, $U = 244$, and the probability that the two samples were drawn from populations with the same mean was less than 0.01. For the comparison between fallow fields and salt mounds, $n_1 = 12$, $n_2 = 14$, $U = 23$, and the associated probability was less than 0.001. Thus, construction mounds have larger rim sherds than fallow fields, which, in turn, have larger rim sherds than salt mounds.

There are at least two possible explanations for this observed

4. SYSTEMATIC SURFACE SURVEY AT QUACHILCO

TABLE 4.4

MEAN PROPORTIONS OF THREE WELL-DATED CERAMIC CATEGORIES IN SURFACE STRATA AND t-TEST COMPARISONS OF STRATA

		Gray	Quachilco Mica	Coxcatlán Brushed
Mean Proportions of Ceramic Categories	Salt Mounds	34.3%	1.7%	12.6%
	Construction Mounds	46.7%	5.5%	8.3%
	Fallow Fields	32.6%	2.9%	9.1%
t-Test Results	Salt Mounds vs. Construction Mounds	Not Signif.	Signif.*	Not Signif.
	Salt Mounds vs. Fallow Fields	Not Signif.	Not Signif.*	Not Signif.
	Construction Mounds vs. Fallow Fields	Signif.	Signif.	Not Signif.*

Significance level for t-Tests is 0.05. * indicates an F-Test of variances significant at the 0.05 level, questioning the validity of the t-Test (Hays 1963:352).

distribution. First, it is possible that the different ceramic types found at Quachilco break in systematically different ways—large, thick-walled vessels yielding large sherds, and thinner, smaller vessels yielding smaller sherds. Second, the pattern could result from changes to the surface ceramics in different strata because of difference kinds of disturbances.

If the first explanation were correct, then we would expect systematic differences in the proportions of various ceramic types across the site and hence funtional, chronological, or status-related differences between strata. Data were not collected to test directly whether the various ceramic types at Quachilco break in significantly different ways. Had rim sherd weights for each ceramic type from each collection been available, this proposition could have been tested easily; unfortunately, these weights were not taken. Unquantified observations, however, suggest that rim sherds of the various ceramic types average about the same weight. The finer types with less tempering material tend to be used for thinner and smaller vessels and are generally fired at higher temperatures. Coarser types are commonly used for larger, thicker vessels such as ollas, large bowls, or comales. The coarse types (Quachilco Mica, El Riego Plain, El Riego Marble-Tempered, Río Salado Coarse, and Abundant Coarse Temper without Mica) break into smaller but thicker sherds, while the fine types (the Gray group, Coxcatlán Brushed and Teotitlán Incised) yield larger but thinner sherds. Because of these characteristics, the average rim sherd weights for the different types and vessel forms appear similar.

It is also possible to examine directly the percentages of ceramic types in the three largest strata. If these proportions were not significantly different, then differential breakage between ceramic types would not account for the observed differences between strata in average rim sherd weight. The results of a series of t-tests (Table 4.4) show that there are no statistically significant differences in the average proportions of Gray types or Coxcatlán Brushed between the salt mound squares and either of the other two strata. There is a significant difference between construction mounds and fallow fields in the proportions of both Gray and Quachilco Mica ceramics. All in all, the proportions of these (the most common) ceramic types in the various strata do not seem to show enough significant differences (especially between salt mounds and other strata) to account for the observed differences in average rim sherd weight.

The second explanation proposed above for the observed differences in rim sherd weights was that the different strata may represent different patterns of post-depositional disturbance. To examine this proposition, it is useful to divide factors affecting sherd size into two general categories: cultural activities, and natural processes. If salt impregnation and crystallization result in increased breakage, then the areas of the site with more saline soil would have smaller sherds. This would explain the small size of sherds in salt mound collections if the identification of the salt mounds as locations of salt extraction were correct; but it is doubtful that these mounds result from salt extraction (see above). Thus it is useful to examine cultural activities to discover sources for such a pattern.

Excavations at many sites in highland Mexico have shown that mounds with stone and plaster facings are often filled with cultural debris, including broken pottery. Excavations at Quachilco (MacNeish et al. 1972: 205-216, Drennan 1977b and Drennan 1978) have demonstrated this fact in at least some of the construction mounds at this site. Any ceramics which had been incorporated into mound fill in this manner might have broken in the process, but they should have been protected from further breakage by cultural activity. Sherds in fallow field squares, however, have been subjected to repeated breakage by farming activity in the area. Sherds from salt mound squares, where there is actually evidence of adobe construction (Drennan 1977b:26 and 1978:60-62), would have been thoroughly broken up by the brick-making process. These particular cultural activities would seem to account quite neatly for the pattern of average rim sherd weight shown in Fig. 4.12, with sherds from the protected fill of construction mounds being largest, and sherds from the adobe constructions of the salt mounds the smallest. Since natural processes of disturbance do not account for the observed differences between fallow field and construction mound squares, and since adobe constructions were found in the three excavated salt mounds, I conclude that the observed pattern of rim sherd weights results from cultural activity rather than natural processes or physical characteristics of the ceramics found in different strata.

This conclusion has several interesting implications. First, salt mounds with larger than average sherds (Square 17, for example) may represent something other than adobe constructions. Second, construction mounds with smaller sherds may not have been stone and plaster construction over a core of fill (for example, Squares 22 and 74) or may have suffered consider-

4. SYSTEMATIC SURFACE SURVEY AT QUACHILCO

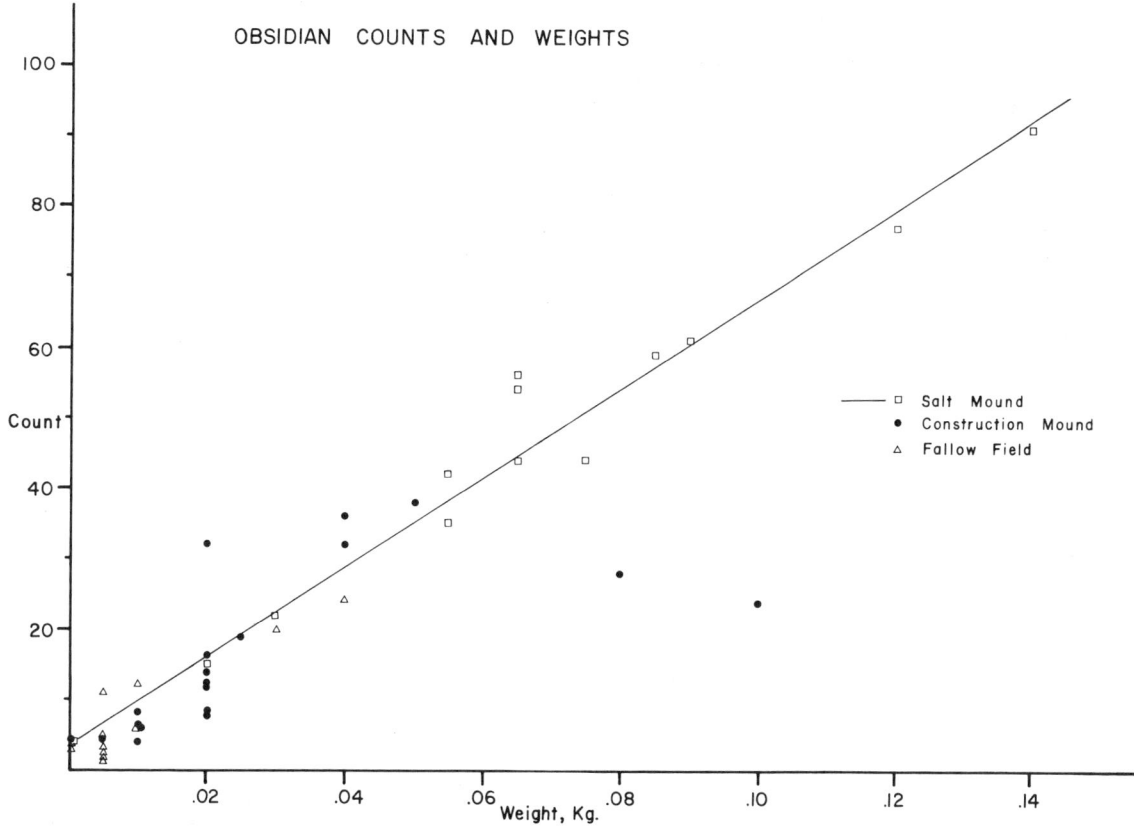

Fig. 4.13. Scatter plot of obsidian counts and weights. The salt mounds form the only surface type that appears to have obsidian fragments of very regular size.

able later disturbance (Square 65). Finally, fallow field squares with the largest sherds (Square 81) may represent areas of the site with little disturbance, while squares of this stratum with smaller sherds (Square 18) could be areas where adobe constructions were once located. Such anomalous surface collections might identify areas of the site which should be investigated if a sample of diversity within strata is desired; they certainly indicate areas which should be avoided if typical deposits from a stratum are the object of excavation. Once the analysis of material from the 1977 excavations at Quachilco is complete, these ideas can be investigated.

Differences between Strata: Average Obsidian Weight

The graph of counts versus weights of obsidian fragments (Fig. 4.13) suggests that the obsidian from salt mound squares is more regular in size than obsidian from other surface strata. The nonparametric Wald-Wolfowitz runs test (Siegel 1956:136-145) fails to show significant differences between the salt mounds and other strata with respect to the average weight of obsidian pieces. (All collections with 20 g or more of obsidian per

100 m² were included; $n_1 = 12$, $n_2 = 15$, $r = 13$, $p > 0.05$.) The Wald-Wolfowitz runs test is, however, of limited power since it tests simultaneously for various kinds of differences between the samples. Accordingly, the variance ratio of the two samples (salt mound squares and construction mound squares, considering only those collections with 20 g or more of obsidian per 100 m²) has been compared to the F distribution (Dixon and Massey 1969:111-112). The F test indicates that the construction mound squares show a higher variance in average obsidian piece weight than the salt mound squares ($N_1 = 12$, $N_2 = 13$, $F = 0.0285$, $p < 0.0005$). Thus, the obsidian fragments found on salt mounds show more uniformity in weight than those found on construction mounds.

Salt mound collections also reflect a greater rate of consumption of obsidian than construction mound collections. The ratio of obsidian to sherds is higher in the salt mound collections than in the construction mound collections, both by weight and by count. This difference was investigated with the Mann-Whitney U test (Siegel 1956:116-127). The probability of the hypothesis that the salt mound collections derive from a population with a higher obsidian to sherds ratio than the construction mound collections is 0.9890 ($n_1 = 13$, $n_2 = 23$, $U = 80$) in the case of ratios by count and 0.9332 ($n = 13$, $n = 23$, $U = 104$) in the case of ratios by weight. The density of obsidian in salt mound squares, irrespective of sherd quantities, was higher too, and the statistical significance of this difference was even greater. (This was also tested with the Mann-Whitney U: $n_1 = 13$, $n_2 = 23$, $U = 113$, $p = 0.9999$ for the number of pieces of obsidian per m²; $n_1 = 13$, $n_2 = 23$, $U = 120$, $p = 0.9994$ for the weight of obsidian per m².) The salt mounds also had a slightly higher percentage of both blade fragments (27.7% versus 23.0%) and non-banded obsidian (12.6% versus 10.0%).

Moreover, all datable salt mound squares show Venta Salada phase occupations, compared to only 62% of the dated squares in other strata considered together. Of the construction mound squares, 61% show Venta Salada phase occupations. It is possible that all these differences between the salt mound squares and other squares are related.

I would speculate that there was a distinct difference in the way that obsidian was obtained during the two occupations at Quachilco. During Late Santa María/Early Palo Blanco times, the inhabitants of the Tehuacán Valley had unimpeded direct or indirect access to a source of banded black obsidian, presumably from a source on the nearby volcanic peak of Orizaba. This obsidian was probably roughly shaped at the quarry, then brought into the Tehuacán Valley to be made into tools at the locations where it would eventually be used. Sometime during the Palo Blanco phase, the Orizaba obsidian sources came to be exploited less. During the later Palo Blanco and Venta Salada phases, obsidian was imported into the region in the form of blades or fully prepared blade cores through an exchange system controlled by the largest highland political units, initially the one centered at Teotihuacán. Such a regulated system of regional exchange would have provided Tehuacán with obsidian tools manufactured in distant wrokshops from material gathered from a mixture of sources.

Thus, the differences observed between the salt mound collections and other collections at Quachilco would be primarily the result of the greater proportion of Venta Salada phase material in these collections. The higher ratio of obsidian to sherds and the higher obsidian densities on salt mounds would be a reflection of a greater rate of consumption of obsidian, owing to increased availability under a system of intensive regional exchange operating during Venta Salada phase times. The regularity of size of obsidian pieces on the salt mounds could result from the increased standardization of production of tools which could be expected under such a system. Unfortunately, these differences only hint at the processes of obsidian procurement, since the majority of the obsidian from the surface collections at Quachilco comes from collections containing sherds from both occupations. Very little of the obsidian, therefore, can be dated. And none of it has been chemically analyzed to determine its source.

The shifts in obsidian procurement and distribution systems suggested here can, however, be further investigated with excavated data. If the changes outlined above occurred, then Late Santa María/Early Palo Blanco excavation units should have:

a) high proportions of obsidian from the Guadalupe Victoria or Pico de Orizaba sources (Pires-Ferreira 1975; Cobean et al. 1971);
b) blades, points, scrapers, and other tools made of obsidian from the same source;
c) relatively high ratio of debitage to tools (unless tools are made at specialized sites or in restricted areas within sites);
d) relatively high morphological variability within tool categories, especially between sites; and,
e) a relatively high proportion of blades with core preparation scars on their distal surfaces or with areas of cortex visible.

In Late Palo Blanco and Venta Salada excavation units, I would predict:

a) lower proportions of obsidian from the Guadalupe Victoria or Pico de Orizaba sources;
b) different tool types made of obsidian from different sources;
c) a low ratio of debitage to tools;
d) a high degree of morphological standardization within tool types and more marked similarity to contemporaneous obsidian tool types from other regions; and,
e) low proportions of blades with core preparation scars on their distal surfaces or with areas of cortex visible.

Differences between Collections within Strata

Each of the three major surface types was examined individually to see if any patterns of artifact distribution indicated subdivisions within a stratum. This was done by examining histograms and scatter plots of the artifact counts and weights for multimodality. A number of variables showed potentially interesting distributions; these were studied more carefully. The distribution of ratios of selected variables (obsidian to other chipped stone and bowls to ollas, for example) was also examined. Results for each stratum are discussed below.

Stratum 1: Salt Mounds. The most noteworthy fact about the salt mounds has been mentioned previously: the absence of fabric-marked pottery on most of these mounds and the discovery of adobe construction in all three excavated salt mounds mean they were probably not salt production sites. Rather, they seem to have been locations of adobe platforms constructed during the Venta Salada phase occupation of Quachilco, possibly the remains of residences. An examination of the Venta Salada ceramic distribution revealed no significant differences within the stratum. Further detailed analysis of Venta Salada phase artifacts might do so, but major attention here was to the earlier occupation of the site.

Stratum 2: Construction Mounds. These mounds, whose defining characteristic was high weight of building stone on the surface, could not, on the basis of surface data, be divided further into civic-ceremonial structures and residential structures. The lack of systematic differences in the surface ceramics has several possible interpretations: 1) that civic-ceremonial and residential structures were not differentiated; 2) that only one of the two types of structures was represented among the surface features classed as construction mounds at Quachilco; 3) that the materials used for fill in both types of structure came from the same source; or 4) that the civic-ceremonial mounds were built with debris which had accumulated around residential mounds, whereas residential mounds tended more to be accumulations of debris rather than construction with artificial fill.

The mounds forming the central plaza, with their formal arrangement, deliberate orientation, size, and steep sides, were almost certainly conceived of as different from the low, unpatterned scatter of construction mounds west of the plaza. Furthermore, this planning and the attendant effort of building the central plaza make it likely that there were functional differences between the two groups of mounds as well as differences in form. For this reason the first two suggestions above, that mounds with different functions were not differentiated at Quachilco and that all construction mounds had the same function, seem improbable.

The third and fourth suggestions imply different patterns of evidence. If the fourth suggestion above, that residential structures involved less construction with artificial fill, is accurate, then excavations would readily detect this difference. Preliminary reports on excavations at Quachilco (Drennan 1977b and 1978) do seem to show exactly such a pattern, with tall mounds around the central plaza made of deep artificial fill and lower mounds to the west and extreme southeast of it consisting of superimposed layers of more modest structures.

An additional difference implied by the last two suggestions would manifest itself in chronological study of artifacts from the construction mounds. If the third possibility above, that all mounds were built of materials from the same sources, is accurate, then no excavations in any of the mounds would produce ceramics in stratigraphic sequence showing fine-scale chronological change. They would be too mixed and would thus not seriate well. If residential mounds, however, were principally long-term accumulations of debris, then they should produce stratigraphic sequences of ceramics showing fine-scale chronological change. The evidence relevant to this point will, of course, emerge from the study of material from excavations already conducted.

The suggestion that the mounds were all filled with materials from similar sources would explain in part why no status or craft specialization differences were found in the surface collections from construction mounds. Most of the collections were taken from relatively high on the mounds, within the area where fill would be eroding. The lower slopes of the construction mounds might yield material more likely to show results of functional differentiation; in future surface surveys it might be best to make most collections from the skirts of of mounds rather than from near the tops.

Stratum 3: Fallow Fields. The frequency distributions of all but the rarer artifact types were smooth and continuous among collections from fallow fields. The only discontinuity observed was in the total quantity of ceramics, used previously to distinguish zones of different occupational density. It also appeared that almost all of the fallow field squares had a scattering of modern occupational debris, but no indications of any recent use except for farming. This observation leads to the final hypothesis to be presented in this report.

The modern debris in fallow and farmed fields appears to come from household refuse used to fertilize fields. This practice was observed both in the area where collections were taken and in other parts of the Tehuacán Valley. However, to my knowledge, archeological debris has not accompanied such transferral of refuse in this region; the precontact materials found around Quachilco probably do not result from this practice. Thus, I would speculate that the scatter of Late Santa María/Early Palo Blanco, Venta Salada, and modern artifacts in the outskirts of the site represent almost 2,000 years of field fertilization with household trash.

It might be argued that the relatively small population of the site and the large amount of available land would make such labor-intensive techniques unnecessary, for a long fallow system would ensure soil regeneration without fetilization. It may, however, be significant that the area around the site has been improved by the construction of an extensive network of recent and prehistoric irrigation ditches. The older ditches have become "fossilized" through deposition of calcium carbonate from the irrigation water, and thus have been preserved for hundreds or thousands of years (Woodbury and Neeley 1972:127-139). Drennan (1978:77) cited evidence that this irrigation system had been in operation by the Late Santa María phase. With such an irrigation system, it would be worth making a small yearly investment by fertilizing (probably using turkey manure and compost or other organic remains) to avoid making a major investment in extending the irrigation system to areas farther from the site. This practice would have been especially easy in the kind of dispersed occupation Drennan (1978:15-18) described for the area around Quachilco.

There is at least one bit of evidence for precontact fertilization in highland Mexico. Sahagún recorded an omen text (Sahagún 1957:128) describing the kinds of behavior which would protect a farmer from ill fortune:

> And if it were irrigated land, he opened his plot for irrigating. And if he had swamp land, and were a dweller in swamp country, he cultivated and planted maize for tamales, transplanted and set out chiles, and fertilized the land.

While this is certainly not irrefutable evidence of precontact fertilization in a form similar to that postulated here, it does suggest that the practice was known by Postclassic times.

Two kinds of archeological data would support the suggestion that the Late Santa María/Early Palo Blanco inhabitants of Quachilco fertilized their fields. First, test excavations in the outskirts of Quachilco should uncover no evidence of occupation structures. Second, the scatter of prehistoric sherds should coincide with the distribution of fossilized irrigation ditches. In fact, it might even be possible to distinguish the irrigation system of the Late Santa María/Early Palo Blanco occupation from that of the Venta Salada phase by mapping the linkages of fossil canals and comparing the canal networks with the pattern of surface ceramics from the two phases.

Conclusions

The detailed mapping and extensive stratified surface collection of Quachilco have yielded a high return on the time and effort invested. The limits of the site have been defined, and populations for the various phases of occupation have been estimated. Strata within the site have been defined and shown to correlate with certain patterns of artifact variability from the collection squares. In several cases, alternative explanations for these observed patterns have been suggested and procedures for testing the different explanations proposed. A number of these observations bear on the reconstruction of developing social and economic complexity in the Tehuacán Valley. The systematic surface survey has been, then, quite effective in reaching the general goals set for it.

Furthermore, the data collected have by no means been fully utilized. The collection data can be used to test hypotheses derived from excavation data and examined for patterning by using different statistical techniques or different groups of collection units. Finally, the collections provide data useful in dealing with questions that cannot be efficiently studied through excavation. Hopefully other sites in the region will be surveyed in a similar fashion; it appears to be a very productive means of research.

4. RECONOCIMIENTO DE SUPERFICIE SISTEMATICO EN QUACHILCO

por John R. Alden

SUMARIO

Durante la temporada de 1975 un programa intenso de colección de superficie se llevó a cabo en el sitio de Quachilco. Cuadros de 5 por 5 m y 10 por 10 m fueron trazados y todos los artefactos encontrados dentro de estos cuadros recogidos. Se hicieron recolecciones en 90 cuadros distribuídos por todo el sitio (Fig. 4.1). Cada cuadro se asignó a uno de cinco tipos según su superficie: montículos "salados," montículos de "construcción," campos en descanso, campos arados, y áreas que no tenían indicios de haber sido nunca trabajadas.

La densidad de cerámicas encontradas en los cuadros de colección nos proporcionó la base para determinar los límites del sitio, y para distinguir el área central de ocupación más densa. El área central (unas 16 ha adamás de las 4 ha de la plaza central) tenía en exceso de 1.0 kg de tepalcates por cada 100 m^2. Estas densidades se redujeron hasta 0.3 kg por 100 m^2 en las 80 ha restantes del sitio. Las áreas que produjeron menos de 0.3 kg por cada 100 m^2 fueron consideradas fuera del sitio, aunque se debe notar que Drennan (1978) ha definido el sitio en términos más amplios.

Para calcular la población de Quachilco es necesario separar la evidencia de las varias fases durante las cuales el sitio fue ocupado. Hay básicamente tres períodos de ocupación: el primero durante las fases Santa María Tardía/Palo Blanco Temprana; el segundo, una ocupación poco densa durante la fase Palo Blanco Tardía; y el tercero durante la fase Venta Salada. El llegar a conclusiones sobre períodos de ocupación basadas en colecciones de superficie implica varias suposiciones en lo que concierne a la exactitud con que el material de superficie refleja la naturaleze de los depósitos bajo tierra. Hay que considerar hasta que grado los artefactos han sido movidos por acción humana o de la naturaleza y hasta que punto la acción del aluvión ha tapado restos en la superficie. Dos técnicas diferentes fueron usadas en el análisis de colecciones de superficie para determinar que período de occupación estaba representado. Una técnica se basó en las proporciones de varios tipos de cerámica en depósitos excavados de fases particulares. Con esta técnica una ocupación de una fase particular era indicada si la proporción de tipos característicos para esa fase excedía la proporción máxima de esos tipos en depósitos excavados de otras fases. Ya que esta técnica no era precisa con colecciones muy pequeñas, y además no era sensible a tipos raros pero cronológicamente significantes, la segunda técnica simplemente hizo uso de la presencia de un número fijo de tepalcates de cierto tipo para indicar ocupación durante una fase particular. Los resultados de estas dos técnicas probaron, en su mayoría, ser complementarios.

Cálculos preliminares de la población del sitio fueron hechos en la misma manera que los hechos por Parsons (1971:23) en su reconocimiento de la región de Texcoco. Según este criterio la población de la fase Santa María Tardía/Palo Blanco Temprana era de 300 a 650 habitantes. Si se incluye el área que Drennan (1978) considera como parte de Quachilco esta cifra debe ser aumentada. La ocupación durante la fase Palo Blanco Tardía fue minúscula, y la población de la fase Venta Salada fue más o menos un tercio de la de las fases Santa María Tardía/Palo Blanco Temprana.

Dos de los tipos de superficie mencionados son los montículos "salados" y de "construcción." Los montículos salados son amorfos y con poca piedra en su superficie, mientras que los montículos de construccióon son más empinados y con una forma mas regular. Sus superficies están cubiertas con gran cantidad de piedra. Ningún montículo clasificado como montículo salado tenía más de 50 kg de piedra por cada 100 m^2, y ningún montículo de construcción tenía menos de 320 kg. Aunque los montículos de construcción parecen ser los restos de arquitectura de piedra, los montículos "salados" en Quachilco no parecen ser los restos de producción de sal como MacNeish et al. (1972:205) creyeron sino de estructuras de adobe (Drennan 1977:26 y Drennan 1978:60-62).

De los cinco tipos de superficie mencionados arriba campos arados y campos sin evidencia de agricultura están representados por demasiado pocos cuadros para estudiarlos. Entre los otros tres tipos se encontraron algunas diferencias interesantes. Las colecciones de montículos de construcción contienen tepalcates más grandes que los de campos en descanso, y las colecciones de campos en descanso contienen tepalcates más grandes que las colecciones en los montículos "salados" (Fig. 4.12). Consideraciones de las varias razones posibles para esta diferencia nos llevó a la conclusión de que la explicación más probable es que los tepalcates recogidos en montículos "salados" habían sido incluídos en los adobes de los cuales estas estructuras habían sido construídas. En el proceso de manufacturar el adobe estos tepalcates hubieran sido quebrados mucho más que aquellos que habían sido simplemente incluídos en el relleno de las estructuras de piedra, los restos de las cuales son los montículos de construcción. Los efectos del arado pueden ser responsables por el tamaño intermedio de tepalcates encontrados en colecciones de campos en descanso—es decir quebrados en pedazos más pequeños que en montículos de construcción, pero no tan pequeños como en motículos "salados."

Otro rasgo de las colecciones de los montículos "salados" es que los fragmentos de obsidiana son mucho más uniformes en peso que los de otras colecciones. La proporción de obsidiana a tepalcates es también mas alta en montículos "salados" que en ningún otro tipo de superficie. Sugerimos que esto resulta del cambio en la manera en que los residentes del Valle de Tehuacán obtenían la obsidiana. Ya que el material coleccionado de la superficie de montículos "salados" es principalmente de la fase Venta Salada (una diferencia con las otras colecciones) estas diferencias entre colecciones de montículos "salados" y otras colecciones pueden representar diferencias entre las actividades de la fase Venta Salada y de períodos de ocupación más tempranos. La manera de obtener obsidiana durante las fases Santa María Tardía/Palo Blanco Temprana puede haber sido por medio de

4. SYSTEMATIC SURFACE SURVEY AT QUACHILCO 157

acceso directo o indirecto a fuentes cercanas de obsidiana con mucho del trabajo de obsidiana hecho en el propio Valle de Tehuacán. El comercio de obsidiana en la fase Venta Salada era probablemente muy organizado e incluía comercio en navajas o núcleos preparados para navajas. Si este cambio tuvo lugar, este comercio bien organizado en obsidiana hubiera hecho que la obsidiana fuera más obtenible en la fase Venta Salada y por consiguiente más común en colecciones de tiempo tardío (i.e., las de los montículos "salados"). Además, la mayor uniformidad de manufactura asociada con producción en masa y comercio en gran escala en navajas hubiera resultado en menos variedad en el tamaño de los fragmentos de obsidiana en colecciones de tiempo tardío (i.e., las de los montículos "salados"). Estas diferencias en los patrones de la manera de obtener obsidiana pueden, por supuesto, ser probadas con los datos obtenidos en excavación.

La examinación de la distribución de varios tipos de artefactos no reveló ninguna diferencia significante entre las colecciones de los cinco tipos de superficies. La dispersión muy amplia de artefactos que provienen de la ocupación Santa María Tardía/Palo Blanco Temprana requiere más atención. Estos artefactos se encontraron en densidades bajas en áreas adonde no había ninguna otra indicación en la superficie de habitación. Pequeñas cantidades de material moderno también se encontraron en estas áreas. Es posible que, como el material moderno, los artefactos prehispánicos fueron regados con el material orgánico usado para fertilizar los campos. En épocas prehispánicas puede ser que basura casera era usada principalmente en esta forma. Fertilización puede ser particularmente probable en situaciones como la de Quachilco, adonde residencias estaban regadas por las áreas de cultivo y donde una inversión considerable ya había sido hecha en el sistema de irrigación para la mejora de la tierra de cultivo.

En conclusión, este programa de reconocimiento de superficie dió prueba de ser muy útil. Llevó relativamente poco tiempo y esfuerzo y produjo no sólo sugerencias que pueden ser probadas por medio de excavaciones, sino que también un entendimiento del sitio más extenso y completo del que hubiéramos conseguido por medio de una excavación limitada.

APPENDIX TO CHAPTER 4

The table which follows gives a summary of the data from the systematic surface survey at Quachilco. Data are given for each of the 90 squares collected, numbered as they are labeled in Fig. 4.1. The notes provide explanations of the categories of information encoded in the table. Note that in some cases the numbers in the table are counts, in some cases weights, and in some cases codes to various classes of objects.

Square Information

1. NORTH COORD   The north coordinate of the southeast corner of the collection square in the site grid system.
2. WEST COORD   The west coordinate of the southeast corner of the collection square in the site grid system.
3. SURF STRAT   Surface stratum, the five basic conditions of the surface at the time the collections were made. The analysis described above was organized with reference to these strata. Code: 1=Salt mound; 2=Construction mound; 3=Fallow field; 4=Field with no evidence of farming; 5=Plowed field.
4. GRND COVER   Density of vegetation ranked on a scale from 1 (low) to 5 (high).
5. DISTURBANCE   Degree of disturbance of the surface prior to collecting, ranked on a scale from 1 (low) to 5 (high).
6. AREA   The area (in m^2) of the square from which the collection was made.
7. LSM/EPB OCC   Indicates the squares which gave evidence of occupation during Late Santa María/Early Palo Blanco times. Code: 0=No occupation indicated; 1=Occupation indicated by the sherd count method; 2=Occupation indicated by the sherd percentage method; 12=Occupation indicated by both methods.
8. LPB OCC   Indicates the squares which gave evidence of occupation during the Late Palo Blanco phase. Code is the same as for No. 7, above.
9. VS OCC   Indicates the squares which gave evidence of occupation during the Venta Salada phase. Code is the same as for No. 7, above.

Ceramic Summary

10. TOT SHRD WT   The total weight of all sherds (in grams, to the nearest 10 g).
11. DIAGNOST CT   The total number of all diagnostic sherds collected, defined here as rim sherds, basal angles, decorated body sherds, and special forms such as handle, spout, or

		support fragments.
12.	RIM SHRD CT	The total number of rim sherds collected.
13.	RIM SHRD WT	The total weight of rim sherds (in grams, to the nearest 10 g).

Ceramic Types

The types used in the analysis of the pottery for this report correspond, for the most part, to those defined by MacNeish, Peterson, and Flannery (1970). Specific citations are given below to their descriptions and points of departure are noted. The types are listed in approximate chronological order according to the seriation of MacNeish, Peterson, and Flannery (1970:Fig. 7). In all cases, the term "diagnostic sherds" means all rims, bases, decorated bodies, and other special features such as bases, spouts, handles, etc. Plain bodies are excluded.

14.	COATEPEC WH	The number of diagnostic sherds of Coatepec White (MacNeish, Peterson, and Flannery 1970:103-107).
15.	RS CRS OLLA	The number of olla rim sherds of Río Salado Coarse (MacNeish, Peterson, and Flannery 1970:76-78).
16.	RS CRS OTHR	All other diagnostic sherds of Río Salado Coarse not counted in the preceding category.
17.	GRAY BOWL	The Gray type group, as discussed in the text, includes Río Salado Gray, Quachilco Gray, Quachilco Brown, and El Riego Gray (MacNeish, Peterson, and Flannery 1970:78-83, 114-134, and 146-157). This category represents the number of rims of outleaned wall bowls, convex wall bowls, and cylinders of these types.
18.	GRAY OLLA	The number of olla rims of the Gray type group.
19.	GRAY OTHER	All other diagnostics from the Gray type group, primarily basal angles from flat based bowls and "basal flanges" (MacNeish, Peterson, and Flannery 1970:129).
20.	Q MICA OLLA	The number of olla rims of Quachilco Mica (MacNeish, Peterson, and Flannery 1970:110-114).
21.	Q MICA OTHR	All other diagnostic sherds of Quachilco Mica.
22.	QUACH RED	All diagnostic sherds of Quachilco Red (MacNeish, Peterson, and Flannery 1970:155-157).
23.	AB CRS OLLA	Abundant Coarse Temper Without Mica Olla Rims—the number of olla rims of a type of coarse pottery which does not precisely correspond to any of the types defined by MacNeish, Peterson, and Flannery (1970). The descriptive name here tentatively assigned to it indicates its major defining characteristics: very abundant temper occurring in large grains with no visible mica.
24.	AB CRS OTHR	All other diagnostic sherds of this same trial type.
25.	ELRIEGO BLK	All diagnostic sherds of El Riego Black (MacNeish, Peterson, and Flannery 1970:157-160).
26.	ELRIEGO PLN	All diagnostic sherds of El Riego Plain (MacNeish, Peterson, and Flannery 1970:168-170).
27.	ELRIEGO ORN	All diagnostic sherds of El Riego Orange (MacNeish, Peterson, and Flannery 1970:164-168).

APPENDIX TO CHAPTER 4

28. THIN ORANGE   All diagnostic sherds of Thin Orange (MacNeish, Peterson, and Flannery 1970:170-174). These sherds have not been analyzed chemically or petrographically, but the sherds counted in this category all correspond visually to "Group A" of Sotomayor and Castillo Tejero (1963:10-12) and "Core Thin Orange" of Harbottle, Sayre, and Abascal M. (n.d.:15-16).

29. ELRIEGO MRB   All diagnostic sherds of El Riego Marble-Tempered (MacNeish, Peterson, and Flannery 1970:178).

30. TEOT INC BL   The number of outleaned wall bowl and convex wall bowl rim sherds of Teotitlán Incised (MacNeish, Peterson, and Flannery 1970:203-206).

31. TEOT INC OT   All other diagnostic sherds of Teotitlán Incised.

32. COXCAT GRAY   All diagnostic sherds of Coxcatlán Gray (MacNeish, Peterson, and Flannery 1970:189-196).

33. COXCAT RED   All diagnostic sherds of Coxcatlán Red (MacNeish, Peterson, and Flannery 1970:196-199).

34. COX BRSH BL   The number of outleaned wall bowl and convex wall bowl rim sherds of Coxcatlán Brushed (MacNeish, Peterson, and Flannery 1970:178-189).

35. COX BRSH OT   All other diagnostic sherds of Coxcatlán Brushed.

36. RED/BLK-ORN   All diagnostic sherds of Coxcatlán Red-on-Orange and Coxcatlán Black-on-Orange (MacNeish, Peterson, and Flannery 1970:199-203 and 220-222).

37. COX POLYCHR   All diagnostic sherds of Coxcatlán Polychrome (MacNeish, Peterson, and Flannery 1970:218-220).

38. FONDOS SELL   The number of fondo sellado sherds. This very noticeable decorative technique is characteristic of the Venta Salada phase and occurs on the interior bottoms of bowls primarily of Coxcatlán Brushed and Coxcatlán Gray. It is described and illustrated by MacNeish, Peterson, and Flannery (1970:188-190), who refer to such sherds as "stamped bottoms" and/or "molcajetes."

39. XANTILES   The number of xantil fragments. MacNeish, Peterson, and Flannery (1970:225) describe these large, hollow, Venta Salada phase figurines made of various pottery types. They make good time markers for the Venta Salada phase so long as the sherd classifier guards against the possibility of classifying miscellaneous, unidentifiable, possible effigy fragments of all phases into this category.

40. TEXCOCO FAB   All diagnostic sherds of Texcoco Fabric-Marked as described by Tolstoy (1958:51-54), who also discusses the association of this type with the production of salt. MacNeish, Peterson, and Flannery (1970) refer to the same type as "Texcoco Fabric-Impressed" in their sections on trade wares of the Palo Blanco and Venta Salada phases.

41. MODERN SHRD   All diagnostic sherds identifiable to the period following Spanish contact as well as all glazed sherds, some of which are not diagnostics in the sense used here.

42. OTH CERAMIC   The presence of all other ceramic objects indicated by the following code: 1=Spindle whorl; 2=Worked sherd

disk; 3=Ticomán figurine body (MacNeish, Peterson, and Flannery 1970:141-142); 4=Oaxaca trial type 5 figurine (Drennan 1976a:233); 5=Other (unidentified) figurine. Two digit numbers signify the presence of the artifacts indicated by the two digits taken separately.

Nonceramic Artifacts

43. GROUND STN   The presence of ground or pecked stone indicated by the following code: 1=Celt of either of the types described by MacNeish, Nelken-Terner, and Johnson (1967:128-130); 2=Hammerstone; 3=Ornament of ground stone, such as a pendant, bead, or earspool; 4=Whetstone, a stone showing signs that it was used to abrade some other substance. Two digit numbers signify the presence of the artifacts indicated by the two digits taken separately.
44. MANO/METATE   The number of fragments of manos or metates of whatever specific type.
45. BLDG STN   The total weight, in kilograms, of all rocks of fist size or larger which are not manos or metates. Rocks did not have to show positive evidence of use in construction to be weighed in this category.
46. PLASTER   The total weight of all plaster fragments (in grams, to the nearest 10 g).
47. MODERN NONC   The number of objects, other than ceramics, identifiable to the period since Spanish contact. This includes plastic, glass, virtually all metal, etc.

Chipped Stone

48. OBSIDIAN CT   The total number of pieces of obsidian.
49. OBSIDIAN WT   The total weight of all obsidian (in grams, to the nearest 10 g).
50. OT CHSTN CT   The total number of pieces of all chipped stone of whatever material except obsidian.
51. OT CHSTN WT   The total weight of all chipped stone of whatever material except obsidian (in grams to the nearest 10 g).
52. BIFACES   The presence or absence of bifacially worked chipped stone tools of any material according to the following code: 1 or 2=Thin biface (MacNeish, Nelken-Terner, and Johnson 1967:89-92); 3=Tehuacán Point (MacNeish, Nelken-Terner, and Johnson 1967:72-73); 4=Harrell Point (MacNeish, Nelken-Terner, and Johnson 1967:77); 5=Possible Harrell Point; 6=Ensor Point (MacNeish, Nelken-Terner, and Johnson 1967; 73-75); 7=Teotihuacán Point (MacNeish, Nelken-Terner, and Johnson 1967:75-76); 8=Morhiss Point (MacNeish, Nelken-Terner, and Johnson 1967:75). Two digit numbers signify the presence of the artifacts indicated by the two digits taken separately.

53. FINE BLADES   The number of fine blade fragments, following the distinction between fine blades and crude blades made by MacNeish, Nelken-Terner, and Johnson (1967:17-26). These fine blades are all of obsidian.

QUACHILCO SURFACE SURVEY DATA -- VARIABLES 1-27

	VAR. NO.	SQ. 1	SQ. 2	SQ. 3	SQ. 4	SQ. 5	SQ. 6	SQ. 7	SQ. 8	SQ. 9	SQ. 10	SQ. 11	SQ. 12	SQ. 13	SQ. 14	SQ. 15
NORTH COORD	1	1285	1223	1254	1115	1132	1034	1193	775	1117	1078	903	886	843	822	790
WEST COORD	2	2590	2377	2185	2040	1694	1429	1315	1332	1213	1212	1266	1203	1236	1204	1288
SURF STRAT	3	3	3	1	3	3	3	1	3	3	3	3	3	3	2	2
GRND COVER	4	5	4	1	4	2	4	1	2	1	3	1	1	1	1	2
DISTURBANCE	5	1	1	3	2	1	1	3	1	1	1	2	1	1	1	1
AREA	6	100	100	100	100	100	100	100	100	100	100	100	100	50	50	100
LSM/EPB OCC	7	0	0	0	0	0	0	1	1	12	0	12	12	12	12	0
LPB OCC	8	0	0	0	0	0	0	0	0	2	0	0	0	0	0	0
VS OCC	9	0	0	12	0	12	0	12	12	2	0	0	12	0	12	0
TOT SHRD WT	10	200	190	6110	100	840	200	5060	1090	490	170	2700	1020	960	700	950
DIAGNOST CT	11	0	2	120	1	17	5	118	18	15	6	58	24	21	12	19
RIM SHRD CT	12	0	1	103	1	11	3	86	10	9	4	42	19	19	7	10
RIM SHRD WT	13	0	10	910	10	50	30	570	110	60	30	450	180	220	180	160
COATEPEC WH	14	0	0	0	0	0	0	0	0	0	0	0	0	0	0	0
RS CRS OLLA	15	0	0	2	0	0	0	0	0	0	0	7	0	2	1	0
RS CRS OTHR	16	0	0	0	0	0	0	0	0	0	0	0	0	0	0	0
GRAY BOWL	17	0	0	1	0	0	0	19	4	5	0	23	9	9	2	3
GRAY OLLA	18	0	0	0	0	0	0	0	0	0	0	0	0	1	0	0
GRAY OTHER	19	0	0	0	0	0	0	3	2	0	0	4	2	4	2	1
Q MICA OLLA	20	0	0	1	0	0	0	1	0	0	0	7	2	0	0	0
Q MICA OTHR	21	0	0	0	0	0	0	0	0	0	0	0	0	0	0	0
QUACH RED	22	0	0	0	0	0	0	1	0	0	0	3	1	2	1	0
AB CRS OLLA	23	0	0	2	0	0	0	3	1	0	1	0	0	2	0	0
AB CRS OTHR	24	0	0	0	0	0	0	4	0	0	1	0	0	1	0	3
ELRIEGO BLK	25	0	0	0	0	0	0	0	0	0	0	0	0	0	0	0
ELRIEGO PLN	26	0	0	2	0	0	0	1	1	1	0	0	0	0	0	1
ELRIEGO ORN	27	0	0	0	0	0	0	0	0	0	0	0	0	0	0	0

	VAR. NO.	SQ. 16	SQ. 17	SQ. 18	SQ. 19	SQ. 20	SQ. 21	SQ. 22	SQ. 23	SQ. 24	SQ. 25	SQ. 26	SQ. 27	SQ. 28	SQ. 29	SQ. 30
NORTH COORD	1	789	1175	1105	919	910	774	758	663	1179	1133	1081	975	937	932	867
WEST COORD	2	1233	1178	1116	1162	1128	1179	1134	1150	1055	1028	1011	1000	1092	1358	1033
SURF STRAT	3	3	1	3	2	3	2	2	2	3	1	3	3	2	2	2
GRND COVER	4	3	1	2	3	1	3	1	2	1	3	2	1	2	1	3
DISTURBANCE	5	1	3	2	1	1	1	1	1	3	1	1	1	1	1	1
AREA	6	100	100	100	50	100	50	50	100	100	100	100	50	50	50	50
LSM/EPB OCC	7	12	12	1	1	12	12	12	0	12	2	0	12	12	12	12
LPB OCC	8	0	0	0	0	0	0	0	0	0	0	0	0	0	0	0
VS OCC	9	2	12	12	12	2	0	12	0	12	12	0	0	0	0	12
TOT SHRD WT	10	1060	4360	3040	1530	1720	2250	1590	240	2480	530	400	4910	2580	5380	3010
DIAGNOST CT	11	36	81	85	36	24	45	40	6	52	11	7	94	52	107	60
RIM SHRD CT	12	27	55	65	27	21	30	28	3	35	5	4	66	34	75	40
RIM SHRD WT	13	330	700	430	330	290	340	240	30	250	80	40	870	620	1360	760
COATEPEC WH	14	0	0	0	0	0	0	0	0	0	0	0	0	0	0	0
RS CRS OLLA	15	0	0	0	1	2	4	0	0	1	0	0	8	2	1	5
RS CRS OTHR	16	0	0	0	0	0	0	0	0	1	0	0	0	0	0	1
GRAY BOWL	17	15	17	8	2	9	10	9	0	13	2	2	19	17	55	16
GRAY OLLA	18	1	0	0	0	0	0	0	0	0	0	0	0	0	0	1
GRAY OTHER	19	1	11	1	2	0	5	5	1	1	2	0	11	1	20	10
Q MICA OLLA	20	0	2	1	4	1	2	1	0	1	0	0	2	3	12	3
Q MICA OTHR	21	0	0	1	0	1	0	0	0	0	0	0	0	0	1	1
QUACH RED	22	1	1	0	0	1	0	0	0	1	0	0	3	0	1	1
AB CRS OLLA	23	0	2	2	2	0	4	4	0	0	0	0	6	0	0	3
AB CRS OTHR	24	0	0	0	0	1	5	3	0	0	0	0	1	0	0	1
ELRIEGO BLK	25	0	0	0	0	0	0	0	0	0	0	0	0	0	0	0
ELRIEGO PLN	26	0	0	1	0	0	0	0	0	0	0	0	0	0	0	0
ELRIEGO ORN	27	0	1	0	1	1	0	0	0	0	0	0	0	0	0	0

	VAR. NO.	SQ. 31	SQ. 32	SQ. 33	SQ. 34	SQ. 35	SQ. 36	SQ. 37	SQ. 38	SQ. 39	SQ. 40	SQ. 41	SQ. 42	SQ. 43	SQ. 44	SQ. 45
NORTH COORD	1	802	796	695	599	157	22	1659	1565	1506	1349	1191	1028	989	949	940
WEST COORD	2	1073	1075	1035	1012	1082	1015	938	962	979	945	903	981	914	916	949
SURF STRAT	3	2	2	1	3	1	4	3	3	3	3	3	1	2	2	2
GRND COVER	4	2	3	1	3	1	5	3	3	3	5	1	1	2	3	4
DISTURBANCE	5	1	1	2	1	2	1	2	1	1	1	2	1	1	2	1
AREA	6	50	50	100	100	100	100	100	100	100	100	100	50	50	100	50
LSM/EPB OCC	7	12	12	12	12	0	0	0	0	0	0	12	12	12	12	12
LPB OCC	8	0	12	0	0	0	0	0	0	0	0	0	0	0	0	0
VS OCC	9	12	1	12	2	0	0	0	0	0	0	12	12	1	1	0
TOT SHRD WT	10	3760	1510	3770	1370	540	40	30	90	240	190	4230	6420	3360	3330	290
DIAGNOST CT	11	86	45	89	19	8	1	0	2	1	6	111	143	80	89	8
RIM SHRD CT	12	48	31	61	15	5	0	0	0	1	3	79	103	62	66	7
RIM SHRD WT	13	710	360	370	260	30	0	0	0	30	10	480	1360	950	580	110
COATEPEC WH	14	0	0	1	0	0	0	0	0	0	0	0	1	0	0	0
RS CRS OLLA	15	0	1	0	0	0	0	0	0	0	0	4	0	2	0	1
RS CRS OTHR	16	0	0	0	0	0	0	0	0	0	0	0	1	0	0	0
GRAY BOWL	17	18	12	31	8	1	0	0	0	0	1	33	49	44	52	3
GRAY OLLA	18	2	1	1	0	0	0	0	0	0	0	0	2	1	1	0
GRAY OTHER	19	9	2	12	2	0	0	0	0	0	1	11	22	14	15	1
Q MICA OLLA	20	1	2	1	1	0	0	0	0	0	0	2	9	6	7	0
Q MICA OTHR	21	0	0	0	0	0	0	0	0	0	0	0	0	1	0	0
QUACH RED	22	1	0	0	0	0	0	0	0	0	0	3	0	1	0	0
AB CRS OLLA	23	0	1	0	1	0	0	0	0	0	0	0	7	0	0	0
AB CRS OTHR	24	0	0	0	1	0	0	0	0	0	0	0	0	0	0	0
ELRIEGO BLK	25	0	0	0	0	0	0	0	0	0	0	0	0	0	0	0
ELRIEGO PLN	26	0	1	0	0	0	0	0	0	0	0	0	0	1	0	0
ELRIEGO ORN	27	0	0	0	0	0	0	0	0	0	0	0	0	1	1	0

APPENDIX TO CHAPTER 4

QUACHILCO SURFACE SURVEY DATA -- VARIABLES 1-27

	VAR. NO.	SQ. 46	SQ. 47	SQ. 48	SQ. 49	SQ. 50	SQ. 51	SQ. 52	SQ. 53	SQ. 54	SQ. 55	SQ. 56	SQ. 57	SQ. 58	SQ. 59	SQ. 60
NORTH COORD	1	897	885	863	855	833	825	819	786	728	636	524	461	394	307	280
WEST COORD	2	990	939	919	924	952	961	961	914	954	967	994	992	974	935	918
SURF STRAT	3	2	2	3	2	4	2	2	3	1	1	3	3	3	5	3
GRND COVER	4	2	5	3	3	1	1	1	3	2	1	3	3	3	1	4
DISTURBANCE	5	2	3	1	1	1	2	1	2	3	3	1	1	1	1	3
AREA	6	50	15	100	50	25	50	50	100	100	100	100	100	100	100	100
LSM/EPB OCC	7	12	12	12	12	12	12	12	12	12	12	0	0	0	0	0
LPB OCC	8	0	0	0	0	0	0	0	0	0	0	0	0	0	0	0
VS OCC	9	0	0	0	0	0	1	0	1	1	12	12	0	0	2	0
TOT SHRD WT	10	2320	270	1280	980	2420	5730	3690	4570	8140	4950	420	500	590	210	380
DIAGNOST CT	11	34	4	33	19	49	166	68	116	165	124	8	7	14	7	9
RIM SHRD CT	12	21	3	23	13	36	118	52	78	111	93	4	3	12	5	8
RIM SHRD WT	13	420	40	220	240	390	1900	790	980	1050	580	100	40	140	70	120
COATEPEC WH	14	0	1	0	0	0	0	0	1	2	1	0	0	0	0	0
RS CRS OLLA	15	1	0	0	0	0	0	0	2	4	3	1	0	0	1	0
RS CRS OTHR	16	0	0	0	0	0	0	0	1	0	0	0	0	0	1	0
GRAY BOWL	17	11	2	17	8	24	100	40	43	66	47	0	0	1	2	4
GRAY OLLA	18	0	0	0	1	0	3	2	1	1	0	0	0	0	0	0
GRAY OTHER	19	0	1	7	4	6	39	14	13	27	9	0	0	0	0	0
Q MICA OLLA	20	3	0	3	2	4	6	4	5	2	1	0	0	0	0	1
Q MICA OTHR	21	0	0	1	0	0	3	0	0	2	0	0	0	0	0	0
QUACH RED	22	1	0	0	0	1	3	0	0	4	1	0	0	0	0	0
AB CRS OLLA	23	0	1	0	0	0	0	0	3	5	3	0	0	0	0	0
AB CRS OTHR	24	0	0	0	0	0	0	0	4	5	2	0	0	0	0	0
ELRIEGO BLK	25	0	0	0	0	0	0	0	0	1	0	0	0	0	0	0
ELRIEGO PLN	26	0	0	0	0	0	0	0	1	1	1	0	0	1	0	0
ELRIEGO ORN	27	0	0	0	1	1	0	0	0	0	1	0	0	0	0	0

	VAR. NO.	SQ. 61	SQ. 62	SQ. 63	SQ. 64	SQ. 65	SQ. 66	SQ. 67	SQ. 68	SQ. 69	SQ. 70	SQ. 71	SQ. 72	SQ. 73	SQ. 74	SQ. 75
NORTH COORD	1	203	71	1111	1017	946	878	874	956	829	803	738	1167	1083	1105	1002
WEST COORD	2	982	991	862	837	869	805	832	863	809	842	853	784	789	797	757
SURF STRAT	3	4	4	3	1	2	2	3	2	3	3	1	3	1	2	3
GRND COVER	4	4	3	1	1	4	1	1	4	4	2	1	3	3	3	3
DISTURBANCE	5	1	2	1	1	1	1	1	3	1	2	2	1	2	1	2
AREA	6	100	100	100	100	50	100	100	100	100	100	100	100	100	50	100
LSM/EPB OCC	7	0	0	12	12	1	12	12	12	12	12	12	2	12	12	12
LPB OCC	8	0	0	0	0	0	0	0	0	0	1	0	0	0	0	0
VS OCC	9	0	0	2	12	12	12	0	1	0	0	12	0	12	0	1
TOT SHRD WT	10	120	120	1330	6580	2590	6900	3660	18100	3280	7960	8970	800	10410	570	10650
DIAGNOST CT	11	4	8	20	136	72	201	96	483	79	211	201	11	290	15	266
RIM SHRD CT	12	3	4	10	104	52	149	66	320	53	158	141	9	216	13	185
RIM SHRD WT	13	30	10	110	790	490	1680	830	5140	740	1720	1020	120	1640	130	2020
COATEPEC WH	14	0	0	0	1	0	0	0	0	0	0	0	0	0	0	1
RS CRS OLLA	15	0	0	0	0	1	0	0	2	0	7	1	0	9	0	10
RS CRS OTHR	16	0	0	0	0	0	0	0	0	0	0	2	0	0	0	2
GRAY BOWL	17	1	0	6	48	9	88	38	209	36	96	83	3	130	6	112
GRAY OLLA	18	0	0	0	0	2	3	2	12	3	6	0	0	4	0	1
GRAY OTHER	19	0	0	2	18	6	24	17	65	5	18	24	0	27	1	41
Q MICA OLLA	20	0	0	0	6	3	19	7	26	7	11	2	0	11	1	15
Q MICA OTHR	21	0	0	0	3	1	0	1	9	2	0	0	0	0	0	3
QUACH RED	22	0	0	1	1	0	0	2	5	1	1	1	0	9	0	2
AB CRS OLLA	23	0	0	0	5	0	0	2	6	1	0	4	0	0	0	3
AB CRS OTHR	24	0	0	0	3	1	0	0	2	0	0	3	0	0	0	0
ELRIEGO BLK	25	0	0	0	0	0	0	0	0	0	0	0	0	0	0	0
ELRIEGO PLN	26	0	0	0	3	0	0	0	0	0	0	0	0	0	0	0
ELRIEGO ORN	27	0	0	0	0	0	0	3	1	0	0	0	0	0	1	2

	VAR. NO.	SQ. 76	SQ. 77	SQ. 78	SQ. 79	SQ. 80	SQ. 81	SQ. 82	SQ. 83	SQ. 84	SQ. 85	SQ. 86	SQ. 87	SQ. 88	SQ. 89	SQ. 90
NORTH COORD	1	958	828	777	1171	941	890	967	964	941	969	968	969	958	975	959
WEST COORD	2	769	752	766	655	652	693	560	507	424	214	286	152	54	-78	-10
SURF STRAT	3	3	3	3	1	3	3	3	3	3	3	3	3	3	3	3
GRND COVER	4	3	3	3	2	4	3	4	4	5	5	3	4	2	4	3
DISTURBANCE	5	2	1	1	2	1	1	1	1	2	2	2	1	1	1	1
AREA	6	100	100	100	100	100	100	100	100	100	100	100	100	100	100	100
LSM/EPB OCC	7	12	0	1	1	12	12	12	12	0	0	0	0	0	0	0
LPB OCC	8	0	0	0	0	0	0	0	0	0	0	0	0	0	0	0
VS OCC	9	1	0	0	0	12	0	1	0	2	0	0	0	0	0	0
TOT SHRD WT	10	4250	650	590	2380	1670	4470	390	840	130	150	240	290	170	130	180
DIAGNOST CT	11	111	9	9	71	28	101	11	15	0	6	6	3	8	0	4
RIM SHRD CT	12	69	9	7	53	20	62	9	12	0	4	6	1	6	0	4
RIM SHRD WT	13	760	110	100	500	300	980	100	210	0	40	40	10	60	0	20
COATEPEC WH	14	0	0	0	0	1	1	0	0	0	0	0	0	0	0	0
RS CRS OLLA	15	1	0	0	0	0	3	0	1	0	0	0	0	0	0	0
RS CRS OTHR	16	0	0	0	0	0	0	0	0	0	0	0	0	0	0	0
GRAY BOWL	17	41	2	4	9	11	32	6	4	0	1	1	0	3	0	1
GRAY OLLA	18	2	1	0	0	0	1	1	0	1	0	0	0	0	0	0
GRAY OTHER	19	23	0	2	6	3	15	1	0	0	0	0	1	0	0	0
Q MICA OLLA	20	6	0	0	1	1	2	0	1	0	0	0	0	0	0	0
Q MICA OTHR	21	0	0	0	0	0	1	0	0	0	0	0	0	0	0	0
QUACH RED	22	0	0	0	0	1	1	0	0	0	0	0	0	0	0	0
AB CRS OLLA	23	0	2	0	0	3	1	5	0	1	0	0	0	0	0	0
AB CRS OTHR	24	3	0	0	2	1	2	0	0	0	0	0	0	0	0	0
ELRIEGO BLK	25	0	0	0	0	0	0	0	0	0	0	0	0	0	0	0
ELRIEGO PLN	26	1	0	0	4	0	0	0	0	0	1	0	0	0	0	0
ELRIEGO ORN	27	0	1	0	0	0	0	0	0	0	0	0	0	0	0	0

QUACHILCO SURFACE SURVEY DATA -- VARIABLES 28-53

	VAR. NO.	SQ. 1	SQ. 2	SQ. 3	SQ. 4	SQ. 5	SQ. 6	SQ. 7	SQ. 8	SQ. 9	SQ. 10	SQ. 11	SQ. 12	SQ. 13	SQ. 14	SQ. 15
THIN ORANGE	28	0	0	1	0	0	0	2	0	0	0	0	0	0	0	0
ELRIEGO MRB	29	0	0	0	1	0	0	0	0	0	0	0	1	0	0	0
TEOT INC BL	30	0	1	9	0	0	0	16	0	0	0	1	0	0	0	0
TEOT INC OT	31	0	0	0	0	0	0	0	0	0	0	0	0	0	0	0
COXCAT GRAY	32	0	0	13	0	1	0	0	0	0	0	0	0	0	0	0
COXCAT RED	33	0	0	1	0	0	0	5	0	0	0	0	0	0	0	0
COX BRSH BL	34	0	0	36	0	8	0	27	4	3	0	1	5	0	1	0
COX BRSH OT	35	0	0	3	0	0	0	5	1	0	0	0	0	0	1	0
RED/BLK-ORN	36	0	0	0	0	0	0	1	0	0	0	0	0	0	0	0
COX POLYCHR	37	0	0	0	0	0	0	1	0	0	0	0	0	0	0	0
FONDOS SELL	38	0	0	5	0	3	0	2	0	3	0	2	0	0	0	0
KANTILES	39	0	0	0	0	0	0	0	0	1	0	0	1	0	0	0
TEXCOCO FAB	40	0	0	21	0	0	0	0	0	0	1	0	0	0	0	0
MODERN SHRD	41	0	2	0	0	7	3	0	13	0	0	2	0	0	0	10
OTH CERAMIC	42	0	0	0	0	0	0	0	0	0	0	0	0	0	0	0
GROUND STN	43	0	0	1	0	0	0	0	0	0	0	0	2	0	0	0
MANO/METATE	44	0	0	0	0	0	0	0	0	0	0	0	0	0	5	0
BLDG STN	45	2	7	1	2	3	1	1	27	8	5	64	46	236	195	24
PLASTER	46	0	0	0	0	1	1	10	0	0	0	0	0	0	0	0
MODERN NONC	47	0	0	0	0	0	0	1	1	0	0	0	0	0	0	0
OBSIDIAN CT	48	0	0	15	0	1	1	44	3	1	0	6	0	3	1	2
OBSIDIAN WT	49	0	0	20	0	0	0	65	5	0	0	10	0	5	0	0
OT CHSTN CT	50	1	4	166	5	4	0	39	13	2	3	24	14	14	9	8
OT CHSTN WT	51	0	20	1070	80	250	0	190	120	10	30	500	60	610	520	310
BIFACES	52	0	0	1	0	0	0	0	0	0	0	0	0	0	0	0
FINE BLADES	53	0	0	7	0	1	1	18	2	1	0	1	0	0	1	0

	VAR. NO.	SQ. 16	SQ. 17	SQ. 18	SQ. 19	SQ. 20	SQ. 21	SQ. 22	SQ. 23	SQ. 24	SQ. 25	SQ. 26	SQ. 27	SQ. 28	SQ. 29	SQ. 30
THIN ORANGE	28	0	1	2	0	0	0	0	0	2	0	0	0	2	0	0
ELRIEGO MRB	29	0	1	2	1	0	0	1	0	0	0	0	2	0	1	2
TEOT INC BL	30	3	2	15	4	1	0	0	0	0	0	0	4	0	0	0
TEOT INC OT	31	0	2	1	0	0	0	0	0	0	0	0	0	0	0	0
COXCAT GRAY	32	1	1	0	0	0	0	0	0	0	0	0	0	1	0	0
COXCAT RED	33	0	3	0	0	0	0	0	1	0	0	0	0	2	1	0
COX BRSH BL	34	1	14	25	3	3	0	4	0	5	0	0	18	4	0	3
COX BRSH OT	35	0	4	1	0	0	1	2	1	0	0	0	3	0	0	5
RED/BLK-ORN	36	0	0	0	1	0	0	0	0	1	0	0	1	0	0	0
COX POLYCHR	37	0	0	0	0	0	0	0	0	1	0	0	0	0	0	0
FONDOS SELL	38	1	2	1	5	0	0	0	0	1	0	0	5	1	0	0
KANTILES	39	0	0	0	0	0	1	0	0	0	0	0	0	0	0	0
TEXCOCO FAB	40	0	0	0	0	0	0	2	0	0	0	0	0	0	0	0
MODERN SHRD	41	3	3	1	6	0	0	0	6	3	12	18	0	0	16	0
OTH CERAMIC	42	0	0	0	1	0	0	0	0	0	0	0	5	0	5	0
GROUND STN	43	0	0	1	1	0	0	0	0	0	0	0	2	0	0	0
MANO/METATE	44	0	1	0	0	0	1	1	0	0	0	0	2	1	0	0
BLDG STN	45	17	9	48	597	23	156	132	18	1	5	4	297	315	294	436
PLASTER	46	0	0	70	0	0	40	0	0	0	10	0	590	0	0	0
MODERN NONC	47	0	0	0	0	4	0	1	2	0	3	1	0	0	0	1
OBSIDIAN CT	48	1	42	11	0	2	0	4	0	59	0	1	6	3	9	2
OBSIDIAN WT	49	0	55	5	0	0	0	5	0	85	0	0	25	5	10	0
OT CHSTN CT	50	3	112	20	25	13	13	37	0	98	2	1	32	12	29	12
OT CHSTN WT	51	170	1000	370	720	520	450	340	150	510	50	40	810	450	520	180
BIFACES	52	0	0	0	0	0	0	0	0	0	0	0	0	0	0	0
FINE BLADES	53	0	9	8	0	0	0	1	0	22	0	0	1	1	2	0

	VAR. NO.	SQ. 31	SQ. 32	SQ. 33	SQ. 34	SQ. 35	SQ. 36	SQ. 37	SQ. 38	SQ. 39	SQ. 40	SQ. 41	SQ. 42	SQ. 43	SQ. 44	SQ. 45
THIN ORANGE	28	2	2	0	0	0	0	0	0	0	0	2	0	0	0	0
ELRIEGO MRB	29	3	0	1	0	0	0	0	0	0	0	3	0	1	1	0
TEOT INC BL	30	0	0	0	1	3	0	0	0	0	0	5	1	0	0	0
TEOT INC OT	31	0	0	0	0	0	0	0	0	0	0	0	0	0	0	0
COXCAT GRAY	32	2	1	0	0	0	0	0	0	0	0	0	0	0	0	0
COXCAT RED	33	0	0	0	0	0	0	0	0	0	0	2	3	0	0	0
COX BRSH BL	34	14	2	11	1	0	0	0	0	0	1	14	26	2	5	0
COX BRSH OT	35	2	0	1	0	0	0	0	0	0	0	2	1	0	0	0
RED/BLK-ORN	36	0	1	0	0	0	0	0	0	0	0	0	0	0	0	0
COX POLYCHR	37	0	0	0	0	0	0	0	0	0	0	0	0	0	0	0
FONDOS SELL	38	5	1	2	0	1	0	0	0	0	1	2	0	1	0	0
KANTILES	39	0	0	0	0	0	0	0	0	0	0	0	0	0	0	0
TEXCOCO FAB	40	0	0	0	0	1	0	0	0	0	0	0	0	0	0	0
MODERN SHRD	41	0	0	0	11	0	0	2	6	6	2	0	0	0	1	0
OTH CERAMIC	42	0	0	0	0	0	0	0	0	0	0	0	0	0	0	0
GROUND STN	43	0	0	0	0	0	0	0	0	0	0	1	0	0	4	0
MANO/METATE	44	1	2	0	1	0	0	0	0	0	0	0	0	0	0	0
BLDG STN	45	238	297	1	59	1	205	1	1	1	1	1	233	297	41	199
PLASTER	46	0	0	10	0	0	0	3	4	0	0	0	0	160	0	0
MODERN NONC	47	0	0	0	1	0	0	0	0	0	0	0	0	0	0	0
OBSIDIAN CT	48	3	1	35	2	3	1	0	0	0	0	56	8	8	3	0
OBSIDIAN WT	49	5	0	55	5	0	0	0	0	0	0	65	10	5	0	0
OT CHSTN CT	50	17	14	202	8	30	2	0	2	0	0	138	15	21	11	3
OT CHSTN WT	51	885	700	940	100	150	20	0	30	0	0	680	370	540	180	280
BIFACES	52	0	0	0	0	3	0	0	0	0	0	2	0	0	0	0
FINE BLADES	53	3	0	11	2	2	0	0	0	0	0	10	0	1	1	0

APPENDIX TO CHAPTER 4   167

QUACHILCO SURFACE SURVEY DATA -- VARIABLES 28-53

	VAR. NO.	SQ. 46	SQ. 47	SQ. 48	SQ. 49	SQ. 50	SQ. 51	SQ. 52	SQ. 53	SQ. 54	SQ. 55	SQ. 56	SQ. 57	SQ. 58	SQ. 59	SQ. 60
THIN ORANGE	28	0	0	0	0	0	0	0	1	0	2	0	0	0	0	0
ELRIEGO MRB	29	1	0	0	0	1	0	0	2	1	2	0	0	0	0	0
TEOT INC BL	30	0	0	0	0	1	0	0	0	5	5	0	0	2	0	0
TEOT INC OT	31	0	0	0	0	0	0	0	0	0	0	0	0	0	0	0
COXCAT GRAY	32	0	0	0	0	0	1	0	0	0	0	0	0	0	0	0
COXCAT RED	33	1	0	2	0	1	0	0	3	2	2	0	0	0	0	0
COX BRSH BL	34	0	0	0	0	2	1	3	4	10	12	0	0	0	0	1
COX BRSH OT	35	1	0	0	1	0	0	0	1	5	4	0	0	0	0	0
RED/BLK-ORN	36	0	0	0	0	0	0	0	0	0	0	0	0	0	0	0
COX POLYCHR	37	0	0	0	0	0	0	0	1	1	0	1	0	0	0	0
FONDOS SELL	38	0	0	0	1	0	0	0	5	2	0	1	0	1	0	0
XANTILES	39	0	0	0	0	0	0	0	0	0	0	0	0	0	0	0
TEXCOCO FAB	40	1	0	0	1	0	0	0	4	3	0	0	0	0	0	0
MODERN SHRD	41	0	0	0	0	0	0	0	0	0	1	9	5	11	0	2
OTH CERAMIC	42	0	0	0	0	0	0	4	0	0	0	0	0	0	0	0
GROUND STN	43	0	0	0	0	0	0	0	0	23	0	0	0	0	0	0
MANO/METATE	44	0	1	0	0	0	0	0	0	0	0	0	0	0	0	0
BLDG STN	45	439	223	62	263	76	136	82	338	49	1	18	41	133	12	440
PLASTER	46	130	0	0	0	0	90	0	0	50	0	0	0	0	1	2
MODERN NONC	47	0	0	0	0	0	0	0	0	0	0	0	0	0	0	0
OBSIDIAN CT	48	2	0	0	3	4	7	2	4	22	54	0	0	0	0	2
OBSIDIAN WT	49	0	0	0	5	5	20	5	0	30	65	0	0	0	0	0
OT CHSTN CT	50	16	0	9	9	19	53	29	42	87	155	1	1	1	1	2
OT CHSTN WT	51	900	0	170	150	350	1500	440	1250	1120	910	10	20	30	0	45
BIFACES	52	0	0	0	0	0	0	0	5	6	5	0	0	0	0	0
FINE BLADES	53	1	0	0	0	1	2	0	3	6	17	0	0	0	0	2

	VAR. NO.	SQ. 61	SQ. 62	SQ. 63	SQ. 64	SQ. 65	SQ. 66	SQ. 67	SQ. 68	SQ. 69	SQ. 70	SQ. 71	SQ. 72	SQ. 73	SQ. 74	SQ. 75
THIN ORANGE	28	0	0	0	2	0	0	0	0	0	8	3	0	2	0	0
ELRIEGO MRB	29	0	0	1	4	1	1	0	0	0	3	1	0	0	0	1
TEOT INC BL	30	1	0	0	7	1	1	1	3	0	0	5	0	8	0	11
TEOT INC OT	31	0	0	0	0	0	0	0	0	0	0	2	0	0	0	0
COXCAT GRAY	32	0	0	0	1	6	1	0	0	0	1	0	0	1	0	2
COXCAT RED	33	1	0	0	1	0	4	0	4	0	1	1	0	3	0	2
COX BRSH BL	34	0	1	2	8	24	18	1	19	0	1	15	0	18	0	9
COX BRSH OT	35	0	0	2	0	3	2	0	8	1	0	1	3	0	0	2
RED/BLK-ORN	36	0	1	0	0	0	4	0	1	0	0	0	0	0	1	2
COX POLYCHR	37	0	0	0	0	0	0	0	0	0	0	0	0	0	0	1
FONDOS SELL	38	0	1	2	0	6	3	0	3	0	1	3	0	0	0	1
XANTILES	39	0	0	0	0	0	0	0	3	0	0	0	0	1	0	0
TEXCOCO FAB	40	0	0	0	0	0	3	6	45	2	2	2	0	0	0	1
MODERN SHRD	41	0	0	10	18	1	9	2	0	1	2	3	12	1	1	0
OTH CERAMIC	42	0	0	0	0	0	0	0	5	0	0	2	0	12	0	12
GROUND STN	43	0	0	0	0	0	0	0	0	0	0	13	0	13	0	0
MANO/METATE	44	0	0	0	0	0	1	0	5	1	1	0	0	0	2	2
BLDG STN	45	264	166	7	14	538	989	17	712	84	220	18	6	1	228	107
PLASTER	46	0	2	0	10	250	0	0	0	0	0	20	0	0	0	0
MODERN NONC	47	0	0	1	7	0	0	0	0	1	0	0	0	0	0	0
OBSIDIAN CT	48	0	3	2	44	7	19	2	38	3	20	77	1	91	2	24
OBSIDIAN WT	49	0	0	0	75	10	25	0	50	5	30	120	0	140	5	40
OT CHSTN CT	50	0	5	10	80	12	42	22	79	13	72	278	3	170	7	49
OT CHSTN WT	51	0	120	10	660	960	2030	420	2720	510	1790	1870	10	1270	190	1030
BIFACES	52	0	0	0	0	0	0	0	7	0	0	8	0	6	0	0
FINE BLADES	53	0	3	0	11	2	5	0	1	2	7	15	0	22	1	4

	VAR. NO.	SQ. 76	SQ. 77	SQ. 78	SQ. 79	SQ. 80	SQ. 81	SQ. 82	SQ. 83	SQ. 84	SQ. 85	SQ. 86	SQ. 87	SQ. 88	SQ. 89	SQ. 90
THIN ORANGE	28	0	0	0	1	0	0	0	0	0	0	0	0	1	0	0
ELRIEGO MRB	29	0	0	0	0	0	1	0	0	0	0	0	0	0	0	0
TEOT INC BL	30	3	0	0	2	1	2	0	1	0	0	0	0	0	0	0
TEOT INC OT	31	0	0	0	0	0	0	0	0	0	0	0	0	0	0	0
COXCAT GRAY	32	1	0	0	0	0	0	0	0	0	0	0	0	0	0	0
COXCAT RED	33	0	0	0	0	0	4	1	0	0	0	0	0	0	0	0
COX BRSH BL	34	6	0	0	11	0	6	0	3	0	0	3	0	1	0	1
COX BRSH OT	35	1	0	0	8	0	1	0	0	0	0	0	1	1	0	0
RED/BLK-ORN	36	0	0	0	0	0	0	0	0	0	0	0	0	0	0	0
COX POLYCHR	37	0	0	0	0	0	0	0	0	0	0	0	0	0	0	0
FONDOS SELL	38	0	0	0	2	0	1	0	0	0	0	0	0	0	0	0
XANTILES	39	0	0	1	0	0	0	0	0	0	0	0	0	0	0	0
TEXCOCO FAB	40	1	0	0	0	0	0	0	0	0	0	0	0	0	0	0
MODERN SHRD	41	8	1	1	7	7	1	1	2	0	3	2	4	1	0	1
OTH CERAMIC	42	5	0	0	0	0	3	0	0	0	0	0	0	0	0	0
GROUND STN	43	1	0	0	1	0	0	0	1	0	0	0	0	0	0	0
MANO/METATE	44	3	0	2	0	0	0	0	0	0	0	0	0	0	0	0
BLDG STN	45	203	11	23	17	8	32	24	73	23	59	13	5	10	37	7
PLASTER	46	160	0	0	0	0	0	10	0	0	1	0	8	0	3	0
MODERN NONC	47	0	0	0	3	4	0	0	0	0	0	0	0	0	0	0
OBSIDIAN CT	48	12	1	1	61	1	4	2	1	0	0	0	1	0	1	0
OBSIDIAN WT	49	10	0	0	90	0	5	0	0	0	0	0	5	0	0	0
OT CHSTN CT	50	24	8	3	90	8	22	2	7	3	1	1	1	0	3	0
OT CHSTN WT	51	900	200	20	510	110	340	10	180	45	50	5	5	0	10	0
BIFACES	52	0	0	0	4	0	0	0	0	0	0	0	0	0	0	0
FINE BLADES	53	1	0	0	17	0	3	0	1	0	0	0	0	0	0	0

5. EXCAVATIONS AT CUAYUCATEPEC (Ts281)

A PRELIMINARY REPORT

by Robert D. Drennan

This chapter attempts to place the excavations undertaken at the site of Cuayucatepec during 1978 into their context within the Palo Blanco Project, to indicate some of the issues the excavations were designed to help resolve, and to describe in preliminary form some immediate results of the investigations.

The excavations at Cuayucatepec are very much a companion piece to the excavations at Quachilco undertaken in 1975 and 1977 (Drennan 1978). By comparing and contrasting the two sites, the significance of both sets of excavations becomes apparent. Quachilco was the first settlement in the Tehuacán Valley to merit the designation "town." During its occupation it was unique in the Tehuacán Valley for its population size, elaboration of public architecture, and, inferentially, centrality of function. It served as a primitive "central place," probably not for the entire valley, but for the broad central section of it known as the Valle de Tehuacán proper. The inhabitants of the remainder of the valley, then, were not organized into sociopolitical groups possessing such central places.

At about the time Quachilco was abandoned, however, this situation changed. Some half-dozen central places analogous to Quachilco emerged. Each of these seems to have served a subunit of the valley much as Quachilco had served the central portion. Some of these centers are indicated on the map in Fig. 1.2; they have been mapped and surface collected by J.A. Nowack (1977). By this time all inhabitants of the valley were apparently members of one or another of the sociopolitical groups focussed on the central places. The site of Cuayucatepec (281 in Fig. 1.2), founded during the Early Palo Blanco phase and occupied until sometime during the Late Palo Blanco phase, was one of these half-dozen second generation central places. The site was first described by MacNeish et al. (1972:416) and subjected to more intense study by Nowack (1977:39). The excavations conducted during 1978 followed up Nowack's mapping and controlled surface collection.

Cuayucatepec is located in the northern reaches of the Tehuacán Valley: of the half-dozen central places of the region during the Early Classic, it is the northernmost (Fig. 1.2). Like Quachilco, it is located

---

The 1978 excavations at Cuayucatepec were staffed by Joann Christein, John Eddins, Kenneth Kvamme, Verónica Kennedy, Esther Skirboll, and Linda Steinberg. Acknowledging their hard work is small recompense for their many jolting rides along the "road" up the hill to the site.

in a section of the valley broad enough to provide a good-sized concentration of level alluvial farmland—in this case on the order of 100 km². This large concentration, known locally as the Valle de Cinco Señores, is second in size only to Quachilco's Valle de Tehuacán proper. These two largest wide spots in the Tehuacán Valley adjoin each other in the northern and central portions of the valley, separated by a narrower neck of valley floor where the city of Tehuacán is situated today.

Despite the small distance separating them, these two subunits of the valley offer some sharp environmental contrasts. The Valle de Cinco Señores lies about 1750 m above sea level and is subject to winter frosts, while the Valle de Tehuacán, at about 1200 m above sea level, is frost free and suitable for year-round maize agriculture. Precipitation figures for the two subunits of the valley are so similar that they belie the significant differences in the amounts of available moisture in the two regions. In the Valle de Tehuacán, non-irrigated agriculture is regarded by today's inhabitants as impossible. No planting is done if irrigation water is unavailable because the chances of sufficient moisture from precipitation are too slim. In the Valle de Cinco Señores, on the other hand, rainfall agriculture, while not highly productive, is possible. If the rainy reason begins with substantial rains, farmers today plant maize and beans in unirrigated fields.

Casual conversations with local farmers indicate the following modern perception of the situation: In something more than half the years, good precipitation early in the rainy season encourages planting, and, of these years, something more than half continue to provide enough natural precipitation that planting unirrigated fields proves of value. The 1978 rainy season, coinciding with our field season, began with promising rains. As our season concluded, it remained to be determined whether late rainy season precipitation would be sufficient to make worthwhile the considerable planting of unirrigated land that had occurred. The importance of good timing, however, was already evident. Those farmers who had seized the opportunity of planting at the very beginning of the rains (coming uncharacteristically in numerous protracted drizzles, not in the more common pattern of a few short cloudbursts) had crops in late August which, while stunted, would have yielded with sufficient September rain. Those who had waited for some sign that the drizzles would turn to cloudbursts, on the other hand, had fields in which very few seeds had even germinated. Thus, while irrigated agriculture is the only dependable means of raising crops near Cuayucatepec, as it is near Quachilco, non-irrigated agriculture can be today an important supplement at the former. The differences in precipitation, together with differences in evaporation due largely to altitude, also result in a markedly lusher natural vegetation in the Valle de Cinco Señores as well as in a major difference in the species of the wild plant community.

During the prehispanic period, however, the Valle de Tehuacán seems to have had the advantage over the Valle de Cinco Señores in terms of available irrigation water. The Late Sata María phase inhabitants of Quachilco used an extensive canal irrigation system which drew water from one or more of the springs emerging in the valley floor in the upstream section of the Valle de Tehuacán (Drennan 1978:17 and 77). This system

5. CUAYUCATEPEC: PRELIMINARY REPORT

brought water directly to and through Quachilco on the central valley floor for application to fields in the surrounding area. While more copious new sources of irrigation water are available to the modern inhabitants of the area (largely through chain well systems), the water from the same springs used in prehispanic times is still a vital resource for the inhabitants of the nearby modern towns of Chilac and Altepexi in particular.

In the Valle de Cinco Señores the most important source of irrigation water today is the recently constructed Valsequillo Dam. Far less important, but still used, is water emerging from several barrancas, most of which empty into the main valley floor here. One of these in particular is related to the prehistoric center at Cuayucatepec. This barranca empties, not into the main valley, but into a small, internally drained basin at the edge of the valley. The approximately 8 km^2 of level, alluvial farmland in this basin are completely irrigated today by water from this barranca, which flows year-round. The basin is separated from the main valley by a semi-circular ridge reaching some 200 m above the valley floor and joined to the higher mountains forming the edge of the valley by substantially lower passes. The site of Cuayucatepec is located on the highest portion of this ridge, looking out in one direction on the main valley floor and in the other on the small and valuable pocket of easily irrigated farmland (Fig. 1.2).

In its hilltop location (Fig. 5.1), Cuayucatepec differs from the earlier Quachilco but conforms to the pattern for such centers of its own time period. Most other major Palo Blanco centers which Nowack investigated are in such locations (Nowack 1977:37). Some of them, like Cuayucatepec, have substantial walls blocking access to all or part of the site. Defense seems to have become a major consideration in the selection of locations for principal centers during this period.

The map in Fig. 5.2 illustrates Cuayucatepec's hilltop location. The contour lines on the map do not extend down to the level of the valley floor. Thus the position of the site is even more commanding than is apparent from the map. To the north of the map lies the small internally drained basin of irrigable farmland already mentioned. To the south lies the floor of the Valle de Cinco Señores. The Palo Blanco phase center covers the highest part of the ridge dividing these two hydrographic units, providing an unobstructed view over the farmland upon which the prehistoric inhabitants of the locale would have depended for food. A commanding view also extends along the main valley toward the continental divide which forms the northwestern extreme of the Tehuacán Valley in the upstream direction, and toward the scarp just below the modern city of Tehuacán where the Valle de Cinco Señores drops off to the Valle de Tehuacán proper in the downstream direction.

Horizontal control for the excavations was based on a grid system which measured in meters from an imaginary point beyond the boundaries of the site. All coordinates are thus in meters north and west of this point and were measured initially from a datum set at 1000N1000W on top of the largest mound on one of the highest points of the site. Grid squares (1 by 1 m) and test pits (usually 1 m east-west and 2 m north-south) were

Fig. 5.1. View of Cuayucatepec from southeast. Sector II is the highest

named by the coordinates of their southeast corners. The grid was oriented to magnetic north. Vertical control was based on an arbitary elevation established as 1000 m at 1000N1000W. All map contours and all depths in excavations read in terms of this elevation. The 1000 m elevation datum corresponds to approximately 1900 m above sea level.

The heart of the Palo Blanco phase center is in the central and south central sections of the map in Fig. 5.2. This highest section of the ridge contains the greatest residential density and the major complex of civic-ceremonial architecture. Evidence of occupation continues along the ridge spurs toward the east and northeast in the form of a sparser scatter of residences on the reasonably level sections of ridge top. The occupation ends near the tips of these spurs where the slopes drop off rather sharply to levels much nearer the valley floor. On all sides but the northwest, in fact, the occupation is constrained by such precipitous slopes. The only relatively gentle approach to the site is from the northwest, and residences extended down the slopes in this direction to a second complex of civic-ceremonial architecture lying, not at the bottom of the ridge, but at the foot of the steepest slopes supporting the heart of the site. A further sparser scatter of residences extends on beyond the area included in the map down the slopes toward the west and northwest. The total area of occupation is over 30 ha and includes zones ranging from very dense to sparse occupation.

The 1978 excavations began with a program of test pits, each 1 by 2 m. These were scattered throughout the occupied area in an effort to obtain a glimpse of deposits from all parts of the site, both for the artifacts and the kinds of features which might be encountered. Eight of these

5. CUAYUCATEPEC: PRELIMINARY REPORT 173

part of the ridge; Sector I extends to the left, Sector III to the right.

test pits (indicated by letters in Fig. 5.2) were later expanded to larger scale excavations, although the total area excavated remained only a tiny fraction of the total occupied area. For purposes of description in this chapter, the site has been divided into six sectors which are indicated schematically and identified by Roman numerals on the map in Fig. 5.2.

Excavations in Sector I

Sector I includes the principal complex of civic-ceremonial architecture in the site and is the easiest of the six sectors to define. It covers the crest of a ridge spur extending west-southwest from the highest part of the hill and only slightly below it. The complex of public buildings is near the tip of the ridge spur (Fig. 5.3). Toward the south and west this ridge drops off very sharply, marking the edge of occupation. Likewise, a precipitous slope marks the north edge of this sector, although in this case the slope is one side of a deep ravine which separates this ridge from the slightly lower occupied area some 150 m directly to the north. Natural barriers thus divide this sector from all surrounding areas, except to the east where a relatively narrow neck of land connects it to the highest part of the hill. The only reasonable route of approach to Sector I is along this narrow ridge, and a substantial wall cuts across the ridge here, providing a clear eastern boundary for the sector. The remains of this wall are visible on the surface today as a long narrow mound running at a right angle across the ridge and some distance down the steep slopes on each side. Excavations at this wall are described below.

Seven test pits were excavated in Sector I, of which two were later

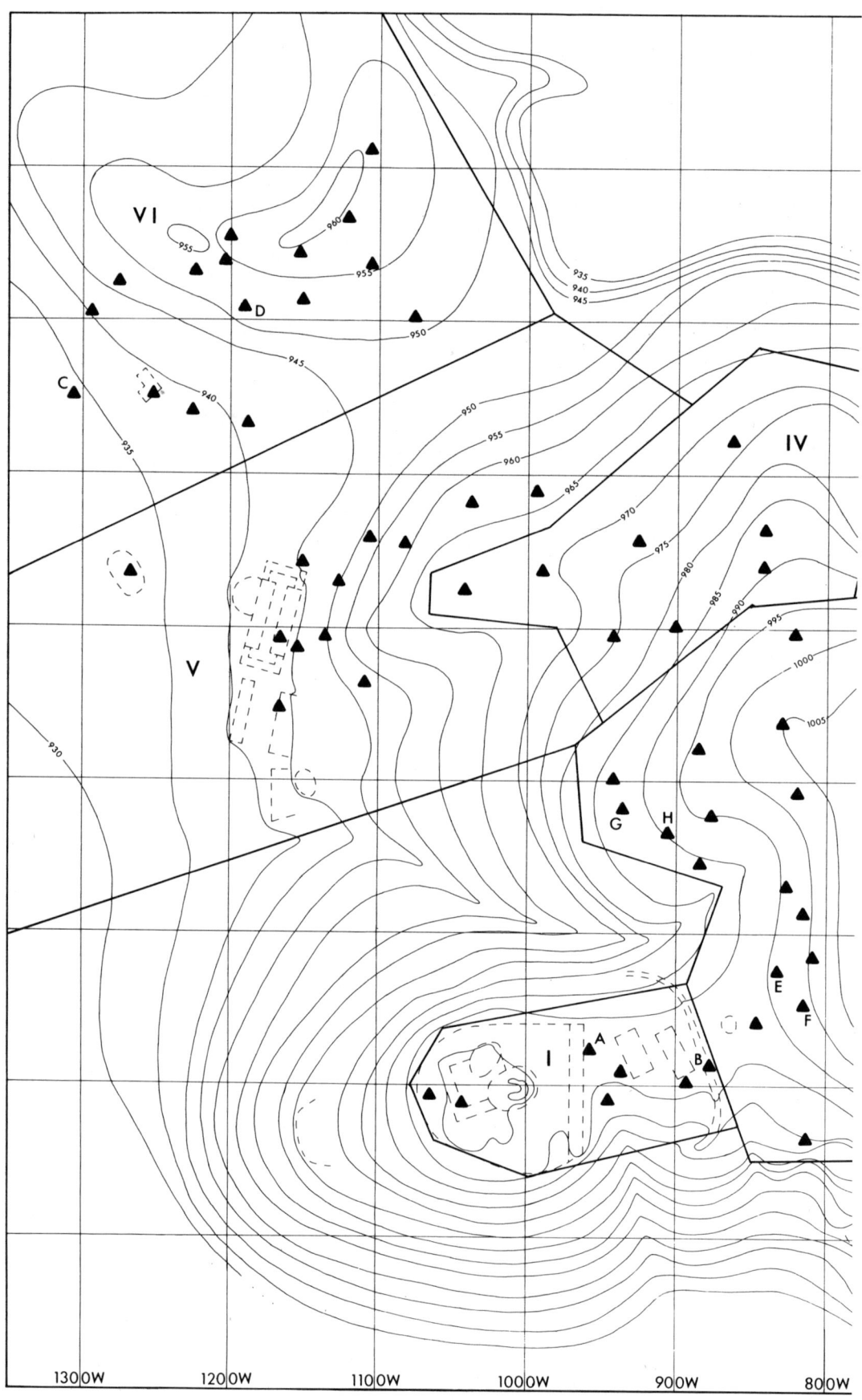

Fig. 5.2. Map of Cuayucatepec. Dashed lines show

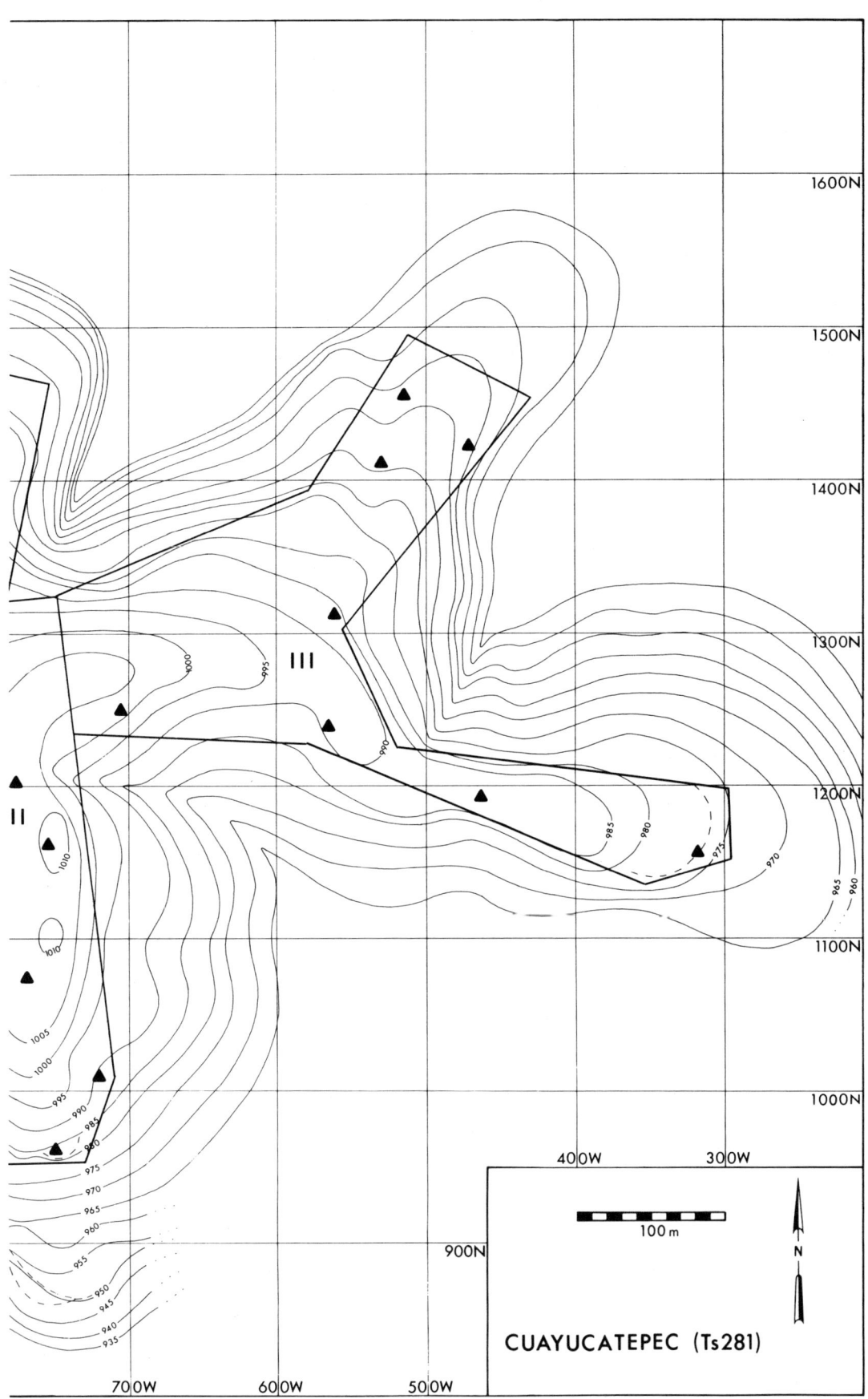

architecture and terraces. Triangles are excavations.

Fig. 5.3. View to the west across Sector I to the Valle de Cinco Señores. Excavations at left are Area B; in center, Area A.

expanded to become Areas A and B. Several major mounds, arranged around plazas and forming the largest architecture of this zone, were avoided in the test pit program; little remained of them after years of local stone quarrying, and exposure of major architecture was not a goal of the excavations. Two test pits, however, were excavated near the tip of the ridge where these mounds are concentrated. One of these pits (at 996N1064W) was near the end of level ground at the tip of the ridge, the other (at 987N 987N1041W) inside one of the plazas formed by the large mounds. Features were limited to a single stone wall foundation, and artifacts were quite sparse in the 30 cm or less of cultural deposits overlying sterile soil.

A test at 1022N959W, later expanded as Area A, was located just east of this major architectural complex. The original test pit encountered a portion of an apparent paving of large flat stone slabs (Feature 3 in Fig. 5.4), the edge of the terrace or broad platform upon which the major mounds rested. Slightly farther east was a rectangular structure of cut stone some 3 by 5 m (Feature 4). These stone walls stood some 40 cm high where best preserved. The entrance must have been near the center of the east side where the walls were not so well preserved. The remains of a well-prepared floor surface of light clay were preserved only near the walls and especially in the corners of the structure. This surface had

5. CUAYUCATEPEC: PRELIMINARY REPORT 177

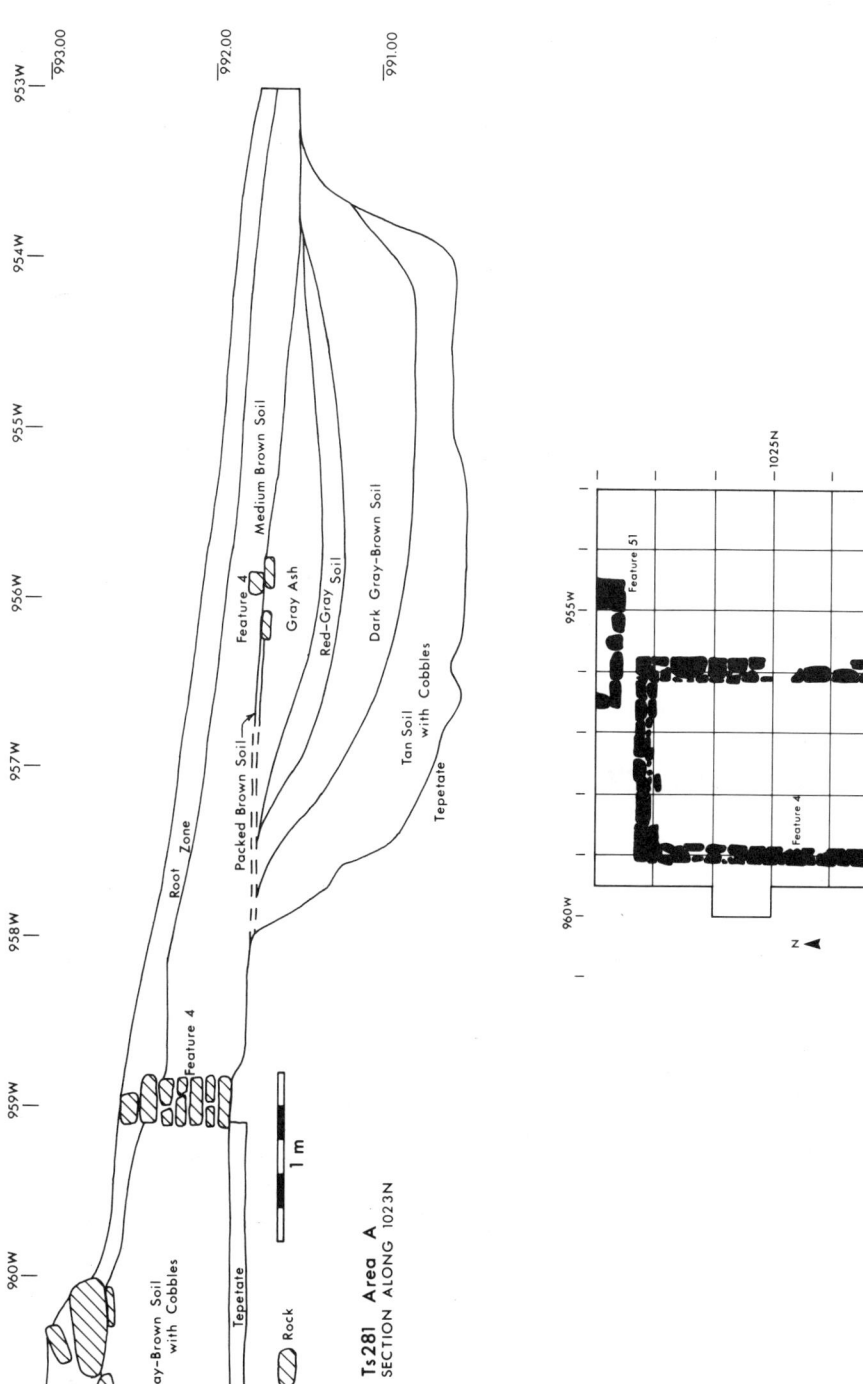

Fig. 5.4. Plan and section of Area A excavations.

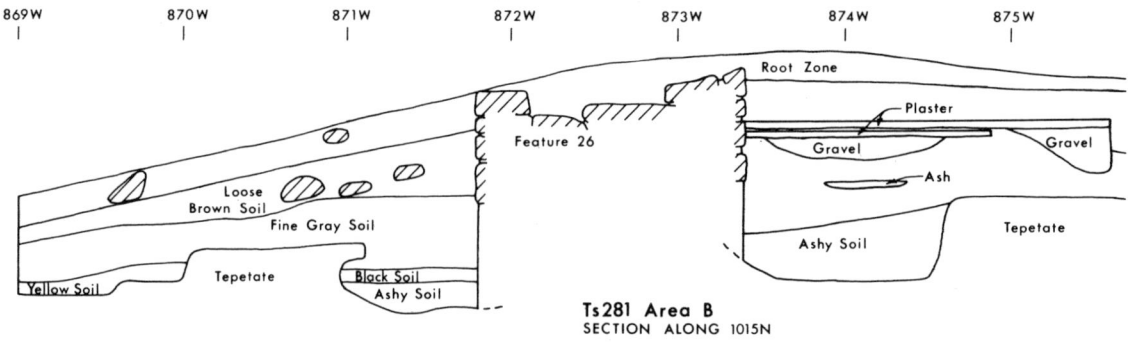

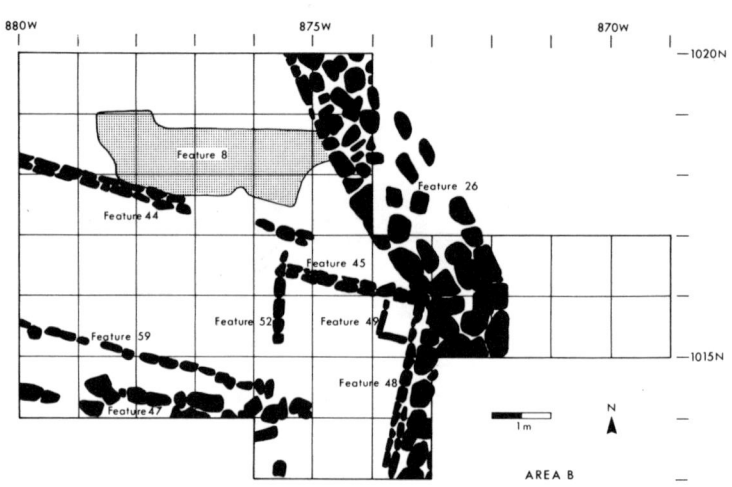

Fig. 5.5. Plan and section of Area B excavations.

apparently worn away through use as the hard-packed floor was discernible throughout, but the lighter coating was not present in the center of the floor. Feature 4 was oriented about 2° west of magnetic north. Features 51 and 54 were other stone walls, probably built later although still during the period when Feature 4 was in use. Since only small portions of the structures which these walls represented occurred in the excavated area, it is impossible to say much about them. Although cultural deposits were relatively shallow at the east and west sides of Area A, a deep trench in the tepetate running down the center of the excavations was filled with cultural material. There was no indication that this trench had been dug; rather, it was a natural depression in which several distinguishable layers of cultural debris had accumulated. All material from the Area A excavations dated to the Palo Blanco phase, with the exception of a small amount of Venta Salada phase material found in a disturbed section in the northern part of the area.

Three other test pits were excavated in the area between the main mound group and the wall which forms the eastern boundary of Sector I. The

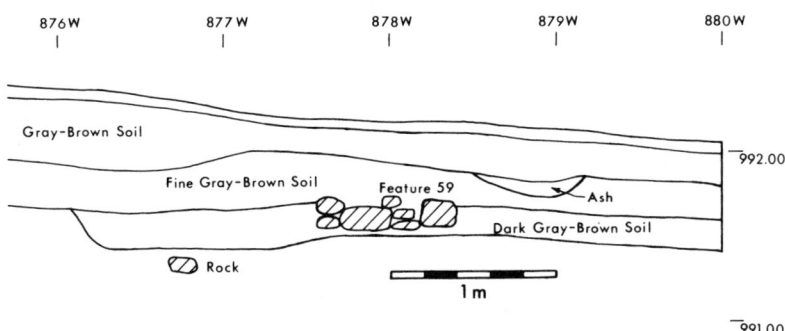

pit at 991N947W, situated on a small terrace slightly below the level of the ridge top, went through some 60 cm of cultural deposits containing moderate densities of Palo Blanco phase artifacts. No features were encountered. The pit at 1009N938W revealed an adobe construction about 40 cm high, apparently part of an attempt to level up the rather uneven surface of the top of the ridge. This was one of the very few examples of adobe construction found at the site. An additional 40 cm or so of cultural material overlay the adobes. All artifacts belonged to the Palo Blanco phase. A test at 10002N894W found only about 20 cm of deposits with sparse artifacts overlying tepetate.

Finally, the Area B excavations began as a test pit at 1018N875W, lying right on the side of the long mound forming the wall that separates Sector I from the rest of the site. This area showed a sequence of intensive use over a considerable period of time. The tepetate which formed sterile soil here was riddled with the remains of excavations of one kind or other. Best-defined of these excavations were several broad and rather shallow bell- or basin-shaped pits. Most of these did not show any clear traces of burning and may have been in use as storage pits. Within the deposits overlying tepetate were parts of a number of structures. The oldest of these, Feature 8 in Fig. 5.5, was an interrupted portion of a low platform surfaced with small rocks and tan clay. It may have supported a residential structure on one side of an open patio, but not enough of the platform remained to be certain. The construction of the main wall bounding Sector I followed that of Feature 8. It thus overlay cultural deposits; and, based on preliminary assessment of artifacts from this area, all of them from the Palo Blanco phase, it was built fairly early on in the sequence of occupation, though not at the very beginning. This wall, represented by Feature 26 in Fig. 5.5, was constructed of large, roughly worked stones and stood over 120 cm high in the sections exposed. The number of similar stones encountered in the excavations on the east side of the wall (stones which had toppled down from the top of the wall) indicate that it originally stood somewhat higher than this. It was a massive construction, some 150 cm across. A slight bend visible at about 1016N was a part of the overall curve described by the wall, which ran perpendicular to the ridge as it crossed its crest but curved back to the west as it descended the two sides of the ridge.

After the wall had been built, no further construction was undertaken to the east (outside) of it. The deposits which covered the wall on this side might all have resulted from erosional processes after the site had been abandoned. In contrast, cultural activities continued to build up deposits on the west (inside) of the wall. Walls of cut stone indicate portions of several different structures (Features 44, 47, 52, and 59) encountered in deposits that, in addition to moderate densities of artifacts, contained a number of small hearths. The continuing intensive use of this area just inside the wall, in fact, disturbed the archeological record to the extent that, of the structures in this area, only the latest (besides the wall itself) was complete enough to describe. This structure, formed by the features numbered 45, 48, and 49 in Fig. 5.5, was a room built into the large wall (Feature 26). Stones of the large wall had been removed or trimmed to allow the corner of this room to intrude. This happened late in the span of occupation at the site, and by this time a considerable depth of deposits had accumulated against the inside of the wall, although on the outside the wall apparently still stood its full height above the contemporaneous ground level. The floor of the structure formed by Features 45, 48, and 49, then, was midway up the inside of the massive wall. The floor of the structure was plaster, with an original surface and one resurfacing evident, and Feature 49 formed a small compartment of undetermined function in the corner of the room.

The overall sequence of use in this area, then, reveals fairly intensive occupation, followed by construction of the massive wall, then by continued intensive use only on the inside of the wall. While cultural deposits accumulated on the inside, the outside was kept clear. The massive wall, then, served as a barrier to movement into Sector I during most of the period during which Cuayucatepec was occupied. An interesting question involves just whom it was intended to block. The wall falls right in the middle of the site; the vast majority of the occupied area is outside it. It might thus have separated two parts of the zone of occupation from each other, creating a clearly defined sector which included the major complex of public architecture together with some (possibly high status) residential area. Perhaps the wall was principally intended to control access to this exclusive and important part of the town. Alternatively, the wall might have been a defensive construction that, together with the steep slopes on other sides, would have restricted access to Sector I. Although most of the twon would have been outside the defended area, such a redoubt is not unheard of—a small, fortified place where large numbers of people can seek refuge in time of attack and which is highly defensible, even though the attackers would have free run of the rest of the town. It might even have been possible for moderate numbers of people to withstand a siege of some duration in such a place. These alternative suggestions are, of course, not mutually exclusive, and a wall setting off and stressing the importance of one sector of the town could also have served a defensive function.

5. CUAYUCATEPEC: PRELIMINARY REPORT 181

Excavations in Sector II

The most intensively excavated of the six areas was Sector II. Surface survey by Nowack (1977) had already made it clear that this sector included the most concentrated habitation in the site—artifacts on the surface were dense, and numerous stone wall foundations were visible. Sector II lies principally on the western slopes of the highest portion of the ridge on which the site is located. To the south and east of this sector, the occupied area is farily sharply bounded by steep slopes where little cultural material is visible on the surface and where three test pits (963N751W, 967N813W, and 1010N721W) produced virtually no artifacts in very shallow deposits overlying sterile soil. To the southwest, Sector II ends at the wall which demarcates Sector I, and it adjoins other zones of occupation on the ridge spurs leading to the northeast and east as well as on the gentler slopes to the west and northwest. Altogether 21 test pits were excavated in the sector, of which four were later expanded to larger scale excavations.

Of the four expanded excavations, two (Areas E and F) are in the area just "outside" the wall which sets off Sector I. Area F is on a

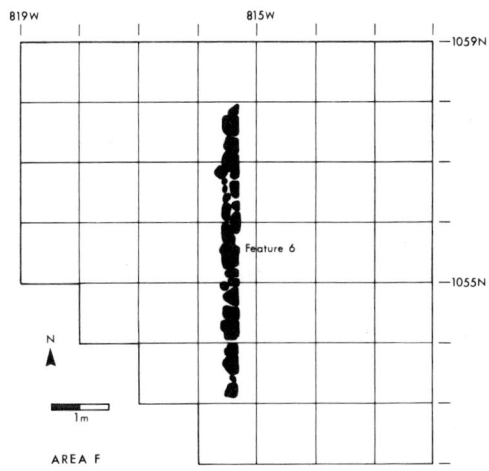

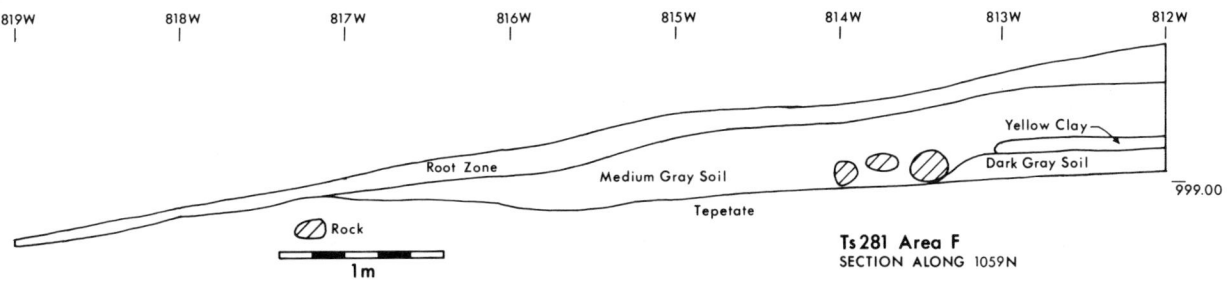

Fig. 5.6. Plan and section of Area F excavations.

moderately steep slope. It was excavated to expose more of a structure whose wall appeared in a test pit at 1054N815W. This wall (Feature 6 in Fig. 5.6) was two or three courses of cut stone high and associated with a floor on each side. This floor was made by leveling and packing the surface of the tepetate which underlay cultural deposits here. The deposits were thus considerably deeper on the uphill (eastern) side of the excavations and tapered to almost no thickness on the west. Moderate quantities of artifacts (all from the Palo Blanco phase) were recovered from the deposits, but the wall itself had been interrupted. Only a few meters of its length remained, and no other portions of the original structure whose wall this had been were encountered.

Area E exposed a longer and more complex sequence of deposition in an expansion from several features encountered in a test pit at 1076N833W. The oldest of these features was a sloping stone wall (Feature 9 in Fig. 5.7) built directly on bedrock. It appears to have been the retaining wall of a low platform or terrace built against the side of the hill. Its height varied up to five or six courses of stones in the westernmost part exposed since bedrock sloped off in that direction. Only a small portion of the Area E excavations were carried to sufficient depth (1.60 m below the present ground surface) to expose this wall. The limits of this deepest part of the excavations determine the end points of the wall as shown in Fig. 5.7; how much farther the wall extended cannot, of course, be determined.

Substantial accumulation of cultural debris subsequently buried this wall, the terrace or platform it retained, and the adjacent area to the north. These deposits, over 1.00 m thick, contained varying densities of artifacts of the Palo Blanco phase, like all others in Area E. Above these deposits were several features which together comprised a single structure that had been rebuilt an undetermined number of times. The several stone walls (numbered Features 5, 70, and 95 in Fig. 5.7) were retaining walls for a platform some 40 cm or less in height. During one stage of construction the stone retaining walls were made in a distinctive fashion with relatively thin dressed slabs placed on edge as facing stones for the low platform. The area inside the retaining walls was filled with rubble and surfaced with plaster. Features 71 and 72 in Fig. 5.7 are the remaining sections of the plaster floor. This type of construction is described in more detail for the best preserved example excavated in Area D (Sector VI). A small cache or offering consisting of a single ceramic vessel was placed inside the fill of the platform. On the downhill or western side of the excavations this structure was eroding out onto the present ground surface.

Near Area F, a test pit at 1043N848W exposed some 80 cm of cultural deposits with moderate densities of Palo Blanco phase sherds and, in the upper layers, a probable corner of a structure like that described for the upper layers of Area E. Two other test pits nearby (at 1085N810W and 1131N828W) produced less than 80 cm of deposits with dense Palo Blanco phase material; one exposed part of the retaining wall of a low rubble-filled platform as well. Between these two pits, however, another at 1113N818W yielded only very sparse artifacts in some 50 cm of cultural deposits.

5. CUAYUCATEPEC: PRELIMINARY REPORT

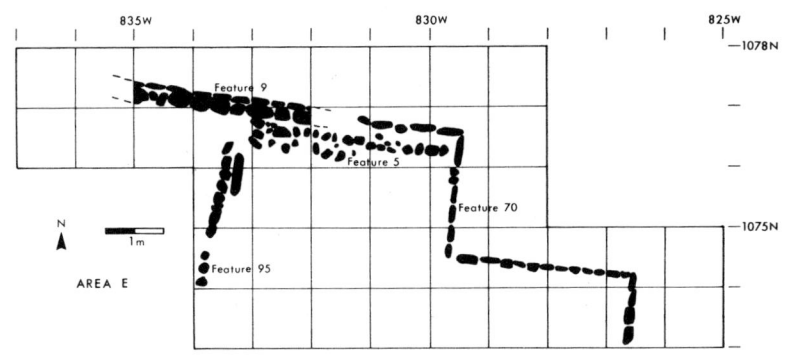

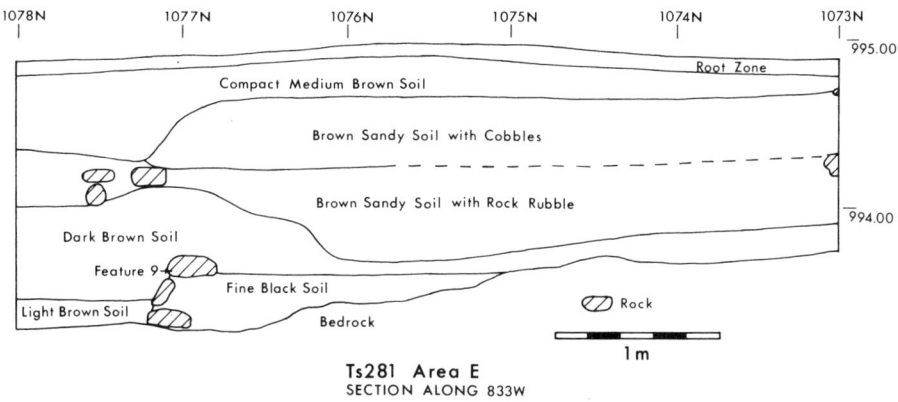

Fig. 5.7. Plan and section of Area E excavations.

Higher up, three test pits along the relatively broad, gently sloping crest of the ridge produced accumulations of primary Palo Blanco phase refuse. Midden debris to a depth of 70 cm was encountered at 1076N770W, and at 1162N755W a sloping retaining wall of dressed stone was exposed. This wall retained a rubble-filled platform or terrace built directly on bedrock near the single highest point on the site. And at 1203N778W a well-preserved plaster floor, bordered on the north by a wall of cut stones, lay less than 20 cm below the present ground surface. This structure had, in turn, been built over an additional 30 cm of cultural deposits.

In the northern portion of Sector II, three test pits at approximately the elevation of Areas E and F and the Sector I ridge indicated a continuation of the zone of dense occupation in that direction. These pits were all located in relatively level sections of an area with occasional steeper slopes. One at 1194N821W was shallow (30 to 40 cm deep) but exposed Palo Blanco phase midden debris with moderately dense artifacts. Another, at 1240N830W, revealed a structure consisting of a platform 60 cm high with a retaining wall of cut stones and surfaces of plaster on top and at its base. Artifacts around this structure were sparse but dated to the Palo Blanco phase. Some 80 to 100 cm of Palo Blanco phase deposits at 1298N822W included pits dug into tepetate and a packed clay floor with

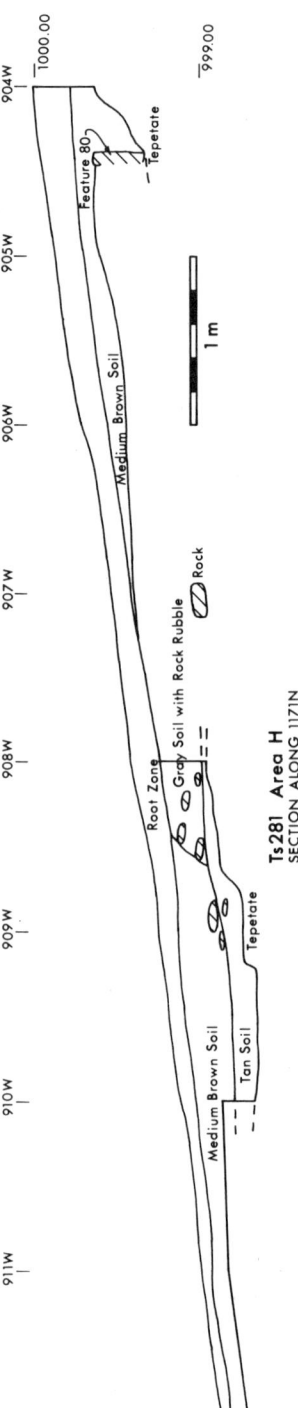

Fig. 5.8. Plan and section of Area H excavations.

traces of burning.

Sector II drops off toward the west of these three pits to somewhat lower elevations. The slopes are, for the most part, relatively gentle and show signs of continued dense occupation. Deposits varied considerably in depth. A test at 1146N887W went through up to 70 cm of Palo Blanco phase midden debris to a stone wall foundation associated with a packed clay floor. In a test at 1179N878W was a large bell-shaped pit dug through 50 cm of cultural deposits and an additional 50 cm into tepetate. The mouth of this bell-shaped pit was buried by some 40 cm more cultural deposit, all with fairly high densities of Palo Blanco phase sherds. In the upper part of the deposits at 1221N888W was the edge of a platform 70 cm high which had been faced with undressed flat slabs of stone set on edge. The surface of this platform had eroded away. The platform dated to the Palo Blanco phase, as did the 30 cm of cultural deposits under it.

The excavations labeled Area H were slightly farther downslope to the west. These began as a test pit at 1166N908W. Although deposits were shallow they contained occasionally dense concentrations of Palo Blanco phase artifacts and a number of features. Two stone walls, Features 13 and 19 in Fig. 5.8, which were noted in the original test pit did not continue much beyond it in the expanded excavations, having been interrupted by later construction. Another short segment of an interrupted wall (Feature 96) extended into the excavated area from the south. Features 79 and 80 were the least interrupted structural remains in the area, at least toward the north and east where the upward slope of the present ground surface left them most deeply buried. Toward the south and west, however, they too were interrupted, since the structure of which they were a part had been built at a level above the present ground surface in the downslope direction. Feature 80 consisted of the stone facing walls of a platform up to 60 cm high. These facing walls were made of dressed stone slabs set on edge, retaining a core of rubble fill. The upper surface of this platform had not been preserved since it was so close to (or even above) present ground level. Feature 79 was evidently an addition onto this structure. Construction technique was similar to that of Feature 80, but the upper surface of this platform was low enough to preserve a section of plaster floor. It was the construction of this platform that seems to have disrupted the structures partially composed of the previously mentioned wall segments. Feature 81, a patch of plaster floor probably originally associated with one of those walls, was also buried inside the fill of the Feature 79/80 platform. All of the construction in this area dated to the Palo Blanco phase.

Not far from Area H, the rambling Area G excavations revealed the most complicated sequence of construction encountered at Cuayucatepec. Area G was in a very level, partly natural, partly artificial terrace. It drops off sharply to the north and west of Area G beyond retaining walls of which Features 72, 87, 88, and 94 in Fig. 5.9 formed parts. Surface remains indicate that the final stage of construction in this area involved buildings around a roughly square plaza some 15 m across. Feature 85 in Fig. 5.9 was the remains of one of these buildings—a low platform built of small stones set in clay, a style in which Cuayucatepec produced other

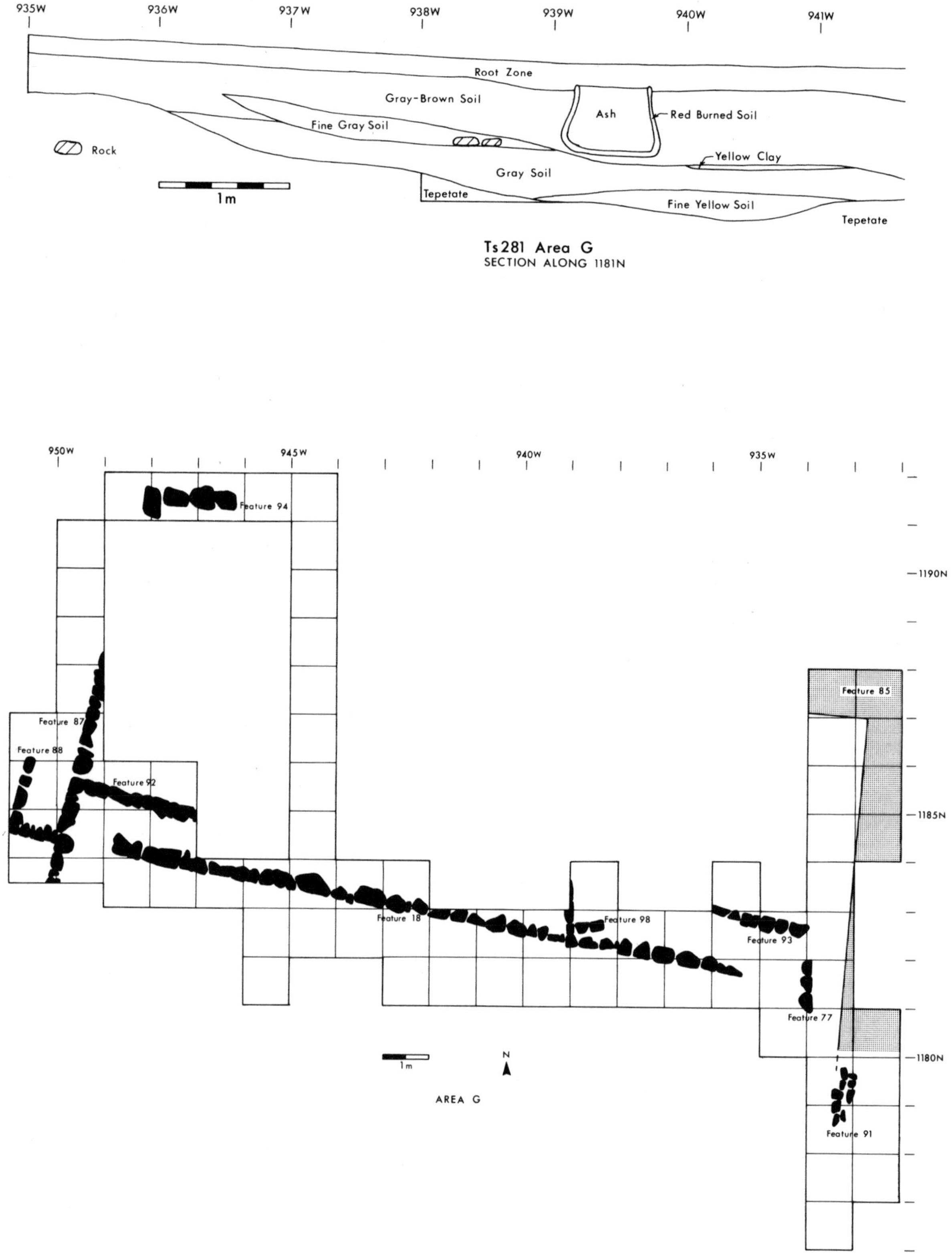

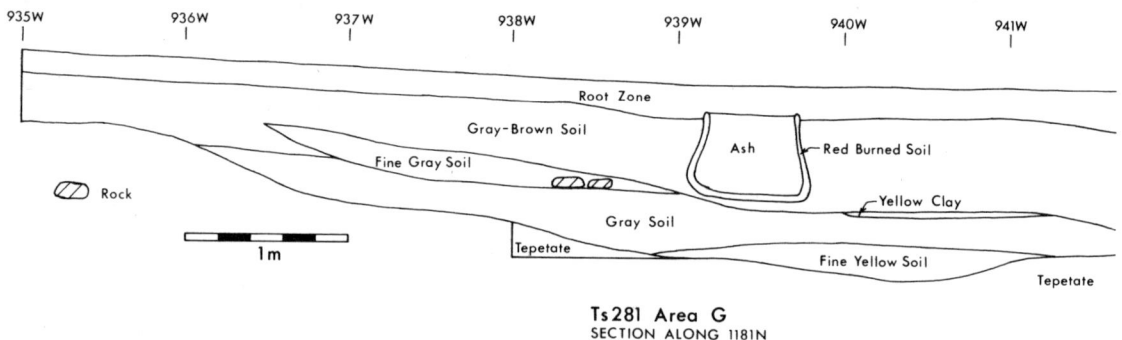

Fig. 5.9. Plan and section of Area G excavations.

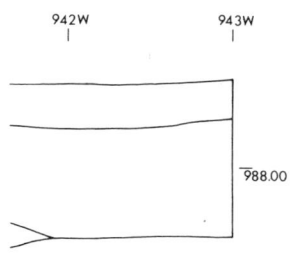

examples elsewhere. The level plaza floor associated with this building lay just above the remains of earlier structures. Chief among these was Feature 18, a stone wall some 14 m long and 40 cm high which retained a platform of rubble fill to the north. Buried inside the rubble fill of this platform were the remains of still earlier structures such as Feature 93 (Fig. 5.9). Feature 98 was the corner of a structure which partially interrupted the Feature 18 wall but predated the plaza floor associated with Feature 85. It was Features 18 and 98 that had originally been exposed by the test pit at 1182N938W of which Area G was the expansion.

A number of bell- and basin-shaped pits had been excavated into the tepetate beneath the cultural deposits of this area. Artifacts all dated to the Palo Blanco phase and varied considerably in density for the several deposits. Other features, such as hearths and additional fragments of interrupted walls, encountered in these deposits are not described here, although some of them are shown in Fig. 5.9.

Finally, a test pit was excavated at 1201N944W on another partly natural, partly artificial terrace immediately north of and lower than the terrace of Area G. In fact, the Area G excavations came within 9 m of this test. The 40 cm of cultural deposits penetrated by this pit produced relatively sparse Palo Blanco phase sherds, and no features were encountered.

Excavations in Sector III

East of Sector II, the main east-west line of the ridge system upon which Cuayucatepec is located continues. The main ridge itself narrows to a very sharp peak and drops off gradually to a series of broader terraces before plunging down a steeper slope. A subsidiary spur drops off fairly steeply toward the northeast to a broad terrace at the edge of a precipitous slope down to the level of the floor of the internally drained basin between the site and the edge of the valley. Sector III includes the two fingers of occupation running out these ridge spurs in which eight test pits were excavated.

A test pit at 1251N707W produced very sparse artifacts in only 20 to 30 cm of cultural deposits overlying tepetate. Three more test pits along this eastward ridge (at 1240N566W, 1195N462W, and 1157N318W) produced similar results. None of the four pits encountered any features. Together, they simply indicate the presence of a very sparse Palo Blanco phase occupation extending out this ridge.

The uppermost excavation on the northeastward spur was not really a test pit at all and consisted of cleaning out a large bell-shaped pit dug into relatively soft bedrock at 1316N564W. The elliptical mouth of this pit, some 100 by 70 cm, was visible on the surface. The pit, only partially filled with debris, reached a maximum depth of 140 cm and had a maximum subsurface diameter of about 220 cm. Although most of the debris in the pit was recent, it seems likely to have been excavated in prehispanic times, probably during the Palo Blanco phase, the only period of substantial occupation of the site.

Three test pits located on a terrace farther down this spur (at 1414N530W, 1422N470W, and 1459N515W) yielded very little cultural material, although a cache consisting of two ceramic vessels was found in one of them. This spur, then, like the one extending eastward, seems to have been the scene of a sparse occupation during the Palo Blanco phase.

Excavations in Sector IV

Sector IV extends in the other direction from Sector II: down the gentler slopes to the north and west which provide the easiest route to the top of the ridge. On the steeper slopes of the upper part of this sector two test pits (1341N843W and 1367N843W) were placed in more gently sloping locations. Both produced small amounts of Palo Blanco phase sherds in 40 to 50 cm of cultural deposits.

Six more test pits were scattered across a broad natural terrace at the foot of these slopes. A pit at 1425N863W yielded sparse Palo Blanco phase material in cultural deposits limited to 15 cm deep, except where a basin-shaped pit had been excavated into tepetate to an additional depth of about 40 cm. A small patch of a poorly preserved plaster floor was included among the Palo Blanco phase deposits of a test at 1359N928W. Sparse sherds and shallow deposits, mixed from plowing which reached to bedrock, were the only results of a test at 1302N901W. At 1298N944W deposits were about 1.20 m deep and artifacts (all of the Palo Blanco phase) were denser, but the test encountered no features. A test pit excavated at 1340N991W in what appeared to be a low mound in a plowed field produced only some 20 cm of thoroughly churned up deposits over bedrock. The broad natural terrace where these pits were sited came to a point near the test pit at 1329N1041W which yielded sparse Palo Blanco phase artifacts in some 20 cm of cultural deposits over bedrock.

Sector IV, then, represents an area where the dense Palo Blanco phase occupation of Sector II has tapered off to an apparent scatter of residences marking considerably less intensive use of this section of the site.

Excavations in Sector V

Sector V includes the lowest slopes of the steepest part of the ridge as well as an area which slopes more gently down to the valley floor without any major impediment to passage. It is thus a relatively indefensible part of the site, being not only outside the wall of Sector I, but also without the protection of the steep slopes cutting off Sectors I, II, and III, and, to a lesser extent, Sector IV. Although the slopes leading up from the valley floor to Sector V are relatively gentle, Sector V is still considerably elevated above the floor. Perhaps the most interesting aspect of Sector V distinguishable from surface survey is a fair density of artifacts on the surface and the remains of several sizeable public or ceremonial buildings. It contains, then, a secondary complex of elaborate architecture (secondary to that in Sector I in size and number of structures).

Sector V was investigated with 12 test pits. One on its upper slopes at 1390N995W went through about 40 cm of Palo Blanco phase deposits, below which were a possible post hole and a large basin-shaped pit excavated into tepetate. Over 90 cm of deposits with dense Palo Blanco phase sherds and a low stone wall were revealed on these same slopes in the test pit at 1386N1039W. Three nearby tests at 1358N1082W, 1361N1107W, and 1332N1128W produced very shallow deposits with little cultural material. More toward the base of these slopes, cultural deposits were somewhat deeper and artifacts more numerous in test pits at 1346N1152W, 1295N1137W, 1289N1154W, and 1266N1110W. Sherds in these four pits were primarily of the Palo Blanco phase, although Venta Salada phase material occurred in some of the upper layers. No architectural features were encountered.

A test pit at 1294N1167W was excavated into one of the mounds forming the side of a ballcourt which had been built into the side of the hill. The surface remains suggest an I-shaped ballcourt some 55 m long with a playing area about 8 m wide. The cross bars at the end of the "I" extended about 5 m to each side beyond the central playing area. The overall orientation of the structure was about 15° east of magnetic north. The centers of the two principal mounds forming the sides of the court stand today about 3 m above the present ground surface for the mound on the uphill or eastern side and about 2 m on the downhill or western side. The mounds forming the ends of the "I" are today slightly over 1 m above the ground surface in the center. The test pit was excavated into the mound on the eastern side with its long axis running east-west or roughly perpendicular to the axis of the ballcourt. Underneath deposits which seem to represent debris from the collapsed upper portions of the structure was a well-preserved plaster floor which was probably the original playing surface. This occurred about 1 m below the present ground surface in the central playing area. Associated with this floor was a part of the actual stone structure of the ballcourt. This consisted of well dressed small flat stones (about 5 cm thick and 10 to 30 cm long) set in clay. They formed the fill and facing of a structure sloping up and back from the playing surface at an angle of about 60° from horizontal. The location of the base of this structure (where it intersected the plaster floor) suggests that the central playing area of the ballcourt was originally some 12 m wide, rather than the 8 m suggested by the modern surface configuration. Since excavations in the ballcourt were limited to this test, it is not possible to estimate how much other figures derived from surface measurements might need to be adjusted. Since the goals of the project did not include large-scale exposure of public architecture, this test pit was not expanded. Sherds were not numerous in this test pit, but they indicate a Palo Blanco phase date for the ballcourt.

Immediately to the south of the ballcourt is an area whose surface remains suggest another ballcourt. In this case a mound some 2 m high forms one side of a long narrow enclosure defined on the other side by the downhill edge of an artificially constructed terrace. This long narrow area, however, lacks the well-defined ends marking the ballcourt described above, and a test pit excavated at 1249N1168W into the terrace edge in a position analogous to that of the test pit in the ballcourt failed to reveal such clear indications of a ballcourt structure. In deposits reaching a maximum depth of 1.20 m were found two stone retaining walls which had formed the front edge of a terrace rising in broad steps. These walls, however, were vertical and of rather different construction from those of the ballcourt. Sherds here also indicated a Palo Blanco phase date for the construction.

Several other small mounds ranging from 1 to 3 m in height are scattered around the ballcourt in the western part of Sector V in no apparent formal spatial arrangement. At 1338N1269W a test pit was excavated into one of these mounds. Deposits here were nearly 2 m deep and dated to the Palo Blanco phase, except for a small amount of Venta Salada phase material in the uppermost layers. This pit provided a cross section through several stages of construction on the site and extended considerably below the ground surface around the mound, whose present height is less than 1 m. The construction exposed consisted of stone wall foundations associated with plaster floors. These remains were probably from residential structures similar to those found elsewhere in the site: houses built on low rubble-fill platforms.

The excavations and surface remains of Sector V make it clear that there was a secondary focus of occupation on the lower slopes of the hill—one that included a fair density of residences, some architecturally elaborate, and other, more imposing structures of probable public or ceremonial character, including the only ballcourt at Cuayucatepec. This zone, of course, was completely outside the major defenses of the site.

Excavations in Sector VI

Along the continuation of the main ridge to the north of Sector V lies Sector VI, partly on gentle slopes in a low place or "saddle" of the ridge and partly ascending the somewhat steeper slopes of a hill to the north. Although it rises above Sector V on this hill, Sector VI is not set off by elevation or steep slopes in the way that Sectors I through IV are. A scatter of low density occupation continues on to the northwest along the main ridge beyond the area which could be sampled by excavation. Sixteen test pits, of which two were expanded to larger excavations, were located in Sector VI.

Two test pits on the gentler slopes (1435N1190W and 1441N1227W) produced around 80 cm of cultural deposits with low densities of Palo Blanco phase ceramics and no features. A third, at 1456N1251W in a very low mound, contained about 1 m of Palo Blanco phase deposits and the poorly preserved remains of a plaster floor stop a low rubble-fill platform. At 1451N1308W a test pit was expanded into the excavations called Area C where a portion of another similar structure was exposed in shallow Palo Blanco phase

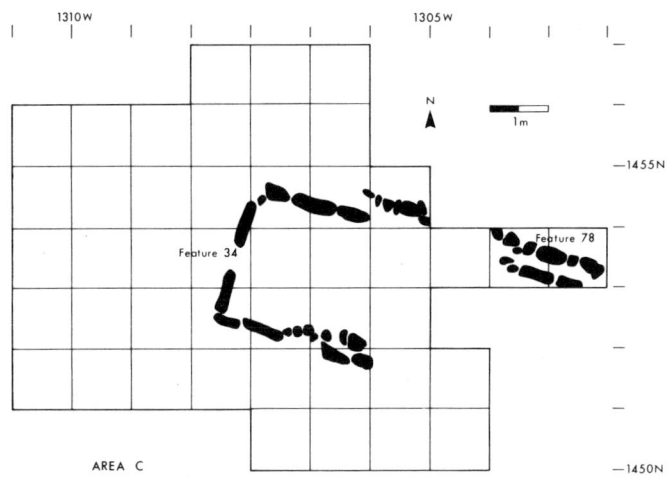

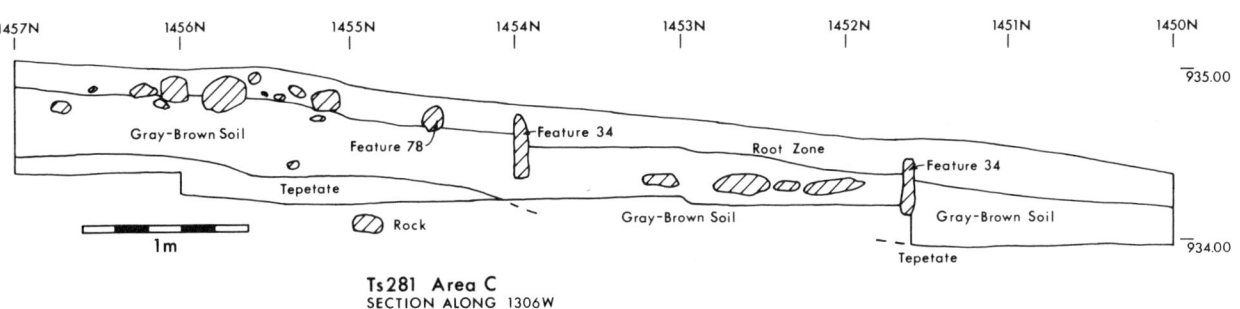

Fig. 5.10. Plan and section of Area C excavations.

deposits. This structure (Feature 34 in Fig. 5.10) was evidently a low platform faced with flat stones of the kind described in more detail below for Area D. No upper surface to the platform was preserved. The wall shown as Feature 78 in Fig. 5.10 was part of a later construction. The deposits in this area also included two well-defined hearths. Just north of Area C, two test pits at 1504N1297W and 1526N1277W yielded moderate densities of mostly Palo Blanco phase sherds and no features.

Farther up the slope, Area D exposed the best preserved and most complete example encountered of a rather distinctive style of house construction. The edge of this structure had been built directly on bedrock, reached only 40 to 50 cm below the surface in a test pit at 1510N1191W. The first stage of construction was part of Feature 29 (Fig. 5.11), a rubble-fill platform using dressed flat slabs of stone as a facing wall. The facing wall went down to bedrock on the north side of this section of the structure (the room located right in the center of the excavations). One dimension of the platform was 5 m, the other at least 3 m. Along the edges of the platform were stone walls extending upward to form the walls of the plaster-floored room supported by the platform. Since no indication of a door remained in the preserved part of the structure, it seems likely that this room faced south, perhaps onto a courtyard. All this side had been destroyed by erosion: this was the downslope direction, and the level floor of the room would have been above the present ground surface here.

At a later date, two additions had been built onto the structure, one to the east and one to the west. The original north-south walls of the first stage of construction were found inside the rubble fill of the final structure at about 1194W and 1189W. The eastward addition added another 4 m or so to the length of this side of the platform and had been built in similar fashion. Wall stubs showed that this addition had contained two separate rooms connected by a narrow doorway, although neither of them communicated with the original room in the portion preserved. The plaster floor of the western addition, unlike that of the eastern addition, was at a slightly lower level than the floor of the original room. The same style of construction prevailed in the western addition, although the stone blocks facing the rubble-fill platform were not so nicely cut. This addition added some 4.5 m or more to the length of the structure, bringing the total to more than 15 m. After the structure had been abandoned, the north-south wall at about 1194W (one of the exterior walls of the original room, but later a partition wall inside the structure) fell over to the west, and its stones were buried by subsequent accumulation of debris. These remains indicate that the wall had been constructed of relatively small, flat stones laid in regular courses to a height of at least 1.50 m. As already mentioned, an undetermined amount of the southern section of the structure had eroded away. Whether the rooms partially recovered originally faced onto a

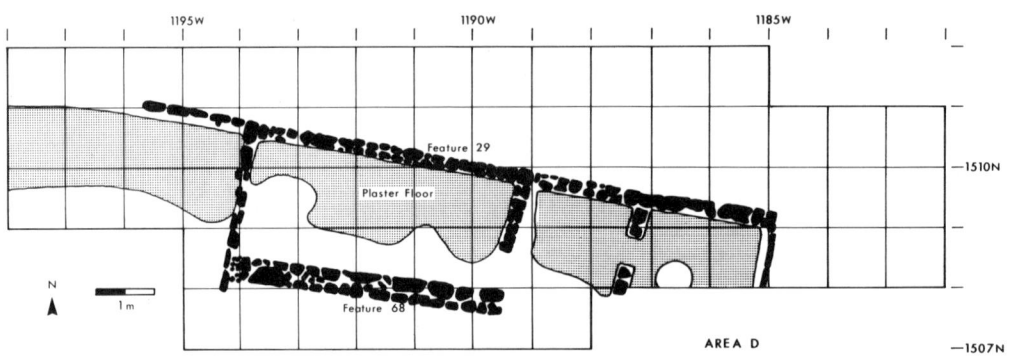

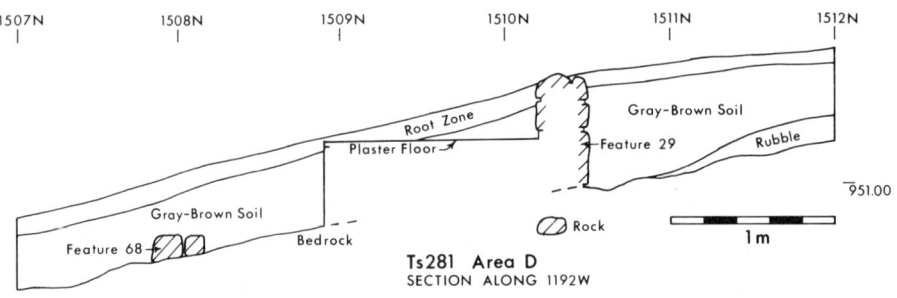

Fig. 5.11. Plan and section of Area D excavations.

patio together with other similar rooms or whether the structure stood alone could not be determined; remains of similar structures elsewhere in the site suggested that such rooms faced on patios in some cases at least. Portions of similar structures were exposed, not only in Area D, but also in Areas C, F, and H, as well as in a number of test pits.

Other remains in Area D included a stone wall (Feature 68 in Fig. Fig. 5.11) from a structure partly destroyed and partly covered over when the original room of Feature 29 had been built; Palo Blanco phase midden debris, including a hearth, accumulated against the north wall of Feature 29; and a cache or offering consisting of two pairs of ceramic vessels.

Although surface remains indicate a moderate number of other structures on the hillside where Area D was located, none of the other tests in this part of Sector VI encountered architectural features. These tests were at 1502N1078W, 1514N1141W, 1534N1225W, 1538N1108W, 1540N1203W, 1544N1153W, 1556N1201W, 1565N1123W, and 1614N1106W. The depth of cultural deposits in these pits ranged from 10 to 100 cm, and most of these deposits produced sparse to moderate Palo Blanco phase artifacts, except for some pits with small quantities of Venta Salada phase materials in the upper layers.

Sector VI, then, was a continuation of the occupied area associated with the secondary focus of ceremonial or public architecture in Sector V. Density of habitation here seems not to have been so great as in portions of some higher parts of the site, such as Sector II, but greater than in Sector III or perhaps Sector IV. There was no indication that any further public or ceremonial structures were located in Sector VI. Occupation tapered off to the northwest of the crest of this lower hill but continued an undetermined distance to the northwest at low density.

Conclusion

Preliminary conclusions from the excavations at Cuayucatepec are unusually difficult to make because such an important part of the research design involved the recovery of samples of artifacts and ecofacts from various locations within the site. The analysis of these and the analysis of their patterns of distribution have only begun at this writing. Nevertheless, some ideas about the site derive from surface remains and from the immediately available results of excavation. Since the excavations at Cuayucatepec were designed to complement those at Quachilco (Drennan 1978), these preliminary conclusions will be phrased in terms of comparisons and contrasts between the two sites.

Although Quachilco constituted the most nucleated population center of its time in the Tehuacán Valley, the later center at Cuayucatepec was still more nucleated. Instead of Quachilco's concentration of occupation around a central plaza with a series of outlying clusters of residences, Cuayucatepec comprised a single zone of relatively dense occupation, compressing probably a larger total number of inhabitants into a smaller occupied area. Perhaps paradoxically, however, the internal structure of the settlement at Cuayucatepec was less centrally focussed than that at

Quachilco. The single architectural focus at Quachilco was a large main plaza where all the largest buildings, and proabably all the buildings of public character, were located. As noted above, two separate complexes of public architecture are apparent at Cuayucatepec, providing two separate foci of residence as well. Neither of these complexes is organized around a single large plaza like the one at Quachilco. The complex in Sector I involves several smaller plazas among the large buildings, and the one in Sector V seems to have slight, if any, formal spatial arrangement of structures.

As at Quachilco, variation in the elaborateness of residential structures at Cuayucatepec seems likely to relate to status differences among the inhabitants. Ordinary houses seem to have consisted of packed clay floors, often created by excavating into tepetate, and stone wall foundations, with upper wall and roof construction undocumented. The more elaborate houses, those with plaster floors and stone walls on low platforms faced with thin slabs of cut stone, seem to have been higher status residences. There is some indication that differences of status were reflected more ostentatiously in residential architecture at Quachilco, although the possibility must be recognized that still more elaborate residences may remain unexcavated at Cuayucatepec. The association at Cuayucatepec of the putative higher status residences with the complexes of public or ceremonial architecture is less clear than at Quachilco where all the most elaborate residences clustered near the central plaza. Those at Cuayucatepec seem more widely distributed through the residential zones tested.

The differences between the locations of the two sites were discussed above. Cuayucatepec's hilltop location suggests a concern with defense unimportant to the residents of the dispersed valley floor settlement at Quachilco.

A number of other topics remain to be explored through the analysis of patterns of distribution of artifacts and ecofacts and comparison of these patterns for Cuayucatepec and Quachilco. Further information on topics mentioned briefly here will, of course, come from such studies as well. More detailed knowledge of ceramic chronology for the Palo Blanco phase will also result, making possible a precise reconstruction of the patterns of founding, growth, and abandonment of the site and of relationships of contemporaneity among the features and structures discussed in this preliminary report.

Clearly, it is pointless to speculate at this stage about the results of such analysis. Nevertheless, one category of artifact may be mentioned: kiln wasters. Nowack's (1977) surface survey of the site recovered from several areas sherds which show the effects of firing problems ranging from poor quality to "fatal" flaws, suggesting that one of the activities centered at Cuayucatepec was the production of ceramics. More such sherds were recovered in the excavations. As was the case with the surface collections, these sherds did not seem to be overwhelmingly concentrated in any single sector of the site; nor were any features exposed which clearly related to ceramic manufacture. The distribution of these sherds within the site will, however, be studied in detail. Also requiring detailed study are the distributions of such materials as shell, greenstone, and obsidian which could not have been obtained in the vicinity of Cuayucatepec. The focus of continuing analysis of the material from this site, then, will be on clarifying the internal organization of such a Palo Blanco phase center in order to contribute to the more general goals of the Palo Blanco Project.

5. EXCAVACIONES EN CUAYUCATEPEC (Ts281)

INFORME PRELIMINAR

por Robert D. Drennan

SUMARIO

Las excavaciones conducidas en el sitio de Cuayucatepec durante el año 1978 tenían como objetivo complementar las conducidas en Quachilco durante 1975 y 1977 (Drennan 1978). Quachilco había sido el primer "lugar central" en el Valle de Tehuacán, y el único durante la fase Santa María Tardía. Aproximadamente cuando Quachilco fue abandonada, alrededor de seis otros centros fueron fundados en varias partes del valle. La forma de organización política centralizada que dichos centros representaban se expandió por el valle durante la fase Palo Blanco Temprana. Cuayucatepec, que continuó ocupado hasta la fase Palo Blanco Tardía, fue unto de estos lugares centrales de la segunda generación.

Al igual que Quachilco, Cuayucatepec está ubicado en una parte del valle suficientemente ancho como para proveer una concentración considerable de tierra nivelada para agricultura. Esta parte del valle conocida localmente como Valle de Cinco Señores, ofrece contrastes ambientales agudos con la zona alrededor de Quachilco. El Valle de Cinco Señores, a 1750 m sobre el nivel del mar, es más de 500 m más alto que Quachilco. Aunque las lluvias en el Valle de Cinco Señores son apenas más copiosas, la diferencia en humedad disponible es tal que el cultivo de tierra no irrigada, imposible en Quachilco, es una operación arriesgada pero posible cerca de Cuayucatepec. Diferencias en la humedad disponible también tienen como resultado comunidades de plantas salvajes diferentes en las dos regiones. Los habitantes de ambas regiones, sin embargo, dependían de la irrigación para una subsistencia agrícola regular. En Quachilco la mayor fuente prehispánica de agua para riego era una serie de manantiales perennes.

Antes de la reciente construccion de la represa de Valsequillo, que es hoy la fuente más importante de agua de riego del Valle de Cinco Señores, la región dependía del agua de los varios arroyos que sirven de desagüe a las montañas, fuente ésta temporal y variable.

Cuayucatepec, a diferencia de Quachilco, estaba ubicada en la cima de una colina, la parte más alta del espinazo que separa una pequeña zona con buena tierra agrícola y desagüe interior del principal Valle de Cinco Señores (Fig. 5.2). La mayor densidad de residencias en la fase Palo Blanco ocurrió en la parte más alta del espinazo (Sector II en Fig. 5.2) con el principal complejo de arquitectura cívico-ceremonial situado en una estribación aislada un poco más baja y al suroeste de él. La ocupación continuó hacia abajo en las únicas laderas suaves y adyacentes (Sector IV), con otro grupo de residencias (Sector VI) y un complejo secundario de

5. CUAYUCATEPEC: PRELIMINARY REPORT 197

arquitectura cívico-ceremonial (Sector V) al pie de la parte más empinada de la colina, aunque aún bastante por encima del nivel del suelo del valle.

Las excavaciones de 1978 comenzaron con la excavación de cuadros de prueba, de 1 por 2 m, ocho de los cuales fueron luego ampliados en excavaciones mayores. El objetivo era hacer un muestreo de los depósitos y elementos arqueológicos a través del sitio y exponer un poco más unas cuantas áreas seleccionadas. No se encontró restos de ocupación anterior a la fase Palo Blanco Temprana y la ocupación principal terminó en la fase Palo Blanco Tardía, con una ocupación poco densa en la fase Venta Salada.

El principal complejo de arquitectura pública, Sector I, fue investigado con siete cuadros de prueba, de los cuales dos fueron ampliados más tarde (Areas A y B). La arquitectura pública, la cual no fue excavada, aparece hoy como una serie de montículos de hasta 7 m de altura situados alrededor de una plaza mayor y de varias más pequeñas. Este sector también fue densamente usado para habitación. Las estructuras residenciales aquí eran de piedra cortada, a veces con piso de estuco. Habían basurales asociados con las estructuras así como pozos de almacenamiento excavados en el tepetate. El sector estaba separado del resto del sitio por una muralla de grandes proporciones que cortaba a través del espinazo que provee el único acceso fácil. Esta pared puede haber sido hecha para controlar la entrada de gente y para enfatizar la exclusividad de esta zona de arquitectura pública y posibles residencias elites, o puede haberse construído para crear una zona de defensa a la cual la población podía escapar al ser atacada aunque la mayoría del sitio hubiera quedado fuera de estas defensas. Las posibilidades no son, por supuesto, mutuamente exclusivas.

Justo fuera de la pared y en la parte más alta de la colina, está el Sector II, sin ningún edificio grande, pero con una gran densidad de residencias. Este sector fue el más intensivamente explorado. Se hicieron 21 cuadros de prueba, de los cuales cuatro fueron luego ampliados (Areas E, F, G, H). Tanto los cuadros de prueba como las posteriores excavaciones revelaron numerosas secciones de estructuras residenciales, basurales asociados con ellas, y elementos arqueológicos tales como hogares y hoyos. La arquitectura residencial en este sector era a veces de piedra cortada con pisos de estuco y a veces de piedra no formada con pisos de tierra apretada o tepetate aplanado. En general, es probable que las paredes, en su parte superior, eran de otro material, no piedra, posiblemente de cañas y barro o de adobe. Los depósitos, en general, representaban una serie de numerosas estructuras en relación estratigráfica, mostrando un largo período de uso residencial intenso de este sector. Esto, por supuesto, también resultó en el trastorno considerable de algunos depósitos tempranos por actividades posteriores, pero también creó la información estratigráfica necesaria como para lograr una cronología detallada que delinee los procesos de fundación, crecimiento y abandono del sitio y los distintos patrones de actividad durante la existencia del mismo.

Los ocho cuadros de prueba en el Sector III, a lo largo de estribaciones del espinazo que se extienden al este del Sector II, revelaron evidencia de muy pocas residencias de la fase Palo Blanco. Al oeste del Sector II, está el único otro acceso fácil a la cima de la colina. En esta zona, Sector IV, ocho cuadros de prueba produceron aún mas escombros residenciales de la fase Palo Blanco. Este sector mostró un uso más intensivo que el Sector III, pero no una densidad de residencias tan grande como en el Sector II. El Sector V está en las laderas mas suaves, en la base de la parte empinada del espinazo. Aunque situado sobre el nivel de la superficie del valle, este sector no está separado del él por laderas empinadas u otras posibles defensas. Doce cuadros de prueba fueron excavados en este sector. Aquí la estructura dominante es un juego pelota en forma de "I," con orientación de 15° al este del norte magnético. La estructura fue construida de pequeñas piedras cortadas colocadas en arcilla: el piso era de estuco. El campo de juego era de aproximadamente 55 m de largo y 12 m de ancho. Varias terrazas sustanciales y montículos de 1 a 3 m de alto llenan este complejo de arquitectura pública que es secundario (en tamaño y elaboración) con respecto al Sector I. Una densidad moderada de estructuras residenciales también ocurre en este sector.

Una densidad residencial moderada también caracterizaba al Sector VI, donde 2 de los 16 cuadros de prueba excavados fueron ampliados en excavaciones mayores (Areas C y D). El mismo tipo de depósitos y elementos arqueológicos que fueron encontrados en las otras áreas residenciales aparecen aquí. Area D también contiene el ejemplo mejor preservado y más completo de un tipo de estructura residencial distintivo, que también se encontró en Areas C, F, y H, al igual que en un gran número de cuadros de prueba. Esta estructura consistía en una plataforma rellena de escombros de unos 40 cm de alto con sus caras cubiertas con planchas planas de piedra tallada. La superficie superior de la plataforma estaba cubierta con estuco y dividida en varias habitaciones por medio de paredes de piedra tallada. Por lo menos dos adiciones se le habían hecho a la estructura original durante el tiempo que se usó. Parece ser que tales estructuras, en otras áreas, tenían patios enfrente, los cuales estaban quizás rodeados de otras estructuras similares. Estas casas eran suficientemente grandes para que ningún ejemplar fuera completamente expuesto, no porque las áreas excavadas eran pequeñas, pero más bien debido a que partes de todas ellas habían sido destruídas previamente, con frequencia por la erosión, dado que los ejemplares descubiertos estaban en las laderas donde sólo las partes que se encontraban cuesta arriba permanecieron enterradas.

La mayoría de la información que las excavaciones en Cuayucatepec debían recoger queda todavía por extraer por medio del análisis de artefactos, de restos naturales, y de la distribución de ellos. A pesar de que el análisis ha apenas empezado, varios hechos interesantes son ya aparentes. Aunque Quachilco había sido el asentamiento más grande y más denso de su tiempo en el Valle de Tehuacán, Cuayucatepec comprimió su aún mayor población en una área de ocupación menor. Sin embargo, quizás paradójicamente, la estructura interna del sitio de Cuayucatepec estaba menos centralizada que la de Quachilco con su única plaza central. En Cuayucatepec habían dos complejos separados de arquitectura pública, ninguno de los cuales muestra el grado de planeamiento formal visto en la plaza central de Quachilco. Considerables diferencias en la posición social parecen reflejarse en la arquitectura residencial de Cuayucatepec, pero

5. CUAYUCATEPEC: PRELIMINARY REPORT

las diferentes clases de casas ocurren frecuentemente juntos en el mismo sector del sitio. Las excavaciones produjeron algunos restos de cerámica mal cocida (ver Capítulo 3), lo mismo que en el reconocimiento del sitio hecho por Nowack (1977), pero esta evidencia de producción de cerámica no parece haber estado concentrada en ninguna área excavada. Una interpretación precisa de la organización de actividades en el sitio dependerá, por supuesto, de un análisis adicional de la distribución de artefactos y del establecimiento de una cronología más precisa para el período de ocupación. El enfoque del análisis que aún continúa, será clarificar la organización interna del sitio como ejemplar de un centro regional de la fase Palo Blanco, para sí contribuir a los objetivos más generales del Proyecto Palo Blanco.

6. FORMATIVE AND CLASSIC DEVELOPMENTS IN THE CUICATLAN CAÑADA

A PRELIMINARY REPORT

by Charles S. Spencer
and Elsa M. Redmond

The Cuicatlán Cañada is a narrow tropical canyon that serves as the only natural corridor between the high semi-arid valleys of Tehuacán and Oaxaca (Fig. 6.1). At the time of the Spanish conquest, the Cañada was occupied by Cuicatec speakers who were ethnically distinct from the Zapotec speakers of Oaxaca and the Chocho-Popolocan speakers of Tehuacán (Hunt 1972). As part of the continuing Palo Blanco Project, a two-phase research program was carried out in the Cañada by the authors of this chapter. The first phase was an intensive survey of the region between the modern towns of Tecomavaca and Dominguillo (Fig. 6.2). Directed by Redmond, this survey involved first locating sites from all time periods through field survey using aerial photographs, and then returning to map and surface collect those sites showing Formative and Classic occupation. The second phase of the project, directed by Spencer, consisted of excavations at the site of La Coyotera near Dominguillo, a site occupied during the Formative and Classic periods. In this brief report, we will first describe the Cañada and the research problem that guided our joint investigations in that region, then summarize the results of the survey and excavation.

The Cuicatlán Cañada

It is in the Cuicatlán Cañada that the Río Salado, flowing south from Tehuacán, and the Río Grande, flowing north from the mountains near the Valley of Oaxaca, join at the headwaters of the Papaloapan River. The floor of the Cañada varies between 500 and 700 m above sea level, unlike the 1500 to 1700 m elevations of Tehuacán and Oaxaca. This fact results in higher temperatures in the Cañada where the mean annual temperature is 24.5° C and where recordings of 40° C and higher are not uncommon, particularly during April and May.

Although there is too little rainfall in the Cañada for successful dry farming (Hunt and Hunt 1974:137), simple floodwater farming (Kirkby 1973:36-41) is possible on some stretches of low alluvium along the Río

---

The research in the Cañada upon which this chapter is based was supported by the National Science Foundation (under Grant No. BNS-77-15805 for the excavations at La Coyotera directed by Spencer), the Wenner-Gren Foundation for Anthropological Research (under Grant No. 3211 for surface survey directed by Redmond), the University of Michigan, and Yale University. We were assisted in the field by Mark King, Richard Lewis, and Glenda Sanchez.

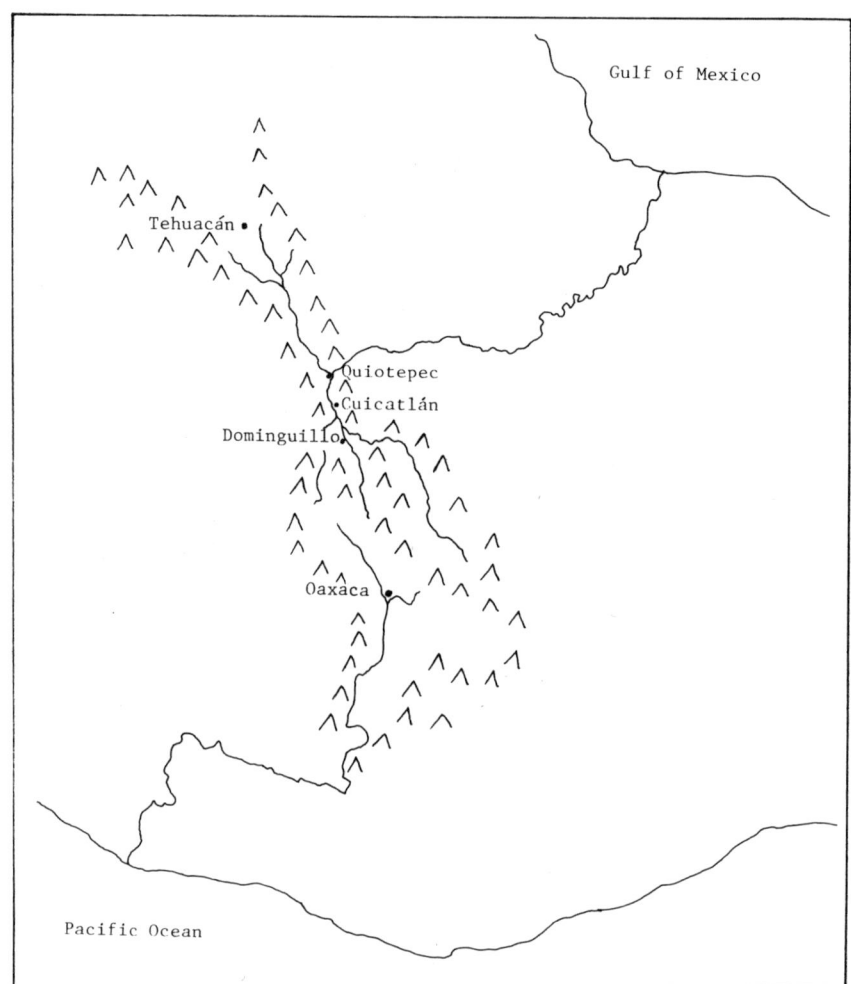

Fig. 6.1. Location of the Cuicatlán Cañada between Tehuacán and Oaxaca.

Grande, and the higher alluvium can be irrigated with water from tributary streams. While the supply of water is virtually unlimited, the amount of alluvium that can be brought under cultivation is limited to four major alluvial fans, formed where large tributaries join the Río Grande and where the canyon widens to produce a relatively wide floor. These four important fans are located near the present towns of Quiotepec, Cuicatlán, El Chilar, and Dominguillo (Fig. 6.2). As Hunt and Hunt (1974:136) quite accurately state, "Elsewhere the terrain is rough, non-irrigable, and uninhabitable." Under irrigation, the alluvium in the Cañada can be extremely productive land. Yields can range up to 2,000 kg of maize per ha per planting, and more than one planting per year is possible. Today much of the alluvium is used for growing tropical fruits such as mangoes, limes, chicozapotes, black zapotes, and ciruelas, delicacies sometimes transported to neighboring highland markets.

The Cañada is, in effect, a pocket of tierra caliente surrounded on all sides by the tierra templada and tierra fría of the southern highlands. Many crops that flourish in the Cañada cannot be grown at all in the Oaxaca

6. CUICATLAN CAÑADA: PRELIMINARY REPORT

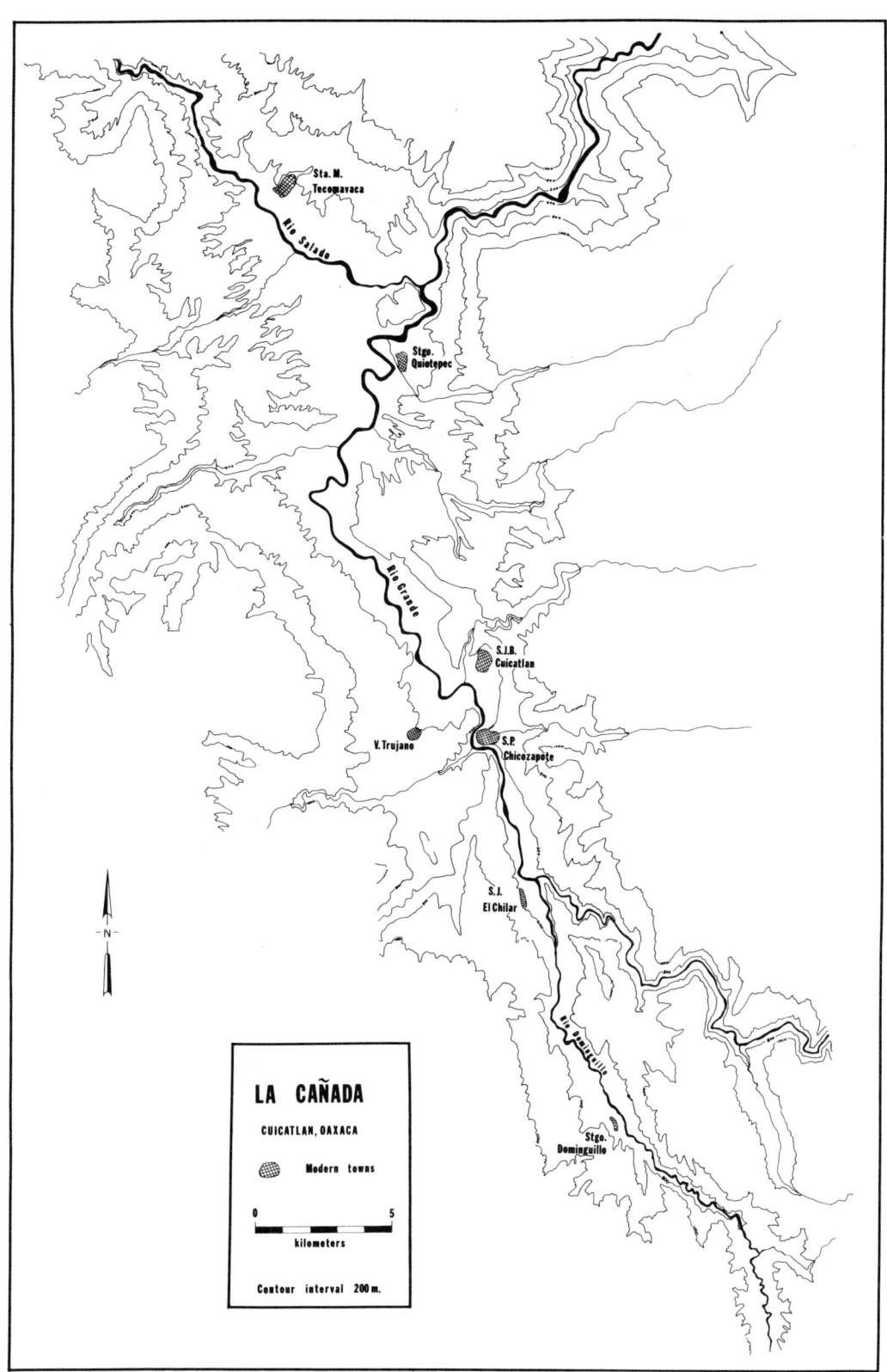

Fig. 6.2. Map of the Cuicatlán Cañada.

or Tehuacán valleys. As we shall see, this difference in agricultural potential figured importantly in the Cañada's relationships with its highland neighbors, particularly with the ancient Zapotec state that emerged during the Late Formative in the Valley of Oaxaca.

A Research Design for the Cañada

There are two major reasons why we selected the Cuicatlán Cañada for archeological investigation. The first was simply a desire to close the gap in archeological coverage that existed between the well-studied valleys of Tehuacán and Oaxaca. Hunt (1972) and Hopkins (1974) had undertaken research in the Cañada, but their studies dealt primarily with the post-Conquest and immediately pre-Conquest (or Postclassic) periods. Our study focussed on earlier time periods in order to provide a linkage between Tehuacán, the Cañada, and Oaxaca during the Formative and Classic periods.

Second, we wished to explore the relationship between the Cañada and the Valley of Oaxaca during the Late and Terminal Formative, the period when the Zapotec state was emerging at Monte Albán. Monte Albán, according to Richard Blanton (1978), was a specialized administrative center, one of whose primary functions was to manage relationships between the Valley of Oaxaca and neighboring regions. Blanton believes that these relationships were militaristic in nature and that the Zapotec actually subjugated much of the countryside surrounding the Valley of Oaxaca. Joyce Marcus (1976) also maintains that Monte Albán was a militaristic state. Her evidence is a series of inscriptions on a Terminal Formative building known as Mound J, located in the Main Plaza of Monte Albán. These inscriptions were identified as "conquest slabs" by Alfonso Caso (1947:21). More recently, Marcus (1976:130), in a study of the place names used in the inscriptions, has suggested that at least one of the glyphs refers to the Cuicatlán Cañada.

Investigators working at Monte Albán, therefore, had proposed that the ancient Zapotec state had been an expansionistic enterprise. Furthermore, one of the regions possibly under domination during the Terminal Formative or Monte Albán II phase had been the Cuicatlán Cañada. In 1976, we began to formulate a research design for the Cañada that would deal with its relationship to the Valley of Oaxaca during the crucial period of Zapotec state formation. We examined the environmental characteristics and economic potential of the Cañada, as well as the ethnohistorical record and archeological data dealing with the region (Hunt 1972 and Hopkins 1974). We then devised a set of four models that we felt subsumed the kinds of relationships that might have existed between the Cañada and the Valley of Oaxaca during the time of Monte Albán. One of these was a conquest model, and it is this model we will briefly, and informally, discuss here. Formal presentations of this model and of our entire research design are in preparation.

Basically, the conquest model explicates how a previous relationship of exchange between the Valley of Oaxaca and the Cañada was replaced during the Late and Terminal Formative by a relationship of subjugation and exaction of tribute. In developing this model, we had to consider why the

6. CUITCATLAN CAÑADA: PRELIMINARY REPORT

Cañada might have attracted the Zapotec, perhaps inducing them to expend the effort necessary to subjugate and control the region. One likely possibility is the Cañada's previously-mentioned potential with regard to frost-free agriculture. By taking over the Cañada, the Zapotec could have regulated the production of tierra caliente agricultural goods according to their own needs, instead of relying upon exchange with the Cañada to provide them with the desired products. For example, the Zapotec might have manipulated the local Cañada economy toward the large-scale production of certain tropical items of interest. Just why the Zapotec would have been so interested in these tierra caliente goods is also a feature of the conquest model, but it will not be dealt with in this report.

Another important consideration for the expansionistic Zapotec probably would have been the strategic location of the Cañada. The Cañada is the major artery connecting the Oaxaca area to the Tehuacán Valley and Puebla basin; moreover, it is narrowly constricted in places by steep mountains. By establishing military outposts in appropriate locations, the Zapotec could have regulated the movement of people and goods through this frontier region.

Let us briefly consider some of the implications of the conquest model. On the regional level, the model would lead us to expect major settlement pattern changes resulting from the Zapotec state's reorganization of the Cañada. We might expect to find evidence for Monte Albán's militarism in the Cañada, as well as for a Zapotec facility concerned with regulating the passage of goods and people through the frontier. On the community level, we would expect to find evidence for a change in the nature of sociopolitical and economic organization due to Monte Albán's intervention. If the Zapotec state manipulated the local economy of the Cañada toward the large-scale production of tropical fruits, we would expect to find evidence for a corresponding shift in the economic activities of the inhabitants of a given community. We might also expect to discover how the Zapotec replaced the traditional political order within such a community with a new form of local administration, one that would respond to the interests of the Monte Albán state.

To collect information on the nature of regional organization, Redmond devised a program of regional settlement pattern survey; all sites found in the course of this regional survey were located by time period on aerial photographs. A second stage of Redmond's survey was designed to collect more precise information on the internal structure of Formative and Classic sites by means of intensive mapping and surface collecting techniques (Redman and Watson 1970 and Flannery 1976c). Finally, one of the sites located during the survey, La Coyotera, was selected by Spencer for excavation. The excavation program was aimed at exploring the nature of local economy and sociopolitical organization at this community before and after the proposed Zapotec take-over of the Cañada.

206

OAXACA	CAÑADA	TEHUACAN
MONTE ALBAN III	TRUJANO	LATE PALO BLANCO
MONTE ALBAN II	LOMAS	EARLY PALO BLANCO
LATE MONTE ALBAN I		
EARLY MONTE ALBAN I	PERDIDO	LATE SANTA MARIA
ROSARIO		

Fig. 6.3. Correspondence of ceramic phases in the Valley of Oaxaca, the Cuicatlán Cañada, and the Tehuacán Valley.

Chronology

Another important goal of the excavations, of course, was the establishment of a ceramic sequence for the Formative and Classic periods in the Cañada. Although much of the necessary analysis remains to be done, we can present at this time a preliminary and partial ceramic sequence for the region (Fig. 6.3). In this chapter we will not describe the sequence in any detail, and we also warn the reader that the chronological framework will be refined and perhaps altered as analysis proceeds.

Fig. 6.3 shows the relationships of contemporaneity between phases in Oaxaca, the Cañada, and Tehuacán. The dates for the phases described below are compromises between the dates which have been assigned to the Oaxaca and Tehuacán phases with which the Cañada phases seem to be contemporaneous.

Three phases in the proposed ceramic sequence concern us here: the Perdido, Lomas, and Trujano phases. The Perdido phase is a late Middle Formative manifestation (ca. 600-200B.C.). Among other characteristics, it has a strong grayware tradition reminiscent of Quachilco Gray in the Tehuacán Valley (MacNeish, Peterson, and Flannery 1970:120-134) and Socorro Fine Gray in the Valley of Oaxaca (Drennan 1976a:21-45). At the moment we consider the Perdido phase to be roughly contemporaneous with the Late Santa María phase in Tehuacán and with the Rosario phase and Early Monte Albán I in the Valley of Oaxaca.

Lomas phase pertains to the Late and Terminal Formative (ca. 200 B.C.-A.D. 200). The dominant grayware of this period is quite similar to that of Late Monte Albán I and Monte Albán II in the Valley of Oaxaca. Our Lomas phase collections include numerous outleaned wall bowls like those of the G.12 category of Caso, Bernal, and Acosta (1967:25-27). Other Lomas phase pottery bears a strong resemblance to the waxy crema wares (for example, C.7 and C.11) of Monte Albán II in Oaxaca (Caso, Bernal, and Acosta 1967: 47 and 68). We would therefore align Lomas phase with Late Monte Albán I and Monte Albán II in Oaxaca, and, by extension, with the contemporaneous Early Palo Blanco phase in Tehuacán.

Trujano phase is a manifestation of the Classic (ca. A.D. 200-700). The grayware of this period bears certain resemblances to both the gray pottery of Monte Albán III in Oaxaca and that of the Late Palo Blanco phase in Tehuacán. Gray bowls resembling the G.35 type of Caso, Bernal, and Acosta (1967:80-82) are common in our Trujano deposits, as are certain vessel forms characteristic of the El Riego Gray pottery type in Tehuacán (MacNeish, Peterson, and Flannery 1970:146-157).

Summary of Results

While the analysis of the survey and excavations is still in progress, we will briefly summarize some of the trends that have emerged to date.

Perdido Phase

There are 11 sites in the Cuicatlán Cañada dating to the Perdido phase. Nine range in size from 1 to 5 ha; two cover 8 and 10 ha, respectively. All the Perdido phase settlements are located on high alluvial terraces overlooking the stretches of low alluvium found at each of the Cañada's alluvial fans. Since we found no irrigation canals or facilities associated with these Perdido phase settlements, we surmise that the low alluvium was cultivated by using simple techniques of floodwater farming.

The sizes of the Perdido phase settlements directly reflect the associated amounts of low alluvium on each of the Cañada's alluvial fans. For example, in parts of the canyon where there are lesser amounts of low alluvium, such as Quiotepec and Dominguillo, the corresponding Perdido phase settlements are small (2 to 2.5 ha). On the other hand, the two largest settlements at this time are found on the two central alluvial fans of the Río Grande, where the amounts of low alluvium are greatest. The site of El Mirador, located on the Cuicatlán alluvial fan, covers about 10 ha, and the site of Hacienda Tecomaxtlahua on the Chilar alluvial fan is just over 8 ha. These two sites have large central plazas with pyramidal mounds up to 4 m in height.

Our excavations at the Perdido phase settlement at La Coyotera, on the Dominguillo alluvial fan, exposed over 1600 m^2 of this community of 2.5 ha. The settlement was organized into a series of large residential compounds, each one measuring about 30 to 40 m on a side and separated from the others by at least 25-35 m of unoccupied space. We were able to excavate one of these compounds entirely and extensively test its neighbor. In so doing we recovered the remains of nearly two dozen complete, Perdido phase houses, along with associated features and burials. The compound we completely exposed consisted of 18 structures arranged around three patios (Fig. 6.4).

A wide variety of plant remains and other items recovered attest to the different kinds of economic pursuits engaged in by the people who lived in this Perdido phase settlement. Craft activities such as shell working and weaving were practiced by some members of the community, and limited numbers of tropical fruits and nuts were cultivated along with the usual staples.

There is evidence for considerable status differentiation among the inhabitants of this Perdido phase community. One of the structures we excavated, for example, turned out to be an elaborate tomb. It contained an adult individual in extended supine position with its head to the north. The body had been painted prior to interment, and was accompanied by 30 ceramic vessels and several shell ornaments, including a shell necklace. By comparison, no other burial we excavated here had more than three associated ceramic vessels.

Unlike the sites of El Mirador and Hacienda Tecomaxtlahua with their large central plazas and pyramidal structures, public architecture at La Coyotera during the Perdido phase consisted of a few low platforms, none of them physically segregated from the area of residence. Certain kinds of ritual paraphernalia were associated with these low platforms and adjacent patios. The ritual activities that took place at this Perdido phase settlement appear to fit within the pattern noted for other parts of Formative Mesoamerica (Flannery 1976a), with an emphasis on costuming, communal dancing, and ritual self-sacrifice.

The Perdido phase community at La Coyotera met a sudden and apparently violent end about 200 to 150 B.C. The settlement on the high alluvium was burned to the ground and completely abandoned at this time.

Lomas Phase

Major changes in the regional settlement pattern of the Cañada took place during the Lomas phase. The most striking of these occurred in the Quiotepec area at the northern end of the Cañada. Quiotepec marks the northern limit of the Cuicatlán Cañada, for here the Río Grande joins the Río Salado flowing south from Tehuacán. A mountain ridge extends west of the river junction and almost seals off the northern Cañada from the Tehuacán Valley. Entry to the Cañada from the north is limited to a narrow pass cutting through this mountain ridge. Immediately south of the natural pass is a major ford on the Río Grande that is still in use today.

In contrast to the 2 ha community of the Perdido phase, Lomas phase settlement at Quiotepec attained a maximum area of 40 ha distributed through five settlement components. The largest of these covers both sides

6. CUICATLAN CAÑADA: PRELIMINARY REPORT

Fig. 6.4. Aerial photograph of the excavated Perdido phase residential compound at La Coyotera.

of the critical mountain pass, and a defensive wall protects a large area of plazas, pyramidal mounds, a ballcourt 70 m long, and associated residential structures. On the alluvial fan directly south of the mountain pass and river ford is a 200 by 210 m plaza delimited by elongated mounds 6 m high, through which any traveler using the ford would have to pass. Additional areas of settlement extend along piedmont ridges overlooking the large plaza on the banks of the river. On all these Quiotepec settlements we found abundant ceramics that show strong similiarities to those of the Monte Albán II phase in the Valley of Oaxaca.

We carried our regional survey north to include the area around the modern town of Tecomavaca, and in so doing discovered that Quiotepec marks the northern limit of the distribution of Lomas phase and Monte Albán II ceramics. At Tecomavaca there is a settlement contemporaneous with the Lomas occupation at Quiotepec, but it is covered with the Palo Blanco phase pottery of Tehuacán.

In the Cañada south of Quiotepec there were also important settlement pattern changes during the Lomas phase. The previous Perdido phase communities on the high alluvial terraces were abandoned at this time, and 11 settlements were established on Piedmont spurs and ridges rising above both the high and low alluvium. These sites are all smaller than 5 ha, and they usually consist of a single small plaza with one or two pyramidal mounds accompanied by a number of residential terraces.

Associated with at least two of these Lomas phase settlements in the central and southern Cañada are the remains of elaborate irrigation canals. These canals evidently channeled water from tributary streams onto the high alluvial terraces previously occupied. It seems clear that the Lomas phase witnessed a great expansion in the scale of agricultural production in the Cañada south of the Quiotepec area.

La Coyotera is one of the Lomas phase sites associated with elaborate irrigation facilities. As happened elsewhere in the central and southern Cañada, the earlier Perdido phase community on the high alluvium at La Coyotera was abandoned, and a new Lomas phase settlement was established atop an adjacent piedmont ridge. The irrigation facility associated with this Lomas occupation at La Coyotera consists of a long and well-built canal that brought water down from a tributary stream behind the community to the expanse of high alluvium below. We traced this canal for much of its original length and located 11 aqueducts where the ancient builders lifted the canal across small arroyos. The canal empties onto the high alluvium at precisely the location of the earlier Perdido phase settlement.

The Lomas phase settlement at La Coyotera differed from its Perdido phase predecessor in a number of striking ways. The organization of residence changed from the earlier pattern of large compounds to one characterized by individual households located on residential terraces. The area occupied by Lomas phase residences, however, is not much greater than the size of the earlier Perdido phase settlement.

Our Lomas phase deposits from La Coyotera suggest that the cultivation of a few special tropical plants was emphasized to a much greater extent than in earlier times. As Judith Smith points out in Chapter 7, two plant species being produced in much greater quantities were the black zapote (Diospyros digyna) and especially the coyol palm (Acrocomia mexicana). Much of the irrigated high alluvium was probably used at this time for cultivating these tropical plants.

The nature of Lomas phase public architecture at La Coyotera represents a real departure from the situation in Perdido times. A single plaza with two pyramidal mounds on an elevated platform was the public focus of the Lomas phase settlement. In front of the larger of these two mounds we found a concentration of 61 human skulls, roughly aligned in rows. At present we interpret this deposit as the remains of a toppled over skull rack, what the Aztec in the Postclassic called a tzompantli. These skull racks were used as symbols of imperial power by the Aztec. They were designed to terrorize a subjugated people and help keep them submissive and responsive to the interests of the imperial state.

Trujano Phase

There are 15 sites in the Cuicatlán Cañada that pertain to the Trujano phase. As was the case during the preceding Lomas phase, these sites extend over hills and piedmont ridges rising above the canyon floor. Some of these sites, in fact, represent a continuation and growth of antecedent Lomas phase communities. With only one exception, all these Trujano phase settlements were larger than their Lomas phase predecessors. The exception is at Quiotepec where the Trujano phase site covers only 8 to 10 ha, a great reduction from the Lomas phase occupation of 40 ha. During the Trujano phase, most of the Cañada population was concentrated at the central alluvial fan near the present town of Cuicatlán where we find 45 ha of settlement distributed along seven hilltops and piedmont spurs. Near El Chilar to the south there are about 20 ha of Trujano phase occupation, and in the Dominguillo area 10 to 15 ha of settlement dispersed over three ridges rising above the canyon floor. During the Trujano phase, therefore, settlement distribution in the Cañada reverted, in a sense, to the situation that obtained during the Perdido phase, with the large alluvial fans of the central Cañada once again becoming the major loci of human occupation.

At La Coyotera, our excavations documented the transition between the Lomas and Trujano phases. During the Trujano phase, occupation continued on the same piedmont ridge, but the area of public architecture was shifted 200 m southeast of the small Lomas phase plaza with the skull rack. Several kinds of public structures were built at this new location, including platforms, pyramidal mounds, and a ballcourt. The plaza that contained the skull rack was apparently not used as a public area during the Trujano phase. The number of house foundations and residential terraces increases greatly between the Lomas and Trujano phases, but the unit of residence remains the individual house on a residential terrace.

Our excavation in the major aqueduct of the irrigation canal suggested that this facility continued to be used throughout the Trujano phase. Trujano phase deposits, however, contained a much lower density of fruit and nut remains than those of the Lomas phase, indicating that the cultivation of these items became less important in Trujano times. Apparently, the irrigated high alluvium was being used mainly to support the community's population, which, during the Trujano phase, grew to be quite large.

Conclusion

In this chapter, we have discussed briefly some of the goals and results of our joint investigation of the Formative and Classic periods in the Cuicatlán Cañada. One of our goals was to explore the relationship between the Cañada and the Valley of Oaxaca during the Late and Terminal Formative, the period of Zapotec state formation. We outlined a model of Zapotec conquest that predicted certain changes in regional settlement patterns, local economy, and sociopolitical organization in the Cañada, compatible with a subjugation of the region by the Monte Albán state.

Although the analysis of the Cañada survey and excavations is far from complete, we can state now that many of the original expectations of our conquest model were in fact borne out by the archeological data we collected in the field. The results tentatively suggest that during the Lomas phase the Cañada was subordinate to the Monte Albán state. The process of subjugation evidently began around 200 B.C., that is, during the Late Monte Albán I phase in Oaxaca, and the condition persisted until the end of the Monte Albán II phase in Oaxaca, or about A.D. 200.

Our continuing analyses will clarify further the relationship that existed between the Cañada and the Monte Albán state. As our understanding of this relationship improves, we hope to gain a unique and important insight into the nature of the early Zapotec state itself.

6. DESARROLLO FORMATIVO Y CLASICO EN LA CAÑADA DE CUICATLAN

INFORME PRELIMINAR

por Charles S. Spencer
y Elsa M. Redmond

SUMARIO

La Cañada de Cuicatlán, que es angosta y posee un clima tropical, contituye el único corredor natural entre los valles de Tehuacán y Oaxaca (Fig. 6.1). Durante 1977 y 1978 Redmond estuvo a cargo del reconocimiento de superficie de la región entre los pueblos de Tecomavaca y Dominguillo (Fig. 6.2). Sitios correspondientes a todos los períodos fueron localizados por medio de un reconocimiento de campo con fotos aéreas, y de esos sitios con ocupación Formativa y Clásica se hicieron mapas, así como también sistemáticas colecciones de superficie. Durante 1978 Spencer dirigió excavaciones en el sitio de La Coyotera, cerca de Dominguillo, que pertenece al período Formativo y Clásico.

La cantidad de lluvia que cae en la Cañada no es suficiente para permitir agricultura seca, pero cuando la tierra es irrigada con el agua del Río Grande, que es amplia, la Cañada es muy productiva. La cantidad de tierra aluvial llana que puede ser irrigada está, sin embargo, limitada a cuatro áreas aluvionales que ocurren donde los tributarios se unen al Río Grande. La Cañada, que posee una elevación de 500 a 700 m sobre el nivel del mar, es en efecto una cuenca de tierra caliente rodeada de la tierra templada y la tierra fría de las altiplanicies del sur.

Una de la razones de los trabajos en la Cañada es que representaba un blanco en los conocimientos arqueológicos de las mucho más estudiadas regiones de los valles de Tehuacán y Oaxaca, especialmente para los períodos Formativo y Clásico. Otra razón para estos trabajos es que la Cañada puede haber sido conquistada durante el Formativo Terminal por el naciente estado zapoteco con su centro en Monte Albán (Marcus 1976:130). El naciente estado zapoteco puede haber deseado el control de la Cañada por sus varios productos tropicales, los cuales no podían ser producidos en el Valle de Oaxaca y por su posición estratégica conectando el Valle de Oaxaca con la Cuenca de Puebla. Si esta conquista ocurrió en realidad, se espera encontrar cambios en el patrón de asentamiento así como también en la organización de las comunidades asociadas con la nueva organización política y los atentados a controlar el pasaje en este corredor natural. Si la adquisición de frutas tropicales era uno de los objetivos en esta conquista, se espera encontrar evidencia de producción de estos productos en gran escala.

Una cronología cerámica tentativa ha sido delineada durante este análisis preliminar, para los períodos Formativo y Clásico en la Cañada

(Fig. 6.3). La fase Perdido del Formativo Medio (ca. 600-200 a.C.) muestra similitudes con la fase Santa María Tardía del Valle de Tehuacán y con la fase Rosario y Monte Albán I Temprana en el Valle de Oaxaca. La fase Lomas (ca. 200 a.C.-200 d.C.) es bastante similar a Monte Albán I Tardía y a Monte Albán II y contemporánea (pero menos similar) a la fase Palo Blanco Temprana en Tehuacán. La fase Trujano (ca. 200-700 d.C.) parece ser contemporánea con Monte Albán III en Oaxaca y con la fase Palo Blanco Tardía en Tehuacán. Debe entenderse que la descripción que sigue es preliminar, ya que el análisis de la información recogida ha comenzado apenas y la continuación de este análisis puede causar cambios en las interpretaciones que son aquí presentadas.

Nueve sitios de la fase Perdido, en la Cañada, varían en tamaño de 1 a 5 ha, y los otros dos son de 8 y 10 ha respectivamente. El tamaño de las poblaciones y sus distribuciones parecen estar relacionados a las cantidades de tierra agrícola que se encuentran en cada una de las cuatro áreas aluvionales formadas por los tributarios del Río Grande. Los dos sitios más grandes tenían plazas con montículos piramidales, de hasta 4 m de altura, a sus lados.

En el sitio de La Coyotera, más de 1,600 m^2 de los 2.5 ha de la comunidad de la fase Perdido fueron excavadas. La comunidad estaba compuesta de grandes conjuntos residenciales de unos 30 a 40 m por lado, separados unos de otros por unos 25 a 30 m de espacio vacío. En esta comunidad se hacían objetos de concha así como también tejidos. Una cantidad limitada de frutas y nueces tropicales eran cultivadas junto con los productos agrícolas usuales. Diferencias de status considerables entre los residentes son deducibles de los entierros, uno de los cuales fue una tumba con 30 vasijas de cerámica y varios ornamentos de concha. En este período, La Coyotera no poseía la plaza central ni las grandes estructuras piramidales.

En la fase Lomas una comunidad de unas 40 ha fue fundada en Quiotepec cerca de donde el Río Salado, fluyendo de Tehuacán, se une al Río Grande que baja de la sierra zapoteca. Este sitio efectivamente controlaba el pasaje del Valle de Tehuacán hacia la Cañada. Este sitio que estaba fortificado con grandes e impresionantes complejos de arquitectura pública, también marca el límite norte de cerámica de la fase Lomas con su fuerte similitud a Monte Albán II. Los 11 asentamientos de la fase Lomas en la Cañada al sur de Quiotepec son todos de menos de 5 ha y fueron localizados en lomas y espinazos. Estos asentamientos estaban usualmente centralizados en plazas pequeñas cada una de las cuales tenía uno o dos montículos piramidales. En esta época también se construyeron elaborados sistemas de irrigación.

En el sitio excavado de La Coyotera, la comunidad de la fase Perdido fue abandonada y una nueva comunidad fue fundada durante la fase Lomas, arriba de un espinazo cercano. Un largo canal traía agua de un río tributario atrás del espinazo, para irrigar la tierra aluvional que quedaba enfrente. Residencias dejaron de estar en grandes conjuntos y pasaron a ser casas individuales, situadas en terrazas, a las orillas del espinazo. El zapote negro (Diospyros digyna) y el coyol (Acrocomia mexicana) eran mucho más común que antes. En una plaza principal con dos montículos piramidales se encontraron los restos de 61 calaveras humanas que aparentemente eran

6. CUICATLAN CAÑADA: PRELIMINARY REPORT

parte de un estante de calaveras o tzompantli similar a los que son conocidos para los aztecas.

Durante la fase Trujano el sitio de Quiotepec se redujo a 8 o 10 ha mientras que otras comunidades de la fase Lomas crecieron en tamaño. La población se encontró otra vez distribuída entre las cuatro áreas de tierra aluvional depositada por los cuatro ríos tributarios. Estas cuatro áreas constituían la mayoría de la tierra agrícola. En el sitio de La Coyotera la plaza con el tzompantli de la fase Lomas fue abandonada y un nuevo complejo de arquitectura publica fue construído unos 200 m al sudeste. La población del sitio creció, pero las residencias continuaron siendo casas individuales. El largo canal de irrigación continuó en uso, pero las frutas y nueces tropicales eran menos numerosas entre los restos vegetales.

Aunque el análisis del reconocimiento de superficie y de las excavaciones en la Cañada aún no está completo, nuestra interpretación preliminar es que la evidencia arqueológica soporta la idea de que el estado de Monte Albán conquistó la Cañada alrededor de 200 a.C., durante Monte Albán I Tardía. Esta dominación parece haber terminado alrededor de 200 d.C., al final de Monte Albán II. Continuación del análisis clarificará aún más la relación que existió entre la Cañada y Monte Albán, y esperamos que mientras nuestro entendimiento de esta relación adelante, podremos lograr una comprensión importante y especial de la naturaleza del mismo estado zapoteco.

7. CARBONIZED BOTANICAL REMAINS FROM QUACHILCO, CUAYUCATEPEC, AND LA COYOTERA

A PRELIMINARY REPORT

by Judith E. Smith

One body of data important to the achievement of the goals of the Palo Blanco Project is the botanical material recovered by excavation. The project has included extensive excavations at three sites: Quachilco or Ts218 (Drennan 1978) and Cuayucatepec or Ts281 (Chapter 5), both in the Tehuacán Valley, Puebla, and La Coyotera (Chapter 6), located in the Cuicatlán Cañada, Oaxaca. Processing, identification, and analysis of the carbonized plant remains from each of these sites have been carried out, and this chapter presents the initial results of such work.

Primary emphasis here rests on presenting a roster of the identified species of botanical remains for each site. For the most part, only edible species, mainly represented by carbonized seeds, are discussed. Brief preliminary assessments of the role of each species in human subsistence systems and their ecological relationships are also offered.

This chapter should be considered preliminary for several reasons. First, while the majority of botanical identifications have been made, a small part of the material remains unidentified or requires more specific identification. Second, a detailed analysis of the morphology of some plants, particularly the cultivars, has not yet been completed. Thus, certain evolutionary developments of the plants themselves and their possible clinal distributions over space have not yet been worked out. Third, the large quantity of identified wood charcoal from all sites awaits statistical analysis and thus has not been included at all in this paper. These data will be crucial in the understanding of environmental variables and patterns of land use.

Finally, application of the basic data presented here to the wider research goals of the Palo Blanco Project will be the subject of a much more extensive, future report. The intra- and inter-site distribution of the botanical remains, taken in conjunction with other archeological data, will help in testing specific hypotheses regarding the evolution of complex society in this area. Botanical data should provide information about the

---

In addition to the N.S.F. support for the Palo Blanco Project (see Chapter 1), the work described in this chapter was supported by a University of Michigan Rackham Dissertation Assistance Grant. I would like to thank Lauro González Q. and the staff of the paleobotany laboratory of the Departamento de Prehistoria, I.N.A.H., for their assistance. Richard Ford and Joyce Marcus read the manuscript and offered valuable suggestions.

following subjects: the availability of different subsistence goods to differing segments of the population on both local and regional levels; the potential influence of man-made changes in the physical landscape upon cultural variables; the ways in which systems of production and distribution of subsistence goods may affect (or be affected by) societal organization and management; and, the role of food products of botanical origin in exchange networks.

Thus, this chapter on the basic botanical data forms only the first step of analysis. Even in this preliminary form, however, it adds to the very small body of information on subsistence at Late and Terminal formative and Early Classic sites in Mesoamerica.

The carbonized plant remains were recovered by hand-screening and by water separation (flotation). Virtually every piece of carbonized organic material that did not pass through the 6 mm mesh screens was saved during excavation at all three sites. Additionally, 185 flotation samples were taken at Quachilco, 160 at Cuayucatepec, and 79 at La Coyotera. Each sample was up to 4 l in size (exact sample size was recorded in each case). All ashy or very carboniferous features and deposits were sampled intensively. Samples were also taken from all deposits where flecks or pieces of carbon were scattered through the matrix. After some experimental sampling in areas where little or no carbon was visible to the naked eye, it was concluded that the tiny yields of plant material would not repay much investment of time and labor, and therefore such deposits received only minimal sampling. Water separation followed procedures described by Minnis and LeBlanc (1976). This method proved effective in the complete recovery of carbonized material in very good condition.

Identifications of the prehistoric plant remains were made in the project laboratory in Tehuacán with the aid of a dissecting microscope. Comparative botanical material was collected by the author locally from markets and in the field. Additionally, I was kindly given access to the comparative collection of archeological plant remains at the paleobotanical laboratory in the Departamento de Prehistoria (I.N.A.H.) in Mexico City.

Preservation of plant material at all three sites was by carbonization alone, not by dessication. Thus, all botanical remains described and discussed below are carbonized.

Quachilco

Quachilco was initially settled early in the Late Santa María phase and became the first and only Late Formative center in the Tehuacán Valley. Palo Blanco Project research at Quachilco, which began in 1975, has determined that a 20 ha area of large-scale architecture and dense, internally complex occupation was surrounded by a much larger area of sparse occupation with scattered clusters of dwellings (Drennan 1978). Occupation of the site continued into Early Palo Blanco times, after which it was abandoned and a

7. BOTANICAL REMAINS: PRELIMINARY REPORT

number of Classic period centers established throughout the valley. Later Postclassic occupation at Quachilco was not a focus of the current research.

Located in a central position on the valley floor at an altitude of about 1210 m above sea level (Fig. 1.2), Quachilco is in an area of extreme aridity. The average annual precipitation (recorded between 1955 and 1974) was only 385 mm (Boletín Hidrométrico 1974). No river or stream flows near the site. Numerous mineral springs, however, are found at various locales throughout the northern half of the Tehuacán Valley, and a series of such springs is situated atop a high escarpment near Quachilco. Fossilized canals which run down the escarpment and criss-cross the level land around the site attest to the use of the spring waters for cultivation in prehistoric times. Today, tracts of land which are not irrigated by waters from the spring have a sparse cover of cactus and thorn-scrub vegetation.

Excavation at Quachilco included tests and expanded excavations at the central plaza, in areas of dense surface remains of architecture outside the central plaza, in open spaces without surface remains of architecture but within the core area of the site, and at small occupational clusters in the peripheral sections. Floatation samples and carbon from the screen were collected at all these localities. Two sections of the site produced almost no carbonized material: the peripheral zone "Southeast Barrio" (Areas H and I and tests), and the westernmost small patio of the core area (Area M and tests). Tests in the "South Barrio," in the floor of the central plaza, and in a Venta Salada phase mound (Area C) yielded only small amounts of wood charcoal. Substantial amounts of charcoal were recovered in all excavations at other parts of the site. Most fruitful in producing carbonized remains of edible plant species were areas outside of the central plaza proper but within the densely occupied core of the site (Areas B, F, G, K, L, and N). Preliminary description of the excavations at Quachilco is available in Drennan 1978.

A description and preliminary discussion of all of the plant remains from the site (excluding wood charcoal) follows. All of the material under consideration here belongs to the Late Santa María/Early Palo Blanco occupation. For convenience, plant species have been divided into four categories representing different types of production or procurement: first, cultivated plants (those species believed to be the products of native agricultural or horticultural practices, excluding arboreal fruits); second, arboricultural products (fruits of trees that were manipulated by humans); third, edible "weeds" (disturbed habitat plants growing spontaneously in cultivated fields or near dwellings and believed to have been food sources); and fourth, wild plant foods from species native to the area in undisturbed zones or in unused fields where succession has taken place over extended periods of time.

Cultivated Plants

Maize. As might be expected, maize was the most common food plant found in the excavations at Quachilco. Carbonized cob fragments, kernels, and cupules were all recovered. The largest amounts of maize were from the deep midden of Area G and from a series of alternating clay floors and thin ash lenses in Area N. Remains of maize in more moderate quantities were recovered from Area F (particularly from a thick midden-like deposit), from throughout the deep depositional sequence in Area K, and from the rubble around the series of stone walls in Area L. Small amounts of maize were also found in the Area B midden and in a test pit in the South Barrio. Several pits containing ash also contained remains of maize (Features 11, 23, 37, and 47). All of the above proveniences date to the Late Santa María/Early Palo Blanco time period.

A detailed analysis of the morphology and intra-site distribution of the maize from Quachilco will appear in a later report, but a brief summary of the characteristics of Quachilco maize taken as a whole follows.

Of the carbonized cob fragments recovered, none was sufficiently intact to permit the determination of length. Diameter and row number, however, could be established for 54 of the cobs. Most were strikingly small: 37% were less than 6 mm in diameter, 70% were below 7 mm in diameter, and 93% had diameters under 9 mm. The majority of the cobs (56%) were 10-rowed, with others, in order of frequency, 12-, 14-, 8-, and 16-rowed. Eight cobs showed irregular rows and/or weak pairing. Five of these and one other displayed the primitive feature of stiff, prominent glumes. These examples all had row numbers other than ten. Three cobs had longitudinally elongated cupules and two had unusually great cupule spacing. The remaining 42 cobs (78%) with complete diameters, however, displayed regular rows with average pairing and no primitive features. A sample of ten cobs of this latter group was kindly examined by Carlos Alvarez of the paleobotanical laboratory of the Departamento de Prehistoria (I.N.A.H.) in Mexico City. Nine of the cobs were identified as slender pop (cf. Mangelsdorf 1974:177-178), and one as Chapalote.

Measurements of cupule width were made on the intact cob fragments and also on 113 loose cupules recovered by water separation. The average cupule width for all of the Quachilco maize was 3.143 mm.

Thirty-eight kernels and fragments of kernels were recovered at Quachilco both in water separation and dry screening. Thirteen were globular in shape; four were "kernel-shaped" (that is, with front and back flattened); the shapes of the remaining kernels could not be definitely classified. The 25 kernels whose widths could be measured ranged from 2.2 to 7.0 mm wide, with an average of 4.32 mm. Height could be measured on six kernels and ranged from 3.0 to 6.2 mm, with an average of 4.23 mm. The average thickness of 15 kernels for which this dimension could be ascertained was 3.61 mm, with a range of 2.2 to 5.0 mm.

Beans. Among the more surprising results of the archeobotanical analysis of Quachilco was the virtual absence of the remains of beans at the site. Only one partial cotyledon of Phaseolus vulgaris was found, even though the same techniques yielded large quantities of beans at Cuayucatepec. The single cotyledon fragment came from the botanically prolific thick midden of Area G. It measured 6.5 mm in width, and its incomplete length was greater than 9 mm which is at the upper end of the size range of beans found at Cuayucatepec (see below). The outer edge of the bean fragment was

7. BOTANICAL REMAINS: PRELIMINARY REPORT

convex and the inner (hilum) edge straight, a shape repeated in several examples at Cuayucatepec. The single Quachilco cotyledon was undoubtedly from a cultivated bean, but the uniqueness of the find casts doubt on its cultivation in the Quachilco vicinity. It may represent an import to the site designed only for limited consumption.

Chile Peppers. Considering the importance of the various kinds of chile pepper in the diet of present-day peoples of Mesoamerica, it is somewhat puzzling that its remains are not found more frequently at prehistoric sites. Today, the preparation of dried chiles frequently involves a brief toasting on the comal which often causes the dried fruit wall to crack open and the seeds to scatter into and near the cooking fire. Given similar preparation methods in prehistoric times, the seeds of the chile have a fairly good chance of being preserved by carbonization and recovered by flotation.

At Quachilco, five carbonized chile pepper seeds (Capsicum annuum) were recovered along with maize remains from a roughly circular pit located near the bottom of a thick midden deposit in Area G containing ash and large pieces of wood charcoal (Feature 23). An additional chile seed was found toward the bottom of the long sequence in Area K (Fig. 7.1), again accompanied by the remains of maize. The chile pepper seeds from Feature 23 had burned to such a degree that only the outer edge of each seedcoat was preserved, forming an open circle around the area where the thinner interior of the seedcoat had completely burned away.

Chile pepper cultivation in the Tehuacán Valley probably began as early as the Coxcatlán phase (C.E. Smith 1967:248), and the chile remains from Quachilco are here considered to be from cultivated rather than wild plants. The average diameter of the carbonized seeds was 3.15 mm, which, when potential shrinkage due to carbonization is taken into account, approaches the range of some of the smaller varieties of modern cultivated chiles. At Quachilco, irrigation would have been necessary to fulfill the relatively high water requirements of chile cultivation, which today involves rather complicated procedures of transplanting. Considering that chile remains were found at Quachilco in such small quantity, it is possible that the peppers were under cultivation elsewhere in the area and, like beans, were imported for limited consumption at Quachilco.

Physalis or Solanum. One additional seed will be mentioned in this section as possibly representing one more cultivated plant, Physalis sp., the "husk tomato" (tomate de cáscara). This small, green tomato-like fruit is grown, with irrigation, in the Quachilco area today. Unfortunately, the seeds of Physalis are very similar to those of some species of Solanum, and since only a single example was recovered, a positive identification to

Fig. 7.1. Partial chile pepper seed from Quachilco. Scale = 1 cm.

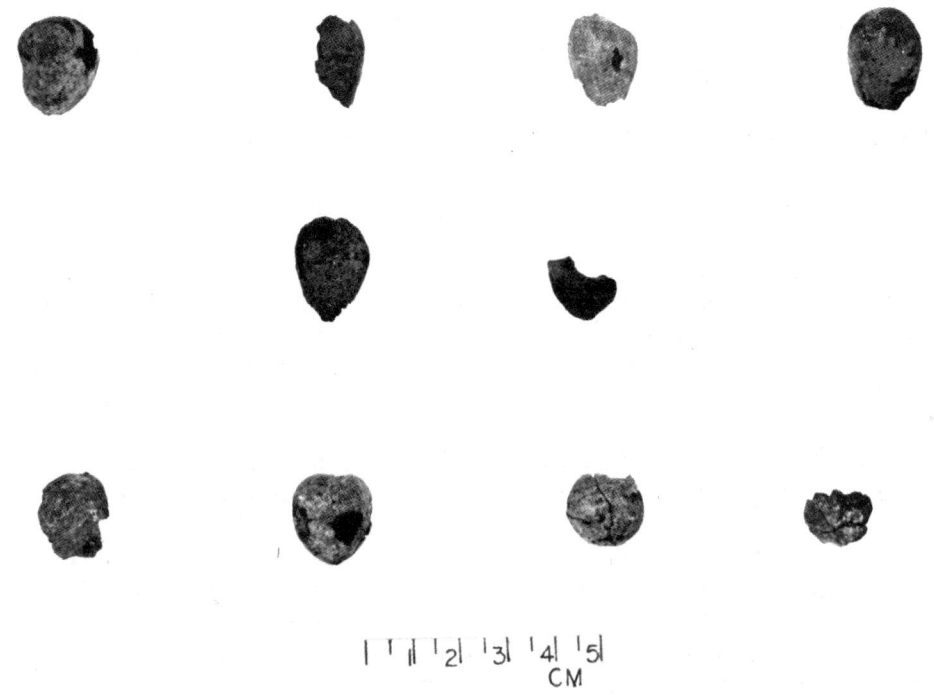

Fig. 7.2. Avocado seeds from Quachilco.

either genus cannot be made. The seed in all probability does represent a food plant as it was found in an ashy circular pit which also contained corn cobs, kernels, and cupules (Feature 11, Area G). If the seed is indeed that of Solanum rather than Physalis, it well may be that of Solanum nigrum, a plant bearing edible leaves and having medicinal applications.

Arboricultural Products

Avocado. Next to maize, avocados are the most common food plant found at Quachilco. Numerous pieces of carbonized avocado seeds, representing at least 56 individual fruits, were recovered (Fig. 7.2). These came from all of the Late Santa María/Early Palo Blanco areas that produced any other edible plant species and were most frequently from midden deposits.

Avocados are not native to the dry valley floor environment of Quachilco. Although the area is not a local center for avocado cultivation today, it could have been at the time of the occupation of the site. Altitude, seasonality of precipitation, and temperature are compatible with the requirements for the variety of avocado represented by the Quachilco specimens, Persea americana var. drymifolia. The relatively high rainfall needed is not present, but the necessary irrigation would have been completely possible.

7. BOTANICAL REMAINS: PRELIMINARY REPORT

From a study of the long temporal sequences at Coxcatlán Cave and other rock shelters, C.E. Smith (1966) has demonstrated that avocado seeds increased in size and changed in predominant shape through time in the Tehuacán Valley, presumably due to selection in cultivation. Although the Quachilco avocado seeds were of a variety of sizes and shapes, no systematic change through time could be discerned. This result was not unexpected since a tree crop such as the avocado requires a considerable period of time to display changes through selection. It is interesting, however, that, taken as a group, the Quachilco avocados were smaller than those from the Tehuacán caves from Santa María or Palo Blanco times.

Many of the avocado seeds from Quachilco were too fragmentary to permit meaningful measurement. The 12 seeds for which length could be measured ranged from 18 to 23 mm long; most of the unmeasurable fragments would have fallen within this range, although some were obviously from even smaller seeds. In 14 specimens for which width could be determined, the width ranged from 8.5 to 18.5 mm. A size index was computed by multiplying length by width for eight seeds (none of which was among the smallest); it ranged from 315 to 391.

Questions of size of prehistoric avocado seeds must take into account the degree of shrinkage resulting from carbonization (as at Quachilco) or dessication (as in the Tehuacán caves). About 20 avocado seeds collected by William Merrill in Oaxaca in 1974 were measured when fresh and again after carbonization in heated sand in the laboratory. The seeds showed an average of 25% shrinkage (cf. Ford 1976:266). Shrinkage in the dessication process has been calculated by C.E. Smith, who compared the sizes of the outer seed coats (for which shrinkage is minimal) with the cotyledons themselves in eight dessicated avocado seeds from the Valley of Oaxaca. He found that dessication resulted in 36% shrinkage (C.E. Smith 1969). Thus, for present purposes, the carbonized seeds from Quachilco and the dessicated seeds from the Tehuacán Valley caves may be treated as roughly comparable. Size comparisons are presented in Table 7.1.

At Quachilco, there were no avocado seeds that approached the largest from the cave deposits of the same time period, and the smallest Quachilco examples were smaller than any found in the caves. Whether by

TABLE 7.1

Persea americana SEED MEASUREMENTS

	Quachilco	Tehuacán Caves	
	Late Santa María/ Early Palo Blanco	Santa María phase	Palo Blanco phase
Mean length	20.5 mm	23 mm	21 mm
Mean width	15 mm	19 mm	18 mm
Size index (max.) (length x width)	391	780	1050

Source for Tehuacán cave data: C.E. Smith 1966.

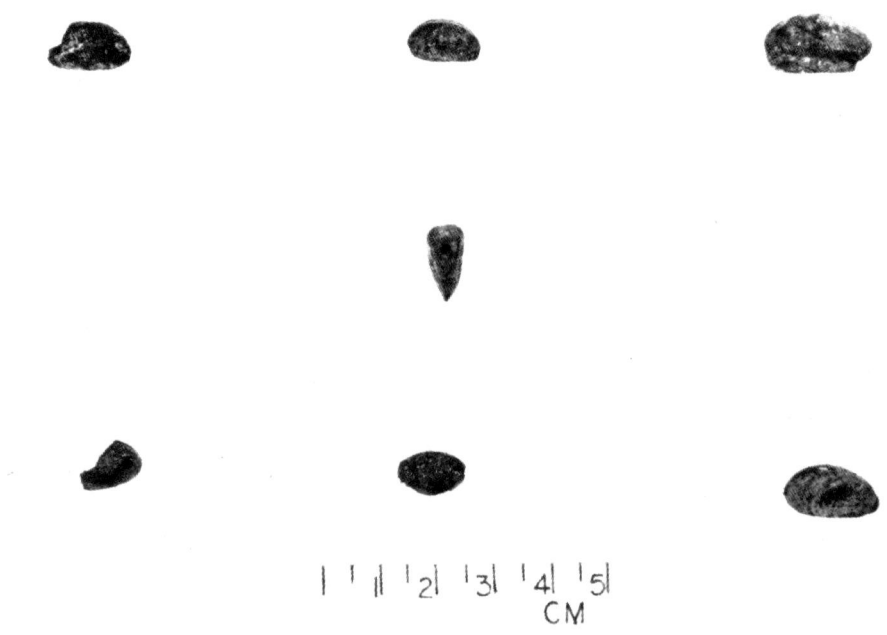

Fig. 7.3. Black zapote seeds from Quachilco. The seed in the center is shown in cross sectional view.

accident or design, inhabitants of Quachilco were not taking advantage of the selective procedures in avocado cultivation applied in other sections of the valley.

This conclusion is further supported by the shapes of the avocado seeds, which can be classified into two basic categories, spheroid and elongated (oblate or conical). C.E. Smith (1966:173) has discovered that, in the Tehuacán Valley cave sites, selection resulted in a dominance of elongated over spheroid seeds (the former possibly introduced from Oaxaca at an earlier time). At Quachilco, however, the two shapes appeared in approximately equal numbers. Seed shape could be determined for 24 cotyledon pieces: 11 were spherical and 13 were elongated.

The elongated seeds were the largest of the avocado seeds at Quachilco; eight out of ten measurable elongated seeds were at least 20 mm in length. The spherical seeds were more variable in size and seemed to fall into two categories. Three examples were very small, round seeds, only about 1 cm in diameter or slightly larger. The remaining measurable seeds, also spherical, were all 17 to 20 mm in diameter, intermediate in size between the large, elongated types and the very small, round types.

Black Zapote. Diospyros digyna is a large tree of the Ebenaceae

7. BOTANICAL REMAINS: PRELIMINARY REPORT

family that grows in Mexico in areas with abundant rainfall and elevations between sea level and about 1500 m. In the fall it produces an edible fruit, the black zapote, which is more or less spherical, about 8 cm in diameter, and dark green in color. Within the thin skin of the fruit is a dark brown pulp, very soft and mushy, with a somewhat sweet flavor. Each fruit contains several (1 to 10) seeds, each about 2 cm long. The black zapote is eaten raw; today in Mexico it is often preferred when mixed with orange juice and sugar.

Nineteen seeds or partial seeds of black zapote were found at Quachilco, 17 of which were in definite association with the Late Santa María/ Early Palo Blanco occupation at the site (Fig. 7.3). Since cooking is not involved in the consumption of these fruits, seeds would most likely have become carbonized in burned trash heaps. Indeed, about half of the seeds came from the thick, midden-like deposits of Areas B, F, and G. Additionally, two seeds were from clay floors in Areas J and N. One example was present in the large, Late Santa María phase, bell-shaped pit that had been excavated into sterile soil in Area D. The remainder of the seeds were from various deposits in Areas F, L, and N.

The Quachilco black zapote seeds ranged from 12 to 20 mm in length. The examples at the lower end of this size range are smaller than seeds of modern cultivated black zapotes. Slight shrinkage during carbonization may account for some of the difference, although some selection for larger fruits may have taken place since the Late and Terminal Formative.

The black zapote is not native to the Tehuacán Valley, but its seeds were present in valley caves by Coxcatlán times (C.E. Smith 1967:247). It could have been cultivated extensively at Quachilco, given sufficient water from irrigation. Or the black zapote may have been grown as it is today in the valley—in more limited quantities as a popular dooryard tree, watered and tended by individual households.

Coyol Palm. Fragments of nutshells (endocarps) of the coyol palm (Acrocomia mexicana) were found in small amounts at Quachilco. A full description of this species and potential uses of its fruits appears later in this chapter with the discussion of plant remains from La Coyotera, where coyol endocarps were found in great abundance.

At Quachilco, deposits containing rock rubble between the preserved foundations of the walls of several structures in Area L yielded the greatest amount of coyol (ten small pieces of carbonized endocarps of the fruit). Interestingly, this same context also produced the largest quantity of cactus fruit seeds found at the site (see below). A total of six more coyol endocarp fragments were found scattered in other excavations (Areas B, F, G, and K).

The coyol palm is not native to the Quachilco area and has not been planted there in recent times. In fact, in all of the Tehuacán Valley, only a few examples of this tree could be tracked down, all toward the southern end of the valley. At present, commercial cultivation of this fruit appears to be confined mainly to lower altitudes in Mexico; coyol sold in the Tehuacán city market is imported, primarily from Veracruz. In all likelihood, the relatively small quantities of coyol remains at Quachilco represent the importation of these fruits from areas to the south, possibly from the low altitude Cuicatlán Cañada, where the fruits were produced in quantity at at least one site of comparable time period (see below). The association of coyol with wild cactus fruits in Area L makes for an interesting combination if the coyol was indeed an import.

Other Fruits. A number of carbonized seeds and seed fragments from Quachilco remain unidentified at this writing. From the general size and shape, several of these appear to be fruit seeds of woody species.

One complete seed of unknown species was recovered from the thick, yellow clay floor of Area J, along with a complete seed of black zapote. The unknown seed was ovoid in outline and round in cross section, with four longitudinal grooves that gave the appearance of dividing the seed into four equal quadrants. The seed measured 1.6 cm in length. It may belong with the Sapotaceae or Palmae.

Four examples of another unknown seed strongly resembled the cotyledons of the peanut in size and shape, but were harder and denser than the oily peanut seed and had a tubular rather than squarish radical area. Seeds of this unidentified species ranged from 15.5 to 19 mm in length and 10 to 11 mm in width. One nearly complete specimen consisted of two cotyledons that separated fairly easily; the other three examples were single cotyledons, all from different seeds. In three instances, fragments of a thin smooth "shell" of a size and curvature similar to those of the unknown seeds were found in the same excavation units and perhaps were the bony seedcoats or fruitcases of these seeds.

Several fragments of apparent fruit seeds were found in Area F deposits that also contained identified fruit seeds. These fragments had durable, slightly roughened exteriors and porous interiors, and, judging from their curvatures, were from large, ovoid seeds. They resembled a type of seed found at La Coyotera which was tentatively assigned to the palm family (see below), but were too incomplete for definite placement in this family.

One excavation unit in Area F that contained nine fragments of this latter seed also produced two good-sized pieces of what was apparently a carbonized fruit. Although incomplete in length, its width was measured at 2.8 cm. It was spheroid to slightly ovoid in shape. The seed of this fruit was not present, although a hollow area on the interior of the fragments probably formerly contained a single seed. The fruit itself was very porous and fragile in its carbonized state and had undoubtedly undergone considerable change in size and shape in the carbonization process. No identification was made.

Another carbonized seed (from the Area G midden) resembled the seed of Mammea americana but measured 2.5 cm in length, only one-third the size of seeds of the mamey. The seed remained unidentified.

7. BOTANICAL REMAINS: PRELIMINARY REPORT

About ten other fragments appeared to be from seeds large enough to be from arboreal fruits (though not from avocado, black zapote, or coyol palm), but the fragments were too small for identification. A large majority of these fragments were from Areas F and G.

In summary, then, definite evidence exists for the use of fruit tree products at Quachilco. We know that these fruits include the avocado, black zapote, and coyol palm, but a number of other fruits, as yet unspecified, were also available in small amounts. The small quantities of unidentified fruit types may be further examples of exotic imports to Quachilco and not products that were locally cultivated.

Edible Weeds

"Weedy" plant species that grow spontaneously in cultivated fields and other disturbed areas can be significant sources of food and beneficial nutrition in the Mesoamerican diet (cf. Messer 1972). Good evidence exists for the use of these by-products of cultivation in Mexico in precolumbian times (for example, J.E. Smith, in press). At Quachilco, the genus Chenopodium, one such edible weed, was utilized: four carbonized seeds of Chenopodium were recovered. The consumption of edible weeds may be under-represented in the archeological record since many species are harvested for their leaves while immature, and preservation of any part of the plant would be very unlikely. On the other hand, some species, including Chenopodium, produce seeds that may be added to certain dishes or ground into flour. The Chenopodium seeds recovered at Quachilco indicate that the plant was harvested at maturity, either for the seeds or for the mature leaves, which could have been added to other foods as a spice, just as Chenopodium ambrosioides (epazote) is used today. The Chenopodium remains were found only in Area K, in ashy lenses that were interspersed in a stratigraphic series of clay floors. Despite the small number of seeds recovered, their accidental introduction to these lenses, which contained other edible species, is quite improbable.

One other disturbed habitat plant might have found similar use at Quachilco. This was a small-seeded, herbaceous legume, of which three seeds that have not been specifically identified were found. Two of the seeds came from an ash lens in the same series of Area K clay floors that produced the Chenopodium. The third example was likewise from an ash lens within a similar series of floors in Area N. Crotolaria pumila is a herbaceous legume (with seeds similar, but not identical, to the Quachilco specimens) whose leaves are, in Mexico, consumed even when harvested from mature plants (Messer 1972). The seeds found at Quachilco may have been from a similar genus that was considered edible by the inhabitants.

Edible Wild Plants

Good evidence was found at Quachilco for the utilization of two general categories of wild plant foods: cactus fruits, and the seeds and/or pods of tree legumes. Both would have been available locally, in areas of the valley floor that had not been cleared for cultivation or where succession on old fields was relatively advanced.

Cactus Fruits. Cactus fruits, eaten out of hand or made into a beverage, are pleasant tasting and have long been popular in Mexico. Various species of cacti with edible fruits undoubtedly grew on the dry soils of unirrigated land around, or even within, the site. For convenience's sake, certain types of cacti may have been planted from vegetative cuttings in dooryards and along fence-rows as they are today. But no direct evidence for this simple "cactus horticulture" is available.

Twenty seeds of cactus fruits were recovered by flotation at Quachilco. Six of these were from tunas, as the fruits of Opuntia spp. cacti are known. Two species of Opuntia were present. The remaining 14 seeds were of Cereus types of cactus fruits, usually called pitahayas (again, at least two different types were present). Of the 20 seeds, 13 were found in Area L, scattered in the layers of rock rubble amid the preserved foundations of several stone walls of structures. The remaining seeds were found in much smaller quantities in ash lenses of Areas F, J, K, and N, where they may have become carbonized by the burning of trash containing bits of the fruits.

Tree Legumes. Ten seeds of tree legumes and the end of one pod were recovered at Quachilco from a variety of Late Santa María/Early Palo Blanco contexts, including the Area L levels where the cactus fruit remains were found. In virtually every instance, these tree legume seeds were unearthed in deposits that also contained remains of plants that were definitely food products. Thus it seems most reasonable to assume that the seeds and/or pods of certain leguminous trees were items in the Quachilco diet.

Various kinds of tree legume pods, known as guajes, are consumed in the area at present. Most commonly appearing in the Tehuacán market are the guajes of Leucaena spp. While most of the Quachilco seeds were smaller than those of Leucaena, they must have belonged to this genus or one closely related (cf. Acacia, Mimosa, Pithecolobium). The pods would have been obtained easily from trees native to the valley floor. Such useful trees would have been left standing when they occurred near residences and would, most likely, not have been removed from fields when they were being cleared for cultivation.

Cuayucatepec

The Early Palo Blanco phase witnessed the abandonment of Quachilco and the establishment of at least six densely occupied hilltop centers in the Tehuacán Valley. Expanded excavations at Cuayucatepec, one such Classic center, are described by Drennan in Chapter 5.

The location of Cuayucatepec in the northern section of the geologically "stepped" Tehuacán Valley places it at a higher altitude than Quachilco; the cultivated land at the base of the hill atop which Cuayucatepec was built has an elevation of 1750 m. The proximity of the Cuayucatepec hill to the western fringes of the Sierra de Zongolica confers certain environmental benefits on the site. The piedmont (about a half-hour walk from the site) and the interior of the range (about a two-hour walk),

7. BOTANICAL REMAINS: PRELIMINARY REPORT

although both badly deforested today, could have provided a variety of plants unavailable on the valley floor, particularly arboreal species, in prehistoric times. Further, intermittent streams originating at higher elevations in the Zongolica flow through barrancas in the piedmont near the site.

Today the land surrounding Cuayucatepec is more extensively cultivated than that in the vicinity of Quachilco, although this is partly due to the irrigation waters provided to some areas around Cuayucatepec by the Valsequillo Reservoir near Puebla. Although rainfall is not quite as low as at Quachilco, it is still not plentiful: an average of 446 mm annually was recorded for the 14 years between 1961 and 1974 (Boletín Hidrométrico 1974). Nevertheless, in wet years successful crops can be produced on land watered by rainfall alone.

Sandwiched between the Zongolica piedmont and the Cuayucatepec hill is an inlet of surprisingly level, fertile land, an estimated 800 ha in extent, known locally today as the tecajete. Located directly below the site, the tecajete was probably one of the primary agricultural zones supplying the population of prehistoric Cuayucatepec. In modern times, waters from springs in the piedmont and intermittent streams flowing down barrancas to this area have been diverted to portions of the tecajete by small dams and canals; the same procedures could have been followed easily during the Classic.

Carbon recovered in the screen and soil samples for water separation were collected from the tests and expanded excavations at Cuayucatepec described in Chapter 5. Most prolific in terms of the carbonized remains of food plants were the two expanded excavations in Sector I (Areas A and B). Areas C and G also yielded a number of economically important species. Expanded Areas D, E, F, and H provided very little carbon (including wood charcoal).

A description and discussion of the Cuayucatepec plant remains, again excepting wood charcoal, follows. Species have been organized into the same production/procurement categories that were used in the previous section.

Cultivated Plants

Maize. The carbonized remains of maize were recovered in considerable amounts at Cuayucatepec, the great majority from the two excavations located in Sector I (Areas A and B). The midden deposit outside of and underneath the rectangular structure in Area A produced the greatest number of preserved kernels; 175 kernels were distributed throughout this deposit, along with 11 measurable and 16 unmeasurable cob pieces. The layers of rubble fill within the rectangular structure itself also yielded small numbers of kernels and cob fragments. In Area B, maize was found in a number of features. Three apparent hearths (Features 46, 58, and 61) contained carbonized cob fragments and kernels in varying quantities. Three more or less bell-shaped pits (Features 56, 57, and 62) yielded good quantities of both cobs and kernels. A few cob fragments were also associated with a plaster floor (Feature 53). Maize remains were scattered throughout the remaining deposits in Area B, with two major concentrations (one containing 16 measurable cobs, over 50 cob fragments, and 2 kernels and the other containing 19 measurable cobs and 40 fragments). Much smaller quantities of maize remains, mostly cupules and small cob fragments, were found in Areas C, E, and G. One kernel turned up in a ceramic vessel in Feature 75 in Area D.

The maize from Cuayucatepec will be analyzed in detail at a later date. However, a few general observations can be offered here.

For the most part, cobs and kernels were larger than those from Quachilco. Only a few examples of the very small cob variety predominant at Quachilco were present at Cuayucatepec. The average maximum diameter of the 59 measurable cobs from Cuayucatepec was 10.13 mm. Only five 10-rowed cobs, so common at Quachilco, were found at Cuayucatepec. Instead, 14- and 16-rowed cobs predominated in approximately equal numbers. Some 12-, 18-, and 20-rowed cobs were also present. Twelve Cuayucatepec cobs had weak pairing and/or irregular rows. One of these, plus two others, had prominent glumes. On three cobs, cupules were widely spaced or vertically elongated. The remaining 44 measurable cobs (75%) displayed regular rows, average pairing, and no primitive features.

A total of 244 kernels was recovered. Of those complete enough to reveal shape, 42 were globular and 39 were "kernel-shaped" (that is, front and back flattened). The 59 kernels that could be measured for height ranged from 2.5 to 9.4 mm high, with a mean of 5.3 mm. The 187 kernels that had completely preserved widths averaged 5.4 mm wide, with a range of 2.6 to 8.0 mm. Average thickness on 128 kernels was 4.47 mm, ranging from 2.4 to 6.5 mm. These average measurements were larger than those of the Quachilco kernels for all dimensions.

Beans. Cuayucatepec was the only site in the current investigation that yielded the remains of Phaseolus in significant quantity. Interestingly, the area around Cuayucatepec is now an important center of bean cultivation; both bush beans and vining types of P. vulgaris are grown on irrigated and unirrigated lands.

At the archeological site, 80 discrete pieces of Phaseolus, representing approximately 56 beans, were found in all. Of these 56, 49 were sufficiently intact to permit measurement on at least one dimension (that is, length or width). In 32 cases, shape could also be ascertained. Almost all (90%) of the Cuayucatepec beans came from the thick midden located outside of the rectangular structure in Area A. The remaining examples were all from Area B, including two found in a large bell-shaped pit (Feature 62).

Considerable variability in size and shape of the beans was evident (Fig. 7.4). Delineation of varieties and even determination of species was difficult, however, because carbonization had destroyed the hilum, seed coat, and of course color of every specimen. An attempt was made, nonetheless, to define separate varieties on the basis of size and shape.

5. BOTANICAL REMAINS: PRELIMINARY REPORT 231

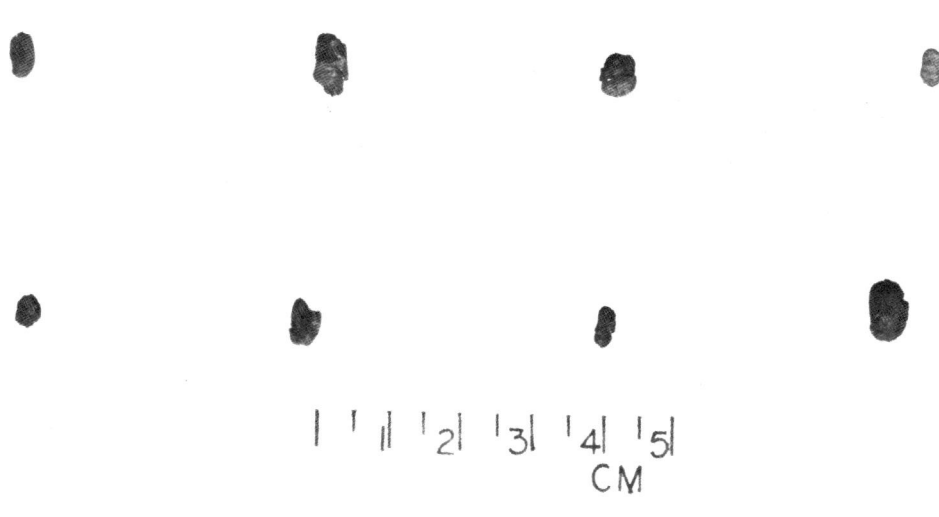

Fig. 7.4. Beans from Cuayucatepec

Five varieties were thus delineated, each of which was represented by at least three examples. A few beans which were all single examples of a particular size/shape combination were not assigned to any of the five varieties; these represented either other varieties that were not common quantitatively, or rare extensions of the range of variation of one of the five designated types.

All of the beans were either P. vulgaris or P. acutifolius. The lack of preserved hila and the small size of some P. vulgaris types from this time period made the separation of the two species difficult; but in some cases a tentative species identification could be made, again on the basis of size and shape.

Table 7.2 presents a list of the cotyledons found in each of the five varieties. Most common was Variety 1, small oval beans judged to be P. acutifolius. Specimens of Variety 2 were on the average only slightly larger (their size range overlapped with that of Variety 1), but were identified as small examples of P. vulgaris on the basis of their mildly reniform shape. Larger than either of the above (size ranges not overlapping) and the largest type at the site were the Variety 3 beans, P. vulgaris, which displayed a straight hilum edge and a convexly curved outer edge. Variety 4 specimens were rectangular in outline, larger than Varieties 1 and 2 but smaller than all but one of the Variety 3 examples. It was not clear whether Variety 4 beans were P. acutifolius or P. vulgaris. Unlike the first four varieties, in Variety 5 the length of the bean was always more than twice its width, resulting in a long, narrow outline. Variety 5 beans had straight, parallel sides and rounded ends. They showed

TABLE 7.2

TENTATIVE VARIETIES OF Phaseolus AT CUAYUCATEPEC

Variety	Shape of outline	Mean length (mm)	Mean width (mm)	Mean thickness of 1 cotyledon (mm)	Individual beans		
					length	width	thickns.
1	oval	6.5	4.5	2.3	6.4+ 7.0 6.9 5.5+ 5.5+ 5.2 7.5 6.5 6.8+ 6.2	3.5 5.0 5.0 5.0 4.8 3.9 4.3 4.5 4.8 4.5	1.4 3.0 2.3 2.7 2.6 2.2 2.6 2.5 2.1 2.1
2	mildly reniform	7.0	4.3	2.3	6.0+ 7.5 6.0+ 5.5 6.8 8.0	5.0 3.7 4.0 3.5 4.9 5.0	2.5 1.9 2.0 2.8 2.4 4.4
3	hilum edge straight; outer edge convex	9.7	5.6	2.75	8.1 9.7 8.9 12.0	5.0 5.5 6.0 6.0	2.5 2.2 3.3 3.0
4	rectangular	8.65	5.2	2.7	8.5 inc. 8.8	4.9 inc. 5.5	2.8 2.0 2.6
5	long and narrow	7.4	3.4	2.0	4.7 9.0 8.0 6.0 8.0+ 9.2	2.2 4.0 3.6 3.0 3.8 4.0	1.1 2.9 1.9 1.7 2.2 2.0

Means are based on the number of complete measurements available and thus exclude incomplete ("inc.") specimens and measurements with a "+" sign, indicating a broken specimen whose dimension was greater than the measurement given.

7. BOTANICAL REMAINS: PRELIMINARY REPORT   233

the greatest variation in size; most of the examples were longer than the beans in Varieties 1 and 2, but their widths were narrower on the whole. Variety 5 probably belonged with P. vulgaris; long narrow examples of the common bean are grown in Mexico today, although they are now much larger.

The assemblage of beans from Cuayucatepec provided an interesting contrast to the specimens found in the dry rock shelters by MacNeish's Tehuacán Archaeological-Botanical Project. Although a number of different varieties of beans were present in the Coxcatlán and El Riego caves, most did not appear until late in the Palo Blanco phase or until the Postclassic (Kaplan 1967:204). Only four specimens of P. vulgaris, all of a single variety, were found in all deposits older than the Late Palo Blanco Zone D of the East Niche of El Riego Cave. These four beans were most like Cuayucatepec Variety 1 but were larger. Cuayucatepec Variety 1 actually most closely resembled another variety from the caves (Variety 13) that only appeared in the Postclassic (Kaplan 1967:204 and 207). Examples of the largest type of bean at Cuayucatepec (Variety 3) were nevertheless smaller than the most similar type from the caves, partly due to carbonization of the former, but also probably because the cave beans were more recent. In summary, then, both quantity and range of variation of P. vulgaris were considerably greater at Cuayucatepec than in contemporaneous (Early Palo Blanco) levels at the rock shelters. Interestingly, the most common type of bean for the Early Palo Blanco phase in the caves was a rhomboidally shaped P. acutifolius (Kaplan 1967:204 and 207) that was not present at Cuayucatepec at all.

It is reasonable to assume that beans were cultivated locally at Cuayucatepec in Early Palo Blanco times as they are today. The quantity and variety of Phaseolus present in the archeological remains indicate that beans were probably a crop of considerable importance at this site.

Chile Peppers. The only evidence for the presence of chile peppers at Cuayucatepec was the recovery (by water separation) of a single carbonized seed, probably Capsicum annuum, from Area G. One corn cupule was the only other example of an edible plant from this context, associated with some scattered human bones. It seems most likely that the chile seed and single cupule were simply in the same fill with the bones and were not food items interred with the dead.

The Capsicum seed measured 2.8 mm in diameter and must have come from a small variety of chile. It is not altogether certain where in the Tehuacán Valley chile cultivation was practiced, nor can it be definitely ascertained that the single small seed from Cuayucatepec was indeed from a cultivated plant.

Arboricultural Products

Preserved remains of avocados were virtually absent at Cuayucatepec. One seed of uncertain identification may be that of a small avocado (length: 14.5 mm; width: 11.2 mm). Its exterior surface and easily separated double cotyledons resembled features of avocado seeds, but the embryo attachment area lacked any trace of the plumule usually preserved in carbonized avocado seeds. But regardless of the identification of this single specimen, it is clear that the inhabitants of Cuayucatepec were consuming few, if any, avocados.

Avocado seeds are one of the most common ethnobotanical finds at Mesoamerican sites where plants have been preserved by carbonization. Their size and density encourages carbonization rather than disintegration to ash, especially in the reduction atmosphere of burned trash heaps. Since there was no lack of other food plant remains in the extensive excavations that included several middens, the absence of avocado seeds should not be attributed to accidents of preservation or vagaries of excavation sampling.

Certain climatic variables may have inhibited the successful cultivation of avocados at Cuayucatepec. While the area meets basic requirements of altitude and soils, and while irrigation water would have been available, the temperature was probably too low. The native Mexican variety (Persea americana var. drymifolia), the avocado most resistant to cold, requires a median winter temperature no lower than 15° C, and irreversible damage can occur if temperatures drop below -6.7° C (Solares 1976:36). In 1974 (to take one example for which data is handy), the mean temperature recorded at a station near the base of the Cuayucatepec hill from October through March was only 10.7° C; temperatures below -6.7° C occurred during five months of that year, the lowest being -13° C (Boletín Hidrométrico 1974). If such temperatures occurred even once every few years prehistorically, the Cuayucatepec area would have been too cold for avocado cultivation.

The avocado is an excellent source of vegetal fat and vitamins—particularly the B group and also vitamins A and E (Hodgson 1950:287). Present day Mexicans as well as a number of prehistoric groups for which we have evidence (cf. Ford 1976 and J.E. Smith, in press) regularly include avocados in their diet. It is thus of note that the Classic period inhabitants, who could not grow avocados locally, were apparently not importing them either. Good avocado producing zones in areas of lower altitudes and higher temperatures were, due to the topography of the valley, not far away from the site. Avocados picked before they are fully ripe are not particularly perishable. To date, however, the avocado has provided no evidence of subsistence goods exchange in the Tehuacán Valley.

The situation is the same concerning other fruit trees. Not a single fragment of black zapote or coyol palm fruit was found. In fact, other than the possible avocado seed discussed above, all excavations at Cuayucatepec produced only one fragment of an unidentified seed that could possibly have been from an arboreal fruit. It is evident that the arboriculture that took place at Quachilco and, as will be seen, at La Coyotera was not practiced at Cuayucatepec, nor were products of arboriculture in other areas of the valley imported to Cuayucatepec.

Edible Weeds

Different groups of people may regard different species of weedy plants growing in fields and other areas of disturbed soils as edible. As mentioned previously, one genus considered edible in Mesoamerica is

7. BOTANICAL REMAINS: PRELIMINARY REPORT 235

Chenopodium. Two seeds of Chenopodium were recovered at Cuayucatepec, one in the Area A midden, the other accompanied by maize and other seeds in Feature 56, a slightly bell-shaped pit in Area B. Additionally, another genus of the Chenopodiaceae family, Atriplex, was present in the form of two carbonized seeds from Area B contexts that also included maize. The seeds and leaves of some species of Atriplex are considered edible in parts of North America and may have been a food source at Cuayucatepec.

A small-seeded herbaceous legume was represented by five carbonized seeds, one from Feature 56, one from another partially belled pit in Area B (Feature 62), one from the Area A midden, and two from Area G. In each case maize and other food plants were recovered from the same flotation sample. Not yet specifically identified, these seeds were not from the same leguminous herb present at Quachilco, although, like that herb, this plant may have been easily collected from disturbed soils and utilized for food.

Finally, one seed of another field weed not usually considered edible, Argemone mexicana, was present, and, interestingly enough, this poppy seed came from a hearth (Area B, Feature 58). While the single seed could have been introduced unintentionally, it is also possible that the plant was purposely brought to the site because it was viewed as useful for food, medicine, or ornament.

Edible Wild Plants

The remains of wild plant species with potentially edible parts were not particularly numerous at Cuayucatepec, but a few scattered seeds did indicate that some local wild products had been used in a limited way.

Seeds of cactus fruits were less common than at Quachilco. Seeds of organ cactus fruits (pitahayas) were completely absent at Cuayucatepec, presenting the possibility that the land around the site had been cleared and cultivated to such an extent that fruits of the columnar cacti were not readily available. Three recovered seeds of Opuntia indicated, however, that tunas had formed a minor part of the diet; a few Opuntia cacti may have been left growing in otherwise cleared territory, or their growth may have been encouraged only in dooryards. The three tuna seeds were from the botanically productive Area A midden, the slightly belled pit in Area B (Feature 56), and Area G.

Only two guaje seeds were found, both in the Area A midden. As the use of guajes was apparently limited, it is probable that the trees were not located nearby. Again, they might have been removed when lands were cleared for cultivation, although today the sight of a useful tree, such as a leguminous one, left standing alone in the middle of a cleared field is not uncommon.

A single partial seed from Area C has been tentatively identified as Prunus capuli, the small Mexican cherry. The small quantity indicates that this plant was probably not especially available and found infrequent use in the diet at Cuayucatepec.

Miscellaneous Seeds

Five ovoid to globular seeds from Areas A and B have been assigned to the family Euphorbiaceae. A number of genera of this family currently grow in the Tehuacán Valley, and until more specific identifications are made, the potential economic significance of these seeds cannot be determined.

A single carbonized Cyperaceae seed (cf. Eleocharis) was recovered by flotation from the Area A midden. This sedge must have been growing in the wet soils immediately adjacent to a spring or stream originating in the Sierra de Zongolica. The presence of this seed, the only example found of a truly wetland species, indicates that a permanent water source was available during the period of occupation of the site. It is not known whether the sedges, which must have been present only in very limited quantities, were utilized in any way.

An Area B hearth (Feature 58) yielded one seed of Geranium sp. It is likely that ornamentals were planted in different localities within the site, and the geranium may be one example of such plantings.

Solanaceae. A number of seeds of an unknown genus of the economically important family Solanaceae (nightshade family) were recovered by flotation. The distinctive coiled embryo was very apparent in these seeds, which were round in outline and measured 1.3 to 1.5 mm in diameter in the carbonized state. They were lens-shaped rather than flat in cross section, with a smooth rather than reticulate surface; these features ruled out identification to Physalis, Lycopersicon, and some species of Solanum.

The quantity of these seeds and the contexts in which they were found indicated that they were from a useful species that was not introduced to the site accidentally. Twenty-five seeds came from two 4 l flotation samples taken from the test pit which later became Area G. In Area B, one seed was found in a hearth (Feature 58), one in a slightly belled pit (Feature 56), and one in a midden deposit. The seeds of Solanaceae were accompanied by remains of maize in all of these contexts.

Hopefully, a generic or specific identification of these seeds will eventually be made. Until that time, they cannot be assigned to any of the above production/procurement categories since the Solanaceae family includes cultivated, weedy, and wild members.

La Coyotera

La Coyotera is located toward the southern end of the Cuicatlán Cañada, a long narrow canyon immediately southeast of the Tehuacán Valley. Despite the close geographical connections between the two regions, they differ environmentally because of the much lower altitude of the Cuicatlán Cañada. La Coyotera, at approximately 750 m above sea level, is, for example, about 500 m lower than Quachilco and almost 1000 m below Cuayucatepec. In essence, the alluvial floor of the Cuicatlán Cañada is an

7. BOTANICAL REMAINS: PRELIMINARY REPORT

isolated strip of hot lowlands carved into the mountains that surround it on all sides. Although precipitation in the Cañada may be slightly greater than that of the Tehuacán Valley, it by no means reaches levels found in the humid lowland regions of Mexico. Distinct winter dry seasons and summer wet seasons occur. The average annual rainfall at La Coyotera between 1956 and 1974 was only 453 mm (Boletín Hidrométrico 1974), and with the high regional rate of evapo-transpiration, useful precipitation was significantly less.

The natural vegetation on the floor of the Cañada has been altered greatly by centuries of agricultural activities. Today the alluvial lands are devoted to the large-scale cultivation of tropical fruits (many not native to Mexico or even the Western Hemisphere) which flourish with irrigation in the Cañada's frost-free climate.

The 1978 excavations at La Coyotera are described in preliminary form in Chapter 6. Carbonized plant materials were recovered through usual dry screening procedures, and flotation smaples were collected, both for later processing and analysis by this author.

A fair amount of plant remains was recovered from the extensive excavations in the Perdido phase occupation (Areas A/B and C). This community, which was roughly contemporaneous with the Late Santa María phase in the Tehuacán Valley sequence, consisted of a series of large, compact, residential compounds located on the canyon floor. Plant remains were primarily recovered from middens and house fill. The Lomas phase occupation (Early Palo Blanco) was located atop a piedmont spur with individual households situated on residential terraces. Excavations here happily included a thick midden deposit on one such residential terrace (Area F). This midden, extremely rich in carbonized plant material, was a primary deposit that dated securely to the Lomas phase. Excavations of the succeeding Classic period occupation at La Coyotera (Trujano phase) were not concentrated in residential areas, and thus few plant remains dating to this time were recovered.

Cultivated Plants

Maize. The most interesting aspect of the maize from La Coyotera was its scarcity. The Lomas phase midden in Area F yielded 43 cupules, two kernels, and one measurable cob. Two more small cob fragments came from secondary fill just above this midden. If remains of maize were scarce at the site as a whole, more remarkable is the fact that a single cupule from a small stone-lined hearth was the only evidence for the presence of maize in all of the Perdido phase community.

The explanation for this paucity of maize at La Coyotera, particularly at the Perdido phase settlement, is at present a matter of conjecture. It is possible that the small amount of preserved maize actually represents little use of maize at the site. But in view of all that is known of Middle and Late Formative subsistence in Mesoamerica, this proposition is untenable. It is more likely that the explanation involves the processes through which the archeological deposits were formed. For example, it is possible that there was some special refuse disposal method for maize which either did not lead to its carbonization or removed it some distance from the main residential areas which were the targets of excavation. Perhaps cultural beliefs dictated that maize cobs never be used for fuel in hearths. Perhaps Perdido phase middens excavated in association with the residential compounds were but a small percentage of the garbage heaps in use at the site, many of which could have been located farther from the living areas and for some reason may have been preferred for maize disposal.

The small sample of Lomas phase remains from Area F indicated a small-cob variety of maize similar to that common at Quachilco. The cob fragment was 12-rowed and 6.9 mm in diameter, with no primitive or irregular features. The 23 measurable loose cupules averaged 3.33 mm in width. The only measurable kernel was 3.8 mm wide and globular. Additionally, a larger cob variety, represented by one 12-rowed cob fragment with a diameter of 10.3 mm, was present in the secondary fill above the Lomas phase midden and probably belonged to a later time period.

Remains of other cultivars (with the exception of arboricultural products) were totally absent. Not a single chile pepper seed or fragment of bean cotyledon appeared. This absence is less surprising than the scarcity of maize, but it is still puzzling, even though these cultivars produce no bulky disposable parts such as the corn cob or the large fruit seed; garbage disposal methods may again be responsible.

Equally conspicuous by their absence were the field weeds, such as Chenopodium and the herbaceous legumes. Not a single example of any of the small seeds of the common, disturbed habitat plants was found.

Perhaps the scarcity at La Coyotera of non-arboreal cultivated products and the edible weeds usually accompanying them in the fields is a reflection of a different kind of production/utilization system that resulted in different patterns of archeological deposition and preservation.

Arboricultural Products

Coyol Palm. Of all the edible plants found at La Coyotera, most abundant were the remains of coyol palm, Acrocomia mexicana (Fig. 7.5). Fifty-one excavation units contained carbonized endocarps of the coyol seed in varying amounts.

Acrocomia mexicana is a medium sized to large palm, densely armed with dark spines. In the winter and early spring, each tree produces one to several large clusters of fruits (the number of fruits per cluster can reach a hundred or more). Each spherical fruit, or coyol, measures about 3 to 4 cm in diameter and consists of a thin, hard, outer husk surrounding a fibrous, mucilaginous, white pulp. Within the latter is a single spherical seed, or nut, which is composed of a very hard shell (endocarp), 2.5 to 3 mm thick, pierced by three more or less equatorial germ pores, enclosing an oily white kernel, about 1.5 cm in diameter, that resembles coconut meat in texture and flavor. In the archeological record at La Coyotera,

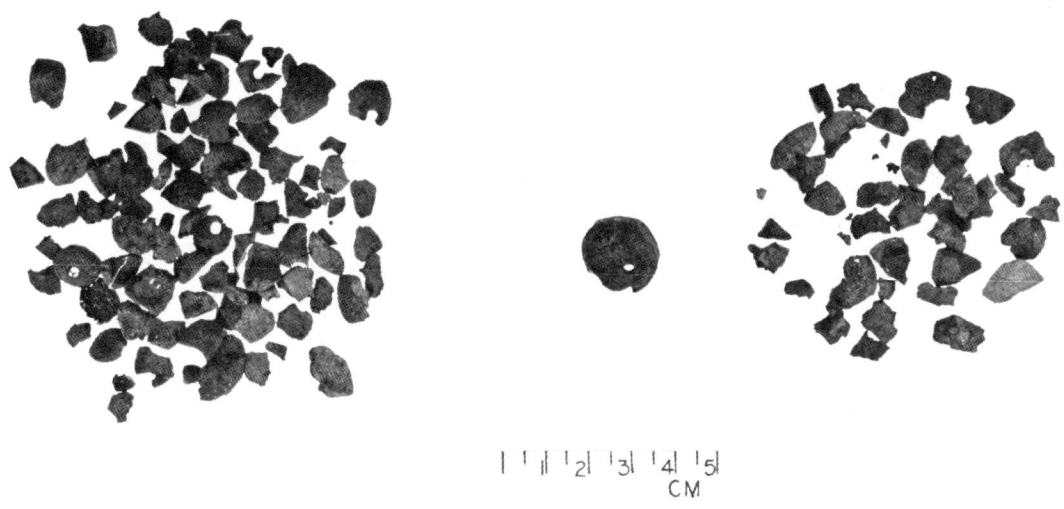

Fig. 7.5. Coyol palm endocarps from Lomas phase midden at La Coyotera. The seed in the center has been reconstructed.

coyol fruits were represented exclusively by pieces of broken-up nutshells (endocarps), a number of which included one or more germ pores.

Today in Mexico, both the fruit pulp and the kernel of the seed are consumed raw. The manner of eating a coyol is as follows: the thin, brittle husk is removed by hand rather easily (particularly if the fruit has become somewhat dried out), and the entire fruit is sucked for its mucilaginous, sweet juice. The remaining seed, to which much of the fibrous portion of the pulp always tenaciously adheres, is sometimes discarded but often is cracked open (with some difficulty), and the small kernel is then eaten. The inhabitants of La Coyotera may have been making use of the coyol fruits in this way. None of the carbonized endocarps, however, had any trace whatever of pulp fibers remaining, and these are almost impossible to remove. My experiments show that, if present, these fibers still adhere to the seed, even after the endocarp is carbonized. But when the fruits are left undisturbed on the ground, the outer rind and pulp disintegrate through the action of the elements and attacks by insects, leaving a clean nut ready for germination. In Paraguay, where another species of Acrocomia is common, native peoples frequently collect the clean nuts from the ground and crack them open to consume the kernels or dry and store them for long periods during which little or no deterioration occurs (Markley 1956:25). At La Coyotera, the clean carbonized nutshells indicated similar collection procedures, and the fibrous pulp was probably seldom, if ever, utilized.

It was obvious from the fragmentary condition of the archeological endocarps (not a single nut was found intact) that the kernels within the seeds had been extracted, probably by breaking the nutshell with a stone. It is possible that the small kernels were valued as a food source: kernels of the similar fruits of Acrocomia totai have a protein content of 12.6% (Markley 1956:21). However, although no direct evidence can be cited, it ceems equally likely that the kernels were used in the production of oil. The glyceride oil content of the kernels is very high, at least 40% (Martinez 1959:447). Kernels of a number of other species of Acrocomia are used in their native regions in the production of oil used in lamps or in cooking. The use of coyol for oil is one possible explanation for the numbers of its nutshells at La Coyotera, especially since the very small kernels, each difficult to extract from its shell, would have been time-consuming dietary alternatives to maize and the fruits other than coyol present at the site. Furthermore, other plant species with a high content of readily extractable oil are rare in pre-contact Mesoamerica.

To extract the oil from the coyol kernels, a technique may have been followed that is used in much of Central and South America where oilpalms, including Acrocomia, are found. The kernels are first roasted, then ground, and the ground meal is boiled with water to release the oil which floats to the surface (Markley 1956:25). The glyceride oil would have made a good fuel for burning in lamps. It could also have been used in cooking, although in its unrefined state it would not have stored well since, after a time, chemical changes result in the conversion of neutral oils to free fatty acids which produce unpleasant flavors and odors (cf. Markley 1956).

Other potential uses of the coyol palm should be mentioned. The sap obtained from a cavity excavated into the top of the trunk (or in several places along the trunk of a felled tree) is, in various regions of Mexico, fermented into an alcoholic beverage known as taberna (Martinez 1959:447 and Corner 1966:125). From this practice arose the English name for coyol: the Mexican wine palm. The production of an alcoholic beverage from coyol would be difficult to document archeologically. The leaves of coyol were probably used as are those of other palms—in the construction of shelters and the manufacture of mats, baskets, brooms, ornaments, and many other objects.

A total of 92.7g of the carbonized endocarp pieces of this widely useful fruit were recovered in the La Coyotera excavations. Endocarps of modern specimens were carbonized in the laboratory, and the average weight of endocarp pieces from one entire coyol seed was found to be 2.2 g. Thus the remains from La Coyotera came from a minimum of 42 fruits; the actual total was probably considerably larger, since pieces came from many excavation units and very seldom could fragments, even from the same units, be pieced together.

Less than one-tenth of the coyol was from Perdido phase contexts; about 5% of the total weight was found in Area A/B, including scattered pieces from the fill of seven different houses and small quantities from each of the large middens. Another 3.6% was from a large midden in Area C. The remaining nutshells (90%) were from the thick Lomas phase midden in Area F. These figures provide a good indication that coyol was much more common in the Lomas phase, although the relative quantities may be somewhat exaggerated since the Area F midden was the only one excavated for this phase and may, for some reason, have contained an above-average amount of the fruit.

The coyol palm was probably not part of the native vegetation of the Cuicatlán Cañada. Martínez (1959:446) listed A. mexicana as most common along the Pacific coast of Mexico, and Standley (1920:83) located the species in Yucatán as well as along the Pacific coast south of Sinaloa. The hot climate and relatively low elevation of the Cuicatlán Cañada would have provided an ideal situation for the coyol, but the broad mountain range between the Cañada and the coastal homeland of the tree makes man the only likely agency for its importation. But once introduced, the coyol probably flourished in the environment of the Cañada, along watercourses and with the aid of irrigation (for which there is direct evidence in the Lomas phase). Large numbers of trees could have been grown on the alluvium with minimal effort. Wild trees of Acrocomia totai reach densities of 150 trees per ha on formerly cultivated lands in Paraguay (Markley 1956:12). The extensive root system of the tree, however, extends far from its base for soil nutrients and water (Markley 1956:27); coyol growing areas must have been entirely separate from fields of other cultivated crops. Nevertheless, simply watering the trees without intervening in their reproduction would have resulted in good yields. Thus, La Coyotera (and other sections of the Cuicatlán Cañada as well) had the potential to become a center of coyol production for the surrounding high-altitude region.

Black Zapote. Black zapote (Diospyros digyna), the soft, dark-pulped, several-seeded fruit that was present at Quachilco, was well represented at La Coyotera, exceeded in quantity only by coyol among all edible plant species. Ninety-five seed fragments were found for a total of about 48 individual seeds. Most (32 seeds) were from the Lomas phase. A number of seeds were from the Perdido phase community (seven from the Area C midden and seven from Area A/B). A small quantity (two seeds) of black zapote was recovered from Classic period deposits (Trujano phase), indicating its continued use at this time.

Black zapote is a tree native to areas with year-round precipitation. It would not have succeeded in the Cañada's regimen of alternating dry and wet seasons without supplementary water during the dry season at the very least. It is thus safe to conclude that the seeds from La Coyotera are from cultivated fruits. The few measurable seeds ranged from 15 to 17 mm in length, making them about the same size as carbonized seeds taken from modern cultivated fruits. Considering the quantity of black zapote remains at La Coyotera, particularly in the Lomas phase, cultivation was probably conducted by residents of the site on alluvial lands nearby with irrigation water provided by the Río Grande. It is impossible to say whether the trees were planted in orchards, along field borders, or simply scattered about. It is unlikely, however, that they were dooryard trees, a possibility considered for Quachilco. The compact arrangement of the Perdido phase residential compounds would have left little space for these large trees, and Lomas phase residential terraces

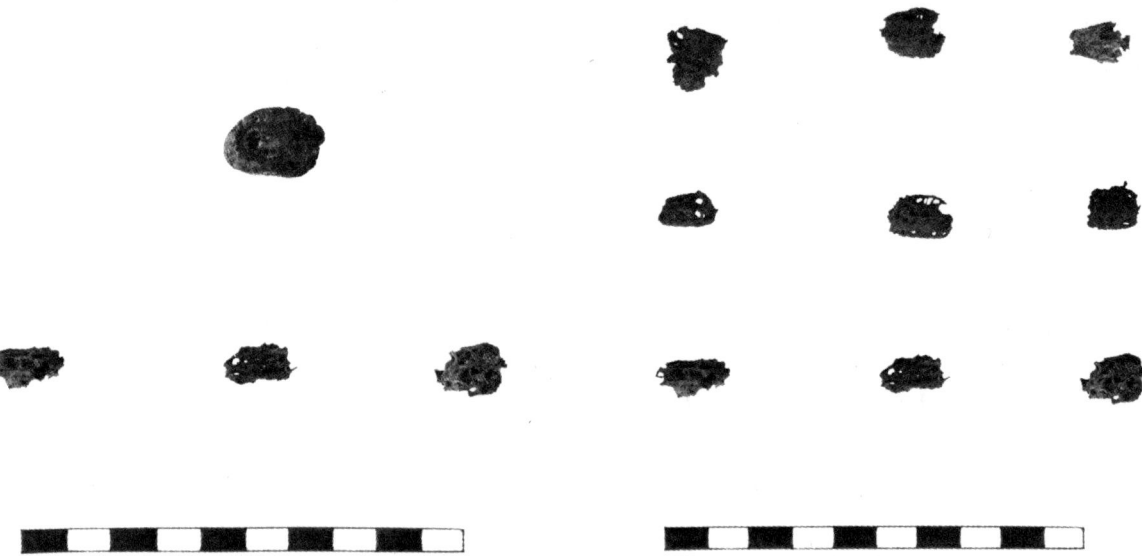

Fig. 7.6. Ciruela from Lomas phase midden at La Coyotera. The upper specimen in the left hand group is a carbonized fruit; the others are carbonized seeds. Scale = 10 cm.

were too far removed from water supplies.

It is certain that the black zapote was introduced to the area of La Coyotera by the Perdido phase and that it was a major product of native arboriculture during the Lomas phase. Its use at the site continued into the Trujano phase as well.

Ciruela. La Coyotera was the only site in the current study at which ciruela, or "hog plum" (Spondias mombin), occurred (Fig. 7.6). One of the more interesting finds at the site was a carbonized ciruela fruit with the seed still in place within it. Additionally, 19 of the distinctive seeds were found. All of the ciruela remains were from Area F. The fruit and 16 seeds were from the thick Lomas phase midden that contained so many plant remains. Two more seeds were from the mixed layer just above this midden. A single seed was from an upper deposit in the same area that dated to the Classic.

The ciruela is another tree that requires rainfall more evenly distributed throughout the year than the pattern of dry and wet seasons that occurs in the Cuicatlán Cañada. Thus, it was not native to the area and was probably introduced as a cultigen requiring irrigation. The low altitude of La Coyotera undoubtedly provided an ideal environment for the cultivation of these fruits, which are susceptible to frost and would not have done as well at the surrounding higher elevations.

Further proof of the introduction of ciruela arboriculture at La Coyotera comes from the complete absence of ciruela seed fragments in the Perdido phase community, where the fruits certainly would have been used had they been available locally. During the Lomas phase, then, the cultivation of ciruela would have been easily incorporated into an economy that already included techniques for growing several other arboreal fruits. The single seed from the Trujano phase attests to the continued cultivation of Spondias during the Classic occupation of the site.

Avocado. The remains of avocado were not very plentiful at La Coyotera. Twenty-four seed fragments were found in four excavation units in the Area F midden deposit, but these were judged to be from a total of no more than eight or nine individual seeds. Four seeds were elongated in shape and averaged 20 mm in length and 14 mm in width. Of two spheroid examples, one was small (15 by 16 mm), the other fairly large (22 by 22 mm). One additional avocado seed came from a somewhat disturbed section in Area A/B. This example was elongated and measured 17.5 by 12 mm. Most of the above avocado remains, which were from both the Perdido and Lomas occupations, were consistent in size and shape with some of the varieties found at Quachilco.

It is reasonably certain that the avocado seeds at La Coyotera were from cultivated fruits. It is much less certain that their cultivation was conducted at the site or even anywhere in the Cañada. Irrigation would have been available, and danger from frost was not a problem. But sudden heat waves, especially when accompanied by low humidity, can interfere with the fruit set of the avocado or cause extensive shedding of young fruits (Hodgson 1950:226). Heat may thus have been a factor prohibiting successful avocado cultivation in the Cañada. The avocado is a tree at home in higher elevations, particularly Persea americana var. drymifolia which is usually grown between 1000 and 1800 m, and to which the specimens from La Coyotera can be assigned. No data are available as to when varieties specifically adapted to lower elevations were first developed.

These facts suggest that the avocados present at La Coyotera were imports to the site from higher elevations to the north or south. If such importation did occur, it took place on a larger scale during the Lomas phase than in Perdido times.

Miscellaneous Fruits. In addition to coyol, black zapote, ciruela, and avocado, a few other types of fruit seeds which have not yet been positively identified were present at La Coyotera.

Of primary concern in this category is one type of large seed that is certainly from a single-seeded fruit (Fig. 7.7). Fragments of these seeds were quite common, especially, as might be expected, in the Area F Lomas phase midden, where 118 fragments weighing 18.6 g were recovered from 13 different excavation units. Fragments also occurred in Houses 3, 11, and 12 of Perdido phase Area A/B. The most complete example of this unknown seed appeared to be almost half of the entire seed and measured 3 cm in length and 2.5 cm in width. The whole seed apparently was spherical or slightly oblong. It was characterized, in its carbonized state, by a porous rather than dense interior with elongated, narrow, hollow pockets throughout. The exterior surface was smooth in some places and slightly roughened in others but had no distinguishing features. One informed observer (who had no prior knowledge of the presence of coyol at the site) suggested that the seed appeared to be that of a palm. Thus all

Fig. 7.7. Seed fragments of unidentified fruit from Lomas phase midden at La Coyotera. Scale = 10 cm.

the fragments of this type of seed received the tentative designation "Palmae." Should this identification prove correct, it would be of much interest that two types of palms had been present at La Coyotera, particularly if the unknown genus were also a good source of oil.

At least two other unknown nut or fruit seed types were recovered in small quantities and in fragmentary condition. One was an oblong seed, 10 mm in length and 7 mm in width, with a faint pattern of parallel curved lines on the exterior surface. The other was represented by small pieces of nutshells or thick seedcoats with well-defined ridges on the exterior surface. Additionally, some small undistinguished fragments of other seeds might have been from fruits, but none was sufficiently intact for identification. All the above unknowns were found in the Lomas phase midden in Area F.

Wild Plant Foods

Cactus fruits and guajes were again the two examples of wild food categories. Both would have been available locally as part of the vegetation native to the area. As mentioned earlier, either of these groups may also have been cultivated, that is, planted and tended by simple techniques to increase quantities or accessibility; but as no direct evidence for such practices can be cited, these plants remain classed as wild food sources. All of the cactus fruit and guaje seeds were from the Lomas phase midden.

The most popular of the cactus fruits were the pitahayas of the columnar cacti (Cereus types). Thirty-two carbonized seeds of these fruits were recovered by flotation. Additionally, three Opuntia seeds indicated that tunas were also used, even if in smaller quantities.

A number of well-preserved guaje seeds, 23 in all, were present in the Lomas midden. These were oval seeds between 4 and 5 mm in length, probably of the genus Leucaena. Two more tree legume seeds were slightly larger and more angular in outline; they could represent different types of guajes produced by other genera of pod-bearing trees.

Summary

The extensive body of data presented in the preceding sections is briefly summarized here through a comparison of the botanical assemblages recovered at the three sites under investigation. It must be kept in mind, however, that such comparisons will become meaningful only after variables in addition to the plant remains themselves are incorporated into the analysis.

Of the cultivated plants (that is, those species that were certainly the products of horticultural or agricultural practices), only maize was present at all three sites. At La Coyotera, however, little is known of the character of the maize because the quantity recovered was so small. This is an unfortunate circumstance in view of the site's unique lowland setting. There is no doubt, however, that maize was an important cultivar and a significant dietary element at the two Tehuacán Valley sites. The predominant type of maize grown at Quachilco—a very small cob, 10-rowed variety with globular kernels—was not common at Cuayucatepec. At the latter site, larger 14- and 16-rowed cobs with either globular or flattened kernels represent the principal type of maize under cultivation, although variations occurred. Only a small percentage of the maize at both sites showed primitive features. No signs of teosinte introgression were present in any of the samples, and no teosinte was recovered at any of the three sites.

The best evidence concerning the other cultivars (excluding for the moment arboreal products) is for bean cultivation at Cuayucatepec. Here, at least five different varieties of Phaseolus vulgaris and Phaseolus acutifolius were raised. Bean remains were scanty at Quachilco and absent from La Coyotera; I suggested above that beans were not under cultivation at these sites, although they may have been imported, at least to Quachilco, from other areas. Evidence for chile peppers was found at both of the Tehuacán Valley sites, but not in sufficient quantities to suggest cultivation at either site. One additional cultivated species that may have been in use at Quachilco is the husk tomato, but evidence is not definite. It should be mentioned here that no remains of gourd or any type of squash were found at any of the three sites. This absence is rather surprising since these fruits have durable husks that are prime candidates for carbonization in trash heaps.

While beans were under cultivation at Cuayucatepec, arboreal fruits were not. Good evidence for arboriculture was found, however, at both Quachilco and La Coyotera. Each site emphasized different tree species. At Quachilco, the avocado was of prime importance, with several types under cultivation. While the avocado was also present at La Coyotera, it was of relatively minor importance and was probably not grown locally. Instead, a number of tropical fruits were of central concern at La Coyotera. During the earliest occupation of the site, these introduced fruits included the coyol and perhaps one other palm, and the black zapote; later the cultivation of these trees increased in importance, and the ciruela was added to the list of arboricultural products. All of these fruits, with the exception of the ciruela, were present in much smaller quantities at Quachilco as well, but some of them (particularly coyol) may have been imported, not locally produced. The coyol palm may have enjoyed such great popularity at La Coyotera because its nuts were an excellent source of oil.

Evidence for the collection and consumption of various field weeds was present at the two Tehuacán Valley sites. The most common kinds of plants in this procurement category were two genera of the Chenopodiaceae family and two herbaceous species of the Leguminosae. The absence of disturbed habitat plants in the archeological record at La Coyotera might be related to the scant preservation of non-arboreal cultivars at that site.

The use of local wild food plants was documented at all three sites. Fruits were collected from prickly pear and organ cacti. Edible pods were provided by one or more genera of leguminous trees. The Mexican cherry may also have been available at Cuayucatepec.

Preliminary results of the analysis of the botanical assemblages at the three sites excavated by the Palo Blanco Project show interesting differences and similarities in the nature of the botanical subsistence systems at the three locations. Continued investigation will aim to isolate factors in the environmental and sociocultural contexts of the three sites which help to explain these differences and similarities.

7. RESTOS BOTANICOS CARBONIZADOS PROVENIENTES DE QUACHILCO, CUAYUCATEPEC, Y LA COYOTERA

INFORME PRELIMINAR

por Judith E. Smith

SUMARIO

Este capítulo presenta los resultados preliminares del análisis de los restos botánicos recuperados en los tres sitios extensamente excavados por los miembros del Proyecto Palo Blanco. El énfasis principal es sobre especies comestibles de plantas y su papel en los sistemas de subsistencia. La preservación de restos de plantas en los tres sitios fue solamente por carbonización; así que todos los restos arqueológicos descriptos están carbonizados. Durante las excavaciones, pedazos de material carbonizado que no pasó por las zarandas de 6 mm usadas para casi todos los depósitos fueron guardados. Adicionalmente muestras de tierra fueron tomadas para flotación (Minnis y LeBlanc 1976) de todos los depósitos cenicientos y de todos los depósitos con pedazos visibles de carbón. Unas muestras iniciales de flotación en depósitos donde no había carbón visible revelaron que el pequeño retorno de tales muestras de tierra no valía la pena.

Quachilco, el primer "lugar central" en el Valle de Tehuacán fue ocupado durante las fases Santa María Tardía/Palo Blanco Temprana (Drennan 1978). Está situada en una parte muy árida del valle donde agricultura de lluvia no es posible. Hoy, como en el pasado, la agricultura depende de irrigación, para la cual la mayor fuente de agua es una serie de manantiales minerales.

Entre los restos de comida en Quachilco, plantas cultivadas incluyen maíz, frijoles, chiles, y tomate de cáscara. Los restos más comunes son los de maíz. Todavía falta hacer estudios morfológicos sobre el maíz, pero ya es aparente que las mazorcas eran bien pequeñas: 36% tenían un diámetro de menos de 6 mm, 70% de menos de 7 mm, y 93% de menos de 9 mm. Solamente unas pocas mazorcas poseen rasgos primitivos. De diez mazorcas examinadas por Carlos Alvarez del laboratorio paleobotánico del Departamento de Prehistoria (I.N.A.H.), nueve fueron identificados como "slender pop" (Mangelsdorf 1974:177-178) y uno como Chapalote. Cinco semillas de chile (Capsicum annuum) han sido recolectadas. Se encontró también una sola semilla del tomate de cáscara (Physalis), aunque esta identificación es bastante tentativa, ya que las semillas de algunas especies de Solanum se le parecen mucho. Tal vez el hecho más sorprendente es que sólo se encontró un fragmento de frijol (Phaseolus vulgaris), una planta cultivada tan comunmente.

De los arboles cosechados, el aguacate (Persea americana var. drymifolia), representa la segunda especie más común entre todos los restos

carbonizados en Quachilco. Hay gran variedad en el tamaño de las semillas
de estos aguacates; pero el promedio es más pequeño que el de los aguacates
del mismo período recuperados en las cuevas de Tehuacán (C.E. Smith 1966).
Esta diferencia no parece ser debida a que los ejemplares de Quachilco
están carbonizados mientras que los de las cuevas fueron preservados al
secarse, ya que el proceso de secamiento, parece reducir los ejemplares
más que el de carbonización. El zapote negro (Diospyros digyna) está
representado por 17 semillas en depósitos de las fases Santa María Tardía/
Palo Blanco Temprana. Esta planta no es indígena al Valle de Tehuacán,
aunque sus restos aparecen ya en la fase Coxcatlán. En Quachilco se hubiera necesitado cantidades considerables de agua, y puede ser que era,
tal como en el presente, un siembro cerca de las casas. Un total de 16
fragmentos de coyol (Acrocomia mexicana) fue encontrado en Quachilco. El
coyol será discutido en más detalle luego, ya que grandes cantidades de
coyol fueron encontradas en La Coyotera; pero parece ser que el coyol en
Quachilco representa, no su cultivo en la vecindad inmediata, sino que su
importación de elevaciones más bajas, tal vez de la Cañada de Cuicatlán.
Varias otras semillas de frutas provenientes de Quachilco nos quedan por
identificar.

Hierbas silvestres de tierra de cultivo utilizadas por los habitantes de Quachilco incluyen Chenopodium y otra semilla con similaridades
a Crotolaria pumila. Frutas de otras plantas silvestres incluyen tunas
(Opuntia) y pitahayas (que provienen de cactus de tipo Cereus), así como
también guajes (probablemente del tipo Leucaena, aunque es posible que
sean Acacia, Mimosa, o Pithecolobium).

En Cuayucatepec, que queda algunos 500 m más alto que Quachilco
Fig. 1.2), y que recibe un poquito más de lluvia, pero que pierde menos
por evapo-transpiración, la comunidad de plantas silvestres es diferente,
y mientras agricultura con irrigación es necesaria para una subsistencia
segura, en algunos años se puede sembrar dependiendo sólo de la lluvia
(Capítulo 5). Agua para irrigación proviene principalmente de pequeños
riachuelos que bajan de la Sierra de Zongolica. La ocupación de este sitio
está fechada a la fase Palo Blanco.

Otra vez maíz es la planta cultivada que se encuentra más a menudo
entre los restos carbonizados. Las mazorcas son más grandes que las de
Quachilco, y tienen un promedio de 10.13 mm de diámetro. Mazorcas con un
número mayor de hileras son también más comunes; pocas mazorcas muestran
rasgos primitivos. En contraste a Quachilco, Cuayucatepec produjo gran
cantidad de frijol (P. vulgaris y P. acutifolius). Se pueden definir unas
cinco variedades de frijol en los restos, aunque no es siempre posible
decir a cual de las dos especies una variedad pertenece. Se puede decir
que en Cuayucatepec el frijol era una cosecha importante tal como lo es
ahora. Una sola semilla de chile (probablemente Capsicum annuum) representa la única otra cosecha encontrada en Cuayucatepec.

Frutos de árboles en Cuayucatepec están representados solamente por
una posible semilla de aguacate y otro fragmento de semilla que todavía
queda por identificar. Es probable que aguacates no eran cultivados en
Cuayucatepec ya que las temperaturas de invierno son demasiado bajas.

7. BOTANICAL REMAINS: PRELIMINARY REPORT 249

Parecen, al igual que el zapote negro y el coyol, no haber sido importados en cantidad de regiones más bajas.

Hierbas silvestres recuperadas en Cuayucatepec incluyen Chenopodium y otro género de la misma familia, Atriplex. Otra hierba que no se considera usualmente comestible Argemone mexicana está representada por una semilla; también se encontraron cinco semillas de una legumbre de semilla pequeña que no ha sido identificada. Pitahayas no se encontraron en Cuayucatepec, pero tres semillas de Opuntia indican algún uso del nopal. Dos semillas de guaje representan los árboles de tipo leguminosa. Un número de semillas de la familia Solanaceae no han sido todavía identificadas en cuanto a género y especie.

En la Cañada de Cuicatlán, La Coyotera está situada a unos 500 m bajo la elevación de Quachilco y 1000 m bajo la de Cuayucatepec. Al igual que en Quachilco, la agricultura es posible sólo con irrigación, pero una gran cantidad de agua está disponible del Río Grande y sus afluentes. La ocupación excavada aquí cubre un período largo que incluye los de Quachilco y Cuayucatepec y fue contemporánea con la de ambos sitios (Capítulo 6).

Restos de maíz son muy escasos en La Coyotera. La única mazorca que se pudo medir tenía 6.9 mm de diámetro, 12 hileras, y ningún rasgo primitivo o irregular. Ningún otro resto de especies cultivadas (excepto las de árboles) y ninguna hierba silvestre fue encontrado.

Tal vez lo más interesante entre los restos botánicos de La Coyotera fue la gran cantidad de coyol (Acrocomia mexicana). Esta palmera de grandes proporciones produce una fruta comestible de cuya semilla se puede extraer aceite para cocinar y quemar. De su savia se puede hacer una bebida alcohólica. Los restos carbonizados de coyol provenientes de La Coyotera pesan un total de 92.7 g y son aparentemente el resultado de la cosecha intensiva de esta palmera, probablemente para exportación a áreas más elevadas donde el coyol no puede crecer. Otro árbol, el zapote negro (Diospyros digyna) era también de importancia en esta agricultura especializada en árboles. Spencer y Redmond discuten esta producción y su importancia en el Capítulo 6. Ciruela (Spondias mombin) era otra cosecha de árbol producida por los residentes de La Coyotera, aunque en cantidades más pequeñas que el coyol y el zapote negro. Un pequeño número de representantes del aguacate (Persea americana var. drymifolia) fueron posiblemente importados de lugares más elevados, ya que el calor de la Cañada no hubiera permitido su cultivo aquí en este tiempo. Por lo menos tres especies de frutas todavía no identificadas se encuentran entre los restos botánicos de La Coyotera.

Pitahayas del cactus tipo Cereus son más comunes que las semillas de Opuntia, pero estos dos tipos de fruta fueron aparentemente usados por los habitantes de La Coyotera. Semillas de guaje, probablemente, del género Leucaena, eran también comunes.

Los tres sitios excavados por los miembros del Proyecto Palo Blanco nos muestran, entonces, algunos contrastes bastante grandes así como también similaridades en cuanto a los restos botánicos carbonizados. Maíz fue la única planta cultivada en todos los tres sitios. En Cuayucatepec frijoles también eran una cosecha importante, pero no en los otros dos sitios. En Quachilco, con sus elevaciones bajas, aguacates constituían una cosecha principal. En La Coyotera, con elevaciones aún más bajas, el enfoque agrícola parece haber sido en cosechas de árboles tales como el zapote negro, y el coyol, los cuales se encuentran ya en los depósitos más tempranos que excavamos y que aumentan considerablemente en número, en el tiempo en que la región parece haber sido dominada por Monte Albán. Hierbas silvestres de tierra de cultivo también fueron usadas en los tres sitios. El análisis que continúa tiene como propósito principal aislar los factores en los contextos ambientales y socioculturales de los tres sitios que ayuden a explicar estos patrones.

REFERENCES CITED

Adams, Robert McC.
   1966 The Evolution of Urban Society. Aldine. Chicago.

Alden, John R.
   1977 Surface Survey at Quachilco (Ts218). In Drennan, ed., 1977.

Armillas, Pedro
   1949 Notas sobre sistemas de cultivo en Mesoamérica: cultivos de riego y humedad en la cuenca del Río de las Balsas. Instituto Nacional de Antropología e Historia Anales 3:85-113. Mexico, D.F.

   1951 Tecnología, formaciones socio-económicas, y religión en Mesoamérica. In Sol Tax, ed., The Civilizations of Ancient America: Selected Papers of the XXIXth International Congress of Americanists. University of Chicago Press. Chicago.

Blanton, Richard E.
   1978 Monte Albán: Settlement Patterns at the Ancient Zapotec Capital. Academic Press. New York.

Boletín Hidrométrico
   1974 Boletín Hidrométrico. Comisión del Papaloapan, Secretaría de Recursos Hidráulicos. Mexico, D.F.

Boserup, Ester
   1965 The Conditions of Agricultural Growth. Aldine. Chicago.

Bordaz, Jacques
   1964 Pre-Columbian Ceramic Kilns at Peñitas, a Post-Classic Site in Coastal Nayarit, Mexico. Ph.D. Dissertation, Columbia University. University Microfilms. Ann Arbor, Michigan.

Brunet, Jean
   1967 Geologic Studies. In Douglas S. Byers, ed., The Prehistory of the Tehuacán Valley, Vol. 1: Environment and Subsistence. University of Texas Press. Austin.

Byers, Douglas S.
   1967 Climate and Hydrology. In Douglas S. Byers, ed., The Prehistory of the Tehuacán Valley, Vol. 1: Environment and Subsistence. University of Texas Press. Austin.

Caso, Alfonso
   1947 Calendario y escritura de las antiguas culturas de Monte Albán. In Miguel Othón de Mendizábal, Obras completas, tomo 1: Homenaje. Mexico, D.F.

Caso, Alfonso, Ignacio Bernal, and Jorge R. Acosta
    1967 La Cerámica de Monte Albán. Instituto Nacional de Antropología e Historia Memorias No. 13. Mexico, D.F.

Cobean, Robert H., Michael D. Coe, Edward A. Perry, Jr., Karl K. Turekian, and Dinkar P. Kharkar
    1971 Obsidian Trade at San Lorenzo Tenochtitlan, Mexico. Science 174: 666-671.

Corner, H.J.H.
    1966 The Natural History of Palms. University of California Press. Berkeley.

Dixon, Wilfrid J. and Frank J. Massey, Jr.
    1969 Introduction to Statistical Analysis. McGraw-Hill. New York.

Drennan, Robert D.
    1976a Fábrica San José and Middle Formative Society in the Valley of Oaxaca. University of Michigan Museum of Anthropology Memoirs, No. 8. Ann Arbor.

    1976b A Refinement of Chronological Seriation Using Nonmetric Multidimensional Scaling. American Antiquity 41:290-302.

    1977a Ceramic Chronology. In Drennan, ed., 1977.

    1977b Test Excavations at Quachilco (Ts218). In Drennan, ed., 1977.

    1978 Excavations at Quachilco: A Report on the 1977 Season of the Palo Blanco Project in the Tehuacán Valley. University of Michigan Museum of Anthropology Technical Reports, No. 7. Ann Arbor.

Drennan, Robert D., editor
    1977 The Palo Blanco Project: A Report on the 1975 and 1976 Seasons in the Tehuacán Valley. R.S. Peabody Foundation for Archaeology. Andover, Mass. And University of Michigan Museum of Anthropology. Ann Arbor.

Erasmus, Charles
    1965 Monument Building: Some Field Experiments. Southwestern Journal of Anthropology 21:277-301.

Flannery, Kent V.
    1972 The Cultural Evolution of Civilizations. Annual Review of Ecology and Systematics 3:399-426.

    1973 The Origins of Agriculture. Annual Review of Anthropology 2:271-310.

REFERENCES CITED

Flannery, Kent V.
    1976a Contextual Analysis of Ritual Paraphernalia from Formative Oaxaca. In Kent V. Flannery, ed., The Early Mesoamerican Village. Academic Press. New York.

    1976b Empirical Determination of Site Catchments in Oaxaca and Tehuacán. In Kent V. Flannery, ed., The Early Mesoamerican Village. Academic Press. New York.

    1976c Sampling by Intensive Surface Collection. In Kent V. Flannery, ed., The Early Mesoamerican Village. Academic Press. New York.

Flannery, Kent V., Anne V.T. Kirkby, Michael J. Kirkby, and Aubrey W. Williams, Jr.
    1967 Farming Systems and Political Growth in Ancient Oaxaca. Science 158:445-454.

Flannery, Kent V. and Joyce Marcus
    1976 Evolution of the Public Building in Formative Oaxaca. In Charles E. Cleland, ed., Cultural Change and Continuity: Essays in Honor of James Bennett Griffin. Academic Press. New York.

Ford, Richard I.
    1976 Carbonized Plant Remains. In Drennan 1976a.

Fowler, Melvin L.
    1969 A Preclassic Water Distribution System in Amalucan, Mexico. Archaeology 22:208-215.

Fox, Dennis and Kenneth Guire
    1976 Documentation for MIDAS. University of Michigan Statistical Research Laboratory. Ann Arbor.

Fried, Morton H.
    1967 The Evolution of Political Society. Random House. New York.

Friedman, Jonathan
    1974 Marxism, Structuralism, and Vulgar Materialism. Man 9:444-469.

    1975 Tribes, States, and Transformations. In Maurice Bloch, ed., Marxist Analyses and Social Anthropology. Halsted Press. New York.

Gibbons, J.D.
    1971 Nonparametric Statistical Inference. McGraw-Hill. New York.

Harbottle, G., E.V. Sayre, and R. Abascal M.
    n.d. Neutron Activation Analysis of Thin Orange Pottery. Mimeo. Dept. of Chemistry, Brrokhaven National Laboratory. Upton, N.Y.

Hays, William L.
    1963 Statistics. Holt, Rinehart and Winston. New York.

Hodgson, Robert W.
    1950 The Avocado—A Gift from the Middle Americans. Economic Botany 4: 253-293.

Hopkins, Joseph W.
    1974 Irrigation and the Cuicatec Ecosystem: A Study of Agriculture and Civilization in North Central Oaxaca, Mexico. Ph.D. Dissertation. University of Chicago.

Hunt, Eva
    1972 Irrigation and the Cuicatec Cacicazgos. In Frederick Johnson, ed., The Prehistory of the Tehuacán Valley, Vol. 4: Chronology and Irrigation. University of Texas Press. Austin.

Hunt, Robert C. and Eva Hunt
    1974 Irrigation, Conflict, and Politics: A Mexican Case. In Theodore Downing and McGuire Gibson, eds., Irrigation's Impact on Society. University of Arizona Press. Tucson.

    1976 Canal Irrigation and Local Social Organization. Current Anthropology 17:389-411.

Johnson, Gregory A.
    1973 Local Exchange and Early State Development in Southwest Iran. University of Michigan Museum of Anthropology Anthropological Papers, No. 51. Ann Arbor.

    1978 Information Sources and the Development of Decision-Making Organizations. In Charles L. Redman, et al., eds., Social Archeology: Beyond Subsistence and Dating. Academic Press. New York.

Kaplan, Lawrence
    1967 Archaeological Phaseolus from Tehuacán. In Douglas Byers, ed., The Prehistory of the Tehuacán Valley, Vol. 1: Environment and Subsistence. University of Texas Press. Austin.

Kappel, Wayne
    1974 Irrigation Development and Population Pressure. In Theodore Downing and McGuire Gibson, eds., Irrigation's Impact on Society. University of Arizona Press. Tucson.

Kirkby, Anne V.T.
    1973 The Use of Land and Water Resources in the Past and Present Valley of Oaxaca, Mexico. University of Michigan Museum of Anthropology Memoirs, No. 5. Ann Arbor.

Leach, Edmund
    1959 Hydraulic Society in Ceylon. Past and Present 15:2-26.

    1961 Pul Eliya. Cambridge University Press. Cambridge.

REFERENCES CITED

Lees, Susan H.
   1973 Sociopolitical Aspects of Canal Irrigation in the Valley of Oaxaca. University of Michigan Museum of Anthropology Memoirs, No. 6. Ann Arbor.

MacNeish, Richard S., Melvin L. Fowler, Angel García Cook, Frederick A. Peterson, Antoinette Nelken-Terner, and James A. Neely
   1972 The Prehistory of the Tehuacán Valley, Vol. 5: Excavations and Reconnaissance. University of Texas Press. Austin.

MacNeish, Richard S., Antoinette Nelken-Terner, and Irmgard W. Johnson
   1967 The Prehistory of the Tehuacán Valley, Vol. 2: Nonceramic Artifacts. University of Texas Press. Austin.

MacNeish, Richard S., Frederick A. Peterson, and Kent V. Flannery
   1970 The Prehistory of the Tehuacán Valley, Vol. 3: Ceramics. University of Texas Press. Austin.

Mangelsdorf, Paul C.
   1974 Corn: Its Origin, Evolution, and Improvement. Harvard University Press. Cambridge, Mass.

Marcus, Joyce
   1976 The Iconography of Militarism at Monte Albán and Neighboring Sites in the Valley of Oaxaca. In Henry B. Nicholson, ed., Origins of Religious Art and Iconography in Preclassic Mesoamerica. University of California at Los Angeles Latin American Center Publications. Los Angeles.

Markley, Klare S.
   1956 Mbocaya or Paraguay Cocopalm—An Important Source of Oil. Economic Botany 10:3-32.

Martínez, Maximino
   1959 Plantas Utiles de la Flora Mexicana. M. León Sánchez. Mexico, D.F.

Messer, Ellen
   1972 Patterns of "Wild" Plant Consumption in Oaxaca, Mexico. Ecology of Food and Nutrition 1:325-332.

Millon, René
   1962 Variations in Social Response to the Practice of Irrigation Agriculture. In Richard B. Woodbury, ed., Civilizations in Arid Lands. University of Utah Anthropological Papers, No. 62. Salt Lake City.

   1973 Urbanization at Teotihuacán, Mexico, Vol. 1: The Teotihuacán Map, Part 1: Text. University of Texas Press. Austin.

   1976 Social Relations in Ancient Teotihuacán. In Eric R. Wolf, ed., The Valley of Mexico: Studies in Prehispanic Ecology and Society. University of New Mexico Press. Albuquerque.

Millon, René, Clara Hall, and May Díaz
    1962 Conflict in the Modern Teotihuacán Irrigation System. Comparative Studies in Society and History 4:494-524.

Minnis, Paul and Steven LeBlanc
    1976 An Efficient, Inexpensive Arid Lands Flotation System. American Antiquity 41:491-493.

Neely, James A.
    1967 Organización Hidráulica y Sistemas de Irrigación Prehistóricos en el Valle de Oaxaca. Instituto Nacional de Antropología e Historia Boletín 27:15-17. Mexico, D.F.

Nowack, Judith A.
    1977 Surface Survey at Major Palo Blanco Sites. In Drennan, ed., 1977.

Nuttall, Zelia
    1904 A Penetential Rite of the Ancient Mexicans. Papers of the Peabody Museum of American Archaeology and Ethnology Vol. 1, No. 7. Harvard University. Cambridge, Mass.

Orlandini, Richard
    1967 A Formative Well from the Valley of Oaxaca. Paper presented at the 32nd annual meeting of the Society for American Archaeology, Ann Arbor, Michigan.

Palerm, Angel
    1955 The Agricultural Basis of Urban Civilization in Mesoamerica. In Julian H. Steward, ed., Irrigation Civilizations: A Comparative Study. Pan American Union Social Science Monographs I. Washington, D.C.

Palerm, Angel and Eric R. Wolf
    1957 Ecological Potential and Cultural Development in Mesoamerica. Pan American Union Social Science Monographs III. Washington, D.C.

Parsons, Jeffrey R.
    1971 Prehistoric Settlement Patterns in the Texcoco Region, Mexico. University of Michigan Museum of Anthropology Memoirs, No. 3. Ann Arbor.

    1976 The Role of Chinampa Agriculture in the Food Supply of Aztec Tenochtitlan. In Charles E. Cleland, ed., Cultural Change and Continuity: Essays in Honor of James Bennett Griffin. Academic Press. New York.

Pires-Ferreira, Jane W.
    1975 Formative Mesoamerican Exchange Networks with Special Reference to the Valley of Oaxaca. University of Michigan Museum of Anthropology Memoirs, No. 7. Ann Arbor.

REFERENCES CITED

Redman, Charles L. and Patty Jo Watson
  1970 Systematic, Intensive Surface Collection. American Antiquity 35: 279-291.

Sahagún, Bernardino de
  1957 General History of the Things of New Spain, Book 4: The Soothsayers; and Book 5: The Omens. Charles E. Dibble and Arthur J.O. Anderson, trans. School of American Research. Santa Fe, New Mexico. And University of Utah. Salt Lake City.

Sahlins, Marshall D.
  1963 Poor Man, Rich Man, Big-Man, Chief: Political Types in Melanesia and Polynesia. Comparative Studies in Society and History 5: 285-303.

  1972 Stone Age Economics. Aldine-Atherton. Chicago.

Sanders, William T.
  1968 Hydraulic Agriculture, Economic Symbiosis, and the Evolution of States in Central Mexico. In Betty J. Meggars, ed., Anthropological Archeology in the Americas. Anthropological Society of Washington. Washington, D.C.

  1972 Population, Agricultural History, and Societal Evolution in Mesoamerica. In Brian Spooner, ed., Population Growth: Anthropological Implications. M.I.T. Press. Cambridge, Mass.

  1976 The Agricultural History of the Basin of Mexico. In Eric R. Wolf, ed., The Valley of Mexico: Studies in Pre-Hispanic Ecology and Society. University of New Mexico Press. Albuquerque.

Sanders, William T. and Barbara J. Price
  1968 Mesoamerica: The Evolution of a Civilization. Random House. New York.

Shepard, Anna O.
  1956 Ceramics for the Archaeologist. Carnegie Institution of Washington, Publication 609. Washington, D.C.

Siegel, Sidney
  1956 Nonparametric Statistics for the Behavioral Sciences. McGraw-Hill. New York.

Solares, Martín
  1976 El Aguacate: su cultivo. Editores Mexicanos Unidos. Mexico, D.F.

Smith, C. Earle, Jr.
  1966 Archeological Evidence for Selection in Avocado. Economic Botany 20:169-175.

  1967 Plant Remains. In Douglas Byers, ed., The Prehistory of the Tehuacán Valley, Vol. 1: Environment and Subsistence. University of Texas Press. Austin.

Smith, C. Earle, Jr.
    1969 Additional Notes on Pre-Conquest Avocados in Mexico. Economic Botany 23:135-140.

Smith, Judith E.
    in   Formative Botanical Remains at Tomaltepec, Oaxaca. In Michael E.
    press Whalen, Evolution in a Formative Community in the Valley of Oaxaca, Mexico: Excavations at Santo Domingo Tomaltepec. University of Michigan Museum of Anthropology Memoirs, No. 11. Ann Arbor.

Sotomayor, Alfredo and Noemí Castillo Tejero
    1963 Estudio petrográfico de la cerámica "anaranjado delgado." Instituto Nacional de Antropología e Historia, Departamento de Prehistoria Publicaciones, No. 12. Mexico, D.F.

Standley, Paul C.
    1920 Trees and Shrubs of Mexico. Contributions from the United States National Herbarium, Vol. 23, Part 1. Smithsonian Press. Washington, D.C.

Steward, Julian H., ed.
    1955 Irrigation Civilizations: A Comparative Study. Pan American Union Social Science Monographs I. Washington, D.C.

Tolstoy, Paul
    1958 Surface Survey in the Northern Valley of Mexico: The Classic and Postclassic Periods. American Philosophical Society Transactions, Vol. 48, Part 5.

Tolstoy, Paul and Suzanne K. Fish
    1975 Surface and Subsurface Evidence for Community Size at Coapexco, Mexico. Journal of Field Archaeology 2:97-104.

Vaillant, George C.
    1941 Aztecs of Mexico. Doubleday. New York.

Winter, Marcus C. and William O. Payne
    1976 Hornos para cerámica hallados en Monte Albán. Instituto Nacional de Antropología e Historia Boletín 16:37-40. Mexico, D.F.

Wittfogel, Karl A.
    1938 Die Theorie der orientalischen Gesellschaft. Zeitschrift für Sozialforschung 7:90-122.

    1957 Oriental Despotism: A Comparative Study of Total Power. Yale University Press. New Haven, Conn.

    1972 The Hydraulic Approach to Pre-Spanish Mesoamerica. In Frederick Johnson, ed., The Prehistory of the Tehuacán Valley, Vol. 4: Chronology and Irrigation. University of Texas Press. Austin.

REFERENCES CITED

Wolf, Eric R.
    1959 Sons of the Shaking Earth. University of Chicago Press. Chicago.

Woodbury, Richard B. and James A. Neely
    1972 Water Control Systems of the Tehuacán Valley. In Frederick Johnson, ed., The Prehistory of the Tehuacán Valley, Vol. 4: Chronology and Irrigation. University of Texas Press. Austin.

Wright, Henry T.
    1977 Recent Research on the Origin of the State. Annual Review of Anthropology 6:379-397.